Ready for the Real World

William C. Hartel
Marietta College

Stephen W. Schwartz
Marietta College

Steven D. Blume
Marietta College

John N. Gardner
University of South Carolina

Wadsworth Publishing Company
Belmont, California
A Division of Wadsworth, Inc.

The Wadsworth College Success Series Editor: Angela Gantner
Director of Marketing/Wadsworth College Success Group: Todd Armstrong
Advertising Project Manager: Sarah Hubbard
Editorial Assistant: Lisa Timbrell
Production Editor: Vicki Friedberg
Text and Cover Designer: Ann Butler
Print Buyer: Barbara Britton
Permissions Editor: Robert M. Kauser
Copy Editor: Tom Briggs
Cover Photo: Paul Barton/The Stockmarket
Compositor: Wadsworth Digital Productions
Printer: Malloy Lithographing

 This book is printed on acid-free recycled paper.

THE SENIOR YEAR EXPERIENCE is a service mark of the University of South Carolina. A license may be granted upon written request to use the service mark THE SENIOR YEAR EXPERIENCE in association with educational programmatic approaches to enhance the Senior year. This license is not transferable and does not apply to the use of the service mark in any other programs or on any other literature without the written approval of the University of South Carolina.

International Thomson Publishing
The trademark ITP is used under license.

Printed in the United States of America
1 2 3 4 5 6 7 8 9 10—98 97 96 95 94

Library of Congress Cataloging in Publication Data
Ready for the real world / [edited by] William C. Hartel . . . [et al.].
    p.   cm.
    Includes bibliographical references and index.
    ISBN 0-534-17712-3
    1. College seniors—United States—Attitudes. 2. College graduates—Employment—United States. 3. College students—United States—Social conditions. I. Hartel, William C.
LA229.R38   1994
378.1'981—dc20   93–40729

Acknowledgments

We would like to thank our partners at Wadsworth Publishing Company, who continue to support our efforts with insight and enthusiasm. Special thanks to our editor, Angela Gantner, and to Lisa Timbrell, senior editorial assistant; Ann Butler, designer; and Vicki Friedberg, production editor. It is gratifying to work with a publishing team who shares a vision for the future and a deep commitment to education.

We would also like to thank the following reviewers for their helpful suggestions:

Philip Gardner, Michigan State University
Carol Templemen, Baldwin-Wallace College
Gretchen Van Der Vere, University of Maryland

Brief Contents

Ready for the Real World

Titles of Related Interest

The Wadsworth College Success™ Series

College Study Skills: Becoming a Strategic Learner by Dianna L. Van Blerkom (1994)

Integrating College Study Skills: Reasoning in Reading, Listening, and Writing, Third Edition, by Peter Elias Sotiriou (1993)

Mastering Mathematics: How to Be a Great Math Student, Second Edition, by Richard Manning Smith (1994)

Merlin: The Sorcerer's Guide to Survival in College by Christopher F. Monte (1990)

The Mountain Is High Unless You Take the Elevator: Success Strategies for Adult Learners by Laurence N. Smith and Timothy L. Walter (1992)

Right from the Start: Managing Your Way to College Success by Robert Holkeboer (1993)

Toolkit for College Success by Daniel R. Walther (1994)

Turning Point by Joyce D. Weinsheimer (1993)

The Freshman Year Experience℠ Series
John N. Gardner, Consulting Editor

College Is Only the Beginning: A Student Guide to Higher Education, Second Edition, by John N. Gardner and A. Jerome Jewler (1989)

Create Your College Success: Activities and Exercises for Students by Robert A. Friday (1988)

The Power to Learn: Helping Yourself to College Success by William E. Campbell (1993)

Step by Step to College Success by A. Jerome Jewler and John N. Gardner (1987)

Your College Experience: Strategies for Success by John N. Gardner and A. Jerome Jewler (1992)

Your College Experience: Strategies for Success, Concise Edition, by A. Jerome Jewler and John N. Gardner with Mary-Jane McCarthy (1993)

The Senior Year Experience℠ Series
Consulting Editor, John N. Gardner

Ready for the Real World by William C. Hartel, Stephen W. Schwartz, Steven D. Blume, and John N. Gardner (1994)

Detailed Contents

Ready for the Real World

Introduction

Every college student faces two critical transition periods: entering college as a freshman and leaving college as a graduating senior. As seniors, you ultimately managed the transition into college successfully. Now it's time to prepare for life after college. And this book will help you do that.

In *Ready for the Real World* we explore some of the key issues you will need to address in order to ease your transition from college life to life in what college students call the "real world." We hope to prepare you to make informed, positive choices in personal and professional matters and to apply the knowledge and skills you have acquired as an undergraduate to the fullest extent possible.

In terms of higher education, we live in a remarkable nation. Not only does the United States have more colleges and universities than any other country in the world (approximately 3,500), but it spends more on higher education (over $150 billion to educate some 14.2 million students annually). Why do we make such an investment? In part we do so to produce leaders and workers. But we also do so to produce better friends, colleagues, mates, parents, and citizens—people who are more involved in their communities and who act out of a strong sense of civic responsibility.

Ready for the Real World reflects our genuine concern for our future generations of citizens. Our intent is to give you the necessary tools to deal with the issues you are certain to encounter. Simultaneously, we hope to reduce your anxiety about what lies ahead. Undoubtedly, many of you are worried about whether college has adequately prepared you for the next stage of your life. You may wonder whether you will be able to achieve your goals: a satisfying career, a loving relationship, a happy family, a healthy lifestyle, financial security, a better, safer world for your children. While we're not psychologists, we know that lack of information contributes to anxiety. Thus we provide you with the information you'll need to reduce anxiety and take control of the transition process.

In some ways *Ready for the Real World* is not a traditional textbook. For instance, it does not represent the voice of one author. Rather, each chapter was authored or co-authored by individuals from diverse backgrounds and perspectives—professors from various disciplines, college administrators, businesspeople, and so on. In addition, each chapter features the "voices" of college seniors or recent graduates who express some of the same concerns you might have. *Ready for the Real World* is also not a traditional book in that it makes greater demands on you to become involved in it. We will not be asking you primarily to read, memorize, and then recite back the material. Instead, we hope you will use the book to provoke your thinking. We hope you will use it to guide your search for additional information outside of class. If you are using this text as part of a senior year transition course or perhaps a capstone course, we hope you will use it to structure your class discussions, oral and panel presentations, debates, role-plays, simulations, and so on. The more you interact with the book—respond positively to the demands it makes on you to reflect, discuss, research, write—the more you will get out of it. Only by seriously considering the questions and issues raised and by getting involved with your fellow seniors in discussing the book's topics can you ensure that you will indeed be "ready for the real world."

Traditionally, preparing students for life after college has been the exclusive domain of career planning and placement offices. We envision *Ready for the Real World* as a resource that will supplement the valuable guidance provided by these offices. Thus the book takes a comprehensive look at the issues you need to address to become a successful employee, spouse, parent, friend, and citizen. It focuses on your cognitive needs for information and knowledge as well as your affective needs for emotional support to cope with the stress and uncertainty ahead. We hope to help you avoid some of the problems we encountered in our own transitions from college senior to college graduate because this kind of "senior year experience" was not available.

We have a selfish motivation for writing this book as well. We want you to be successful not only for your sake but for ours. We hope you will reflect well on the higher educators who have invested so much time and energy in, and developed so much affection for, you. The bottom line is, we hope you will be a positive reflection on the institutions from which you will graduate—and you are more likely to do so if you take this book to heart.

Ready for the Real World will guide you on a journey during your senior year that may well determine how successful you will be in your future professional and personal life. So we urge you to take the book as seriously as we did in putting it together. We would also like to hear from you regarding the book: What did you like about it? What can we do to improve it? Please feel free to write to Bill, Steve, and Steve c/o Marietta College, Marietta, OH, 45750, or to John c/o University of South Carolina, Columbia, SC 29208.

The fact that you've come this far in college makes us feel optimistic that you'll make the transition to the "real world" successfully. We wish you well.

William Hartel

Stephen Schwartz

Steven Blume

John Gardner

I   The Purpose of College

1 Evaluating Your College Experience

Hilda F. Owens, Ph.D.

Executive Assistant to the President for Planning and Research,
Spartanburg Methodist College

Senior Voices

Wendy

I am very different from the person I was when I began my college experience. I doubt if I'd even recognize the Wendy of three and a half years ago! My religious and political views have not only expanded but been radically transformed. I am much more self-aware and more concerned with the world and all the folks in it.

I feel more in control—in a chaotic sort of way—of myself and my future. I also feel prepared to adapt; I have gained flexibility! I plan to work as a center director for an Appalachian service project. I will be in charge of a summer center in rural Appalachia with three other college students. Each week we will have sixty or so high school kids from across the country there to renovate and construct housing for impoverished families. It is a camplike atmosphere in which the four staffers are in charge of construction, finance, spiritual development programs, community relations, and so on. I will choose the families and construction projects. Anxious? Can I do it forever? Can I do enough? I'm excited; I'm confident; I'm dying to get there. I worked last summer with the project. After this summer, I'm applying for a full-time job with the organization. I am ready! ■

You are about to reach a major goal in your life, completing the requirements for that long-dreamed-of and sought-after bachelor's degree! You are about to become a college graduate, ending one major phase of your life and beginning another.

Few decisions will have as great an impact on the quality and direction of your life as the one to go to college. Attending college has already helped shape who you are, how you think and behave, and what you value. In addition, the college experience will affect your future choices and help write the script of your life's story. In this chapter we want you, the soon-to-be college graduate, to put yourself in the shoes of past college graduates. By looking at how college has affected others, you can better understand its impact on you. This is part of "taking stock"—of assessing the worth of the experience you are about to complete.

What Difference Does a College Education Make?

Why are students willing to forgo immediate earnings to attend college? Why are students and parents willing to commit themselves to a college education despite the spiraling costs? Why do states and the federal government invest large sums of money to help provide facilities, equipment, and instructional resources and personnel, as well as give significant financial aid to help thousands of students who otherwise could not afford to go to college? Why do people make this educational and financial commitment? And what do we expect colleges to do for students?

When you were completing your last years of high school and approaching young adulthood, no doubt you were encouraged by teachers, counselors, parents, friends, and others to go to college. And when you arrived at college and sat through orientation sessions and freshman seminars, you probably heard many reasons for being there. Now you are a senior, and you face the transition from college to employment, graduate or professional school, the military, or another of life's options. A look back at your college experience may help you take that big step.

One of the major academic legacies of the 1960s was the emergence of the study of college student development and the college experience as a legitimate field of academic inquiry. A review of the research on the impact of an undergraduate education may help you assess what changes have occurred in your life—in who you are, what you believe and value, and what you are likely to be able to do as a result of this experience.

Educational Attainment and Income

Social mobility, professional or occupational competence, status, income, and other quality-of-life indicators are inextricably linked to postsecondary education in modern American society. Formal postsecondary

Table 1.1 Differences in Average Monthly Earnings by Educational Level, 1990

Educational Level	Average Monthly Earnings	Increase over Previous Level ($)	Increase over Previous Level (%)
No high school diploma	$492	—	—
High school diploma	1,077	585	119
Vocational training	1,237	160	15
Two years of college *and* an associate degree	1,672	435	35
Bachelor's degree	2,116	444	27
Master's degree	2,822	706	33
Doctorate degree	3,855	1,033	37

SOURCE: U.S. Department of Commerce, Bureau of Census, *Current Population Reports* (Washington, DC: Government Printing Office, 1990).

education plays a critical role in available career opportunities, which in turn significantly influence individual and family life.

Attaining a bachelor's degree has important implications for lifetime earnings. For example, college graduates will earn roughly 50 percent more during their lifetime than will nongraduates. Moreover, the average lifetime income of college graduates today is expected to exceed that of nongraduates by more than $600,000. And U.S. Census Bureau statistics on workers who have earned associate degrees from community and junior colleges show that those individuals earn, on average, 25 percent more than those who did not go beyond high school.

Not only is there a direct correlation between educational attainment and income, but the percentage increase in income is also related to educational level, as shown in Table 1.1. And while white males still earn more than women and blacks with comparable education, a college education may have a particularly favorable impact on career opportunities and earnings for women and for blacks and other minorities. Furthermore, college graduates have a more continuous, less erratic job history, are promoted more often, and are much less likely to become unemployed than are nongraduates. They are also generally more satisfied with their work.

In short, in spite of the possibility that you or some of your friends may have some difficulty in getting the job you want at the salary you want, you have only to look at employment and income patterns of non-college graduates to see that persons with the most education hold a competitive advantage in terms of job opportunities and income levels.

Exercise 1.1

Looking Back and Looking Ahead

List five words or phrases that best described you as an entering freshman in college. Now list five words or phrases that best describe you as you near completion of college. What do the differences between the two lists reveal about the impact college has had on you and your preparation for the "real world"?

Increased Knowledge and Cognitive Skills

It will take more than a high school education to obtain the knowledge and skills necessary to get ahead in the workplace in the 1990s and into the twenty-first century. Among other things, good communication skills, analytical and critical reasoning skills, and the ability to learn and adapt and to retrieve information electronically will be crucial to future success.

Attaining a bachelor's degree should enable you to be more competitive in the workplace and permit you more social mobility. However, the rapidly changing business world may lead you to seek additional formal education to reach your goals.

Research over a fifty-year period demonstrates that students gain significantly in general and specific knowledge during their undergraduate years. According to Pascarella and Terenzini (1991), students gain competencies in general verbal skills, general mathematical and quantitative skills, and specific subject matter knowledge. At this point you might want to think about your own skills and how they have developed since your freshman year.

College graduates generally have improved skills in oral and written communication, abstract reasoning, and critical thinking. They are also more skilled at using reason and evidence to address problems for which there are no verifiably correct answers. Furthermore, they are able to understand more than one side of a complex issue, and they can develop sophisticated, abstract frameworks to solve complex problems. The undergraduate experience clearly has an important influence on general cognitive development. In addition, substantial evidence indicates that college graduates are more inclined to add to their knowledge through serious reading and continuing education, especially concerning interests, capabilities, and values crystallized during their college years.

Exercise 1.2

Assessing Your Cognitive Development

Place a check mark next to each item that accurately describes your progress since you were a freshman or that you believe will continue to develop due to your college experience. (Be honest!)

_____ 1. Increased writing skills

_____ 2. Increased speaking skills

_____ 3. Increased subject matter competence (general areas)

_____ 4. Increased subject matter competence (major field)

_____ 5. Increased abstract reasoning skills

_____ 6. Increased critical thinking skills

_____ 7. Improved ability to deal with conceptual complexity

_____ 8. Improved ability to see both sides of an issue

_____ 9. Improved ability to use reason and judgment in making decisions about controversial issues

Personal Self-Discovery and Emotional Growth

One of the frequently identified purposes of college is to help students to find themselves. Thus a college education goes beyond the cognitive and intellectual development of students. In the words of student affairs professionals and others, colleges help to develop the whole person.

Erikson (1968), Heath (1968), Chickering (1969), Loveinger (1976), and others emphasize the various aspects of psychosocial development in college students. According to the research evidence, college graduates generally have a stronger sense of self and higher self-esteem, a clearer resolution of identity issues, and more clearly forged commitments to a personal identity in political, religious, sexual, and occupational areas. Ego development (that is, the central organizing framework that provides meaning for yourself and your world) is enhanced; academic and social self-concepts (that is, how you evaluate your competencies and skills relative to those of your peers) are stronger; and leadership abilities are improved.

College seniors and graduates tend to be more autonomous, independent, and internally rather than externally directed. For example, aren't you more likely to make decisions on the basis of your personal values than bend to the pressure of your peers? College seniors and graduates also tend to be less authoritarian, less dogmatic, and less ethnocentric in thinking and behavior. Aren't you more likely to make decisions after considering facts or views presented by others? Finally, college seniors and graduates are better problem solvers, are more tolerant of other people and differing viewpoints, are more sophisticated politically, and have a greater capacity for aesthetic appreciation.

Students tend to leave college not only more competent but also more confident than when they arrived. They generally leave with a better sense of who they are, where they fit in the scheme of things, and how they might make a difference in the world about them.

Don

I am the product of the educational and social experiences I have had at this college. I entered with values instilled in me by my friends and family, values that were imposed on me. As I have grown over the past four years, I have adapted these same values to fit my personal beliefs. This school helped me to establish the standards for these beliefs by providing me with factual as well as social knowledge. Interaction in the classroom and around the campus has allowed me to develop into the confident person that I am today. After graduation I will enter the field of pharmaceutical sales. With a strong technical background in biology and chemistry, I am confident that I will be happy and successful in this profession. I am also a little nervous about moving into the "real world." I'm satisfied with my accomplishments to date and with the work I've done to make this transition, but naturally I have anxieties. ■

Exercise 1.3

Assessing Your Personal Growth

Place a check mark next to each item that accurately describes your progress since you were a freshman or that you believe will continue to develop due to the college experience. (Be honest!)

_____ 1. Improved ego development

_____ 2. Improved clarity about one's personal identity

_____ 3. Improved sense of self-esteem

_____ 4. Improved academic self-concept

_____ 5. Improved social self-concept

_____ 6. Increased autonomy

_____ 7. Increased independence

_____ 8. Increased ability to control your own fate

_____ 9. Increased maturity

Exercise 1.4

Looking Ahead

What is the most important principle on which you want to build your life, and why?

Positive Attitudes and Values

Research reveals that people change as a consequence of attending college and not simply as part of the normal maturation process or historical, social, and political trends. (This will be explained more fully in Chapter 13.) Specifically, students usually become more culturally, aesthetically, and intellectually sophisticated, expanding their interest in music, reading, creative writing, philosophy, history, and the performing arts.

College graduates also recognize the intrinsic value of a liberal arts education and exposure to new ideas and de-emphasize the more instrumental and extrinsic view of education as career and vocational preparation. Moreover, the college experience causes attitudes, values, and behaviors to become more open and other-person-oriented; it fosters humanitarian and altruistic values, political tolerance, liberalism, and respect for the rights of others. It promotes equality of men and women—socially, educationally, occupationally, as well as within the family. Finally, college fosters the increased use of principled reasoning in judging moral issues. Although in recent years we've seen a trend toward more conservative social and political attitudes, college graduates historically have been more liberal than society at large.

Exercise 1.5

Assessing Your Values

Place a check mark next to each item that accurately describes your progress since you were a freshman or that you believe will continue to develop due to the college experience. (Be honest!)

_____ 1. Less authoritarian

_____ 2. Less dogmatic

_____ 3. Less ethnocentric

_____ 4. More intellectually flexible

_____ 5. More tolerant of the views and behaviors of others

_____ 6. Less interested in being well-off financially

_____ 7. More interested in developing a meaningful philosophy of life

_____ 8. More interested in being creative, using talents, and finding a challenging, satisfying job than in making lots of money

_____ 9. More clear about how you want to earn a livelihood

_____ 10. More humanitarian and less selfish

_____ 11. More liberal in political views

_____ 12. More liberal in religious views

_____ 13. More liberal in social values

_____ 14. More involved in civic and political activities

_____ 15. More flexible in the perceived roles of women and men in marital relationships and responsibilities

_____ 16. More flexible and open in relations with opposite sex

_____ 17. More flexible and open in relations with same sex

_____ 18. More flexible and open in relations with persons from different races, religions, and cultures

_____ 19. More liberal in personality and value structures

_____ 20. More likely to use principled reasoning to judge moral issues

_____ 21. More likely to act morally

Exercise 1.6

Thinking About Morality

What does it mean to say that something is "right" or "wrong"?

Increased Practical Competence and Quality of Life

One of the expected outcomes of college is improved competence and performance in the practical affairs of life. College graduates tend to be more adaptable and future-oriented, to adopt more liberal views and more ideological thinking, and to develop greater interests in political and public affairs. They are also more likely to vote and to participate in community affairs.

College is a very important influence on family life as well. The stereotypical images of the "appropriate" role of men and women in the family seem to diminish with increased education. As more women work and as working women earn more of the family income (about 60 percent of American women work outside the home), child care and household responsibilities are more likely to be shared or even shifted by marriage partners. College-educated people often delay the age of marriage, become more discriminating with respect to the overall compatibility of a prospective spouse, and reduce the number as well as plan the timing of their children's births. They also tend to allocate more thought, quality time, energy, and money to child-rearing. In turn, the children of college-educated parents generally have greater abilities and enjoy greater achievements of their own than children of non-college-educated parents.

College-educated people characteristically receive greater economic benefits and are more efficient consumers than non-college-educated persons. They tend to save more of their money, make higher-risk investments as a hedge against inflation, and place greater emphasis on long-term savings aimed at the future welfare of their children. (For more details on personal finances, see Chapter 15.) They also tend to spend a greater percentage of available income on developmentally oriented experiences and resources (education, books, magazines, and so forth) and emphasize to their children the importance of educational enrichment and continued learning.

As citizens, college graduates are better equipped to deal with the complexities of bureaucracies at all levels: the legal system, the tax system, and so on. As consumers, they are less vulnerable to false and misleading advertising. They are also more likely to plan for their own future needs and for retirement.

College graduates exhibit different priorities with regard to leisure time activities. They are somewhat more cultured in their tastes for leisure activity, less likely to spend time watching television, and more selective in their choice of movies. They spend more time on intellectual and cultural pursuits, including continuing education, hobbies, community and civic affairs, and family vacations.

Finally, a college education appears to have a positive impact on subsequent health status. Graduates are likely to be concerned with wellness and preventive health care rather than just treatment of physical and mental illness. Diet, exercise, stress management, a more positive attitude, and other factors tend to give them a longer expected life span and fewer disabilities. This attention to preventive health maintenance probably reflects better self-concept and sense of personal worth. (Health care issues are discussed in detail in Chapter 17.)

Exercise 1.7   *Assessing Your Practical Skills*

Place a check mark next to each item that accurately describes your progress since you were a freshman or that you believe will continue to develop due to the college experience. (Be honest!)

_____ 1. Improved leadership abilities

_____ 2. Improved interpersonal interactions

_____ 3. More able to adjust and adapt to new situations

_____ 4. Less dominated by practical considerations

_____ 5. More likely to engage in future formal educational programs and activities

_____ 6. More clearly focused on a career choice

_____ 7. Improved chance of earning a good income

_____ 8. Improved attitude regarding preventive health care

_____ 9. Improved health care practices (diet, exercise)

_____ 10. Improved stress management skills

_____ 11. Increased chance of marriage at a later age

_____ 12. Increased chance of limiting family size

_____ 13. Increased chance of better timing of marriage and children

_____ 14. More discriminating about overall compatibility of future mate

_____ 15. More likely to encourage children to go to college

_____ 16. More likely to save money for children's education and other enrichment purposes

_____ 17. More likely to attend cultural events

_____ 18. More likely to be selective about television programs and movies

_____ 19. More likely to spend some leisure time in reading and adult education activities

_____ 20. More likely to listen to different types of music

_____ 21. More likely to go to an art museum or exhibit

_____ 22. More likely to find life interesting

What Has the College Experience Done for You?

Research over the past fifty years—especially over the past twenty-five years—shows that college-educated persons tend to exhibit considerably different competencies, behaviors, attitudes, and values than persons who did not choose that route after high school. The research findings, of course, are general and do not apply to every individual and in every setting; neither does every individual experience change in all of the areas discussed. The summary of changes that occur during college and the most likely characteristics of college graduates do enable us to predict the expected outcomes of a college education. At the same time, the amount and particular dimensions of change depend on the specific college environment and on the extent to which an individual becomes involved in the various learning opportunities and is willing to change.

As you conclude your undergraduate experience, you should assess how you have changed and what the college experience has done for you. Some of those changes are not easily measurable, and some of those benefits will become more evident with time. Nonetheless, you should find that college has added meaning, focus, and purpose to your life. It should have increased your sense of self, place, judgment, and responsibility. It should enable you over time to identify and articulate those few principles and values on which you will build your life. An educated perspective should also make life much more interesting to you as well as make you more interesting to those who work or spend time with you.

Exercise 1.8

Rating Your Level of Change

Review the four checklists you filled out in this chapter. Based on your responses, identify the ten areas in which you have experienced the most change and the five areas in which you have changed least. Overall, how much would you say you've changed at college?

Exercise 1.9

Talking with College Graduates

Interview several graduates who have been out of college for at least three years to find out how their college experience affected them. Do their experiences correspond to the findings reported in this chapter?

Conclusion

As this chapter demonstrates, college graduates have enhanced knowledge and skills, an increased employment rate, and a higher income level. They develop the flexibility, mobility, and knowledge needed to adapt to the many changing demands of work, life, and relationships. They contribute to increased productivity and enjoy greater job satisfaction. They think more logically, communicate more effectively, behave more ethically, and they feel better about themselves. They participate in a full range of social and cultural activities, and they "work the system" to their benefit. In short, they receive a more-than-reasonable return on the time, energy, and money invested in a college education. Thus, as you near graduation, you should feel gratified by your decision to attend college.

References and Resources

Astin, A. (1977). Four Critical Years: Effects of College on Beliefs, Attitudes, and Knowledge. San Francisco: Jossey-Bass.

Baird, L., M. Clark, and R. Hartnett. (1973). The Graduates: A Report on the Characteristics and Plans of College Seniors. Princeton, NJ: Educational Testing Service.

Bowen, H. (1981). *Investment in Learning: The Individual and Social Value of American Higher Education.* San Francisco: Jossey-Bass.

Boyer, E. (1987). *College: The Undergraduate Experience in America.* New York: Harper & Row.

Chickering, A. (1969). *Education and Identity.* San Francisco: Jossey-Bass.

Council on Policy Studies in Higher Education. (1981). *Twenty Thousand Futures.* San Francisco: Jossey-Bass.

Erikson, E. (1968). *Identity: Youth and Crisis.* New York: Norton.

Feldman, K., and T. Newcomb. (1969). *The Impact of College on Students.* San Francisco: Jossey-Bass.

Heath, D. (1968). *Growing Up in College.* San Francisco: Jossey-Bass.

Katz, J., et al. (1968). *No Time for Youth: Growth and Constraint in College Students.* San Francisco: Jossey-Bass.

Kohlberg, L. (1981, 1984). *Essays on Moral Development,* vols. 1 and 2. New York: Harper & Row.

———. (1981). *The Meaning and Measurement of Moral Development.* Worchester, MA: Clark University Press.

Loveinger, J. (1976). *Ego Development: Conceptions and Theories.* San Francisco: Jossey-Bass.

Owens, H. (1992). "The Value of College." In John N. Gardner and A. Jerome Jeweler (eds.), *Your College Experience: Strategies for Success.* Belmont, CA: Wadsworth.

————. (1989). "The Cost of College: Is It Worth It?" In John N. Gardner and A. Jerome Jeweler (eds.), *College Is Only the Beginning*, 2nd ed. Belmont, CA: Wadsworth.

Pace, C. (1979). *Measuring Outcomes of College: Fifty Years of Findings, and Recommendations for the Future*. San Francisco: Jossey-Bass.

Parks, S. (1991). *The Critical Years: Young Adults and the Search for Meaning, Faith, and Commitment*. New York: HarperCollins.

Pascarella, E., and P. Terenzini. (1991). *How College Affects Students*. San Francisco: Jossey-Bass.

2 Managing Choices

Margaret A. Ross

Professor of Leadership in the McDonough Leadership Program,
Marietta College

Margaret A. Ross

Professor of Leadership in the McDonough Leadership Program,
Marietta College

Student Voices

Steve

Until my senior year in college, I really never made many important decisions. It was a "given" that I would go to college, and my choice of college was easy since I had a good financial aid package. Once I was in college, selecting classes didn't seem that bad, although there were certain classes I was required to take. My major was an easy choice, since the field was one I liked. Classes fell into place, and my advisor was there to help me. Now in my senior year I feel like the decision of what to do next is the first major choice I've had to make, and I'm scared. What if I make the wrong choice? I need to keep in mind that decisions can be changed and that what I do the first year out of college is not necessarily what I will be doing the rest of my life. ■

"Would you tell me, please, which way I ought to go from here?"
"That depends a good deal on where you want to get to," said the Cat.
"I don't much care where," said Alice.
"Then it doesn't matter which way you go," said the Cat.
"So long as I get somewhere," Alice added as an explanation.
"Oh, you're sure to do that," said the Cat, "if you only walk long enough."

—from Lewis Carroll, *Alice's Adventures in Wonderland*

Graduation often is equated with panic! Like Alice you are facing—or perhaps trying not to face—some tough decisions. Indeed, for many of you, your senior year will be the first time in about twelve or thirteen years that you may not be clear about what you will be doing in the fall. In fact, you may be facing what you feel are the most serious choices of your life, the ones that really matter. To this point, your life has gone along on a reasonably smooth path, and school has always been the place to return to when summer ended. While you may have been making choices, they didn't seem as serious as the ones now facing you. For the first time, you are faced with the serious question, "What should (can) I do now?" In this chapter we'll help you answer that question.

Putting the Decision-Making Task in Perspective

Many seniors put off making choices, using the following excuses, which tend to result in poor decision making and poor decisions:

- I can't make up my mind.
- I'll decide now and analyze it later.
- Whatever will be, will be.
- It just feels right.
- I'll think about that tomorrow.
- I know I should, but I just can't get with it.
- If it's ok with you, it's ok with me.

The result of such thinking is a sense of helplessness.

At this stage in their college careers, many students work themselves into a state of panic as they try to project their future. Many seniors I have worked with are paralyzed by the idea of having to make any choice that they believe will shape their lives irreversibly. Herein, of course, lies the problem: The decision you make is *not* carved in stone! It is possible to change decisions as well as circumstances. Always keep in mind that the decisions you make as seniors are tentative. Moreover, the first job you take is not permanent—it is just your *first* job. It is the beginning of your career, which probably will take a number of turns; indeed, research suggests that most people will have four or five careers in a lifetime.

Many seniors also suffer a crisis in confidence that delays their decisions. After four or more years of college, you may wonder what you are trained to do. With some exceptions, the answer in terms of specific careers is that you are not trained for a specific position. Rather, during the course of your college career, you have acquired many different types of skills both within and outside the classroom. For example, in the process of taking a history class, in addition to learning about history, you have also learned how to analyze, write, research, and so forth. Such skills will prove valuable as you begin your career.

As you think about what to do after graduation, what things should you consider? Probably your first consideration should be your degree of mobility. Are there restrictions on where you might search for a position? Do you have personal reasons for wanting (needing) to stay in a specific geographical location? If so, then your possible career choices might be limited. Obviously, the more mobile you are, the more opportunities for career choices you will have.

A second consideration might be your willingness to take a position that might be beneath your educational level. It is not unusual for some organizations to employ new people at the bottom of the career ladder and have them work their way up.

A third consideration might be the graduate school option—now or later. Consider what your opportunities would be. For example, will you be accepted by the university of your choice? What type of financial aid might you receive? Will graduate school enhance your career prospects or, more importantly, is it simply a way of putting off a difficult decision?

Guidelines for Making Choices

Preparing to Decide

A first step in making decisions, one that many people overlook, is preparing to decide. This preliminary step will provide information on and insight into the issue at hand. By answering the questions in the following seven-step "preparing-to-decide" process, you will ensure that your decisions are sound.

1. **Is your objective clearly defined?** Are you trying to make a decision before you have thought through what precisely you are deciding?

2. **Who else is involved in this decision?** Do you need to consult with someone else? If so, involve that person from the beginning.

3. **What are the time factors?** How soon do you need to make this decision?

4. **Do you have enough information?** Have you done all the necessary research?

5. **Have you done a field-force analysis?** Every decision is controlled by forces (people, circumstances, policies, and so forth) acting on it. What forces will be acting on your decision—either for or against?

6. **What are the risks?** Are you willing to accept them?

7. **Is your action plan ready to implement?** Do you have the resources, either financial or human, to act on your decision?

Case Study: Janet.   Janet was a senior accounting major who grew up near the college she attended. After graduation she wanted to stay in the area because she felt secure. She had lived there all her life and was not ready to move away. She didn't want to live at home and thus chose to live in an adjoining community. During her senior year she had a part-time job with a local public accounting firm. While she enjoyed the work and was successful at it, she knew that this was not the type of accounting she wanted to do. She was able to continue in this position after graduation, so she could afford to take her time to look around for the type of position she did want. While continuing to work as a public accountant, Janet kept her file active in the career development center and continued to work actively with the director, who knew what she was looking for. When an advertisement came in for a position that met her requirements, she was notified and she submitted her application. She is now working for the company.

Janet's case illustrates a number of factors involved in the career decision-making process:

1. She was clear in her own mind what she wanted to do and where she wanted to be located.

2. The decision of where she was going to locate involved only herself.

3. Because she was already employed, she could take the time necessary to search for the position she really wanted.

4. By keeping in close contact with the career development center, she assured herself that she would be informed about new job opportunities.

5. By succeeding at her current position, she made herself attractive to potential future employers.

6. Because she was already employed, she kept the risk factors to a minimum.

7. When the opportunity presented itself, she was able to act on it.

A key for Janet was knowing that her initial decision to keep the public accounting position was not a lifetime decision. By working at that job to pay expenses, she could take her time to look around for something she really wanted to do. Janet also knew that she wanted to stay in the area, but she did not rule out the possibility of moving at a later date. For her, the security of living in a familiar area helped to limit the risk factors.

Exercise 2.1

Brainstorming for Alternatives

Most of us have tunnel vision when it comes to making decisions and need practice in uncovering alternatives. In groups of four or five, work together to generate as many ideas as possible for the use of the common wire coat hanger. Do not evaluate the ideas. List all ideas on paper, and when all the groups have finished, post them so that everyone can see the results. No doubt there will be duplications, but there will also be ideas that are unique to groups. This will help you get ready for the next step in decision making.

Making a Decision

To make a sound decision you should take the following steps:

1. **Identify the decision to be made.** Many people falter at this step, and the result is fuzzy thinking.

2. **Generate all the reasons for the decision under consideration.**

3. **Study the reasons you have developed for your choice.**

4. **Reflect on your tentative decision and be aware of how you feel about it.** Are you excited? Are you depressed? Think about how the decision is going to affect your life right now. If you are dissatisfied with the results of your decision, then you need to review the reasons you listed in step 2. Did you leave something out? Were you honest with yourself?

Reviewing Your Options

As graduation looms, you may be mired in uncertainty about what comes next. Are you thinking about going on to graduate school? Getting a job? Taking a year off? In order to make the best choice, you need to follow the decision-making steps outlined previously.

The Graduate School Option

To illustrate how you should go about making such decisions, imagine that, in considering the graduate school option, you gave the following answers to the seven "preparing-to-decide" questions.

1. I am interested in working in the field of psychology.

This answer is much too vague. The field of psychology is very large, so you need to narrow your focus. Do you want to work in the area of human services? Do you want to be a counselor, and at what level? Do you want to teach? Are you interested in doing research? Until you explore these options, you are not ready to address questions 2–7. Thus you can see how important it is to define your objective clearly.

2. I don't need to consult with anyone about this decision. I do need to find out about available financial aid and scholarships.

It never hurts to consult with people whose opinions you value—friends, family, professors—when making important decisions. You will need to develop a plan of action to investigate financial aid and scholarship packages.

3. I need to be aware of deadlines for applications and for any tests I might have to take for my application.

Your response to question 3 depends on the information you will acquire as a result of deciding which area of psychology you wish to focus on and which schools offer that area of specialization. After you find this out, you can write for applications and find out which graduate school tests you need to take. Many of these tests are given only on specific dates, so this information is very important.

4. I need to explore what aspect of psychology I want to go into and then research graduate schools that have programs relevant to my interest.

5. The factors that will help me in this decision include whether I do well enough on the graduate tests, what type of financial assistance I will be able to get, and where the graduate school is located. I also have to think about other kinds of expenses associated with attending graduate school (for example, travel and personal expenses).

Your answers to question 5 also depend on the information given previously. You may wish to explore further your feelings about the location of the graduate school. Which will be more important to you—location or financial aid available?

6. I might not be able to finish my degree or to find employment in the field even if I do. I might also find out I don't want to work in the field or that a degree in that field won't open the door to the type of position I want.

Whether you will be successful in graduate school is not something you can know ahead of time, although your academic success as an undergraduate and your admission to graduate school certainly should be positive indicators. Perhaps you need to think about what might be available in terms of short-term employment. Would it be wise to get some experience before you go to graduate school? For example, maybe you could get employment in a human services position that would provide some exposure to what working in the field would be like. Perhaps you could interview some people who work in psychology to see what they do on a day-to-day basis.

7. I have to consider how much money I will need to take the graduate tests and to visit the schools I'm considering. I also need to consider whether I have the energy to attend school for another two or perhaps six years.

It should be easy to find out how much money you need to take tests since most application booklets contain that information. It would be a good idea to visit the career development office to see what type of information they have. This would also be a good place to get information on different careers in psychology.

The Year-Off Option

A strong case can be made for not going immediately on to graduate school. A major purpose of an undergraduate education is to help young people explore themselves and their interests. In many cases an undergraduate degree is not a terminal degree leading to a lifelong career. Rather, it is a stepping stone. The logical next step is to go to graduate school, but the major question is *when?* Is it always desirable to go straight to graduate school? If you have any doubts, you'd probably be better off postponing the decision for a year or so.

Senior Voices

Susan

Now that I'm a senior, I'm getting a lot of pressure from my folks to get a high-paying job. They don't seem to understand that after seventeen years of school, I want some time off. I know that once I take a job, I will have a limited amount of time to travel and do other things. I just want to wait a few months, if not a year, before I start my career. They think I'm lazy and don't want to work. That is not it at all. I'm really looking forward to my career, and I know I will do better with it if I take some time off now. In talking with the director of career development, I also know that it is not easy to get a job by graduation time. I just think I'll do better if I postpone that decision. ∎

A personal example might help explain why this is the case. When I went to graduate school after fifteen years of teaching, I found myself in the classroom with many young people who had just graduated from college the previous spring. As I listened to them, I had the distinct feeling that, if they had taken some time off to work before attending graduate school, they would have known the answers to many of the questions they were asking. Many answers come not from a professor but from life experiences. By contrast, because of my own experiences, I was able to develop a graduate program that enhanced my knowledge and helped me learn what I believed I needed to know.

Another factor you should consider is the field of study. For many young people that is not always clear. Keep in mind, however, that no law states that your field of study in graduate school must be a continuation of your undergraduate major. In fact, many graduate students choose a new discipline when they return to school. By taking some time off from school before attending graduate school, you can explore what field you want to concentrate on.

In addition to the benefits noted previously, you can use the year off to investigate the advantages and disadvantages of different graduate schools.

The Employment Option

Suppose you are planning to begin working after graduation. Your answers to the seven "preparing-to-decide" questions might be formulated as follows.

1. My objective is to get a job after graduation.

   This answer is too vague. It is not enough to say you want to get a job—you need to narrow this down. A first step could be evaluating your strengths by using a skills inventory (available at your college's career development center). Looking at your major should give you some clues as to the type of work setting you might enjoy. An interactive career development software package called SIGI PLUS™ can also help you define your value system and thus narrow the areas you're interested in. The more you learn about yourself, the better you will be able to focus on the type of career you would like to pursue. You also need to remember that your first job is a stepping stone, not a career terminus.

2. I have a lot of pressure to get a job and become self-sufficient. Other than that I am free to go job-searching wherever I want. There are no geographic limits, only those that I might impose on myself.

3. I would like to get a job by graduation time, but realistically that isn't likely.

   You might consider taking a temporary job to earn living money while you explore career options. If you do this, you would want to narrow down your employment focus and, if possible, find an evening job so that you would have your days free to interview.

4. I would need the following information before I could make a decision: What jobs are available? Am I willing to locate anywhere? What are some of the resources available to me to help look for employment? Is my resume on file in the career development office?

You might check the alumni directory to see who is living in the area you're interested in. Alumni might be able to provide you with some advice on geographic areas as well as write letters of introduction to people they know in the field you are interested in. They might also be a valuable resource on what type of temporary employment is available in their locales. You should talk with your advisor and other professors to ask for their advice and suggestions. You also need to check into what type of networking might be available.

5. I should take advantage of the help available on campus.

For example, you might schedule a mock interview to get feedback on how you interview. You could also investigate other programs on campus that would aid you in the job search.

6. I need to develop a support system among my friends so that they will be there to encourage me. I know that I will probably have to go on a number of interviews before I am offered a job. I will need support to keep from getting discouraged.

7. I need to set up a timetable and list the things I must do before I start my job search. After I have set the timetable, I could consult the career development office to ensure that my timetable is realistic.

Exercise 2.2 *Improving the Decision-Making Process*

Evaluate the responses to steps 2–7. What might you add to make the decision-making analysis more helpful?

Overcoming Psychological Blocks

The decision-making model just outlined seems pretty straightforward, yet students still have difficulty with making decisions. This suggests that we need to look beyond the surface to see what other factors might be impeding decision making.

Certain psychological blocks hinder people from working through the decision-making process. The first is life goal awareness. There is no guarantee that even seniors have gained an awareness of their personal wants, needs, and/or goals. If individuals have not explored this facet of their personality, it will be very difficult to establish a goal. Thus establishing even a temporary goal is a necessary step in the decision-making process.

A second psychological block is the degree of anxiety in making choices. For whatever reason (and there could be many) some people have an extremely difficult time making any decision, let alone one of such magnitude as "What am I going to do after graduation?"

A third psychological block is the belief that there might be a secondary gain in *not* making a decision. In other words, an individual could have a vested interest in not making a decision. This person might be avoiding making a decision simply by virtue of not wanting to grow up.

A fourth psychological block is the individual's dependence on significant others. Habitually deferring decision making to others constitutes a major block for the individual.

The final psychological block is related to a philosophy of life. Some people approach life from the perspective that what happens to them is due either to luck or to fate. They believe that they have no say in their life and that "what will be, will be."

If any or all of these factors are operating, the unwillingness to make a decision is related to psychological blocks. Depending on the seriousness of these blocks, the individual might profit from therapy. Finally, you must recognize that there is no such thing as not making a decision. Rather, the choice is between making an active decision and making a passive decision, between taking charge of your life and letting life happen to you.

Is There Life After College?

The answer is, yes, there is a life after college, but you need to be prepared for some differences. In some ways college is an abnormal environment. Most of you have spent four years surrounded by peers who are in the same general age group. Your day-to-day activities were very similar—living in communal housing, eating in a common place, going to class, hanging out in the student center, and so forth. Your contact with people from different age groups was very limited and to some degree impersonal. It is highly unlikely that you will ever again find yourself in a similar situation.

For many of you graduation also means taking on the responsibilities of finding your own housing, feeding yourself, and developing a social life that is not ready-made. For the uninitiated this can be frightening. How do you make arrangements to find a place to live? What will it be like living alone? How much do you need for start-up costs such as rent deposits, utility deposits, and food? How do you figure a budget? How do you go about meeting new people? All of this involves some major life changes, and you need to prepare yourself for them while you are still in college.

One source of help in making these life decisions is this book. Review the chapters in this book that deal specifically with these questions (for example, see Chapter 14, "Personal Finances," and Chapter 21, "The Final Six Weeks"). Talk with friends who have graduated before you. The more information you can gather ahead of time, the better prepared you will be for life after college.

Another resource is a healthy support system, one that will not contribute to your stress over decision making. Surround yourself with people who are positive in their attitudes about themselves as well as supportive of you. You will find that such people help you develop a strong sense of self and an awareness of what skills you have acquired and what you have been able to accomplish thus far.

Exercise 2.3

Prioritizing Your Choices

As you approach graduation, what choices must you make? Prioritize these choices in terms of those that need to be made before graduation and those that can wait. Take one of the choices you face and use the four-step decision-making method to arrive at a strategy for action.

Conclusion

Over the years I have worked with many students who find graduation intimidating. They fear that life after college will be all drudgery and no fun. If I were they and I believed that, I wouldn't want to leave college either. I can only say, it doesn't have to be that way. The bottom line is that you can make your life interesting and exciting. Indeed, you have the power to make it whatever you want it to be.

Professional Life

3 Career Planning

Larry G. Salters

Interim Director of the University Career Center,
University of South Carolina

Senior Voices

Lynda

With graduation only eight days away, reality has hit me very hard. As I reminisce about the past few years, I realize that my emotions have been running high.

I have been concerned about finding the "perfect job" for as long as I have been in college. I began as a premed, biology major and soon realized that this career avenue was not for me. After much deliberation and soul searching, I decided to change schools and majors. I have worked very hard for four years in order to be better prepared and qualified when looking for a job in my chosen field— marketing.

Anticipation best describes how I am currently feeling. I have a location restriction that has really put a damper on my marketability. This limitation has made my career hunt much more difficult. After four years of schooling, I have finally decided what I want to do with my life. So far, however, no one has had any open positions in my field of choice. This has to be the most frustrating aspect that I have encountered thus far.

I have approached my career search in various ways. I began looking for a position through the campus career placement center during the spring semester of my senior year. This proved to be a valuable experience, but many of the companies interviewing were interested primarily in people who could relocate. I have also contacted a headhunter, who is looking for other opportunities for me. Finally, I have contacted the companies that I am interested in directly. I know that eventually these strategies will result in the career that I'm looking for. But I have to keep reminding myself that it is going to take time, persistence, and patience. My advice to those looking for a career is to start early, *do not give up*, sell yourself, and develop and utilize a networking system. ∎

Congratulations on your upcoming graduation! Perhaps you're thinking about how hard you've worked these past four or five years, about how you deserve a great job with a rewarding salary and lots of opportunity for growth and personal satisfaction.

Reality hits when you begin to realize that employers aren't knocking down your door with job offers, when Mom and Dad keep asking, "What are you going to do now?" and you don't have an answer, when graduate school seems more alluring than ever before. Reality hits again when the news media report that the 1992 job market for seniors was the worst in thirty years, that only 10–15 percent of seniors had jobs lined up after graduation as compared to 40–50 percent in normal economic times. Reality strikes yet another blow when you hear that companies currently downsizing due to the recession will continue to be leaner in the future and graduating seniors will be competing with experienced, out-of-work people for jobs.

Sounds hopeless and bleak, doesn't it? In truth, today's college seniors do face some hard realities. However, if you engage in proper career planning, you can beat the odds even in tough economic times. In this chapter we will show you how you can successfully prepare yourself for today's job market and enhance your chances for that dream job after graduation through proper career planning.

Learning About Yourself

Michigan State University recently published a list of the most noticeable shortcomings of today's college seniors as reported by employers. Do any of the following apply to you?*

- They have unrealistic career aspirations and work expectations.
- They feel they have already "paid their dues" and employers owe them something.

---

*List adapted from Michigan State University, *Collegiate Employment Institute Newsletter* 6(2) (Winter 1992).

- Their writing skills, oral communication and public speaking abilities, and interpersonal competencies are noticeably worse than in previous years.
- Their mathematical skills and problem-solving abilities need improvement.
- They lack career-related work experiences.
- They are overconfident about their abilities.
- They lack tenacity, motivation, and commitment.
- Their resume and interview preparations are insufficient.

Today's employers consistently stress four qualities when looking at new graduates: (1) good grades, (2) career-related work experience, (3) good communication skills, and (4) leadership skills. In order to make a positive impression on potential employers, you must first learn about yourself: your interests, skills, personality characteristics, values, goals, likes and dislikes, limitations, and so on. The college experience, with its myriad activities, courses, and opportunities, is designed to help you accomplish this. In addition, numerous instruments and exercises can assist you in this process, as can your college career center and your professors, parents, and peers.

Exercise 3.1

Identifying Your Interests

To identify what you're interested in, you can take standardized inventories or tests at the counseling or career advising center at your school. You can also do the following:

1. Read through your college catalog and check each course that sounds interesting. Ask yourself why they sound interesting.
2. List all the classes, activities, and clubs you enjoyed in college. Ask yourself why you enjoyed these things.

Exercise 3.2

Identifying Your Skills

Use the following list to help you determine your current skills. First, place a check mark next to the skills you presently have. Then, identify and circle the five skills you are most confident about, those about which you could say to anyone, "I am good at this."

_____ writing	_____ socializing	_____ getting results
_____ reading	_____ working on a team	_____ being neat

_____ conversing	_____ explaining	_____ keeping records
_____ reporting information	_____ helping others	_____ being accurate
_____ interviewing	_____ teaching	_____ asserting self
_____ being creative	_____ entertaining	_____ taking risks
_____ working on machines	_____ speaking in public	_____ negotiating
_____ being sensitive	_____ selling	_____ applying technical knowledge
_____ learning	_____ analyzing	_____ being friendly
_____ building things	_____ evaluating	_____ motivating
_____ repairing things	_____ handling money	_____ managing
_____ operating tools	_____ planning	_____ directing others
_____ observing	_____ solving problems	_____ adapting
_____ listening	_____ scheduling	_____ encouraging
_____ brainstorming ideas	_____ following through	_____ cooperating
_____ being tactful	other: _____	

Select two or three of your strongest skills. Suppose a potential employer asked you to prove you possessed these skills. How would you do this?

_____

Exercise 3.3

Identifying Your Aptitudes

For the following aptitude areas place an X next to those you know you are weak in, a question mark next to those you are not sure about, and a check mark next to those you are strong in. Are they in the same family as the skills you previously checked?

_____ 1. *Abstract reasoning.* People with strong aptitudes in abstract reasoning can interpret poetry, work out scientific problems in their heads, and solve logic problems.

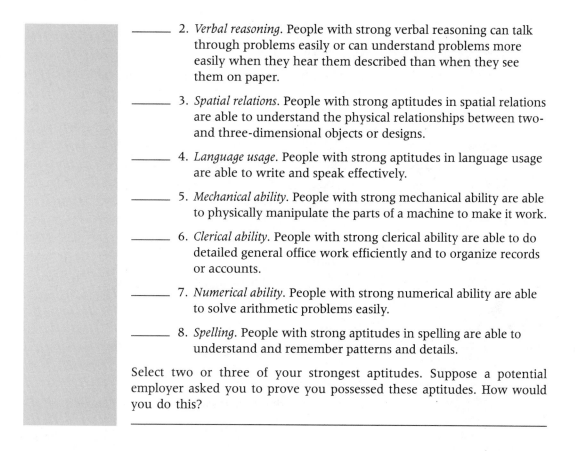

_____ 2. *Verbal reasoning.* People with strong verbal reasoning can talk through problems easily or can understand problems more easily when they hear them described than when they see them on paper.

_____ 3. *Spatial relations.* People with strong aptitudes in spatial relations are able to understand the physical relationships between two- and three-dimensional objects or designs.

_____ 4. *Language usage.* People with strong aptitudes in language usage are able to write and speak effectively.

_____ 5. *Mechanical ability.* People with strong mechanical ability are able to physically manipulate the parts of a machine to make it work.

_____ 6. *Clerical ability.* People with strong clerical ability are able to do detailed general office work efficiently and to organize records or accounts.

_____ 7. *Numerical ability.* People with strong numerical ability are able to solve arithmetic problems easily.

_____ 8. *Spelling.* People with strong aptitudes in spelling are able to understand and remember patterns and details.

Select two or three of your strongest aptitudes. Suppose a potential employer asked you to prove you possessed these aptitudes. How would you do this?

_____

Exercise 3.4

Identifying Your Personality Characteristics

List ten words you think best describe yourself. Ask at least three people who know you well (parents, spouse, brother or sister, close friend, co-worker) to write down ten words they would use to describe you. How do the lists compare?

_____

Exercise 3.5

Identifying Your Life Goals

The following list includes life goals some people set for themselves. This list can help you begin to think about the kinds of goals you may want to set. First, place a check mark next to the goals you would like to achieve in your life. Next, review the goals you have checked and circle the five you want most. Finally, review your list of five goals and rank-order them (1 for most important, 5 for least important).

_____ 1. The love and admiration of friends

_____ 2. Professional success

_____ 3. Good health

_____ 4. A personal contribution to the elimination of poverty and sickness

_____ 5. Lifetime financial security

_____ 6. A chance to shape the future of a nation

_____ 7. A lovely home

_____ 8. International fame

_____ 9. Personal freedom

_____ 10. Professional freedom

_____ 11. A satisfying and fulfilling marriage

_____ 12. A good love relationship

_____ 13. A happy family relationship

_____ 14. A satisfying religious faith

_____ 15. Complete self-confidence

_____ 16. Recognition as the most attractive person in the world

_____ 17. An understanding of the meaning of life

Other: _____

_____

SOURCE: List adapted with permission of the author from James D. McHolland, Human Potential Seminar, Evanston, IL, 1975.

Exercise 3.6

Identifying Your Work Values

The following list includes typical work values—reasons people give for liking the work they do. It can help you begin to think about what you want to receive from your work. First, place a check mark next to each work value you'd like to have as part of your ideal job. Next, review the items you've checked and circle the ten items you want most. Finally, review your list of ten items and rank-order them in order of importance (1 for most important, 10 for least important).

1. *Help society:* Do something to contribute to the betterment of the world.

2. *Help others:* Be involved in helping other people in a direct way, either individually or in a small group.

3. *Have public contact:* Have a lot of day-to-day contact with people.

4. *Work with others:* Have close working relationships with a group as a result of work activities.

5. *Compete:* Engage in activities that pit your abilities against others where there are clear win-and-lose outcomes.

6. *Make decisions:* Have the power to decide courses of action.

7. *Hold power and authority:* Control other people's work activities.

8. *Influence people:* Be in a position to change the attitudes or opinions of other people.

9. *Work alone:* Do projects by yourself, without any significant amount of contact with others.

10. *Hold intellectual status:* Be regarded as a person of high intellectual prowess, an acknowledged "expert."

11. *Create* (general): Create new ideas and programs instead of following an established format.

12. *Supervise:* Have a job in which you're directly responsible for the work done by others.

13. *Experience change and variety:* Have work responsibilities that frequently change.

14. *Be stable:* Have a work routine that is largely predictable.

15. *Be secure:* Be assured of keeping your job and reaping a reasonable financial reward.

16. *Live at a fast pace:* Work in circumstances in which there is a high pace of activity and work must be done rapidly.

17. *Gain recognition:* Be recognized for the quality of your work.

18. *Feel excitement:* Experience frequent excitement in the course of your work.

19. *Find adventure:* Have work duties that involve frequent risk taking.

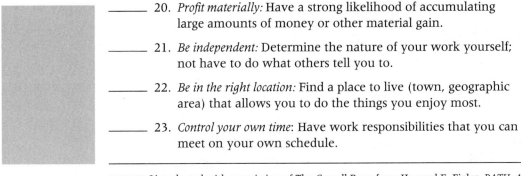

_____ 20. *Profit materially:* Have a strong likelihood of accumulating large amounts of money or other material gain.

_____ 21. *Be independent:* Determine the nature of your work yourself; not have to do what others tell you to.

_____ 22. *Be in the right location:* Find a place to live (town, geographic area) that allows you to do the things you enjoy most.

_____ 23. *Control your own time*: Have work responsibilities that you can meet on your own schedule.

SOURCE: List adapted with permission of The Carroll Press from Howard E. Figler, *PATH: A Career Workbook for Liberal Arts Students* (Cranston, RI: Carroll Press, 1979). Copyright © 1979 by Carroll Press.

If you do a good job of assessing yourself, you should be well prepared to answer that key interview question, "Why should we hire you?" Your answer would focus on three areas:

- **Personal characteristics**. Here you would list your most applicable personality traits, such as ambitious, assertive, people-oriented, and so on.

- **Content areas**. Here you would identify your relevant areas of interest, such as solar energy, urban renewal, labor negotiations, and the like.

- **Transferable skills**. Here you would present the specific talents you possess, such as cost accounting, chemical engineering, research instrument design, and so forth.

Investigating the Job Market

Clarifying your self-concept is a key step in career decision making, but it's not the only one. You must also learn about the work world and understand the job market. To do so, you can draw on three basic resources: (1) the print media, (2) working professionals, and (3) college career centers.

The Print Media

Your college library and career center have numerous resources in which you can find information about the job market in general and individual employers in particular. These resources include the *Encyclopedia of Associations*, the *World Chamber of Commerce Directory*, and publications of the College Placement Council.

Exercise 3.7

Investigating Employers

Select three organizations with which you are interested in seeking employment. Utilizing resources in the career center, the library, or the community, compile information on the following:

1. Name of the organization
2. Parent company and subsidiaries
3. Primary locations
4. Age, growth history, and growth potential
5. Major goods/services
6. Current problems/issues facing the organization
7. Position you would apply for in the organization
8. Position requirements
9. Average starting salary

Working Professionals

People who are already employed in areas of interest to you are another good source of information. You may wish to shadow someone who is doing the kind of work you hope to do; in fact, many colleges have formal programs to facilitate shadowing alumni and other friends of the institution. Or you may choose to do some information interviewing—that is, visiting with someone who is working in a job you would like to explore. The information-gathering interview enables you to become more knowledgeable about your field(s) of interest and allows potential employers to get to know you in a pleasant, low-stress setting. This type of interview will greatly increase your chances of a satisfying job placement. To have an effective information interview, you should take the following steps:

1. **Clarify your goals.** Write a brief summary of your abilities, interests, and values. Conclude with a short statement about the kinds of organizations that you think may match your statement.

2. **Select some places to visit.** Use the Alumni Community Referral file, the Yellow Pages, alumni directories, Chamber of Commerce listings, friends, faculty, and so on to generate the name of at least one organization to visit. One name will be sufficient, for it will soon lead to others.

3. **Set up an appointment.** Contact directly the person who is actually doing the job you are interested in, rather than going through the personnel office or the receptionist. If you have done your homework,

you will not be imposing on the person's time. It's important, however, that you show genuine interest in what your target person is doing. To illustrate, suppose you are exploring the career of advertising director. You contact the advertising director of company X (whose name was given to you by an alumnus). You might begin as follows:

"Mr. Simpson, my name is ———. I was given your name by ———. I'm very much interested in advertising, but feel like I don't have enough current information on the field. I thought that if I could talk to someone knowledgeable in advertising, like yourself, I would have a clearer picture of the profession.

"I've heard that your department has been doing some very creative things, particularly with your recent radio-TV campaign. I would like very much to get your personal opinion about corporate advertising and would enjoy the opportunity of coming to your office to discuss your views."

If the target person cannot see you, ask to talk for a few minutes on the phone. Also ask for names of others you might contact in the same career field.

4. **Prepare for the interview.** Research the organization by consulting the print media and by talking to people who are acquainted with the organization. Draw up a list of questions for the person you will interview. And be sure to dress appropriately.

5. **Conduct the interview.** Remember, this is *not* a job interview! Certainly, you want to make a positive impression, but your prime purpose is to acquire information. You are the person in control of the interview; you are asking the questions. These questions might include the following:

   a. What types of careers exist in this field?

   b. What is the future outlook for this career field?

   c. What kinds of persons do well in this field? What skills, interests, or values are important?

   d. Is choice of major important in this field?

   e. How important is graduate school to this occupation?

   f. What are the most significant pluses/minuses about working in this field?

   g. How did you (the interviewer) enter this field? What previous jobs led to this one? What do you like/dislike about the field?

   h. What would I do in an average day working in your organization?

   i. Where might I be after five years with your organization? What about movement?

j. If I left this career field after five years, what other occupations might be open to me?

k. Who are other people with whom I could talk to learn more about this career field?

l. What kind of training is necessary for this career field?

m. What are typical salaries in this career field?

n. What is the top job one can land in this career?

o. What special advice would you give a young person entering this field?

p. What is the best way to obtain a position that will start me on a career in this field?

q. Can you give me information on job specifications and descriptions?

6. **Write a thank-you letter.** Don't forget this courtesy! It will impress the interviewee and remind him or her of your pleasant conversation. It may also help your job-finding campaign later on.

7. **Follow up.** Keep a record of the organizations you visit. For each, note opportunities/problems that you feel your skills could help solve. Also, contact the people referred to you by the interviewee and interview them.

Exercise 3.8

Conducting an Information-Gathering Interview

The information-gathering interview provides an opportunity for you to learn about yourself and about possible career options appropriate for you. Using the guidelines above, conduct an information interview relevant to your career goals.

The College Career Center

Whether you are graduating from a large university or a small private college, you will want to use the resources of your college career office. Many career centers offer orientations for seniors on how to use the various systems for researching the job market and securing employment. Your college may have an on-campus recruiting system where employers visit the campus and interview students. Or you may have access to a Career Day when employers conduct interviews on campus. Many campuses have resume referral services, bulletin boards, computer networks, job bulletins, alumni networks, and other sources for making contacts with employers. These mechanisms are only one means of securing employment and should be maximized along with your own self-directed job search.

After you have researched yourself and researched the world of work, you are ready to synthesize this information, make a choice, and begin preparing for a satisfying career. The career decision-making and job search process is outlined here:

1. **Clarify your career goals.** It will be very difficult to find a job when you are not sure what you are looking for. For assistance make an appointment with a counselor or attend a career objectives workshop.

2. **Write your resume.** Attend a resume-writing workshop or watch a videotape on resume writing in the career library. (Resumes are discussed in detail in the next section.)

3. **Attend a career center orientation for seniors.**

4. **Identify employers.** Consult the career library to assist in identifying appropriate employers directories. Also, CPC (College Placement Council) annuals can assist you in your job search.

5. **Establish a network.** Identify a person in each organization who can give you insight into their needs. For ideas about networking, attend a job search workshop or watch a videotape on job search strategies.

6. **Research the employer.** Read literature in the career library to learn about companies and industries.

7. **Make an appointment to talk to a potential employer.** If you are unable to schedule an appointment, send a resume and cover letter to the appropriate person. Be sure your cover letter is strong and reflects your research. (Cover letters are discussed in detail in the next section.)

8. **Follow up with a telephone call.** At this time arrange for an interview.

9. **Prepare for the interview.** Review research material, attend an interviewing workshop, watch videotapes on interviewing, or participate in a mock interview. (Job interviews are discussed in detail later in the chapter.)

10. **Follow up.** After the interview send a thank-you note and, within an appropriate time, make a phone call.

11. **Seek help.** If you need any help or have any questions, make an appointment with a counselor in the career center.

Writing Resumes and Cover Letters

Now that you've clarified your self-concept and learned something about the job market in general and potential employers in particular, you need to put together your resume. In addition, you need to craft a cover letter to accompany the resume.

Resumes

You will need a resume to present your qualifications to a potential employer. The word *resume* means "short summary." It is a marketing tool whose sole purpose is to secure an interview. Resumes commonly are organized according to (1) chronology or (2) skills.

Chronological Resume.   Recent college graduates and career changers with related experience often use a chronological resume, which organizes information in reverse chronological order. The content of the resume may vary, but whatever you do include should highlight your strengths. The following list outlines the sections you might incorporate into a chronological resume; Figure 3.1 shows how one such resume might look.

- **Career objective**: A one- or two-line description of the position sought or specific job interest. Avoid long or overly broad descriptions.
- **Education**: Degree(s) earned and major, minor, or cognate, as well as school and graduation date. List the most recent degree first. Include the proportion of college expenses earned and GPA/GPA in major if 3.0 or better.
- **Selected courses**: Courses that support the objective. Include areas of concentration if impressive. This information might also appear in the Education section. Do not use if course work is assumed according to the degree earned.
- **Honors/awards**: Scholarships, fellowships, academic honors, and so on. If there are less than three, list elsewhere on resume.
- **Experience**: Job title, location, and dates. List the most recent first. Describe duties using action verbs. Include summer, part-time and full-time work, internships, and cooperative education work. List accomplishments and skills developed.
- **Activities**: Membership and leadership in organizations, and volunteer work, on campus or in the community. Include a description of duties and offices if relevant.
- **Interests**: Hobbies, sports, and so forth. List these especially if they are common in the field sought (for example, golf and banking).
- **References**: May simply state, "Available upon request." Alternatively, list names, addresses, and telephone numbers of references on a separate sheet.

Keep in mind that these guidelines are only for the purpose of beginning your resume. Individuals may want to change the order of categories or add/delete categories based on their background. Ask yourself, What makes the best statement of who I am and what I can do? Then ask, Does this format give the strongest picture of my assets?

Figure 3.1   Sample Chronological Resume

JOHN Q. PUBLIC
3130 Appian Way
Oldtown, NY 70001
808-555-4321

OBJECTIVE

Seeking entry-level management position utilizing managerial experience, organizational abilities, and interpersonal skills; particular interests in production.

EDUCATION

Bachelor of Arts in Psychology, May 1988
Minor: Business Administration/Management
- GPA in major 3.2
- Worked 20 hours per week while full-time student
- Financed 60% of educational expenses

SELECTED
COURSES

Introduction to Management
Principles of Production Management
Advanced Managerial Theories
Principles of Supervision
Fundamentals of Accounting I & II

EXPERIENCE

Assistant Manager, Pop's Deli, July 1984–present
- Supervised waiting staff of 10
- Ordered $1,000 in supplies weekly
- Trained new employees
- Increased sales by 10% during time as assistant manager

Manager's Assistant, Swift Pool, May–July 1984
- Assisted with the supervision of a locally popular pool facility
- Organized and ran concession stand that sold up to $300 of food daily

ACTIVITIES

President, Zeta Zeta Zeta Fraternity
- Organized and supervised work of 10 committees
- Allocated annual budget of $15,000
- Interacted with university, city, and state officials
- Fraternity membership increased 10% during presidency

Chairman, Interfraternal Council
- Convened and led weekly meetings of fraternity representatives
- Appointed representatives and supervised work of all committees
- Organized three fund-raising activities yearly that raised $25,000, the most money ever raised by interfraternal council in one year

American Management Association
Waterskiing Club
Equestrian Club

INTERESTS

Golf, tennis, English literature, numismatics

REFERENCES

Available upon request

Skills Resume.   The skills resume is appropriate for individuals who do not have experience or education related to their objective but who have mastered the skills necessary for the position desired. Career changers might use this format if their previous experience is not directly related to their desired goals. The following list outlines possible components of a skills resume; Figure 3.2 shows how one such resume might look.

- **Objective**: Description of position sought or job area interest. Avoid overly broad or general descriptions. Also avoid double objectives. Use two separate resumes if you have two career directions. You may use a long-term objective if it fits the natural progression (for example, "Bank trainee position leading toward branch management")

- **Education**: Degree(s) earned, major, minor, school, and graduation date. List the most recent degree first.

- **Skills**: A general statement of at least three important skills related to the career objective. For each skill provide specific documentation: full- and part-time employment, internships, cooperative education experiences, and so on. Use action verbs in documenting these skills.

- **Experience**: A reverse chronological listing of jobs, employers, location, and dates employed. Information may be arranged according to strength (that is, job title first, employer first, or organization first).

- **Activities**: Membership in organizations, offices held, volunteer activities, and the like.

- **Interests**: Hobbies and areas of special interest.

- **References**: May simply state: "Available upon request." Alternatively, list names, addresses, and telephone numbers of references on a separate sheet.

This style of resume is used to translate your potential in your chosen career field when that potential may not be obvious from your specific background. Thus, for example, it may be helpful in applying for a job outside of your major. The statements under each specific skill area should be pulled from the description of duties or collateral courses or honors/awards—that is, from *facts* in your background—and should not appear in other resume sections.

Again, note that these guidelines are only intended to help you begin your resume; individual formats vary greatly. For examples of a variety of resume layouts, consult your campus career center.

Cover Letters

A good cover letter is essential to the job search when you cannot make face-to-face contact with the prospective employer. In most cases the cover letter has three major goals, one per paragraph: (1) to introduce

Figure 3.2   Sample Skills Resume

MARY L. PUBLIC
39 Sherman Avenue
Newtown, NJ 30003
515-987-6543

OBJECTIVE   Seeking hospitality-related managerial position utilizing sales initiative, organizational abilities, planning skills, and supervisory experience

EDUCATION   Bachelor of Arts in English, May 1987
• Managed own business while a full-time student
• Financed 100% of educational expenses

SKILLS   **Initiative**
• Developed and promoted summer pool parties and banquets
• Established and managed in-home dining service
• Developed marketing strategy and arranged promotions
• Within one year, profits reached $200 weekly

Organization
• Organized parties for up to 500 area residents
• Hired and trained staff of 6
• Designed promotional materials for newspaper, TV, and radio release
• Ordered supplies

Supervision
• Supervised staff of 10 hired for New Year's Eve party
• Hired and trained staff of 4 for own dining business, operated while a full-time college student

EXPERIENCE   **Self-Employed,** June 1984–August 1987
Diner's Delight
• Managed a local in-home dining facility while a college student

Self-Employed, August 1982–May 1984
Parties Plus
• Organized parties for local civic groups

Bagboy, May–August 1982
Wee Pig Food Store
• Bagged groceries for customers in locally popular shopping facility
• Received 6 monthly awards for providing the most courteous service

ACTIVITIES   American Management Association
Volunteer, American Red Cross
Literacy Volunteers of America
Equestrian Club
Whitewater Rafting Club

INTERESTS   Golf, hunting, tennis, skiing, chess

---

yourself, (2) to present relevant qualifications, and (3) to establish a personal link.

In the first paragraph you explain the circumstances under which you are writing. This can range from simply stating the sources and date of the advertisement you are responding to (least desirable) to mentioning mutual acquaintances, past conversations, or specific facts about the company or its products that attract you. The more personal the connection, the better (for example, "I read in the Wall Street Journal . . . " or "Bill Smith suggested I write you . . . ").

In the second paragraph you list your skills, experiences, and special attributes as they relate to the needs of the company or organization. This is a good place to highlight material not necessarily on the resume, such as commitment to a common goal, special experiences supporting that goal, product knowledge, and the like. You may also want to highlight material on your resume, but do not simply repeat information.

In the final paragraph you initiate direct contact with the person reading the letter. Stating a date on which you will contact the recipient of the letter assures some level of direct interaction and presents you as an individual willing to show an appropriate level of initiative. By contrast, the "contact me at your convenience" phrase common to cover letters presents a passive attitude.

Although there is no single perfect way to write a cover letter, there are some general guidelines:

1. **Address it to an individual.** Find the name of the appropriate individual—it will pay off! One letter to the right person is more productive than ten "to whom it may concern" letters.

2. **Keep it brief and simple.** Use words that work for you rather than trying to impress with quantity or fancy language.

3. **Be professional.** Type the letter on high-quality paper, use good business letter principles—and don't forget to sign it!

4. **Use brief examples.** When stating specific skills, keep it simple and to the point.

5. **Avoid using a form letter for every application.** A letter that doesn't fit the company or the circumstances does more harm than good.

6. **Proofread it carefully.** Mistakes in grammar, spelling, punctuation, or fact make you look unprofessional. It's also a good idea to have someone else read the letter—he or she is likely to spot things you missed.

7. **Don't repeat your resume.** A cover letter should expand on and add to the resume.

8. **Avoid cliches.** Phrases such as "opportunity for advancement," "a challenging position," "position offering security," and "rewarding, challenging career utilizing my skills" have already been used to excess. Try to keep your language fresh and original.

As with resumes, your campus career center should be able to provide you with a number of examples of cover letters.

Rajan

My senior year was one of the most paradoxical experiences of my life. I wasn't sure if I should be excited because I was finally graduating or scared because life after graduation was one big question mark.

Not one night passed without my thinking about the future. My mind was flooded with anxieties, fears, confusion, and, above all, questions about where I would be three months after graduation. Every time I was asked, "So whatya doing after school?" I dodged the question. Frankly, I hadn't a clue.

The last time I had to go through this was when I was a senior in high school. I thought that would be the last time I would have to be subjected to such a fear of the unknown. How wrong I was. At least in high school, the unknown was simply where I would go to college. Now, it's not so much "where I would be" but more "what I would be doing."

I was constantly turning to friends, professors, and especially other seniors just to talk about the future. I now realize that all I was trying to get from them was reassurance and support. I wanted to hear other seniors dodge the questions about life after college, hoping to find that I wasn't the only one. I just needed someone to tell me, "Everything is going to be ok."

I read just about every book I could find on career planning, resume writing, graduate school, and interviewing. I also forced myself to attend many career workshops and seminars during my senior year. I guess I thought the answer was to be found in one of these books or seminars. Unfortunately, each book and seminar only left me with more questions. Little did I know that this was the objective—that the process was preparing me to find my own answers.

Ironically, no matter how much I prepared and investigated my options, I constantly felt that I was behind everyone else and that I should have started six months earlier. Everything I was being put through boiled down to wanting a sense of security after graduation.

The senior experience was at times a tumultuous one: too many questions, not enough answers. Planning a career was definitely one of my most challenging endeavors. It is only after going through the entire process, emotionally and practically, that I can say I really learned something about myself. I have finally realized that, if I approach such decisions with a mature, positive attitude and a sense of responsibility, everything is indeed going to be ok. ■

Interviewing for a Job

Now that you have received that important phone call and the interview time is set, what do you do next? Naturally, you may be apprehensive and nervous, but you can enhance your chances of success by (1) preparing for the interview, (2) knowing what to expect, and (3) learning how to negotiate a salary.

Preparing for the Interview

The first step in the job interview process is analyzing your strengths and weaknesses, your background, your academic performances, your vocational interests, and your personal aspirations and values. In other words, you need to begin formulating in your mind not only what you would like to do but also what you feel you are best prepared to do.

Exercise 3.9

Anticipating Interview Questions

The following are commonly asked interview questions. Think of a specific job you would like to have, and then answer the questions.

1. What are your short-term career objectives?
2. What are your long-term career objectives?
3. Why does our company/organization interest you?
4. Why did you choose your particular area or field?
5. What are your interests and activities?
6. Why did you choose this college?
7. What do you expect from this job?
8. What do you feel you have to offer this company/organization?

These questions are important ones. If you had trouble answering them, your campus career center can help.

The Initial Interview

Although each job interview takes on its own shape and tone, certain features have come to be regarded as standard, and your awareness of them can make your interviews more positive. Table 3.1 outlines the initial interview process—both topics covered and responses expected.

Table 3.1 Stages and Topics of the Initial Interview

	Interview Topics	Interviewer Expectations
First Impression	Introduction/greeting Small talk about traffic, the weather, the basketball team	Firm handshake, eye contact Appearance and dress appropriate to the business, not campus setting Ease in social situations, good manners, poise
Educational Record	Reasons for choice of school and major Value of education or preparation Grades; effort required for them Courses enjoyed most and least, and why Special achievements, toughest problems High school record, SAT scores Reaction to teachers	Intellectual abilities, breadth and depth of knowledge Relevance of course work to career interests Value placed on achievement Willingness to work hard Special or general interests Ability to cope with problems Relation between ability and achievement Reaction to authority
Work Experience	Nature of jobs held Reasons for taking them Level of responsibility reached Relations with others Supervisory experience Duties liked most and least	Sensible use of resources High energy level, vitality, enthusiasm Leadership, interest in responsibility Ability to get along with others Ability to motivate oneself, to make things happen
Activities and Interests	Role in extracurricular, athletic, community, and social service activities Personal interests: hobbies, cultural interests, sports	Diversity of interests Awareness of outside world; social conscience, good citizenship

Negotiating a Salary*

At this stage of your life, getting a job is probably more important than earning a high salary. Nonetheless, you must earn enough to at least get by in an increasingly tough economic climate. While salary is usually more negotiable for experienced candidates than undergraduates, certain

---

*Discussion based on guidelines developed by Ronald C. Pilenzo, *National Business Employment Weekly*.

	Interview Topics	Interviewer Expectations
Type of Work Desired	Successes/failures Skills/deficiencies Immediate objectives Long-term objectives Interest in this company	Realistic knowledge of strengths and weaknesses Preparation for employment Knowledge of opportunities Seriousness of purpose Career-oriented rather than job-oriented
	Other companies being considered Desire for further education/training Geographic preferences and limitations Attitude toward relocation Health factors	Knowledge of the company Real interest in the company Company's chances to get and keep you How might health affect job performance
The Company	Company opportunities Where you might fit Current and future projects	Appropriate but not undue interest in salary or benefits Informed and relevant questions Indications of interest
Conclusion	Further steps you should take (application form, transcript, references) Further steps company will take; explanation of how application will be handled, when you will be notified of decision Cordial farewell	Candidate's attention to information as a sign of continued interest

techniques can help you win a desirable offer. Keep in mind, too, that salary is more than the money in your paycheck; benefits are usually worth at least one third more than base pay.

Negotiating a salary is an art. The following pointers should help guide you through this unfamiliar terrain.

1. **Let the interviewer bring up salary.** This is especially applicable if you have already gotten a job offer. If you must name a figure, give a range that you are comfortable with, perhaps within $5000.

2. **Do your homework on what the job is worth.** You can get this information from salary surveys and marketplace interviews, and, if possible, by finding out what the previous person made.

3. **Find out about performance reviews and salary administration.** This will tell you how often you can expect raises.

4. **Don't always push for more than is offered.** If you do ask for substantially more than the company is offering, you must be able to back up your counteroffer with reasons you are worth what you are asking.

5. **Consider the benefits as well as the salary.** In other words, look at the total package when you evaluate an offer.

6. **Begin salary negotiations even before the interview.** When you fill out the employment application, don't specify a figure, even if you have one in mind. Under "salary requirements," write "open" or "negotiable."

7. **Ask what you can look forward to in terms of promotions.** Although it may not seem salary related, job progression affects salary. Assuming you do a good job, what's the next step? How are promotions handled? If there is not a progression, does the company offer the opportunity to move into other jobs? (Interviewers may not volunteer this information because they are interested only in filling the vacancy; you have to ask.) You may be faced with a dilemma: an interesting job with an appealing salary, but no room for advancement.

What you and the interviewer are striving for is the best possible job match between you and the organization. Keep in mind, too, that each situation is different and that there is no right or wrong way to negotiate a salary. Somehow, you will reach a mutually satisfactory agreement.

Interviewing: Some Points to Remember

The job interview is a major life step. The following tips should help you prepare for—and succeed in—this process.

1. **Analyze strengths and weaknesses.** In preparing for interviews, start by doing some solid, honest soul searching. Analyze your strengths and weaknesses, your background, your academic performance, your vocational interests, and your own mind.

2. **Read employer literature.** Study your prospective employers. It is important that you have some knowledge about their policies, philosophies, products, and services. Failure to do your homework before an interview can be the kiss of death—nothing turns recruiters off faster.

3. **Dress in good taste.** Although most employers are becoming more liberal in their standard of dress and appearance, let basic good taste

be your guide. If a beard or "Alice in Wonderland" look is going to jeopardize your chances for a job, at least be aware of that and proceed accordingly. With some employers, appearance could be the deciding factor. The question you have to ask yourself is, "How important is it?"

4. **Be yourself.** Your attitude is going to influence the interviewer's evaluation. Don't try to be something you aren't; just be yourself. Emphasize your strong points and remember that the recruiter is looking for inherent personal energy and enthusiasm. The interview is your opportunity to sell a product, and that product is you!

5. **Dwell on the positive.** Try always to dwell on the positive. While past failures and shortcomings need not be volunteered, don't try to cover them up or sidestep them. Should the recruiter ask about them, try to explain the circumstances rather than give excuses or blame others. Remember, the interviewer is human, too, and probably has made a few mistakes. You'll create a better impression by being honest and open.

6. **Ask questions when indicated.** If appropriate, ask meaningful questions, particularly if you're not clear about the details of the job, the training program, or other job-related concerns. However, don't ask questions just because you think that's what is expected.

7. **Follow up.** Provide whatever credentials, references, or transcripts are requested by the prospective employer as soon as possible. Be sure to write down the name, title, and address of the recruiter. You may want to consider writing a brief letter of thanks for the interview.

Weighing Your Options in Tough Economic Times

A recent newspaper cartoon depicted a new master's degree holder flipping burgers for a fast-food chain; her supervisor tells her she can't wash dishes until she has a Ph.D. Unfortunately, many recent college graduates have been forced to take jobs that are beneath their level of education and skill, especially in recessionary times. If this happens to you, you should develop a plan to move on before you get locked in by personal and financial obligations or before you become typecast. You should look for ways to advance with your present employer, but if that is impossible, recognize it and find yourself a new employment situation in which you have more options for growth.

Other options may include traveling, getting a temporary job before continuing with your education, or just resting awhile. You should consider how each option relates to your long-range career development plan. Ask yourself where you want to be five or ten years from now and how this option fits into the master plan. You should also think about how "stopping out" looks to a future employer and how you will explain such gaps or lapses in your work history in future interviews.

If you should find that you've somehow fallen off the track to that ideal high-paying, high-status job, there's no reason to despair. Teaching, human service occupations, and public service areas offer rewarding career options. Although the rewards are often more intrinsic than financial, they are sufficient to provide a fulfilling and satisfying career. Your campus career center should be able to help you find out about careers in these areas.

Conclusion

The skills you develop in college in knowing and selling yourself, in researching employers, and in networking will continue to benefit you throughout life, especially when you are confronted with a career change. Many colleges offer alumni assistance with this process as well. In a very literal sense your preparation as a senior for the job market or life after graduation is really preparation for life. Good luck!

References and Resources

Bolles, Richard N. (1985). *The Three Boxes of Life*. Berkeley, CA: Ten Speed Press. If there are any modern-day classics in career literature, this book by the author of *What Color Is Your Parachute* (see below) is surely among them. It's big, opinionated, and every bit as valid today as in 1978 when it was first published. The subtitle, *An Introduction to Life/Work Planning*, is too modest. It's actually a complete course—"a rich and rewarding guidebook that provides literally hundreds of opportunities for growth" (*Library Journal*), "truly a monumental work which provides a wealth of information" (*Journal of College Placement*).

————. *What Color Is Your Parachute?* (1992). Berkeley, CA: Ten Speed Press. On the twentieth anniversary of its first publication, this new edition offers invaluable, realistic advice and suggestions for job hunters and those interested in changing careers. Appendices include career-planning activities, a state-by-state listing of career counseling groups, and job-hunting tips for people with disabilities.

Figler, Howard. (1988). *The Complete Job-Search Handbook*. New York: Henry Holt. What distinguishes this book is its coverage of topics not found in other books, a program using twenty basic lifetime skills that come into play in the job search, and Figler's clarity, humor, and reassuring good sense. This text includes the hidden nine-point agenda of every job interview, special strategies just for the liberal arts graduate, ways to determine the correct salary, and the most common ways job hunters trip themselves up. Intelligent, practical advice for the bored, the aimless, the depressed, and the panicked.

Jackson, Tom. (1990). *The Perfect Resume*. New York: Doubleday. This is one of the most complete guides to resume writing available—with fifty-five samples of job-winning resumes, a variety of resume formats for different job objectives, easy-to-use resume drafting forms, and a section on cover letters. The text includes job-finding tips and salary negotiating strategies plus special resume information for women entering the job market and college students seeking first jobs.

Jud, Brian. (1991). *Job Search 101*. Avon, CT: Marketing Directions. This guide gives step-by-step directions for planning, implementing, and evaluating a professional job search, including tips on how to use proven principles of marketing in your search. The five stages of the interviewing process are covered, as is writing resumes and cover letters. This text is billed as "the practical way to find a job, written by someone who has been on both sides of the interview desk."

Michelozzi, Betty Neville. (1992). *Coming Alive from Nine to Five*. Mountain View, CA: Mayfield. This handbook is a practical guide that demystifies the career search process and meets the needs of a wide range of people, from students beginning college to professionals changing careers. The challenges, options, and opportunities in the twenty-first century are explored, as are the problems of balancing work and family. In addition, key labor statistics and other time-sensitive data have been thoroughly updated, including new information on job sharing and self-employment.

Stair, Lila B., and Dorothy Domkowski. (1992). *Careers in Business*. Lincolnwood, IL: VGM Career Books. This nicely organized book focuses on how to choose the right business career: accounting, data processing, finance, insurance, real estate, marketing, production and materials management, human resources, public relations, management, and consulting. The authors discuss specific positions within each of these broad areas, providing data on salaries and benefits, career paths, employment outlook, educational and training sources, and sources of additional information.

Managing the Transition from College to Career

Human Resource Manager with General Electric's Polymers and Specialty Chemicals, Parkersburg, West Virginia

Keiko

Being in a transitional period right now, I'm learning to adapt the skills I learned in college to the work world. These are not merely the academic skills of writing and analyzing, but skills of relating. In college, a student needs not only intelligence and determination to succeed, but also the ability to recognize what a teacher is asking for and then to supply it. The same applies to the workplace: One needs to listen and learn to understand exactly what a manager needs or a task requires. And, as in school, one is most noticed and appreciated when one not only does the job as needed but also adds a personal touch or an extra bit of polish.

Another college skill that has helped me during this transition is the ability both to master and apply what I already know and to ask questions so that I learn new things. The first makes you feel more secure about your ability to perform your job, and the second expands that ability, sometimes in small but exciting ways.

The hardest part of adapting to the work world has been getting myself out of a short-term-goal mode. In school, time is structured according to when a paper is due, when this quarter ends, when one graduates to the next level after so many months or years. One can get promoted or change jobs, but the outlook is not quite the same. The key thing to remember is that after sixteen years of school life, adapting to work life will not happen overnight. ■

The transition from college to professional full-time employment is both exciting and frightening. New employees express real satisfaction at landing a job, relocating to a new environment, and finally beginning their careers after completing college. At the same time, these employees come face-to-face with the real world, probably for the first time, and have to cope with a myriad of new experiences that college has often not prepared them to confront.

Most people look on the transition to the "world of work" as a period of tremendous personal growth—a chance to test their coping skills and an opportunity to learn from their mistakes. This new world is full of challenges from budgeting one's time, to adapting to a world without course syllabi, to dealing with conflicting expectations and adjusting to a workplace filled with individuals who differ in terms of age, experience, and educational levels. This is a period of enormous social and professional growth.

In this chapter we will examine tools that others have used to smooth this transition and present some tips for finding help, seeking solutions, and achieving success.

New Employee Experiences

I recently had the opportunity to facilitate a roundtable discussion with ten members of the New Employee Action Team at a General Electric Plastics manufacturing site in West Virginia. These new engineers, chemists, accountants, and human resource professionals—or transitional employees—focused their discussion on the following four questions:

1. What was the most difficult transitional issue that you encountered in joining the professional work force?
2. What was the best part(s) about this transition?
3. What was the most pleasant surprise about this transition?
4. What advice would you like to have had prior to making this transition?

All of these new employees were anxious to share their personal experiences, and all had advice for college seniors or graduate students who were preparing to take the plunge from academic life to the workplace and from the college social scene to the real world.

Outside the Workplace

All members of this group stated that some aspects of the transition had gone easier than they had anticipated, but that for the most part the transition had been relatively difficult. They all agreed that adjusting to a new community and having to develop a new professional and social support network was very emotionally challenging.

Each team member had attended college full-time and had really enjoyed the college environment, surrounded as they were by people the same age and with similar interests. In college most had found it fairly simple to make friends and get dates. By contrast, when they moved to a new community to begin their careers, they suddenly found themselves cut off from familiar social connections and experienced panic. This sense of aloneness was alleviated only when they took the initiative and found ways to get involved in the community. Most of these employees quickly joined a health club, started attending a local church, volunteered their time to a nonprofit organization, or signed up for graduate classes. In these ways they addressed their needs to be involved with other people and to fill nonwork hours.

On the Job

Manager/Worker Relations.   The need to fill time was also an issue on the job, particularly as these new employees were initially assigned to their new tasks. A key discovery was that very few managers knew how to work well with new employees and to provide the right blend of guidance and freedom. Even though most of these individuals came to like their supervisors, they found it much more difficult to develop this relationship than they had with their college professors. Most learned that they had to invest the time to learn how to work effectively with their new managers. They had to study the manager's reactions to various situations as well as listen to the experiences of other employees. And pleasing the boss seemed to be a real challenge.

"Buddies."   The most successful of the new employees were those who had associated themselves with a "buddy." A buddy was described as a slightly older person who had been through the transition in recent years. This buddy served as a support network, helped to introduce the new employee around, and guided the employee through the world of industry by showing how to get things done and make things happen. At the same time, several transitional employees advised caution in choosing a buddy. Because new employees are often judged by the company they keep, it's important to find a buddy whose reputation is compatible with the image that you hope to create.

Communication.   Another challenge for these new employees was communicating with others. They noted that they had to learn to really listen to others and to seek advice rather than immediately trying to prove themselves. In addition, several mentioned encountering animosity when they began working with the blue-collar work force and occasionally received similar treatment from fellow professionals, who seemed threatened by their age, education, or perceived connections (for example, "You must think you're really smart since you went to college" or "I was making quality products before you were even born, so don't try to tell me what to do"). They discovered that the best way to deal with these comments was to really listen to people, to respect people for their knowledge and experience, and to honestly believe that experience is as good a teacher as a college education. Another key was to not overreact—the new employees who became either defensive or sarcastic were targeted even more strenuously. It is important to take time to build trust and develop a working relationship.

Several of the new employees stated that they had gone out of their way to ask questions and to show genuine interest. They quickly learned that people like to share their knowledge; moreover, by listening, they really did learn. This approach required that the employee possess enough self-confidence to move cautiously rather than try to prove him- or herself immediately upon entering the work force. Indeed, new employees need to learn the organizational structure, understand business and personal needs, and learn to build consensus before trying to push their own agenda.

Teamwork. The new employees were also surprised by the amount of teamwork required. In college most of their work had been completed either alone or in small groups. In fact, they had been competing with other students rather than seeking collaboration. These employees found that in the workplace they had to constantly consider the wants and needs of others and that very few projects were actually the result of individual effort. They were surprised to find that seemingly good projects could be brought to a standstill because of poor communication or the lack of commitment of some group or individual.

Politics and Bureaucracies. With regard to the corporate political environment, most of these students admitted that they were unprepared to deal with it when they left college. Most stated that they had been initially confused as to who within the organization held power and how much attention they needed to pay to how one communicated, how one acted, and how one determined which person was responsible for making decisions. They agreed that they had encountered more bureaucracy than they had anticipated or were prepared to handle. As one young man stated, to be successful one had to "play the game"—to learn the rules and understand the other players. Among other things, one had to be careful what one said, concerned about one's image, and aware of whom one was talking to. One young woman offered a great piece of advice: "Be careful what you say, never talk bad about anybody!" Others emphasized the importance of choosing one's battles carefully, not "spouting off on every issue," and dealing in a professional manner with others. "Take the time to really listen and seek input of others," they advised.

Mentors.   Finally, these new employees suggested that new people take the time to associate with people who had a good reputation, to watch their actions and learn why these particular people have been well received. Along these lines, they pointed out the benefits of having a mentor, someone who has been in the organization for a period of time. Such an individual can help the new employee learn the ropes, understand and interpret the culture, and provide the necessary "air cover" and visibility to further one's career and make the right decisions. Mentors can be particularly useful in illuminating organizational issues and needs.

Making the Transition

As a former college counselor and student services administrator and a member of various human resource departments within the General Electric organization, I have had the opportunity to work with a great number of new employees in my seventeen-year professional career. I have watched with pleasure as some of these students quickly made the transition to productive and successful employees, and with dismay as others did less well. What distinguished the successes from the failures, and what do you need to do to be numbered among the former?

Evaluating Yourself

The first step is to evaluate yourself—to take a serious inventory of your strengths and weaknesses, and know what you are capable of accomplishing. You must never sell yourself to a new organization as having the capability to do something that you cannot. Organizations are relatively patient about teaching new employees their processes and procedures but have very little tolerance for individuals who overstate their skills.

Making a Good First Impression

It is important to make a good first impression in an organization. The best way to do this is by listening to and respecting others, and by taking the time to learn something about the organization's history. You need to develop sound relationships with co-workers before you try to change them or sell them on new ideas and methods.

At the same time, you don't want to act overly confident or to brag about your past exploits. This is a relatively delicate balancing act that new employees must play. By asking for regular feedback from others, you should be able to discern whether you are maintaining the appropriate balance. You want to be perceived as being keenly interested and as having experiences that are of value to the company.

By keeping your eyes and ears open, you will pick up feedback in a variety of forms. If the feedback is not what you hoped for, however, don't become defensive; rather, use this information to determine how to improve relationships in the future. Reality truly is what people perceive. Thus you need to know what people are thinking and saying about you.

Fitting into the Team

As was discussed previously, you need to enter the organization not only as a cooperative employee but also as a good listener. It is quite appropriate to watch others and take your cue from them. It is equally important that you take the time to learn who in the organization is respected and how this respect was earned. Once you understand this, you will know how to adapt your behavior for maximum benefit.

Some new employees view this assimilation process as frustrating. They have spent years trying to be themselves, and having to adapt to organizational styles or cultures somehow seems wrong. Although you need not sacrifice your individuality, as a new employee you want to be viewed positively—as an asset, not a detriment, to a team trying to achieve certain goals. Diversity of opinion is vital to an organization's success; however, one must be respected in order to be heard.

In college the major goal was to educate students, and therefore you were the main focus (even if this did not always seem to be the case). In business the focus is on profits, and you will be expected to help the organization achieve its goals. This means that you probably will not be treated as special, and your needs or ideas may not be given the consideration that they were in college or that you feel they warrant. Because the bottom line now is profits, you have to begin to sell yourself and your ideas, and to show how your ideas relate to increased profitability or productivity. In short, your fellow workers need to understand what you bring to the table and how your suggestions will contribute to achieving organizational goals.

Building a Relationship with Your Supervisor

As was also discussed previously, how you manage your relationship with your supervisor is critical. Granted, many managers do not take the time or have the skills to be effective mentors to new employees; nor do they realize that they are not meeting all the new employee's needs. For this reason, you must be honest with yourself as to your own needs and wants, and you must let your boss know when additional guidance, clarification, or direction is needed. Even the most empathic supervisor will not be able to read your mind. Therefore, you must ensure that you are expressing your needs in a direct and straightforward manner.

Most supervisors have found that their span of control (number of direct reports) has been increasing in recent years to the point that they have less time to monitor employees and provide close direction. As a new employee perhaps you can suggest times for and methods of getting together, as well as ways for people other than the direct supervisor to help in your training. This is one area in which a "buddy" can be extremely effective.

Getting Involved

As a new employee you may find that you have extra time on your hands or that others are extremely busy while you are not busy enough. This is when you need to be confident enough to get yourself invited to meetings, social gatherings, and other occasions. It is a good time to volunteer to help out on committees and other team activities. The absolute best way to learn the business is by participation. People may not think to invite you, but most organizations will be glad to include you if you ask. Take the initiative in this regard; don't wait to get noticed.

Along the same lines, you should get to know as many people as possible. In addition, you'll want to keep track of the people you meet by name, title, and functions. Ask fellow employees what they do, what they like about their jobs, what projects they are currently involved with, what they see as the future for the business, and what concerns them most about the business. People like to talk about themselves and their jobs, and simply by listening you can learn a great deal. Moreover, by asking questions, you will be viewed as interested and interesting.

Organizations like employees who are active and involved. Thus, you should show enthusiasm and take the initiative. Remember, however, to get the facts before acting. More people fail in organizations by not taking any risks or waiting to be told what to do than by making mistakes. One of the best ways to learn is through getting involved and assisting others.

It's not enough, however, to get involved only in the workplace. Like the new employees discussed previously, you need to get involved in the local community. When you're new to an area, it's easy to fall into a trap of criticizing the local community for being different from or not quite as good as home—and at first it may not be. Nevertheless, you should avoid expressing negative opinions for two reasons. For one thing, this community is home to many people both inside and outside the company, and these people will take your criticism personally. For another, negative comments can become self-fulfilling: If you regard the community as boring, sure enough you will be bored. Focus on the positive both at work and at home by approaching this as a new experience in which you can and will learn.

Remember, while this may be your first full-time job, chances are you won't hold it forever. It's important to treat it as a learning experience and a springboard to your future. If your situation is not totally to your liking, then do what you can to make it better or look for ways to make your assignment more to your liking or more valuable. Most of life's experiences are not wholly great or wholly bad. Focus on the positive.

Taking Control of Your Future

Finally, keep in mind always that you alone are in charge of your own career. You are the one who has the most to gain—and the most to lose. Don't fall into the common trap of blaming others for your dissatisfaction. You're in the driver's seat, and you need to manage yourself in a manner that shows you in the best light and gives you the greatest amount of information to make appropriate life choices. It's your responsibility to find appropriate solutions to problems and to get the most out of your assignments. Sometimes the greatest thing that people get out of their first professional job is the realization that this is not what they want to do for the rest of their life. This knowledge gives them the impetus to seek alternatives and make a sound second choice.

Conclusion

The transition from college to the workplace is both exciting and frightening. The emphasis can be on excitement if you understand what is expected, communicate effectively, and develop the necessary social and professional support network.

Planning, evaluating, and listening will be the keys to success. Taking time to complete the necessary legwork and doing your homework will lead to successful projects. Finding a means to solicit necessary help and guidance will be vital. The knowledge that you alone are the architect of your own career success may seem staggering at first; however, it is also very liberating when you understand that by taking charge of your own direction you can be happy. By learning as much as you can about the organization you are joining, seeking the support and guidance of others within the company, focusing on your particular strengths, and allowing yourself to take educated risks you should be able to make a successful transition and, more importantly, to enjoy the experience.

There are fifty-two Monday mornings every year, so it is vital that you find a means to be able to say, "Thank goodness it's Monday and I get to go to work."

Best wishes and happy beginnings!

References and Resources

Carter, Carol, and Gary June. (1993) *Graduating into the Nineties: Getting the Most Out of Your First Job.* New York: Farrar, Straus & Giroux.

Krannich, Ron, and Carlyle Krannich. (1989). *Network Your Way to Job and Career Success: The Complete Guide to New Opportunities.* Manassas. VA: Impact Press.

McKensie, Alex. (1989). *Time for Success: A Goal-Setting Strategy.* New York: McGraw-Hill.

Ripi, R. R., and G. R. Funkhouser. (1987). *The Ropes to Skip and the Ropes to Know.* New York: John Wiley.

Solomon, Muriel. (1993). *Getting Praised, Raised, and Recognized.* Englewood Cliffs, NJ: Prentice-Hall.

5

Women in the 1990s: Old Barriers, New Opportunities

Judy Goldsmith

Special Consultant to the Chancellor for Equity and Affirmative Action,
University of Wisconsin–Stevens Point

Senior Voices

Jennie

I've only recently become more aware of the issues facing women. Those of us just coming out of college have a lot to be grateful for: The women of the preceding generation have opened up avenues and gained rights that most of the women my age take for granted. There are still many battles for women my age to fight, but our main battle is on a different front than that of the previous generation. Discrimination has gone underground; structures and laws have changed, but attitudes about women and their rights have been slow to follow. We fight a subtle discrimination, one that we may not even be aware of because we have been socialized to accept it.

I was lucky enough to attend a school where most of the teachers and students respected me as a woman and were relatively open to new attitudes concerning women. But I've broken out of that cocoon. Now I have to deal with people like the man on a tour bus who made a snide "joke" about women to his buddy, or people like my mother, who can't be convinced that she should get help with the housework on a regular basis even though she works full-time. We still have a lot of work to do, but many young women now respect themselves enough that they can make others respect them as well. ∎

As a woman of the nineties, you are poised between two worlds; one rooted in age-old stereotypes and assumptions about what women can and can't do; the other a new, freewheeling, high-tech realm with virtually unlimited possibilities. If you view the future with some uncertainty and misgivings, you're in good company.

We are currently undergoing what can legitimately be described as a revolution in relationships between the sexes, moving from a time when women served in support capacities almost exclusively (both in the home and the workplace) to an era in which many women are functioning autonomously. Where it used to be the woman who brought the boss a cup of coffee or the file on the Jones case, now, in greater numbers than ever, women are sitting across the table from men as their professional peers. Such profound changes can be unsettling, but they also present you with rich and exciting possibilities. In this chapter we'll examine both the opportunities and the obstacles facing women in the 1990s, as well as ways to overcome those obstacles.

Shifting Demographics

In many ways, the last decade of the twentieth century is the best possible time for female college graduates to be entering the work force. For example, *Workforce 2000: Work and Workers for the Twenty-first Century*, a frequently cited study by the Hudson Institute, provided some dramatic information about the changing demographics in our nation. Among other things, the study notes that women and people of color will make up more than two-thirds of new entrants to the work force over the next decade. Indeed, women have been moving into the work force over the past four decades in steadily increasing numbers, and according to the U.S. Census Bureau women are expected to comprise 60 percent of the work force by the year 2000. Now, with an anticipated shortage of workers, the need (and competition) for women should be at its highest point ever, especially in scientific and technological fields.

A 1990 *Time* special supplement on women lays out the scope of the changes:

> The U.S. is about to undergo the most wrenching shifts in the composition and quality of its work force in more than a half-century. While most companies have yet to come to grips with the new realities, the cold, hard fact is that corporate America is facing a deepening shortage of skilled labor in the decades just ahead. . . . Over the next several years, women will make up the majority of new skilled and educated workers . . . and smart managers searching for talent are already courting the women,

African Americans, Hispanics, Asians and others whom corporate executives have traditionally discounted or dismissed.

These same trends apply on college campuses. With women now comprising at least half the student body on our campuses (54 percent on average), greater efforts are being made to attract women faculty (currently, only 27 percent of college faculty are women). The concern about that figure is a direct function of our concern about the importance of role models. One study, for example, indicated that in a coeducational classroom with a male professor, males spoke three times as often as females; with a female professor, men still spoke more, but the gap was reduced significantly (Karp and Yoels, 1976). Given that a student who is actively engaged in the learning process is getting a better-quality education, the lack of women faculty is obviously a problem. Moreover, female role models are important not just for women students but for men, too. After all, men will need to be able to relate to women as professional peers (or as authority figures) in their own careers.

Exercise 5.1

Women Past and Present

Interview your mother, or a woman of her generation. What were her expectations of her future as she grew up? Ask her to characterize relationships between the sexes in the home and in the workplace.

Now consider your own childhood. What did you want to be when you grew up? Has it changed? Have your expectations for what you can do changed since that time?

The Leadership Vacuum and Changing Leadership Styles

John Naisbitt and Patricia Aburdene's influential book, *Megatrends 2000* (1990), identifies the 1990s as the "decade of women in leadership." They cite women's growing numbers in the work force and burgeoning entrepreneurial spirit (women are starting businesses at twice the rate of men). But, more importantly, they contend that women are also coming center stage at a time when a new style of leadership, one that is more "female" in character, is coming to be not only accepted but valued:

Today, we are replacing the manager as order giver with the manager as teacher, facilitator, and coach. The order giver has all the answers and tells everyone what to do; the facilitator knows how to draw the answers out of those who know them best—the people doing the job. The leader as facilitator asks questions, guides a group to consensus, uses information to demonstrate the need for action.

This latter phenomenon is especially significant because widely divergent male/female leadership styles have contributed in large part to the impenetrability of the "glass ceiling," the invisible barrier that has kept women from the nation's top-level executive offices, in spite of their increasing numbers in senior positions.

Because leadership positions have, until recently, been held almost exclusively by men, a male standard of leadership behavior has been accepted as the norm. That style has been largely authoritarian and characterized by strong central control and a hierarchical structure. By contrast, a female leadership style is more likely to be collaborative and cooperative; women leaders usually operate (to varying degrees) on consensus. In the past such a style has been regarded as "weak" (that is, indecisive, hesitant, and fearful); in fact, women who wanted to "make it" had no option but to modify their behavior and adopt the male model.

However, as the balance of world economic power shifted and other nations grabbed increasing amounts of global trade, American businesses began to examine some of their previously unquestioned assumptions about how they operate. They noted, for example, that Japan, with its "quality circles" and teamwork approach to production and decision making, was often more productive. The businesses began to experiment with flexibility, decentralized power, and cooperative rather than dictated patterns of operation. (A 1989 *Fortune* magazine article entitled "New Ways to Exercise Power" refers to a survey of top-level executives, who say, "You can't manage today's work force like yesterday's. . . . The military command-and-control model went out with red meat.") At the same time, women were beginning to question whether they had to become "one of the boys" in order to function, whether, in fact, what they had to offer wasn't good enough as it was. It was time, women were proposing, to recognize that the male model was just that—a model, and not the only valid way of doing things—and that women had something equally valid and valuable to add to the mix.

The result (although this is a dynamic, ongoing process) is a greater openness to a leadership style with which women are much more comfortable and which allows them to follow the dictates of their own personal propensities and socialization rather than having to adopt one foreign to their life experiences. A 1990 study done by Russell Reynolds Associates, an international executive recruiting firm, underscores this trend. In seeking to identify leadership in senior executive positions, the researchers expected to find fewer "leader-style" traits among women executives than among men. They found the opposite:

> The years ahead are increasingly seen as a time when educated workers will be in a seller's market and when educated women will have an increased competitive advantage.

The good news for women is not only that they will be even more in demand in the years to come, but that they have proven their ability to excel as "leader-style" executives. . . .

"My belief is that the most competitive organizations will select leaders wherever they find them, no matter what sex they are," states [Malcolm] MacKay [managing director of Russell Reynolds]. "There will be great opportunities for women at the highest levels of corporate leadership."

Exercise 5.2 *Women and Leadership*

Find out from your student government office or the office that deals with student organizations what percentage of student officers are female, and what percentage of presidents of organizations are female. Have those numbers been changing in the last few years?

Find out, too, how many women are in executive or leadership positions on your campus (for example, chancellor, vice chancellors, deans, department heads). Ask one or two of them how things have changed (or not changed) for women leaders in recent years.

Barriers to Women

All of these developments are occurring within the context of opportunities that have opened up over the past twenty-five years. During that time women's rights activism has resulted in the passage of laws and precedent-setting legal cases that have challenged traditionally discriminatory practices. For example, less than twenty years ago, newspaper employment ads read, "Help Wanted—Male" and "Help Wanted—Female," perpetuating a rigidly sex-segregated work force in which working women were systematically undervalued and underpaid. Employers could legally refuse to hire a woman because she was a woman. Schools could limit the number of women they would allow into certain departments (or refuse to allow any in at all). And girls and women faced greatly restricted access to athletics and physical fitness programs. As startling as it may seem, as recently as 1971, in *Hollander v. Connecticut Conference, Inc.,* the Connecticut Supreme Court ruled that Susan Hollander couldn't participate in the boys' cross-country team—there was no girls' team at her school—because, they said, "Athletic competition builds character in our boys. We do not need that kind of character in our girls, the women of tomorrow."

Although laws have been passed outlawing such blatant discrimination, attitudes are slower to change. Indeed, it would be naive to assume that the workplace and the world are now free of such inequities. The most overt manifestations of sex discrimination have been effectively eliminated, but more subtle and deep-rooted ones remain. Thus a woman can still expect to encounter barriers, including (1) wage and occupational discrimination, (2) sexual harassment, and (3) the fact that men and women, in a sense, occupy "different worlds."

Economic Disadvantage

You've heard about the wage gap—the difference in pay for women and men (currently it is at 71 cents, which is what women average for every dollar men make, with both working full-time). This phenomenon continues in spite of laws that make such economic discrimination illegal. A woman today is unlikely to be told that she isn't being hired or promoted "because she's a woman," but, as we've just mentioned, discrimination can also be subtle or indirect, or even unconscious.

An example of the economic disadvantage women still experience is revealed in a study by the U.S. Department of Education (*National Longitudinal Study, 1972*). This study tracked 22,652 randomly selected students from the high school graduating class of 1972 over a fifteen-year period through college and into the work world. The researchers found that female students did better in college (in all subjects), worked harder, and generally made a higher-quality investment in their education than their male counterparts. However, when they entered the job market, the men earned more. Specifically, men averaged $25,022 per year, women without children made $18,970, and women with children earned $15,016. Clifford Adelman, senior associate in the office of research at the Department of Education, recommends recasting "the central observation in the dialogue about pay equity: it's not merely the case that women are equally qualified, they are better qualified."

What is more, the wage gap exists in every job category, even in those where women numerically predominate, according to Wider Opportunities for Women, a Washington-based organization dedicated to preparing women for entrance into nontraditional fields. For example, although nursing is still 94 percent female, male nurses earn on average 10 percent more. And when the job is male-dominated, the disparity is even greater. For example, construction work is 98 percent male, and men make 25 percent more than their female co-workers. Finally, in 1988 almost half (46 percent) of employed women earned less than $10,000 per year, compared to 25 percent of men, and only 15 percent of women earned more than $25,000 per year, compared to 41 percent of men.

Speculation about causes of the wage gap continues. Researchers identify such factors as women's more recent entrance into the work force, their lower levels of education, and time away from the work force for childbearing and child-rearing. However, some portion of the gap is not attributable to such factors, and discrimination unquestionably continues to negatively affect women and the employment decisions that are made regarding them.

Exercise 5.3

Addressing the Wage Gap

Discuss with your friends how you feel about the wage gap. Why do you think it exists? What traditional attitudes and practices may have created it? Do you think the practice has ever been justified? What do you think can be done about it?

Sexual Harassment

The issue of sexual harassment burst into the national consciousness in 1991 with Anita Hill's charges against Supreme Court nominee Clarence Thomas, and then again in 1992 with the infamous Navy Tailhook Association scandal. In one short year an issue that had been taken seriously by few people beyond actual victims commanded widespread national attention.

Sexual harassment is illegal according to both federal law (Title VII) and many state statutes. In addition, the Civil Rights Act of 1991 gives women new rights to sue and to collect damages (in addition to back pay). Nevertheless, sexual harassment continues to be a reality of the workplace for a substantial percentage of women (various studies estimate between 40 and 80 percent). Sexual harassment may include off-color humor, suggestive or insulting remarks, inappropriate physical contact, sexual invitations, and pressure for sex. Whatever form it takes, it embarrasses women, erodes their self-confidence and self-esteem, creates an uncomfortable work (or learning) environment, and limits their opportunities. Though it often masquerades as good-natured fooling around (for example, "What's the matter, sweetheart . . . can't you take a joke?"), it is at best inconsiderate and at worst abusive. In short, it focuses on sexuality at times or in situations in which references to sexuality are irrelevant or inappropriate.

Sometimes sexual favors are made a condition of continued employment or promotion; other times sexual harassment takes less direct forms. Much sexual harassment, however, is the result of miscommunication and the very different ways in which men and women can view the same situation. It has been estimated that no more than 5 percent of men are "intentional harassers," whose actual intent is to embarrass or demean women. Behaviors that some women may regard as inappropriate or demeaning may be intended by men as flattering or complimentary. In such situations the individual who is experiencing what she regards as harassing behavior should communicate her disapproval directly to the harasser. That can be done through oral communication (for example, "I'm sure you intended that remark as a compliment, but I really don't appreciate comments about my appearance when I'm concentrating on my work") or in writing, which may also have the advantage of putting someone who is being persistent "on notice." In other cases, especially where the harassment is coming from a superior, it may be preferable to talk to a third party who could intervene.

Finally, keep in mind that while the overwhelming majority of sexual harassment is directed by men toward women, harassment of men by women does happen, as does same-sex harassment. The gender of the two parties in no way affects the fact that the behavior is both reprehensible and illegal.

Exercise 5.4

Investigating Sexual Harassment

If you don't know what your school's sexual harassment policy is, find out. Does it spell out clearly how and where to file harassment charges? (When you are employed, you will want to be sure you know what your employer's harassment policy is—and, of course, to be sure there is one.) Also, take an informal poll asking people what their definition of "sexual harassment" is. Do the definitions vary by gender? How?

Two Different Worlds

Some of the challenges women face involve more subtle kinds of obstacles than those mentioned previously and are important to know about. Many of them have to do with the fact that women and men experience very different realities in our society. For example, as boys and girls we grow up associating little with each other, and so we perceive many things differently. Many women watching the all-male Senate committee that questioned Professor Hill said, "They just don't get it," when the senators expressed confusion about her reactions to the harassing behavior. Similarly, many men who were questioned by investigators of the Tailhook scandal (in which women were mauled and sexually molested by partying naval aviators) asked, "What's the big deal?" There is no question that men and women have some profoundly different perspectives on the world around us. Sexual harassment may be a particularly dramatic example, but there are many others.

As human beings we tend to be more comfortable with people who are "like us," who have had the kinds of experiences we've had, who speak the same language. That doesn't mean, of course, that as men and women we don't or can't enjoy each other or take pleasure in the differences. However, the differences make it difficult to establish productive or collegial working relationships. One problem is that most men have had little experience relating to women in anything other than a support capacity (for example, as secretary or assistant). Now they find that women are their professional peers, and that reality may take some getting used to and require behaviors that are not in their repertoire. Women may find themselves not being taken seriously or not being included in meetings or settings in which they legitimately have a place.

In addition to these problems, most women also face the challenge of managing home and family. Current studies show that, on average, women continue to do approximately 70 percent of domestic chores, including child care. And while some women choose to stay at home, especially during child-rearing years, others have no choice but must work to support or contribute to the support of their families.

All of these problems are additionally complicated for women of color, the handicapped, older women, single mothers, and lesbians. All are doubly jeopardized (or more) by other societal biases that compound the challenges they face.

Survival Strategies for Women

The problems that women still face are significant. However, there are ways to deal with all of them: maintain a support system, know your rights, become a student of communication, nurture yourself, avoid the role of "superwoman," and learn to love change.

Maintain a Support System

Being connected is the most important strategy you can learn for growing and thriving in whatever environment you enter. Whether friends, family, or colleagues, your connections provide support and keep you "rooted." It is a good idea, particularly when you've started some new phase of your life (for example, a job, a move, a promotion), to compile a list of the people who make up your personal network. Ask yourself the following:

1. Who can I call just to talk to?
2. Who can help me get organized?
3. Who shares my interests and is fun to be with?
4. Who is a good person to give me a "reality check"?

Some types of connections are particularly important. For instance, most professionals, especially women, find that mentoring is critical to career success and satisfaction. A mentor is an individual, usually a senior person in your company (or organization or academic department), who will help you to learn your way. He or she will, among other things, acquaint you with the unwritten rules that may govern conduct in your situation and put you in touch with the people you need to know.

Professional networks are also important. Generally, these are informal structures of people in your field (traditional "old boys' networks" are being supplemented these days by "old girls' networks") that are often an excellent source of support for people starting out or new to a position. Networks can also fill in gaps in your mentoring needs.

Use your research skills to identify resources that will help you get off to a good start and pursue a life that provides you with a sense of accomplishment and gratification. And, when you are on your way, complete the cycle by helping others.

| **Exercise 5.5** | *Building a Support Network* |

List the people who might be personal or professional resources: friends, family, teachers, professionals, and so on. Brainstorm: Are any of them in businesses or careers that may be helpful to you (including as mentors)? Do they know anyone who is? Can any help you get relocated if you're moving? Can they compile resource lists for you? Put down everyone you can think of—don't edit anyone out—and think of all the ways in which they might be helpful to you. Don't worry about "using" people; you'll be a resource for others, too.

Know Your Rights

You don't need to be an expert on federal, state, and local laws regarding sex discrimination. Sex discrimination is prohibited at all levels, from federal to institutional, as part of basic civil rights. The following nondiscrimination clause is typical: "There will be no discrimination on the basis of gender, race, religion, ethnicity, and sexual orientation."

If anything happens to you that you believe constitutes sex discrimination (including sexual harassment), see your local chapter of the American Civil Liberties Union or consult representatives of the state/local Human Rights Commission. And if you do decide to take legal action, be sure to keep careful records and a written log of all interactions. Weigh the pros and cons carefully, however; legal action can be difficult, costly, and time-consuming. This is where your support system will be particularly important.

Keep in mind, too, that discrimination may be unconscious or unintentional. We learn biased attitudes virtually from birth, and we learn them from people who are usually not aware that they're teaching them to us. Consequently, while overt discrimination certainly occurs, some discriminatory behaviors merely reflect those old, unconscious attitudes. In such cases (which will usually involve relatively minor problems) the problem may be resolved by pointing out to the person involved why his (or her) conduct makes you uncomfortable or seems unprofessional.

Indeed, resolving problems mutually builds goodwill—some people genuinely appreciate an opportunity to correct behaviors in a cooperative way, leaving their dignity and self-esteem intact. Don't ever fear, however, to take stronger action when reason doesn't prevail. While it is not the easiest course to take, it is usually the only one that can effect significant change.

Become a Student of Communication

You will have a substantial advantage in your career and in life if you learn how to "hear" what people are saying beyond the words themselves. Body language, facial expressions, pitch, tone, volume, and vocabulary all convey meaning. In addition, gender scripts affect the communication process.

One currently developing body of knowledge involves differences in men's and women's communication styles. Emerging research affirms that men and women come from two very different cultural perspectives (boys and girls having grown up in two different worlds), so that we often miscommunicate because the same words (or expressions or body language) may mean different things to us (Tannen, 1990). For example, men grow up in a competitive, adversarial world, and for them language is often primarily a matter of contest or display. For women, however, language serves to reinforce connections and build relationships. Men tend to be on guard; women want to share. Male communication is characteristically firm, assertive, and confident; female communication is much more likely to be tentative, qualified, and supportive.

It is especially important to be aware of these differences because the male mode of communication remains the norm in the public arena—in business, in politics, in the classroom—though we may expect some modifications in the norm as more women enter public life as peers. Consequently, women need to be aware of the differences in styles in order to avoid putting themselves at a disadvantage by sending messages that may communicate uncertainty, submissiveness, or powerlessness. This does not mean that you have to "talk like a man," but learning any new language (whether Chinese, French, or "male") enhances your ability both to understand the speakers of that language and to communicate effectively with them.

Because relationships between the sexes are changing so dramatically, in both personal and professional contexts, an improved understanding of each other is going to be critical. Many of the traditional styles of relating are becoming obsolete, and, while the changes may be unsettling, they also have the potential to produce new relationships in the home and workplace that are better, richer, and more egalitarian.

Exercise 5.6

Communication Between Men and Women

Listen to two or three conversations involving both males and females. What gender differences do you observe in terms of amount of participation, tone of voice, pitch, volume, vocabulary, body language, facial expressions, and listening style? What impressions does each style convey? What would it be like if the males spoke in the female style and the females in the male style? What significance would such a role reversal have?

Nurture Yourself

Traditionally, women in our society have been conditioned to be self-sacrificing. This behavioral model may have a certain appeal, especially to those who benefit from it, but it is not particularly healthy for women, whose real needs are often shortchanged in the process. Working hard and caring for those around you is gratifying and important, but it should not be at the expense of your own well-being. You are your own most important natural resource. Thus taking care of your needs is responsible, not self-indulgent.

Caring for yourself falls into several categories:

- **Physical needs.** This relates to everything your mother taught you—eat well, get plenty of sleep, exercise (do something you enjoy so you really do it), and avoid drugs and alcohol.

- **Social needs.** Even if your work is a genuine pleasure, other interests (including varied social relationships) are vital to maintaining balance and perspective in your life. You really can't see the forest if you never get outside of the trees.

- **Psychological needs.** Nurturing is important for everyone, including you. Do nice things for yourself when you're under pressure. Be at least as gentle and understanding with yourself as you are with others.

Exercise 5.7

Taking "Minivacations"

Make a list of three things each that you could do (and would really enjoy) for a ten-minute break, a half-hour break, an hour, an afternoon, and a day off. Keep that list near you and revise it as needed. Learning to take such "minivacations," during which you take a real break from responsibilities, can be a life-saver.

Avoid the Role of "Superwoman"

As women have moved rapidly into the work force over the past two decades, there has been much talk about the value of "having it all," of combining career with family. While many women have, in fact, done that, the cost has usually been considerable. Too often, "having it all" has meant performing at least two full-time jobs rather than one—holding a job, raising a family, being a wife, maintaining a home. The strains associated with trying to fill this "superwoman" role have been immense.

In our society men who work have generally had a support system available to them—a wife, who would see to it that all domestic needs, including child-rearing, were attended to. Today, however, working women lack such support systems. Fortunately, this is one of the social realities that is undergoing significant change, as women and men are beginning to recognize the need for shared responsibilities. Women will continue to be employed; they need to work, and our society needs their talents, skills, and abilities. Thus our traditional assumptions about domestic relationships will have to change.

Fairness requires a more equitable division of labor in the home. In addition, both parents must be fully involved in and responsible for their children's well-being. The same applies to care for the elderly, which traditionally has fallen disproportionately to women. In short, the times are changing—and when the dust has settled, we may hope that we will see a society with a healthier balance of family roles for both men and women.

Learn to Love Change

Some of us who are older—and not even that much older—were born into a time when the pace of change was much slower than it is now. Television had only recently been invented and wasn't yet commercially available. Automobiles and air travel were still a novelty, and people had one telephone at most. In this era people could make life plans and assume with some certainty that things would go along pretty much as they had planned.

Today, however, technological, demographic, and social changes occur with dizzying speed. Whereas once the only things that were certain were death and taxes, now we have to add "change" to the list. Therefore, in the workplace as in the rest of our lives, flexibility has become a virtue to be cultivated.

In her extraordinary 1990 book *Composing a Life*, Mary Catherine Bateson talks of the need to view life in this new way:

> In many ways, constancy is an illusion. After all, our ancestors were immigrants, many of them moving on every few years;

today we are migrants in time. Unless teachers can hold up a model of lifelong learning and adaptation, graduates are likely to find themselves trapped into obsolescence as the world changes around them.

Bateson speaks, too, of an advantage that she feels women may have in this regard: "The physical rhythms of reproduction and maturation create sharper discontinuities in women's lives than in men's. . . . As a result, the ability to shift from one preoccupation to another, to divide one's attention, to improvise in new circumstances, has always been important to women." Thus, as women, you have a chance to reap the full benefits of our changing world.

Conclusion

As you prepare to graduate from college, you are at an important threshold in your life. Coincidentally, our society—in fact, our planet—is also at a critical turning point. Changes are occurring so dramatically and so rapidly that few guideposts or roadmaps exist. The introduction to the 1990 *Time* special supplement on women says it clearly: "All that was orthodox has become negotiable." And you are going out into the world at a time when, although biased attitudes and sex discrimination still exist, they exist alongside unparalleled opportunities for women. It's an exciting prospect. Good luck and best wishes!

References and Resources

Adelman, Clifford. (1990). "NLS/72 Women at Thirtysomething: Paradoxes of Attainment." Washington, DC: U.S. Department of Education, Office of Research. Adelman details the results of a fifteen-year longitudinal study of 22,652 randomly selected 1972 high school graduates, with emphasis on a comparison of male/female performance in college and the workplace, and on compensation patterns.

Bateson, Mary Catherine. (1990). *Composing a Life.* New York: Plume Books. This book is a vitally important roadmap through modern times for anyone, but for women in particular. Using the stories of five women (including her own) as examples of lives characterized by "discontinuity," Bateson explores the dynamics of change and our relationship to it.

Hall, Roberta M., and Bernice R. Sandler. (1983). "Academic Mentoring for Women Students and Faculty: A New Look at an Old Way to Get Ahead." Project on the Status and Education of Women of the Association of American Colleges. Washington, DC. This paper provides an excellent introduction to mentoring: its importance and functions, the problems women encounter in finding mentors, and ways to fill in gaps in mentoring needs. Though designed to address the realities of an academic environment, it is applicable to other settings as well.

Helgesen, Sally. (1990). *The Female Advantage: Women's Ways of Leadership*. New York: Doubleday Currency. This is an instructive and insightful analysis of women's leadership styles as observed in "diary studies" of four women leaders in diverse business and nonprofit settings.

Hudson Institute. (1987). *Workforce 2000: Work and Workers for the Twenty-first Century*. Indianapolis, IN: Hudson Institute.

Karp, David A., and William C. Yoels. (1976). "The College Classroom: Some Observations on the Meanings of Student Participation." *Sociology and Social Research* 60.

Naisbitt, John, and Patricia Aburdene. (1990). *Megatrends 2000*. New York: William Morrow.

Pearson, Carol S., et al., eds. (1989). *Educating the Majority: Women Challenge Tradition in Higher Education*. New York: American Council on Education/Macmillan. This is not only an important collection of essays geared primarily to women college students but a vital resource for any woman going into higher education.

Ries, Paula, and Anne Stone, eds. (1992). *The American Woman, 1992–93: A Status Report*. New York: Norton. The fourth (and current) in a series produced by the Women's Research and Education Institute in Washington, DC, this volume focuses on women in politics. Other books in the series examine women in specific fields as well as provide a comprehensive overview of the current status of women.

Russell Reynolds Associates. (1990). "Men, Women, and Leadership in the American Corporation." New York: Russell Reynolds Associates.

Tannen, Deborah. (1990). *You Just Don't Understand*. New York: William Morrow. Tannen's book, both scholarly and readable, offers a valuable context within which to better understand cultural barriers to communication between men and women, in both personal and working relationships.

Time. (1990). Special issue, "Women: The Road Ahead" (Fall).

Wider Opportunities for Women. (1990). "Risks and Challenges: Women, Work and the Future." Washington, DC: Wider Opportunities for Women.

6

Written Communications in Organizations

Charles Pridgeon, Jr.
Professor of English and Business and Technical Writing, Marietta College

Senior Voices

Evelyna

During the summer of 1990, I worked as an intern for Colgate-Palmolive in Cambridge, Ohio. Colgate-Palmolive manufactures household and personal care products, and emphasizes a changing and challenging environment for its employees. The philosophy of the Cambridge plant is that every individual is an important part of the team; everyone is treated as an equal, including management. The only divisions that exist in the plant are maintenance technicians and operator technicians. For example, each maintenance technician at the plant can perform numerous jobs that in many plants would take three or four people. Moreover, the company believes that job rotation helps to foster a well-rounded employee. Thus I was involved in writing a user-friendly, reader-centered, and comprehensive procedures manual so that technicians and newly hired employees could better track the inventory. This experience taught me to appreciate how tactful, clear written communications contribute to the social cohesion and sense of community within a company. Written communications such as memos and procedures manuals have helped to build a team-focused and people-centered environment at the Cambridge plant.

After my summer internship, I returned to college to complete my English degree. The major difference between writing for a company and writing for a professor is that in a company one must be aware of all the different readers. In the classroom the professor comprises an audience of one. However, as I look ahead to my future prospects of writing for a company, the knowledge and information I gained at college as well as from my internship at Colgate-Palmolive will be invaluable to me. ■

Whatever career field you are planning to enter, you probably assume that your college experience has been preparing you to develop as a professional—a person who will maintain a certain level of specialization and be committed to a certain level of performance. You may also have assumed that your college experience has been preparing you to practice your professional skills within an organization, as one person among a number of people who have specific responsibilities and are united for a particular purpose. Implicit here is a particular meaning of "professional," distinguished by four characteristics:

- Commitment to the conscientious practice of specialized skills in serving the goals of the organization

- A sense that the practice of specialized skills includes habits that express sensitivity to people

- An awareness that working in an organization is a collaborative activity

- A realization that, whatever product or service it provides and whatever its size, the activity of an organization is intricately attached to the communities that make up the larger world

Such a professional outlook should guide your behavior in all phases of your work in an organization. The premise of this chapter, though, is that this outlook is nowhere more important than in the way you approach and give shape to written communications.

When, Why, and What Will You Be Writing?

You may already know that, even at entry levels in organizations, you will be called on to write regularly, perhaps frequently. Surveys agree that you may spend from four to over sixteen hours out of a forty-hour work week in writing activities alone (Anderson, 1985). Feedback from graduates further suggests that, whether you write once a month or once a day, writing well will be essential and perhaps crucial to your success. However much you write, keep in mind that the quality of your on-the-job writing offers compelling evidence of your potential and character as a professional.

The types of writing required of you will vary in length, form, and degree of formality, but will include some or all of the following: memos, letters, instructions, informational and analytical reports, proposals, minutes of meetings, scripts for oral presentations, and articles. As you think ahead to your writing responsibilities in the workplace, bear in mind the following major purposes of written communications:

- To analyze the causes and effects of a problem, and often to suggest a solution
- To report on the status of a situation or project, such as to update progress
- To explain a process or procedure, so as to show both why and how it happens or is done
- To set forth instructions for carrying out a procedure
- To examine the feasibility of a change in policy, procedure, equipment, facilities, product, and the like
- To propose an expenditure to cover a method for implementing a change in policy, procedure, equipment, facilities, product, and so forth
- To record data or proceedings for your or others' future reference
- To evaluate yourself, others, a procedure, a product, and so on
- To establish or reinforce relationships, whether with colleagues, employees, customers/clients, or the general public
- To share specialized information and knowledge, especially as part of the exchange that characterizes a collaborative organization

As you survey these purposes for writing within an organization, remember that they generate communications of widely varying scale, from an interoffice memo of one paragraph to a report of several hundred pages.

Exercise 6.1 *Your Profession and Writing*

With your future profession in mind, try to identify the purposes that are likely to prompt you to write on the job. Can you cite specific situations that would call for written communications? As you research your career field and particular employers, make it a point to investigate the frequency and purposes of writing. Sharing questions and findings about on-the-job writing can be a helpful group discussion activity.

Writing as a Collaborative Activity

As the purposes for writing just listed might suggest, most writing within an organization is a collaborative activity. You may compose and write out a communication by yourself, but you will have depended on others in gathering information. On complex reports or proposals you may well be part of a team that must collaborate in planning, researching, and writing. In these cases the meshing of interpersonal and writing skills is essential. In the future you can be sure that professionals will be partners in collaborative writing efforts. Effective management practices increasingly emphasize the efficiency of such cooperative activities. In addition, computer networking and programming facilitate rapid exchange of information, social interaction, and hence the group writing process itself.

Exercise 6.2	*Investigating Collaborative Writing*

Investigate the nature of writing in your future profession. Find out what role writing plays in collaboration.

Writer and Reader as Collaborators

While the writing you do in an organization may well involve collaboration, your interactions with your readers are even more collaborative. There are two levels to this interaction, one common to all sound writer/reader relationships and one specific to relationships within an organization.

You and your readers collaborate to shape meaning. Your words on a page or a screen achieve meaning only with the active cooperation of your readers. Although this may seem obvious, far too often, without even being conscious of it, we write *to ourselves* and not *for others*. Our readers, even if we know them by name, too often remain shadowy, passive receivers of "our" meanings. It takes conscious effort to maintain the awareness that as we choose words, organize sentences, and order paragraphs, we are developing a collaborative relationship.

In an organization such relationships take on special importance in helping both you and others reach common goals. Chances are, when you have written papers, lab reports, and essay exams, your sense of collaboration with the professor or grader has been different from that which you will seek to develop with readers in the work setting. In college you and your readers are normally bound by some understanding of learning objectives. In the work setting you and your readers should be bound by a common understanding of organizational needs. For example, you and your readers might be bound by the need to analyze critical problems (such as growing client dissatisfaction) or to strengthen routine operations by writing clear instructions. In short, in the work setting the outcome of what you write is likely to influence both you and your readers.

Moreover, in college you probably have assumed that, in order to evaluate your work, your readers know more about your subject than you do. Within the organization, however, you may not make that assumption—you are the "authority" in the relationship. This is true even when you are asking for information, since you will frame such requests in terms of situations with which you are familiar and that generate your need for a particular kind of information. This points toward a final aspect of this writer/reader relationship. In the work setting your readers will evaluate what you have written on the basis of how much they have learned and how readily this assists them in achieving an objective—even if this objective is to provide you with appropriate information toward the solution of your problem.

Exercise 6.3	*Analyzing the Writer/Reader Relationship*

Analyzing the Writer/Reader Relationship

Based on the discussion of the writer/reader relationship, analyze a piece of writing you have done outside of class, perhaps for a Greek organization or a club. How did the collaboration between you and the reader help to shape meaning and to serve organizational needs and objectives?

Developing a Reader-Sensitive Outlook

Awareness that you and your readers share a collaborative relationship provides the foundation on which you can build a reader-sensitive outlook. In general terms, being sensitive means being alert and receptive to other people's feelings, attitudes, and circumstances. In particular, being reader sensitive means giving your readers identities and bringing them to life. We talk about sympathizing and empathizing with characters in novels, movies, and television dramas; sympathy and empathy also play a key role in writer/reader relationships in an organization. Thus, to develop reader sensitivity, you need to (1) think of readers as whole persons and (2) identify specific writer/reader ties.

Thinking of Readers as Whole Persons

Your readers may be machine operators, managers, clerical or technical assistants, salespersons, engineers, maintenance workers, customers, or the public. They may be in your office or small business; in another department, section, branch, or regional facility; in another organization; or in either the local or larger community. They are male and female. They hold beliefs, look at the world from unique perspectives, and have developed a sense of values. They live in a variety of social and economic circumstances. They may have strong political or religious commitments. They may have clear racial, ethnic, national, or regional identities.

But whoever and wherever they are in relation to you, they read your written communications as people who are concerned about details of their personal lives, who have emotions and feelings of self-esteem. Remembering this when you write is a major step toward reader sensitivity. Finding out all you can about your readers is another. Making sensitive writing choices in light of what you know is still another.

Exercise 6.4

Developing Reader Sensitivity

First, choose a small group of classmates with whom you are familiar, and think about them as potential readers. Using this section as a basis for analysis, list their characteristics as readers of a written communication. Second, try to imagine a reader in two or three specific work settings. In both cases how do the components of a "whole-person" reader affect the writer/reader relationship?

Identifying Writer/Reader Ties

In developing a reader-sensitive outlook, you try to empathize with your readers—that is, to imagine them as whole people and to put yourself in their situations. From your vantage point in an organization, whatever its size, you can locate your readers in either any one or some combination of five relationships. Each of these relationships identifies a social tie and a set of responsibilities; each involves the perspectives that you and your readers have on the subject about which you have information. Three of these ties have a direct bearing on the collaborative operation of the organization; two of them mesh with the encompassing organization of communities that make up the larger world.

Collaterally Supportive Ties. At one level "collateral" means side-by-side or parallel. Hence we can say that collateral relationships tie you to your peers within your organization and perhaps within other organizations as well. You and they may be peers in that you share similar specialized backgrounds (for example, programmers, engineers, accountants), similar responsibilities (for example, managers, administrative assistants, marketers, systems analysts), or special interdependencies (for example, those between buyers and suppliers or sales and technical people).

At another level "collateral" implies a supportive and reinforcing professional relationship. When you are writing to your peers, you are most likely concerned about coordinating general responsibilities or specific work projects. Often your communications will figure in problem-solving processes. You may be offering or requesting information. You may be trying to reconcile disagreements or misunderstandings. Whatever the case, you share with your peers a commitment to joint effort and common understanding. This spirit of collaboration is highlighted in recent management practices that emphasize the critical role of clear, tactful communication in the production of quality goods and services. Thus you are entering a work setting in which writing increasingly seeks to foster collaterally supportive ties.

Strategically Supportive Ties.   Every organization, regardless of size, should have a strategic vision and a plan for working toward these goals and the concept of organizational identity they define. Everyone in an organization ought to have a sense of this collaborative strategy. There are, of course, people specifically responsible for giving expression to this vision and making key decisions to implement it. Strategically supportive ties relate you to those who plan budgets, shape policy, and determine priorities. You may well write to these planners and decision makers to report on the status of a project, to propose the solution to a problem, to suggest the feasibility of a change, to request an expenditure, to report your own development plans and progress, and perhaps to contribute information toward the updating of the organization's strategic plan.

Some of these people were trained in traditional business fields, others have moved from technical fields (such as engineering) into management positions, and still others must combine management responsibilities and other technical expertise (such as a chief engineer). As readers they are interested in cost effectiveness; time use; productivity; production/service standards; organizational, industry, and governmental regulations; employee morale; and the image of the organization. They depend on you and your writing to help them give definition and direction to the organization.

Tactically Supportive Ties.   Organizational strategies do not take on specific shape until they are defined as tactics and do not come to life until these tactics become actions performed by people. From your vantage point in the organization, your role here is to provide tactical support. Thus your written communications are directed to those crucial persons who may operate office or assembly line machinery, maintain files, keep the work environment clean and orderly, provide security, or meet the public in a range of service roles.

This relationship is special because in a sense you serve as an intermediary who explains, interprets, and applies your organization's strategic plan and the ways in which it gives a unifying sense of purpose to what people do. On the one hand, this tie involves you in the challenge of writing clear instructions and constructive performance evaluations; on the other, it offers you the challenge of showing how the details of doing a job can express the mission of the organization.

Senior Voices

Richard

As I begin my search for employment in an uncertain job market, I have often wondered to myself what skills I possess that will separate me from thousands of other college seniors and land me that "dream" job. After numerous interviews with various companies in the marketing and banking industry, I have realized that my experience in business writing seems to have given me an edge over some of my competitors. In fact, my prospects have been further bolstered by an experience in which I actually used my writing skills in a business environment.

During my second semester I was involved with the Small Business Institute (SBI), which is a government-funded co-op program in which groups of students consult with local businesses. Our three-member group worked with a hotel management firm that owns and operates seven hotels in the eastern United States. Our project was to put together a proposal to show the company how it could improve its efficiency and cut costs without sacrificing customer services. After a month spent reviewing corporate reports and interviewing personnel, we targeted the areas that we felt needed improvement: marketing and accounting. Since I had business writing experience from my "Writing for the Professions" English class, I volunteered to edit the proposal for the group. I took each individual piece and placed it into the overall puzzle that would become our proposal by using various styles of cause-effect analysis and a uniform business-type format. Ultimately, our group won the Bert T. Glaze award for the outstanding proposal in our SBI class.

As I have learned during my job search, experience is everything. Now, whenever I interview for a potential job, I can point to a situation in which I used business writing in an actual business environment. Moreover, I have come to understand the importance of writing in the workplace. Recruiters from banking firms have told me that knowing how to write well is a fundamental part of the everyday skills needed in their field. And marketing firms have said the same. Thus, no matter what field I enter after graduation, I now know that writing in the workplace will be an essential part of my career. ■

Patron-Supportive Ties.   It is hard to imagine an organization that does not depend on people who use its products or services or who support its efforts through votes, contributions, or the voicing of opinion. It is equally hard to imagine that your organization would be indifferent to these patron-supportive ties. In one sense or another, your patrons compose a "market" and therefore are a crucial community of readers.

Any tie you share with them would involve you in some phase of the process that attracts, serves, satisfies, and retains patronage. Your patron-supportive writing might be part of a marketing or public opinion study, an advertising or promotional campaign, a direct sales effort, an information program, a customer relations process, or the routine efforts to help patrons understand or properly use a product or service. Surveys; letters that inform, promote, or handle complaints; newspapers; product or service specification material; sales proposals; instruction manuals—all such forms of written communication could tie you to your organization's patrons. And even if you are not directly involved in producing such communications, you may be providing information and thus collaborating with peers who are responsible for promotion, sales, service, and public relations.

Community-Supportive Ties.   In large organizations writing communications that strengthen community ties is often the responsibility of people who specialize in public relations (perhaps the field you are going into). Information or public relations offices or agencies write press releases and other literature that describe personnel, operations, technology, and the nature of the product or service offered by the organization as well as its commitment to the cultural, recreational, educational, and environmental well-being of the community.

Although strengthening community ties is the specific responsibility of public relations departments, each person writing within an organization should be sensitive to the place of the organization in the local, national, and international communities. Even if you are not writing directly to the community or collaborating with one of your peers who is, you can write to reinforce community-supportive ties. Be aware that what your organization does has broad social, economic, and environmental impacts.

Exercise 6.5

Analyzing Your Audience

As you look ahead to your writing activities in an organization, find out or speculate about the kinds of written communications you will be addressing to each of the reader groups. As a group activity, compare and question your findings and speculations about how what you write will be responsible for reinforcing the five relational ties. This will help you appreciate all the more that writing is one of the most productive social activities in the work setting.

Cultivating Writer/Reader Ties

Having identified the basic writer/reader ties found in an organization, we can reflect on several reader-sensitive practices that reinforce these ties. Reader-sensitive writers should (1) give special attention to the role that attitudes play in written communications, (2) take into account the importance of the environment and circumstances in which people read communications, and (3) think about the degree to which readers are familiar with subjects and bodies of information.

Assessing Attitudes

A writer's attitude toward subjects and readers results in tones that can work for or against communication. A clearly organized, soundly developed memo, report, or set of instructions can easily be undermined by insensitive attitudes that alienate readers and thus discourage a spirit of collaboration. Thus you should avoid attitudes that weaken the five ties discussed previously and break down collaborative efforts. Such attitudes might include the following:

- Peers are mainly to be competed with.
- Bosses should be told only "what they want to hear."
- Support staff should be talked down to.
- Patrons are to be manipulated.
- The community is to be fooled.

Your skill in conveying reader-sensitive attitudes and avoiding insensitive ones depends on your ability to imagine your readers as whole persons who bring their own attitudes to their reading. Writers must be aware of the attitudes they convey in their writing, and they must be willing to nurture those that are positive and change those that might impede communication. Doing so can be an important step toward developing a collaborative relationship with your readers.

Assessing Reading Conditions

If you are training in the fields of public relations or advertising, you appreciate the importance of studying the situations in which communications are likely to be read. In the work setting, however, it is important to be sensitive to the conditions in which any communication is read. Are your readers in a private office? Among the steady activity of twenty desks? In front of a bulletin board next to clattering machinery? Moreover, you need to keep in mind the range of responsibilities and duties that can either focus or distract your readers' attention. In one sense, you are explaining to yourself what stake your readers have in whatever you are trying to accomplish. Are they predisposed to appreciate the mutual benefits of collaboration? Will they see explicit or detect implicit criticism of their job performance? How will they feel if what you write changes a procedure that they follow or alters the nature of their responsibilities?

Reading, then, is an activity that takes place in a particular environment and within a set of circumstances. Imagining and evaluating these conditions are indispensable in developing the empathy that characterizes reader sensitivity.

Assessing Reader Familiarity with Your Subject

Commonly, writers in both academic and work settings either attribute to their readers greater familiarity with a subject than they actually possess or give no thought at all to this key element in writer/reader ties. In the work setting you should consciously take into account the nature of reader familiarity with your subject at two levels.

At one level you need to concern yourself with how much your readers—including support people, patrons, and citizens of larger communities—know about the specialized concepts in your communication. At a second level you should consider your readers' familiarity with the reasons behind your communication and the information you are providing. In putting yourself in their places, consider that familiarity with a subject may also pertain to how readily readers can link information to larger contexts or recognize the relevance of what you say to their own needs. As a general rule, remember that, whatever their status within or outside of the organization, no readers can reap the full benefits of your familiarity with a subject unless you help them.

Exercise 6.6

Developing Reader/Writer Ties

To bring reader/writer ties into perspective, imagine that in your job you have to write an explanation of, and then instructions for, a new or revised work procedure. What attitudes are you likely to bring to this task? In order to reinforce tactically supportive ties, try to role-play your readers. Dramatize as specifically as you can their reading environment, their stake in the situation, their familiarity with the subject, and their likely attitudes. If you need help in identifying an appropriate situation, ask your professor. Complete the exercise by discussing the task in small groups.

Putting Reader Sensitivity on the Page

A reader-sensitive outlook helps to secure your readers' agreement with you. They are likely to take the action you desire not only because you have helped them to understand but also because you have encouraged them to feel like agreeing and acting. Moreover, reader sensitivity in an organization is a matter of thoughtfulness and courtesy—a means for creating the quality of social contact that prompts collaborative effort. To achieve reader sensitivity, you should (1) plan and revise thoroughly, (2) treat readers as well as information as your subject, (3) provide signals to highlight key points, and (4) choose appropriate language.

Planning and Revising for and with Readers

From brief memos to extended reports, all written communications deserve careful planning and revision. Whether this process takes twenty minutes or several days, it should produce a reader-sensitive communication. To ensure reader sensitivity, share an outline or, better yet, an advanced draft with one or more of your peers as well as with someone among the relational group for whom the communication is intended. Make it clear to these readers that you value their response and advice and are not looking for an automatic stamp of approval. Ask them not only whether they understand but also how they feel after they have read your communication. This is an important way to make the writing process collaborative and to cultivate one or more of those five social ties basic to an organization.

Putting Readers into Your Subject

As you write, bear in mind that your "subject" is not only the "matter" under consideration (such as a new step in an office procedure) but also your readers. Putting these people into your subject means, among other things, writing introductions in which you address one or a combination of reader-sensitive concerns. In these introductions, you might do one or all of the following:

1. Review the background of the situation prompting the communication.
2. Survey your readers' stake and interest in the situation.
3. Summarize your understanding of your readers' position on any issues involved.
4. Explain how what you have to say will serve your readers' needs in this situation.

Notice that these four concerns address both the cognitive level by setting forth helpful material that provides background and context and the affective level by emphasizing mutual and collaborative involvement. When the spirit of these introductory comments carries over into the body as well as into the concluding summary and your recommendations, you are shaping a communication that is likely to inform and motivate.

Signaling Your Readers

Creating a well-organized communication depends on your critical thinking skills and your grasp of material. You create organizational structure as you decide how to group and sequence information for the convenience of your readers. Up to a point, this structure takes form in your preliminary outlines, but its sense is not completed until you turn it into signals that help your readers *process*, *remember*, and *locate* information. Providing signals is one of the most direct means of forming ties with your readers; unfortunately, it is a means that many writers do not employ. Here are four signaling guidelines:

- **Preview signaling.** At the beginnings of the overall document, of subsections, and of paragraphs, provide your readers with signal statements that announce your main ideas and their component parts. By offering your readers such frames of reference, you help them to anticipate and thus to process your information.

- **Review signaling.** At the ends of the overall document, of subsections, and of paragraphs, summarize and draw conclusions. Always give your readers the opportunity to pause and, with your help, draw ideas together before moving on.

- **Linkage signaling.** Use a word, phrase, sentence, paragraph, or subsection as a linkage signal to help your readers make connections and transitions. These linkage signals may take the form of a heavy-duty paragraph that bridges two subsections or a short statement that announces a thought connection ("as a result"), a subset in a sequence ("third"), or an explanatory tactic ("for example").

- **Reinforcement signaling.** Throughout a document use graphic devices to reinforce preview, review, and linkage signaling. Headings and subheadings; numbering and lettering systems; spatial and typographical devices, such as indentations and bullets (•) to set off and emphasize material; abstracts that precede and summarize longer communications; tables of contents; charts, graphs, and other visuals—all of these are forms of reinforcement signaling. Not only do these help in the reading process, they give your documents a professional look.

Signaling is a practical and courteous way of helping people process, remember, and locate information. It assists not only in a full reading of your communication, but also in two other situations. First, clear preview, review, and reinforcement signaling help people to scan what you have to say as a preliminary or follow-up to or as a substitute for a complete reading of the communication. Second, in helping people locate material quickly, clear signaling assists in discussions where your communication is being used as a reference. In any case, effective signaling is likely not only to speed the movement of ideas into actions but also to cultivate goodwill.

Choosing Words for Your Readers

Whether you are writing a memo, a set of instructions, or a formal report, keep in mind that the words you choose not only serve to sharpen or blur meaning but also to either strengthen or weaken your relationship with your readers. Each time you write, take a close look at your vocabulary to check its level of formality and technical specialization.

In the work setting too many people assume that a formal vocabulary is essential to convey a writer's sophistication, authority, and seriousness of purpose. On occasion, a choice of more formal terms like *ascertain*, *transpire*, or *parameters* rather than *discover*, *happen*, and *conditions* may actually cause your readers to misunderstand the communication. More importantly, though, such formal expression creates an effect of overly elegant writing or a tone of impersonality that can be offputting and thus weaken the tie with your readers. For example, compare *commence* to *begin*, *alleviate* to *reduce*, *utilize* to *use*, *requisition* to *request*, and *designate* to *name*. The more formal words are unlikely to help you strengthen any of the five relational ties that make up an organization.

Perhaps even more troublesome, however, are the roles that technically specialized terms play in these relationships. Clearly, a certain percentage of specialized vocabulary in any field is necessary and, depending on the background and situation of the readers, useful in written communications. If you will be working in financial accounting, for example, you could probably feel comfortable that fellow accountants and both middle- and upper-level managers could relate to *balance sheet*, *assets*, and *liabilities*, and that such basic terminology readily conveys meaning as well as positive feelings associated with shared knowledge. But you would want to ensure that other readers such as clients, support people, and people in the larger community understand the meaning that *you* assign to such basic vocabulary (for example, that *liabilities* means not only debts but also obligations like work paid for but not yet delivered).

If you have been studying in a field that involves complex procedures and theory, be especially careful in your use of terminology. From the field of production and operations management the terms *inventory* and *break-even point* would readily convey specialized meaning to some readers and general meaning to many others, but a communication peppered with words or phrases like *polycentric attitude*, *Therblig*, *heuristic*, and *Poisson prob-*

ability distribution, and acronyms like *CRAFT* and *COFAD,* would more than likely test even collaterally and strategically supportive ties and certainly undermine the bases for tactical, patron-, and community-supportive ties. While not put into practice nearly enough, the implicit policy in many organizations is to keep both formal and technical vocabulary to a minimum and to make certain when such terms are used that writer and reader reach a common understanding of meaning.

You can get computer assistance with the mechanics of putting reader sensitivity on the page. Proofreading/editing programs not only can help you correct grammatical and spelling errors, smooth out sentence structures, and replace cliches and other inappropriate wording, but also can give you guidance in checking some levels of signaling and in determining appropriate vocabulary for given reading audiences. Despite the potentially valuable assistance of such interactive programs, however, a reader-sensitive communication grows out of your outlook and expresses the quality of your thoughts and feelings.

Exercise 6.7

Building Stronger Writer/Reader Ties

Carry Exercise 6.6 a step further by drafting an explanation of the revised or new procedure that you can share with others. Take care to put your readers into the subject, to signal them in all four ways, and to keep them in mind as you think about the formality and technical specialization of your vocabulary. Group reinforcement is a must here!

Conclusion

I f you have taken a business or technical writing course, you most likely have been able to relate what you learned there to what has been said in this chapter about reader sensitivity. If you have not taken such a course and still have the opportunity, by all means do so. Whatever the case, take an active, positive interest in the writing you will do in an organization. In your job search look for information about on-the-job writing in company literature and show your interest in your resume and in interviews. Beyond this, equip yourself with both a handbook and textbook in business or technical writing, which you can order through your college bookstore. Consider, too, computer software that can help you in proofreading and editing your work. Above all, however, keep in mind that writing meshes inseparably with collaborative activities in successful organizations and that a reader-sensitive outlook enhances the likelihood that writing will play a positive role in this collaboration. Ultimately, you can cultivate a reader-sensitive outlook only over a course of time and as part of an encompassing effort to develop as a professional.

References and Resources

You might want to select from the reading materials used in a technical or business writing course at your college, or order materials from the works suggested here. In either case, you will not go wrong if you do some serious reading about written communication in the work setting and supply yourself with two or three helpful resources.

Handbooks. Alphabetical organization, topical keys, and indexes make Charles T. Brusaw's *Handbook of Technical Writing*, 4th ed., and *Business Writer's Handbook*, 4th ed. (New York: St. Martin's, 1993), handy resources that can help you answer a wide range of questions about the form, style, and mechanics of written communication.

Textbooks. Textbooks can be useful beyond the classroom in helping you to think in some depth about the process of writing and about giving shape to memos, letters, reports, proposals, and instructions. Some of the many available textbooks are in various ways concerned with the collaborative nature of writing and with reader sensitivity. Examples are Paul V. Anderson's *Technical Writing: A Reader-Directed Approach*, 2nd ed. (San Diego: Harcourt Brace, 1991), and *Business Communication: An Audience-Centered Approach* (San Diego: Harcourt Brace, 1989), as well as Rebecca E. Burnett's *Technical Communication*, 3rd ed. (Belmont, CA: Wadsworth, 1994).

Anthologies. Anthologies collect articles and excerpts from books that zero in on key principles and issues of writing in the work setting. Kevin J. Harty's *Strategies for Business and Technical Writing*, 3rd ed. (San Diego: Harcourt Brace, 1989), does this and offers a bibliography listing over 300 works on technical and business communication.

Computer Software. Several writing improvement programs on the market can help you proofread and edit your writing and can indirectly reinforce a reader-sensitive outlook. Among the software available are Gram.mat.ik IV (Reference Software, San Francisco) and Macproof (Lexpertise Linguistic Software, Salt Lake City).

Anderson, Paul V. (1981). "Organizing Is Not Enough." In Dwight W. Stevenson, ed., *Courses, Components, and Exercises in Technical Communication*. Urbana, IL: National Council of Teachers of English, 163–84.

————. (1985). "What Survey Research Tells Us About Writing at Work." In Lee Odell and Dixie Goswami, eds., *Writing in Nonacademic Settings*. New York: Guilford Press, 3–85.

Britton, W. Earl. (1978). "What Is Technical Writing?" In W. Keats Sparrow and Donald H. Cunningham, eds., *The Practical Craft: Readings for Business and Technical Writers*. Boston: Houghton Mifflin, 8–13.

Clauser, H. R. (1978). "Writing Is for Readers." In W. Keats Sparrow and Donald H. Cunningham, eds., *The Practical Craft: Readings for Business and Technical Writers*. Boston: Houghton Mifflin, 148–58.

Flower, Linda. (1989). "Transforming Writer-Based Prose into Reader-Based Prose." In Kevin J. Harty, ed., *Strategies for Business and Technical Writing*, 3rd ed. New York: Harcourt Brace, 53–63.

Paxson, William C. (1989). "Non-Discriminatory Writing." In Kevin J. Harty, ed., *Strategies for Business and Technical Writing*, 3rd ed. New York: Harcourt Brace, 110–12.

Phelps, Lonnie D., and Debbie D. DuFrene. (1989). "Improving Organizational Communication Through Trust." *Journal of Technical Writing and Communication* 19(3): 267–76.

Pickens, Judy E., et al., eds. (1977). *Without Bias: A Guidebook for Non-Discriminatory Communication*. San Francisco: International Association of Business Communicators.

Shurter, Robert L. and J. Peter Williamson. (1978). "Some Principles of Business Communication." In W. Keats Sparrow and Donald H. Cunningham, eds., *The Practical Craft: Readings for Business and Technical Writers*. Boston: Houghton Mifflin, 4–7.

7 Oral Communication in Organizations

R. Glenn Ray

Director of the Institute of Education and Training for Business, McDonough Center for Leadership and Business, Marietta College

Senior Voices

Erica

It has been my experience that the strength of people's communication skills can determine their ability to achieve. Community volunteers, teachers, engineers, campus leaders, coaches, editors—all can move ahead in their fields when they take the time to learn to facilitate group discussions. Few organizations need a loner, but all desire the inputs of even a single member who knows how to produce effective interactions.

A Civil Liberties in America class I took last year used the four stages of group development in bringing the class together. As noted in this chapter, when groups forgo the forming, storming, norming, or performing stages, they are often not productive. But in this class the professor made sure the group got off to a sound start. He began by asking us each to tell the rest of the class why we had signed up for this course. At the time, this seemed like a simple formality, but as the group progressed, I could see that he had allowed us to each make a contribution to the purpose of the class. We had each described an intent that increased our commitment to learning throughout the semester. Vocalizing the fact that there was a reason for taking the course made the class more meaningful for me.

In using the various techniques outlined in this chapter, a group member can emerge who facilitates achievement. Even the simplest of questions or activities can impact a group's performance. Thoughtful use of communication skills can be your impetus for productivity in all types of group situations. ∎

Interpersonal communication is a socially learned skill—we are not naturally effective in our communication. In addition, communication is a process, not a static event. Due to the variety of role models from whom we learn these skills, we have a spectrum of abilities. Ultimately, however, communication is a skill that can and must be developed. As one CEO commented, "My top managers don't fail because of the lack of technical skills. It is their inability to get along with their people."

In this chapter we focus on the dynamics of the group communication process in organizations. Specifically, we'll examine the communication skills involved in solving problems, making decisions, building consensus, and managing meetings. In addition, we'll outline the structures that improve the effectiveness of organizational interactions.

The Four Stages of Group Communication

Work groups go through phases to reach their most effective level, much as a child goes through developmental phases to reach adulthood. According to Tuckman (1965), a group must experience four phases in order to be the most effective: (1) forming, (2) storming, (3) norming, and (4) performing. In the forming stage the team members say hello and get acquainted and comfortable with one another. In the storming stage they determine their roles within the group, and in the norming stage they set the operating rules of the group. Finally, the group is ready to perform the task at hand. The length of these stages will vary from group to group and from meeting to meeting. What's most important, however, is that the group experiences each successive stage—groups that skip the early developmental steps tend to communicate poorly and to end up with unfinished business.

Exercise 7.1	*Defining Organizational Communication*

Write down a definition of organizational communication. Then, as a group, synthesize a unique definition that incorporates the elements of each individual definition.

The Forming Stage

An expectation check is a useful icebreaker in the forming stage. Any group member can begin by suggesting that each member tell a little bit about him- or herself and describe what he or she expects to achieve or get out of involvement in the group. This process allows the members to understand the objectives and potential contributions of individuals in the group. And you don't have to be the group leader to suggest doing this.

Another important task in the forming stage is to achieve consensus on the ground rules of interaction. As a group facilitator I develop a set of interaction ground rules early in the session. Often, I will begin by asking the group members for suggestions as to how the group should interact. After posting on a flip chart their list of rules, I ask the participants to modify or delete any items on the list or add additional rules. Of course, these rules can be changed at any time in the group's life. After I have agreement upon the ground rules, I tape them in a prominent place on the wall so that I can refer back to them if the meeting gets out of hand. The following is a list of ground rules I have suggested to groups in my sessions:

1. Be on time to meetings.
2. Be a good listener.
3. Focus on the present and future rather than the past.
4. Keep an open mind, and don't be negative.
5. Don't be defensive if your idea is criticized.
6. Participate in the discussion.
7. Ask for clarification when unsure.
8. Keep inputs short and to the point.
9. Give everyone a chance to speak.
10. Be prepared to take responsibility for group decisions.

The key to the forming stage is that each member have an opportunity to meet every other member and acknowledge one another as group members.

The Storming Stage

Next, the roles—formal and informal—of each member should be discussed and agreed on. Some roles emerge from one's past experience or personality while others are strategically selected.

Role Assignment. Roles may relate to either task or relationship maintenance functions. Task functions involve communication about the job to be accomplished by the group. Examples of task functions include asking the initial question about the group's task, seeking information about the task from others, giving information about the task, elaborating on someone else's thoughts about the task, and clarifying and summarizing statements about the task. Maintenance behaviors involve communication that deals with group relationships. Examples of relationship maintenance functions include statements that support and encourage other group members, that harmonize group interactions, that provide feedback about another member's effectiveness, and that reduce tension. At this stage most behavior involves relationship maintenance: members of an effective team will demonstrate some of both types of communication functions.

Transition Teambuilding.　As a new organizational member, you must consciously communicate your expectations to others and to clarify others' expectations of you. A process called Transition Teambuilding (Looram, 1978) can accomplish this for a new work group; a variation of the process is also useful for intact work groups. Each time I use this technique with work groups, I redesign the technique with the new manager to meet his or her priorities. There are several steps to the process.

The meeting should begin with a short teambuilding exercise to enhance the communication to come. If possible, the former manager should have an opportunity to describe the state of the unit and to explain the progress that the group has made. Then the new manager can explain his or her vision for the group: goals, objectives, improvements, and so on. Next, each member of the team should list his or her duties as he or she sees them or as they have been performed in the past. Then team members can outline the resources and information they need from the leader and from one another to accomplish the leader's vision. Finally, the leader or a facilitator should summarize the day's communication. Follow-up action-planning sessions on strategy are often useful as well.

Assimilation Meetings.　The General Electric Company has a variation of this process called an assimilation meeting. Here an outside facilitator meets with the work group but without the new manager. The purpose of this meeting is to elicit a set of questions to be posed to the new manager. These questions are posted on the wall for all to see. Then the facilitator clarifies the questions privately for the new manager, who frames his or her responses. Next, the manager introduces him- or herself, describes new organizational objectives, and responds to the questions of the group. Finally, the new manager answers any additional questions from the group. In this way nothing is left to chance.

Exercise 7.2　　*Identifying Group Expectations*

Form mock intact work groups, and assign one group member the role of new leader. Each team member and the leader should write down their expectations of self, leader, and peers. As a class, discuss what was learned during the process.

The Norming Stage

In this stage the group identifies its norms. According to Burke (1982), "Norms are concepts that represent standards or rules of conduct to which people conform." Norms have a great impact on the effectiveness of a group. By this point in a group's life, the trends and patterns in its interactions comprise its norms. In an effective team, members of the group have learned how to deal with conflict. They demonstrate more self-disclosing behaviors, and they cooperate rather than compete. In short, the group has begun to gel.

Usually, these norms are not discussed. A useful technique to clarify the norms is to ask each member of the group to identify three norms that have evolved in the group. Then, ask the group members to prioritize the norms based on the norm's impact on the group's task. Next, ask each group member to share the norms he or she has observed with other group members. With this process the group can validate the positive norms and remedy those that are found to be counterproductive.

The Performing Stage

If the group has progressed effectively through the previous three stages, they can efficiently accomplish the task at hand—that is, they can perform. Many times, organizations and managers attempt to push the group into the performing stage while ignoring the earlier stages. The result may be wheel-spinning in which group members revert unconsciously to the forming, storming, or norming stages. For example, questions will be asked to find out who the other group members are and why they are there. Group members will be concerned about individual and group responsibilities. People will be hesitant to act because the group norms have not been discussed or demonstrated. In essence, the group may spend more time reverting to unanswered questions than they would have spent had they progressively addressed each stage.

Exercise 7.3   *Group Communication*

In class have a small group perform some task. Then discuss how well the group performed. Did it progress through the four stages of group development? Were the stages identifiable? What task and maintenance behaviors were demonstrated?

Managing Meetings

A great deal of an organizational member's life is spent in various meetings. This is also the single event about which people most often complain. Indeed, many meetings generate no positive or concrete results and thus are a waste of time. Fortunately, there are several techniques for improving the productivity of a team meeting.

A basic but often overlooked meeting tool is the agenda. There are several ways to compile an appropriate agenda. If the purpose of meeting is for ongoing problem solving or information sharing, the agenda for the next meeting can be the final agenda item for every meeting. You can quickly set the date for the next meeting and decide what should be addressed. For the first meeting of a group, the Delphi technique (described in the next section) is an effective means of consolidating the individual needs of the group members. If group members have input on the agenda, their commitment to the group product will be greater. Regardless of the method of developing a list of meeting topics, the agenda should be distributed in advance of the meeting. Ground rules are also critical to the group effectiveness.

Action planning should end every meeting. This can be accomplished by summarizing the content of the meeting and resolving a few basic issues. The first is identifying who will be responsible for each activity agreed on in the meeting. It is important that one person takes this responsibility—group responsibility is too ambiguous and often results in no action. Other group members who are willing to contribute in a supporting role should also be identified.

The second issue is determining the resources this individual will need to accomplish the task. If these resources are not available, then actions to obtain them or to modify the plan must be undertaken. Resources may consist of people outside the group as well as equipment, funds for research, or facilities like a team meeting room.

The third issue is defining the time frame. Depending on the scope of the task, a PERT (program evaluation and review technique) chart may be useful. This technique identifies all of the steps or milestones and time frames in the task as well as allocation of resources and concurrent tasks. In any event, it is important to agree on an appropriate deadline. This enables the responsible person and the group to identify when the task is complete and to measure the success of the effort.

Solving Problems, Making Decisions, and Building Consensus

Common problem-solving and decision-making techniques include brainstorming and the nominal group technique. Consensus-building strategies such as Delphi technique and affinity diagraming are also gaining popularity.

Brainstorming

Brainstorming is an effective way to stimulate and capture creative thoughts for use in the problem-solving process. In a brainstorming session four basic ground rules should be observed:

1. **Don't allow criticism.** Participants should withhold judgment, evaluation, and analysis during the idea-generation stage.
2. **Think freely.** Everyone has something to offer, and even the most "off the wall" idea should be accepted.
3. **Quantify.** The more ideas generated, the better!
4. **Build on the ideas of others.** Embellish, combine, or improve on generated ideas in an effort to generate further thoughts.

It is important to allow sufficient time—at least an hour—to carry out the brainstorming session. A note should be sent to every member identifying the topic to be considered and the purpose of the meeting well before the meeting begins. During the meeting itself, a facilitator should be appointed to record all ideas generated by the group on a flip chart or chalkboard. Remember that at this point ideas should not be evaluated. It's important, too, to maintain a free flow of thoughts by establishing and maintaining a rapid pace until "the well is dry." Finally, be sure to reflect on ideas already listed and ask if a new idea differs from one already listed.

After the group has generated its full list of ideas, the ideas need to be evaluated. This means combining, consolidating, and embellishing listed ideas, and then reviewing the summarized list in terms of the following:

- **Practicality**: Can this be done?
- **Workability**: Will it work?
- **Usefulness**: Will it be useful?
- **Value**: Will it be valued by others?

At this point the group can eliminate from further consideration any ideas that don't meet these criteria. The ideas that remain can then be discussed further as potential solutions to the problem under consideration.

The Nominal Group Technique

Nominal Group Technique (NGT) is a variation of brainstorming with some unique characteristics. In NGT, after the problem statement has been listed on the flip chart and is understood by all participants, the group does the following:

1. Generate ideas in writing.
2. Prioritize ideas.
3. List participants' ideas on flip chart in their order of priority.
4. Continue listing ideas until all are exhausted.
5. Briefly discuss and clarify the listed ideas.

The major value of this technique is the equalization of input. In open brainstorming the most vocal participants get their ideas listed while more reticent members may not contribute to the spontaneous idea generation. Thus, potentially, the best idea might be missed in open brainstorming. The down side of NGT is that you lose some of the synergy that occurs as ideas pour out and are built on by group members.

Exercise 7.4

Brainstorming

As a class, examine a Styrofoam cup closely. Then brainstorm on all of the possible uses for this cup. After you have reached one hundred uses, rephrase the question. That is, imagine that the cup is four feet in diameter at the lip. Now what uses can the cup serve? After the well has run dry or you have reached a one-hour time limit, discuss how the brainstorming went, and how it would have differed if the nominal group technique had been used.

The Delphi Technique

This technique differs from brainstorming in that group members do not have to be together in one place. The Delphi is an especially useful technique for problem-solving groups that are in distant geographic locations or whose members are on different shifts. The technique involves the following steps:

1. Choose a group of experts on the problem to be considered. Select one person to serve as the hub—to distribute questionnaires and consolidate responses.

Round One

2. Distribute a questionnaire consisting of several open-ended questions on the problem to each panel member. Encourage panel members to be as creative and wide-ranging as possible at this point.

3. Complete the questionnaire and return it to the hub.

4. Consolidate the responses into unique items.

Round Two

5. Redistribute to the panel members a new questionnaire containing the unique items. Have panel members prioritize the items in order of importance.

Round Three

6. Analyze the responses of the panel members and send a summary of responses to the panel members. Have panel members reprioritize their responses in light of the group responses.

Round Four

7. Drop the lowest-ranked items. Distribute the new questionnaire to the panel members for prioritization.

8. Repeat the process until consensus is reached.

The turnaround time of the questionnaires by the panel members and the hub is the critical element in this process. Thus, if the hub uses a unique color of paper for the distribution, panel members will be able to identify and respond to the Delphi questionnaire quickly when it comes across their desks.

The Affinity Diagram

Another variation on brainstorming is the affinity diagram. This problem-solving tool is used to generate and organize data around a problem or situation. First, the problem statement is clarified as in the other brainstorming processes. Next, each group member silently lists independent solutions on separate Post-it notes. As members exhaust their alternatives, the items are distributed across a blank wall. When all the participants' alternatives are on the wall, items are sorted into groupings that seem to naturally relate or have common areas. However, items should not be forced into a category. In addition, if an item is moved more than ten times, it should be placed to the side by itself. Once all the items have been sorted, header cards should be created to describe each grouping.

The Multivoting Technique

This technique helps a group reduce the number of items to be considered in a way that tends to eliminate individual's "ownership" of items. For example, suppose a ten-member group is voting on twelve items. The multivoting technique would proceed as follows:

First Vote

1. Vote for as many items as desired.

2. Circle the items that receive six or more votes.

Second Vote

3. Vote on the top vote getters (those items that received six or more votes). This time each person gets a total of three votes (one per item).

4. Circle the items that receive six votes or more.

Third Vote

5. Vote on the top vote getters from the second voting (items receiving six or more votes). This time each person gets just one vote.

It's generally best to discontinue the multivoting process when the list is pared down to three items. At that point the group should discuss the merits of the items to seek consensus.

The Effect of Physical Structures on Communication

Even buildings and offices impact the nature of communication in organizations, though the effect will vary from organization to organization. To illustrate, let's contrast two corporate headquarters that house two very different cultures. The first featured high, sound-proof walls, so that while walking through the hallways, people were unable to look into or communicate with those in the offices. Moreover, the ceilings were equipped with a special series of fans to muffle human interactions. Employees described the atmosphere as being similar to a morgue. Communication was hushed and subdued, and morale was low. The office design made people feel as though they were working in solitary confinement; those who desired interpersonal contact had to purposefully seek it. Indeed, even joke telling was discouraged by top management, who feared that such activity would make employees less comfortable with the present office culture.

The headquarters of the other organization was constructed with all-glass interior walls. No one could totally block out the communication that occurred in their office. In addition, organizational members felt free to walk into any office (including the president's) in the building to give feedback and express opinions. Not surprisingly, these employees were far more satisfied with the communication in the company, and this satisfaction positively impacted the productivity of all employees.

In both cases the physical environment was purposefully designed to reflect a corporate communication strategy. One office was control-oriented; the other promoted open communication. As you step into your potential employer's office for your job interview, notice how open the communication seems. Are people smiling? Do you hear laughter? Also, notice how you feel throughout your visit. Pay attention to these feelings because they will determine your personal comfort with the organization's style of communication.

Conclusion

The single most significant factor impacting your future success or failure in your professional life is your communication skills. Your present level of interpersonal functioning can be developed and improved. But it is up to you to analyze your current skills and focus on developing your weakest areas. Then, you need to undertake further research and practice some more. In short, be proactive with your communication skills and you will surely reap the benefits for a lifetime.

References and Resources

Burke, W. Warner. (1982). *Organization Development: Principles and Practices.* Boston: Little, Brown.

Looram, James. (1985). "The Transition Meeting: Taking over a New Management Team." *Supervisory Management,* 29–36.

Tuckman, B. W. (1965). "Development Sequence in Small Groups." *Psychological Bulletin* 63(6).

8 Applied Ethics

Michael B. Taylor

Associate Professor of Management, Marietta College

Michael B. Taylor

Associate Professor of Management, Marietta College

Senior Voices

Douglas

When I initially signed up for the Business Ethics class, I had no idea what I was getting myself into. I knew that the class dealt with ethics in business, but I am a psychology major. So, I naturally assumed that the material would be irrelevant to me. I was wrong.

Ethics are principles of morality that appear in every profession including psychology. In fact, psychologists are given a casebook that outlines all of the ethical principles of psychology that they must follow in order to be a member of the American Psychological Association and not be in violation with the Ethics Committee. Obviously, ethics are a top priority in professions other than business.

I consider myself a person who sees situations and issues in a black-or-white/right-or-wrong way. However, I found in Business Ethics that this type of thinking is impossible. I started the class believing that certain actions, such as lying, cheating, betraying, and hating, were in and of themselves wrong, regardless of the consequences. However, I learned quickly that ethics are relative and that everyone has their own ideas about what is right and what is wrong, as well as different reasons for regarding actions as such. For example, I consider cheating to be equivalent to lying. I knew of a person who had cheated on a particular assignment, and I felt that this person should have been punished severely. However, when I was constructing my resume, I rounded my grade point average up. I justified this to myself as being all right because I had earned those extra points and did not want them to go to waste. In any event, I was doing exactly what the "cheater" had done: I was lying/cheating. Not only was I just as guilty as that person, I was clearly betraying my own ethical standards. This caused me to have a much more open mind when considering the reasons for people's actions.

At the same time, there are persons who are devoid of ethics. These individuals simply use other people throughout their entire lives as a means to their ends. They couldn't care less how you are after they get what they want from you.

This leads to another important part of ethics—forgiveness and tolerance. Until very recently, I would carry around this emotional baggage of what a horrible person I was because of the mistakes I had made. I have learned, however, that everyone is human and that mistakes simply go with the territory. Coincidentally, when I was taking Business Ethics, I was also taking a New Testament History course. The New Testament speaks of the need for forgiveness and the fact that God is forgiving. In Business Ethics we learned that we will make mistakes in our lives and that we must forgive ourselves and go on with life. Strangely enough, these two concepts meshed in my mind and I have come to see them as the essence of our survival. In order to be tolerant and loving of others, we must first forgive ourselves for our mistakes.

Finally, I've learned that we can have our morals and ethics, but that they simply aren't black and white and that sometimes gray is a viable resolution. We need to be persons of conviction, but sometimes it is better to be persons of understanding. ■

For many traditional college students the move into the work force as a full-time employee is a major shock. Employers expect not only competence and honesty but also loyalty, which often means putting the interests of the business ahead of other, competing interests. Colleges and universities expect loyalty, but seldom to the degree that an employer does. At times employers expect that you will live by their ethics, at least on company time, and keep your moral reservations to yourself.

Learning how to maintain your own values and self-respect in a new moral universe is a major part of any transition. Many of you remember the struggle you had moving from the moral context of high school and home to the new moral context of college amidst other people with decidedly different moral views. Initially, this was very disconcerting. Gradually, you learned what the institution expected and adjusted to the views of a new set of friends and peers. The same type of situation awaits you as you enter the business world; thus you should recognize that you have already managed this type of transition once before. There are, however, important differences as well as similarities that you should be aware of.

In this chapter we will look at some of the ethical issues commonly faced by people at the beginning of their careers. These issues include bribery, pollution, unsafe products, dishonest advertising, employee rights and responsibilities, and whistle blowing. We will examine how ethical discourse helps us make decisions with some confidence when we are puzzled about what to do and why.

Ethics and Resumes

The first of the new moral situations you will face during and after your transition from student to employee likely will involve the creation of a resume. This document is supposed to introduce you to potential employers by listing, among other things, your previous work experiences, such as part-time employment, summer work, and internships. Some applicants routinely "put on the best possible face" and give grand-sounding titles to rather mundane experiences. For example, a student who acted as a typist, receptionist, and general "go-fer" described himself as an "administrative assistant." A lifeguard described herself as a "personnel administrator." A clerk in a bank's trust department described himself as a "trust officer." A student who played golf all summer listed herself as a "manager at the parks and recreation department."

These examples show job applicants progressively stretching the truth until in the last example the truth becomes falsehood. In the first case an exalted but commonly used title is employed, and the reader is not likely to be misled. In the case of the lifeguard, there is no evidence of any personnel to manage in the traditional sense although a head lifeguard may well do many of the tasks of a personnel manager (for example, hire and fire people, set work schedules, keep personnel files, and train new employees). In the case of the trust officer, the applicant has improperly described his position. The duties commonly handled by a trust officer are not those handled by a clerk in a bank trust department. And in the case of the golfer, the applicant had no job, and the misrepresentation is total.

We have, then, four different situations: first, a grand title that employers know and understand; second, a commonly used title that covers a variety of tasks and responsibilities and may loosely apply to the specific job; third, a job title that has a specific meaning and that has been misused to mislead a potential employer; and fourth, an outright fabrication designed to mislead.

Assessing the Resumes

Which, if any, of these resume writers were justified in making the claims they made? What reasons can you give to support your explanations?

Ethics involves giving reasons to justify actions that affect the welfare of others. Philosophers insist that what constitutes a good reason in one case also is a good reason in all similar cases, so it is important to frame your reasons carefully. Therefore, if you said that the golfer was wrong to claim to have been a manager because that is a lie and it is wrong to tell a lie, then either it is always wrong to tell a lie or you need to explain when it is bad to tell a lie and when it is all right.

Classifying Ethical Systems

Now that you have given your reasons and are ready to defend them, let us see what type of ethic you are employing. Ethicists have become quite expert in classifying ethics in order to assess them on philosophical grounds. Thus we can identify three main types of ethics: (1) teleological, (2) deontological, and (3) ethics of virtue. And by understanding how ethical systems differ, we can recognize some of the sources of disagreement among people.

Teleology

Also known as consequentialist or utilitarian ethics, teleological ethics hold that the action or practice under consideration is justified because it produces the greatest amount of good. In other words, the ends justify the means.

Teleologists often disagree, however, about what the good is and whose good should be considered. In our culture, which is egalitarian in principle, teleologists usually include the welfare of all persons equally, and the disagreement tends to be about the nature of the good. In other cultures the disagreement is often about whose good needs to be considered: Is it family, clan, tribe, race, religion, or nation that has the prime claim on the good?

In both our own and other cultures, some argue that only their own interests should be served. Although they recognize that there are others whose interests could be served, they are concerned only with themselves. These "ethical egoists" are consistently self-serving and believe that self-interest is paramount. In the case of the job titles for the resume, ethical egoists would argue that one should look after one's own interests regardless of the effects on potential employers or other job applicants. (Later on, we will consider to what extent free market capitalism is a modified form of ethical egoism.)

People who believe that one can only look after one's own interest deny the very possibility of ethics, for they are not concerned with the welfare of others and thus do not believe in the possibility of free choice. These "psychological egoists" should not be confused with ethical egoists, who recognize the possibility of choice—that is, that others' interests might be served.

Exercise 8.2 *Justifying Resume "Padding"*

Examine your justification for stretching the truth on a resume and see if consequences are important. For example, if you said that everyone does it, so no one is at a disadvantage or that no one is hurt by the practice, then in some sense you are a consequentialist.

Deontology

Deontologists take the view that certain acts or practices are wrong regardless of the consequences. Most deontologists acknowledge that consequences are one important consideration but deny that consequences are the only morally relevant issue. If you said that some of the resume writers were lying and that lying is wrong regardless of the consequences, you are taking the deontological view that some acts or practices are simply wrong.

People give different reasons for knowing that a particular act or practice is right or wrong. Some believe in commandments given by God. Others trust in intuition. Still others believe that a natural law can be discerned through the correct use of reason.

Ethics of Virtue

Here the focus is on the cultivation of a person's character. Consequently, ethics is about realizing one's potential, not about certain actions or practices. Looking at our resume example, the issue is how such an action would affect the character of the person involved. So, if you said that you would not misrepresent yourself on your resume because you are not a liar and not about to become one, then you may be arguing from an ethics of virtue. More commonly, an ethics of virtue is applied to acts or practices. For example, the practice of capitalism is good or bad to the degree that it helps or fails to help people reach their full potential as free citizens in control of their own futures. In Chapter 17, "Making Your Way Toward Citizenship," Suzanne Morse argues from an ethic of virtue.

Pluralism/Relativism

As you discuss with other people what you think is good or bad, right or wrong, you find that people differ not only in their moral judgments but also in justifications for them. For example, some people believe that abortion is always wrong because it violates God's law against murder. Others see it as morally permissible because a woman has the right as a free person to control her own body. In the United States we have what is referred to as a pluralistic culture, that is, a culture that permits a variety of competing moral views. Disagreements about moral matters are common, and many are long-standing and bitter.

Moral Disagreements and Relativism

When people have trouble agreeing about moral matters, the temptation is to say that there are no moral absolutes, only relative judgments conditioned by time and place. This view, called relativism, takes several different forms. One such view, emotivism, holds that moral claims are simply disguised statements of preference by a group or an individual. Another view, cultural relativism, holds that moral claims are a part of a whole cultural complex that has evolved as a survival mechanism for a group, and that what is right for that group is right for it and it only. Anthropologists and sociologists often take this view.

According to relativism, given a disagreement between two people about a moral judgment, there is no reason to assume that either party is correct or incorrect. Neither should we assume that a third party, an observer, ought to respect the view of one or the other. After all, the observer may be as obstinately wrong in his or her moral judgment as the disputants.

Since it is possible that a person can admit to having been wrong in a moral judgment and can explain the source of his or her error, it is important to understand some of the sources of moral disagreements so that we do not give up too soon in trying to convince one another about the correctness of our views. For example, in our resume case we looked at the "go-fer" who called himself an administrative assistant. One of my students thought this was immoral until he found out that this was the official title given this position by the employer. Once this fact became known, the moral judgment changed. Thus some moral disputes can be resolved by an appeal to the "facts."

Other moral disputes arise from conflicting loyalties, different modes of moral discourse, and different beliefs about human nature, the course of history, and the existence and nature of a deity or deities. If you are a Quaker or a Mennonite, for example, then your loyalty to a tradition of pacifism may be more important than any arguments justifying involvement in war. If you are a consequentialist, convinced that the rightness and wrongness of actions are solely determined by the consequences of those actions, you will have a hard time discussing the morality of a particular action with someone who operates from an ethics of virtue—that is, someone for whom keeping promises and telling the truth are of primary importance. Those who believe that humans are in some sense able to choose freely are frustrated in discussing moral matters with determinists who deny the existence of free will. Correctly identifying the sources of disagreement may result in the resolution of the disagreement, in less frustration, or in the recognition that moral disagreement does not necessarily imply moral relativism. Pluralism and tolerance may reflect the recognition that for all one's certainty one may still be wrong.

The Importance of Tolerance

In a pluralistic culture tolerance is an important value. One need only look at pluralistic societies that do not have a tradition of tolerance to see the difficulties of working together without some consensus about what should be done and how it should be done. In some societies whose populations are divided on religious or racial grounds and that have no tradition of tolerance, violence between groups has been widespread (the former Yugoslavia is one glaring example). Tolerance grows out of respect for others and a recognition that for all one's certainty one may be wrong. Tolerance grows out of humility, not out of certainty. Fortunately, we live in a country that values tolerance and that has developed patterns of living that allow us to coexist with those with whom we disagree on some pretty serious matters.

The Importance of Clearly Defined Roles

The existence of clearly defined roles is another important element in stabilizing pluralistic societies such as ours in which individuals with strong moral disagreements not only live side by side but also work together in cooperative ventures. For example, you don't ask the person at the checkout counter what his or her religious beliefs are before paying for your groceries. This individual rings up your purchases regardless of your sex, creed, or color, and charges you the same price as the other customers even though you do not belong to his or her church. In turn, in your role as customer, you pay promptly and thank him or her for the assistance.

The Role of Student.   One role you are very familiar with is that of student. While it is not easy to spell out all of the expectations of someone filling this role, we can do a rough sketch. From the teacher's perspective, students do not do economically valuable work; hence, they are not paid to be students. Students are to learn from their teachers, who have something worthwhile to teach; hence, teachers are paid. Teachers grade the work of their students; hence, students must do their assigned work on a timely basis. The grades that a student receives are important since work opportunities and further educational opportunities are affected by them. Finally, students are expected to abide by the academic rules laid down by their teachers.

The role of student from the student's perspective looks somewhat different. For example, teachers and their classes are to be endured as a necessary evil. Teachers teach because they are unable to do anything useful. Students have much in common with one another and should band together to make school tolerable. And most of the academic rules are designed to make the teacher's life easier or are arbitrary and capricious acts of power-mongering by the teachers. These rules have no other justification and hence can be ignored whenever possible.

Clearly, the role of student from the student's perspective is a caricature, but it highlights an important point about roles: No single set of expectations exists for any role. Those who occupy a given role may conceive of it somewhat differently from others who occupy the same role as well as from those who occupy another, related role. Obviously, problems will result when clear expectations about roles do not exist. For example, for teachers, cheating and plagiarism are clearly unethical, whereas for some students these practices are not serious matters unless one has the misfortune to get caught. Some students have told me that since they produced a piece of work and freely chose to give it to others, they had done nothing ethically wrong. Other students have been outraged, however, that certain students were getting credit for work they had not done.

The Role of Employee.   In business some of the same role ambiguities exist. In part, doing a good job means knowing what your role is. Although part of your role is contained in your job description, much more will be expected of you than even the most complete job description can detail. For example, most employers expect you to pick up on indirect cues such as praise given to other employees or stories told about past employees who were particularly valued. Or your employer may ask you to work additional hours (with or without pay) and suggest that this is what "team players" do. But what if you have already promised to take your daughter to a baseball game as a reward for her excellent grades. Now you are confronted with a conflict between your role as parent and your role as a "good employee."

But is this a moral dilemma? It's not an easy question to answer. When you took the job, did you implicitly promise to be a "good employee"? How stringent was that promise? So far, we have looked only at the employer's notion of what constitutes a "good employee." How do other employees view the role of "good employee"? In some companies there is a decided split between workers and managers or between managers at different levels. Role conflicts in such circumstances can be quite nasty. And even in organizations where employees and managers share expectations of what makes a "good employee," such conflicts can present moral dilemmas.

Moral Dilemmas in the Workplace

Moral dilemmas certainly arise when your employer asks you to do something that violates your own sense of what is right. For example, an employer might instruct you not to acknowledge the receipt of a bill until a second notice is received and then to write a note indicating that this is the first notice you received. Having been brought up to tell the truth, such a deception may cause you some "pangs of conscience."

Loyalty to an Organization

Suppose your employer asked you to falsify a report to a federal agency so that a new drug could be tested on human subjects in spite of some dangerous side effects experienced by animal subjects. In this case the stakes are higher than in the case of the delayed payment of a bill and an attendant lie. Is the problem that you are being asked to lie or that you may be putting human lives at stake unnecessarily? And what resources can you draw on when your conscience rebels?

Of course, you can quit. Then your conscience is clear—or is it? In the case of late payment, you may just walk away without saying anything, but in the case of the experimentation with human subjects you may feel the need to "blow the whistle." Keep in mind, though, that many people become quite close to and develop a strong sense of loyalty to their co-workers. And loyalty to a group can become loyalty to a company. Thus blowing the whistle on the company is seen as harming one's friends. In short, from outside the company the issue may seem clear-cut, but from inside things become much murkier.

Exercise 8.3

Blowing the Whistle

Suppose you're working for a company that is doing something not only illegal but also potentially harmful to people. Would you "blow the whistle"? Keep in mind that engineers, scientists, and others have ruined their careers because they were concerned about the safety risks their companies were taking with the lives of other people; some of them have been unable to find a job in their fields after turning in their companies. Would this knowledge make any difference?

Loyalty to a Profession

One can also develop loyalty to a professional group, such as doctors, dentists, lawyers, engineers, or accountants. Because these professionals possess skills that are important for the public good and because they are in some sense servants of their communities, they often have codes of ethics governing their behavior.

These codes of ethics can be an important resource for the individual professional facing a moral dilemma. First, the code represents the collective wisdom of the profession and can provide moral guidance in moments of confusion. Second, it can lend support when one feels obligated to do the right thing, even when doing so is difficult. Knowing that others similarly situated would understand and support you is a source of strength. Third, a code of ethics can provide the professional with a bargaining chip if he or she wants to refuse to do something but does not want to quit. After all, if you won't do something because it violates your profession's code of ethics, then no other professional will either.

Professionals take their professions very seriously. One's profession is not just a skill—it constitutes an identity. Codes of ethics are not just pieces of paper but serious attempts to think through obligations to society.

Loyalty to Management

One of the groups we did not include in the list of professions is management, and that was intentional. Why? The manager's role is to promote the interests of the company. In crude terms, they are "hired guns." The really interesting question is not whether they are "hired guns," but who they have been hired by. That is, whose interests should managers serve?

Traditionally, the answer has been that the managers are responsible to the owners. Clearly, if a business owner hires you to manage the business and you give away the profits to charity, you have violated your role. You have not done what you were hired to do no matter how laudable the result. But in the modern corporation, which may have thousands of owners (that is, stockholders) and may handle pension funds for the benefit of present and future pensioners, things get more complicated. For which group of owners does the manager work? One traditional answer has been that the manager should seek to maximize profits for the company since that is what the owners want and what benefits society as a whole. Economists from Adam Smith to Milton Friedman have sought to show that as each individual selfishly promotes his or her own welfare, the interests of all are best served, especially in the economic sphere. This form of ethical egoism has served to justify for some the narrow pursuit of profitability by managers.

Others have objected on various grounds that the modern corporation has obligations to groups other than its stockholders. Currently, "stakeholder theory" suggests that managers also have obligations to customers, suppliers, employees, and local publics, for without the support of these groups the company would not exist. Thus these groups also have some claims on the company, and the manager needs to consider their interests in addition to the shareholders'.

Modern managers must balance the interests of various shareholder groups that may be in fundamental disagreement with one another. They must also consider the often conflicting interests of other stakeholders. Since there is currently no agreed-on manner for resolving such conflicts, there is no managerial ethic to which managers can appeal if their superior asks them to do something they perceive as wrong. The managers can only appeal to personal codes of ethics and give reasons. Managers know that if they resign, replacements wait eagerly in the wings. But the problem remains, since the closest thing to a managerial ethic is the single command to maximize profit. The new managers will be as much adrift as their predecessors.

Ethics and Wisdom

What has wisdom to do with ethics, managers, or, for that matter, anything? Wisdom is going around the block for the second time and remembering what you saw the first time. Wisdom is not making the same mistake twice. Wisdom is recognizing a new mistake before you make it.

Remember, ethics involves giving reasons concerning actions, practices, or ways of living that affect the welfare of other people. Since we are concerned with human welfare, we are concerned in some sense with outcomes. That means that consequences do matter in ethics even if they

Kendra

Ethics is certainly nothing new or unusual to any of us. For years, when we have made decisions, we have asked ourselves, "Should I do this?" or "Is this right or wrong?" However, our business ethics may be tested for the first time. As graduating seniors we are ready to apply business ethics in our new, developing careers.

For many it will begin with the composition of a resume. Graduates should be honest when listing their experiences, activities, and qualifications. Resumes should never contain exaggerations or embellishments of the truth.

However it begins, business ethics will be with us throughout the rest of our careers. We will constantly be faced with decisions and actions that we may find questionable. What we must remember is this: We control our destiny, we make our decisions, and we live with the consequences. Business ethics is the art of making decisions that will benefit all.

We should strive to do this in all of our business dealings. Not only will we remain moral and trustworthy, we will also retain our dignity. The ultimate ethic is, after all, to be at peace with ourselves. ■

are not all that matters. Since consequences do matter, wisdom is a necessary guide to right action.

One way of gaining wisdom is to live a long time and be very active (assuming you pay attention as you go). Most of us want to be moral throughout our life and not just at the end of it. Wherever possible, we want to avoid actions that produce negative consequences and that may give us sleepless nights for the rest of our life. Most of us want some wisdom now rather than later when it may be too late.

Where can we get wisdom now? There are three places to start. First, we can study those accounted wise by previous generations. People like Moses, the Buddha, Socrates, Jesus Christ, the Prophet Mohammed, Sojourner Truth, Abraham Lincoln, Mahatma Gandhi, and Martin Luther King, Jr., have all contributed their spoonfuls to the cup of human knowledge that we can all drink from in times of moral confusion and doubt.

Second, we can talk with those in whose footsteps we can follow. Sometimes, in business, we call them mentors—older people who take a special interest in younger colleagues and offer needed counsel at crucial times. Or they may be friends or family members whose judgment we have come to trust. Having a mentor can be absolutely crucial for someone just starting out. Mentors can provide you with confidence and help you overcome the sense of isolation that impersonal corporations may foster.

Third, some works of literature can teach us harsh lessons without the real consequences that living through something may entail. Such works as *An Enemy of the People, Death of a Salesman, Night Flight, Antigone, Crime and Punishment,* and *A Man for All Seasons* are excellent places to start acquiring wisdom while still young.

One place not to look for wisdom is among those who are also just starting out. The person who has been on the job for a year may appear to have all the answers, all the "ins and outs." Such individuals may indeed have important information, but they probably have little wisdom. Knowing how to fill out a form requires information; knowing when to fill out a form may require wisdom. Wisdom is necessary when judgments are made. Wisdom cannot proceed without information, but information is not enough.

The Need for Forgiveness and Tolerance

Forgiveness may seem like an odd place to end a chapter on applied ethics. It is not. We all make moral mistakes, and at times, we all suffer from moral confusion. Life can be tragic in the sense the classical Greeks understood tragedy when they said, "Call no man happy until he is dead," because we can make disastrous decisions with the best of intentions. Learning to live with our mistakes without losing our will to be moral is tough.

Learning how to live and work with others who make what we believe are moral mistakes is imperative in a pluralistic culture. Learning to be tolerant is particularly difficult because we do not want to abdicate moral responsibility in the process. If you are convinced that what your colleagues are doing may expose others to harm without their knowledge, you may decide to "blow the whistle," the ultimate act of intolerance. But before you do that, you need to be sure you've exhausted all possible internal remedies. In the process you need to listen to others' arguments and views as well as express your own, and be aware that for all your certainty you might be wrong. Ultimately, you have to exercise your judgment and recognize that you did the best you could under the circumstances.

| **Exercise 8.4** | *Thinking About Applied Ethics* |

Think back on your college experience and, specifically, experiences that have presented you with an opportunity to practice "applied ethics." Write about one occasion or incident, taking into account the following questions: What were the dynamics of the situation? How did you handle or resolve the situation? How do you think this may stand you in good stead to deal with life after college? How could college have better prepared you to deal with these types of situations? If you perhaps don't feel tested yet, what challenges do you predict may lie ahead?

Conclusion

Talking about ethics is a lot easier than living morally. Remember that you have already successfully survived an important set of tests. You have worked together with others of different ethical views in a new moral environment. College has been a place of preparation for living and not just a place to pick up valuable information and techniques. You have more wisdom than you realize. You have already been around the block once. You are ready for the next trip.

References and Resources

Bolt, Robert. (1962). *A Man for All Seasons*. New York: Vintage Books. In this play Thomas More is caught between his loyalty to two sovereign lords, King Henry VIII and God. It is a story of a man wrestling with loyalties and with the temptations of wealth and power.

Dostoevsky, Fyodor. (1987). *Crime and Punishment*. New York: Bantam Books. In this classic tale of the interaction of conscience and moral rationalization, the main character, Raskolnikov, thinks it is morally permissible to murder someone until he does so and has to deal with his conscience.

Ibsen, Henrik. (1977). *An Enemy of the People*. New York: Penguin Books. This play (later adapted by Arthur Miller) contains all the elements found in today's newspaper accounts of whistle blowing by employees eager to stop corporations from harming the public. In the play, as is often the case in real life, the motives of the main characters are mixed. In the end the reader may wonder whether motives matter in the judgment of actions.

MacIntyre, Alasdair. (1984). *After Virtue: A Study in Moral Theory,* 2nd ed. South Bend, IN: University of Notre Dame Press. For those inclined toward philosophy, the first eight chapters are an interesting attempt to explain why philosophical ethics has been unwilling and unable to wrestle with the practical moral problems of the twentieth century. It is not easy going, but a thorough reading is well worth it. Two other works by modern philosophers that are worth the effort are Robert Nozick's *Anarchy, State, and Utopia* and John Rawls' *A Theory of Justice*.

Maugham, W. Somerset. (1977). "The Out Station." In *Collected Short Stories*, Vol. 4. New York: Penguin Books. This tragic tale examines what happens when an employee and a "mentor" do not get along because of different backgrounds. Imagine yourself in the shoes of both parties as you read this story and see if there was any other possible outcome. Is there a warning here for modern corporations with vast overseas' networks? Couldn't the same problem occur in the "home office"?

Miller, Arthur. (1976). *Death of a Salesman*. New York: Penguin Books. This play challenges us to think about our lives as totalities and about the consequences of our actions. It suggests that we tend to do as others in our trade do and to think of our business lives as separate from our family lives. And it reminds us that the self is not so easily compartmentalized as role moralities would suggest.

Saint-Exupéry, Antoine de. (1932). *Night Flight*. New York: Harvest/HBJ. At first reading Riviere, the manager, appears heartless. A closer look reveals a man committed to something other than profit or fame. Riviere sees in his work the opportunity to give meaning to his and others' lives, something that mere happiness can never do. This novella takes us back to an era when people believed in "progress" as a way of living, not as a product.

Sophocles. (1947). *Antigone*. In *The Theban Plays*. New York: Penguin Classics. This play is the last of the famous trilogy concerning Oedipus and his family. While we cannot read this play as the ancient Greeks would have, we can readily identify with the moral dilemmas faced by the main characters caught between sound reasons and appropriate loyalties. We like to believe that there is always a "win-win" solution to problems, and the great tragedies are a needed dose of reality for our overly optimistic age.

9 The World of Business

Richard L. Smith

Executive-in-Residence, McDonough Center for Leadership and Business, Marietta College;
formerly Chief Financial Officer for Borg-Warner Chemicals

Senior Voices

Monica

Even as a political science major, I have found that I need a basic understanding of how business works. I completed an internship and plan on a career in the public sector. However, in working for the state, I found that I drew on even my limited knowledge of business every day.

During my internship, I was asked to plan a series of seminars for a segment of the population for which my state agency was unable to provide grant money. Suddenly I found myself planning international marketing seminars for industries in southeastern Ohio. Wait a second, I thought, I'm studying political science, not marketing! However, I found that being a successful public servant sometimes means understanding the needs of constituents, all of whom are affected by the success of business in their area.

Realizing the ways of measuring success in business, understanding the distinction between a bond holder and a stockholder, and being able to elaborate on the differences in finance and accounting are skills that will not only be useful in employment but in social situations as well. Most of the people we meet will work for a business. Being able to converse intelligently or to make some sense of the *Wall Street Journal* just may be the edge you need to make a good impression on a potential employer or social contact.

In studying political science, I have found that public policy is increasingly influenced by global competition. To get the latest information on a political issue often means picking up a business

You are involved in business nearly every day of your life—as a customer, employee, owner (that is, stockholder), lender (that is, bond holder), or critic. Regardless of the form of participation, you will be more effective in your role if you are familiar with the business world. In this chapter we will examine the world of business in terms of its functions—both national and global—its economic and legal systems, and its stakeholders.

The Capitalist Economic System

An economic system determines how a society uses its scarce resources to produce goods and services and to distribute them to consumers. In the capitalist system with which we are most familiar, businesses are owned by individuals, as compared to a communist system, in which the government owns and operates all businesses. For the capitalist system to operate, then, individuals must do the following:

1. Save some portion of their income (the money received as compensation for their production) rather than consume all of it.

2. Invest that savings by lending it or by buying ownership in a business by purchasing stock.

3. Receive rewards (a share of the profits as interest, dividends, or capital gains) for having taken the risk of investment. This provides the incentive to save and invest.

Profit: Incentive for Investment

Why is it important for businesses to generate profits? To attract the financing needed to carry on and expand, a business must earn enough profit to provide a reasonable return to the investor. In light of the many options for investing their savings, investors must balance the degree of risk of an investment and the potential reward for having made the investment: interest earned, dividends received, or capital gains from selling the investment. Investors must also be willing to reinvest their returns in order to provide businesses with the funds to carry on and expand, thereby producing greater profits and greater returns on investment.

The primary ways of measuring the success of a business are the rates of growth in sales and profits and the return on investment generated by the business. Healthy companies require investment in fixed facilities (buildings and equipment), upgrading of facilities to keep pace with technological advances, and working capital (inventories and accounts receivable). Businesses commonly draw on operational profits to finance continuing growth and issue new stock or bonds to finance major expansions.

How much profit do companies actually earn? Critics of American business sometimes claim that companies earn excessive profits (for example, 50 percent or more). Each year, in April, *Fortune* magazine publishes a listing of the largest industrial companies in the United States, called the "Fortune 500." That report measures profit in one of three ways: (1) return on sales, (2) return on assets, and (3) return on equity. In 1990, for example, the median company of the Fortune 500 earned a return on sales of just 4.1 percent, a return on assets of 4.8 percent, and a return on equity of 13 percent. The risk faced by a stockholder in a company is that the company could fail (and many do), resulting in the total loss of the investment. Thus investing in common stock is much riskier than many other types of investments (for example, certificates of deposit or government bonds), but the potential return is higher as well.

Profit: Incentive for Production

The amount of goods and services available for consumption within the capitalist system depends on the productivity of that system. Goods or services consumed by a society must have been produced by that society. Thus the more a society produces, the higher its standard of living and its potential for profit will be. Admittedly, an individual may consume without having produced (for example, a welfare recipient), but this consumption will be underwritten by someone else in that society—specifically, the taxpayers.

Productivity can best be measured as the value of goods and services available for consumption in relation to the units of labor and capital employed. In this measurement the value of goods and services is determined by quality, performance, and price. Therefore standard of living is based not only on the quantity of goods available for consumption but also on their value.

The Role of Global Competition

The world is changing very rapidly, especially in the realm of economics. Markets that were once very clearly separated by national boundaries are now becoming integrated. Moreover, national markets have become global markets as a result of improved and lower-cost transportation, a reduction in protectionist policies such as stiff tariffs, and a sharpening of the abilities of businesses to compete worldwide. Thus, in order for a company to be successful, it must compete not only against other American businesses but also with companies in Japan, Taiwan, Mexico, Spain, Italy, and elsewhere that have developed a competitive advantage. The advantage might be low labor costs, government support of national industries, advanced technology, low-cost raw materials, or something else that enables the company to provide a better product at a lower price. American companies must now take a broader view of competition and adjust their strategies to the new circumstances in order to compete successfully.

The experience of the American automotive industry is a prime example of the effect of global competition. The invasion of the U.S. automotive market by Japanese producers has changed the industry significantly over the past twenty years. For example, General Motors' market share declined from 45 percent in 1980 to 35 percent in 1990 while the Japanese producers increased their market share from 20 percent to 30 percent in that same time period. In the 1960s and early 1970s the "big three"—General Motors, Ford, and Chrysler—dominated the domestic market, but today the Japanese companies, as a group, sell more automobiles than does Ford or Chrysler. If American automotive companies are to survive in this global economy, they must alter their strategies and methods of operation to remain competitive. They must provide the customer with better products at lower prices (that is, a better value for the customer). This will induce customers to buy more from American companies and less from foreign companies. A better product means (1) more desirable features (air bags, higher gas mileage, better handling, more attractive appearance, greater comfort), (2) higher quality (more reliable, less maintenance cost), and (3) longer life (more durable). Lower prices can only be achieved by companies operating more efficiently and at lower operating costs. Better products at lower prices can be achieved through the active participation of employees in the process of operating the company. This requires the application of their creativity, energy, and initiative in a focused way to the objectives of the organization. Only good leadership will cause this to happen. And the automotive industry is a good case study for many American industries since global competition has no industry boundaries, but applies to all business.

Money and Banking

In primitive societies the exchange of goods was limited since each individual or family produced almost everything needed and consumed all that was produced. As societies became more complex, however, individuals began to specialize and to barter their output for the output of others, that is, to trade goods for goods. Because this became a very cumbersome way to do business, a medium of exchange was created—money.

Although money was originally based on a commodity with intrinsic value (for example, gold), today our money has no intrinsic value (it is called fiat money) but is based on faith. Thus, as long as all parties accept it as having value, it is a good medium of exchange. Money has two other key attributes: (1) It is a way to store value easily, and (2) it provides a common denominator for measuring value.

The instrument for the circulation of money is the banking system. The U.S. banking industry is regulated by a central bank, the Federal Reserve System, which is an independent agency of the federal government. The Fed, as it is called, controls the money supply through monetary policy, manages regional and national check-clearing procedures, and supervises federal deposit insurance of commercial banks belonging to the Federal Reserve System. In combination with the federal government's fiscal policies on spending and taxation, the Fed's monetary policy influences the U.S. economy in terms of overall economic growth and inflation. While this influence is not exercised with great precision because of the very complex interacting factors in the economy, it does affect the broad movements in the economy.

Commercial banks are financial institutions that hold deposits in accounts for individuals and businesses and use some of the deposited funds to make loans to individuals and businesses. While commercial banks are the oldest and largest of all banking institutions, many other kinds of institutions provide various financial services. These include savings and loan associations, credit unions, and mutual savings banks as well as insurance companies and pension funds.

The Legal Environment

Business is regulated by a myriad of laws covering the following areas: taxation, bankruptcy, competition, property ownership, commercial transactions, securities transactions, environmental control, workplace safety and health, equal opportunities for employment, and international trade. These laws provide a framework within which any business must be conducted. As long as all competitors in the economy play by the same rules, the competition is fair. However, in some instances foreign competitors play by a different set of rules (laws) and therefore have a competitive advantage over American companies. As we move more and more toward a global economy, legislators will need to become more sensitive to the effect of U.S. laws on the ability of American firms to compete globally.

The Functions of Business

The major role of any business is to satisfy its customers. A business that does this is likely to be prosperous—to grow and earn a good return for its owners. Every business must perform the following functions:

- **General management**: provide overall strategic direction to and coordination of the many functions necessary to business success.
- **Sales and marketing**: acquire and retain customers by planning and executing the conception, pricing, promotion, and distribution of goods and services.
- **Operations**: provide the goods or services desired by customers through purchasing or manufacturing, storing, and transporting them.
- **Finance**: maintain the financial viability of the firm and provide the financial resources needed for successful operation.
- **Accounting**: record, measure, and interpret the results of the operation.
- **Research and development**: create, develop, and test products to satisfy customer needs.
- **Human resources management**: maximize the satisfaction of employees, improving their efficiency, and ensure that the organization has enough employees with appropriate skills to meet organizational objectives.

All of these functions are performed by every business. In a small business, however, several or even all of the functions are performed by the same person; a large corporation requires many people to perform each function.

Labor-Management Relations

During the first half of the twentieth century, labor unions grew rapidly and had a great influence on our industrial economy. These unions represented workers in negotiating with management on such issues as wages, fringe benefits, and working hours and conditions. During this period, management generally opposed the unions, but the unions were powerful enough to secure substantial benefits for workers. Over the past twenty years or so, however, in the context of a faltering economy, unions have declined in membership and influence. In addition, labor-management relations have been adversely affected by the increase in imported goods and the loss of American jobs and industries. Improvement in these relations is one of the changes needed to enable American firms to compete successfully with foreign firms. A new era of cooperation must be developed in which workers take a greater interest in the success of the business and management takes a greater interest in providing jobs that are safe, interesting, and fairly compensated. The overall objective of all parties must be to produce high-quality yet affordable products to satisfy the needs of customers.

To accomplish this goal, management and labor must work together as a team. An excellent example of this kind of behavior change can be found at the Ford Motor Company plant in Atlanta. Not only is this facility the most productive car plant in the United States, it is also a match for the typical Japanese car plant and is far superior to anything in Europe. As *Forbes* magazine writer Jerry Flint put it,

> [I have] never seen such common purpose among union and workers and management. They don't necessarily love Ford, they just said they wanted to do it right and win. No, Americans don't have to become Japanese to compete with the Japanese. But they do need to work harder at what they do best, and they need to build teamwork and trust and keep questioning the old ways of doing things.

J. C. Phillips, head of United Auto Workers Local 882, described the situation this way: "We have good competition and we have to meet it. We can't stick our heads in the sand. We want to eliminate no-value work. We're not expecting anything but a fair day's work for a fair day's pay. Mr. Anderson might be the boss, but it's our company."*

In short, to remain competitive, American companies must change the way they do business. One incentive that might make it easier is profit-sharing for all employees of a company.

Financial Statements

All of the transactions of a business are summarized in three basic financial statements, which are supplemented by varying degrees of elaborating detail. The three financial statements are (1) the income statement, (2) the balance sheet, and (3) the statement of cash flows. In addition, an annual report provides further data on the state of a business operation. The primary users of this information are managers of the business, stockholders, taxing authorities, banks and other lenders, outside financial analysts who follow the trading of the company's stock, and credit rating agencies.

Income Statements

The income statement reflects the profit-generating activities of a business over a period of time known as the accounting period—normally a month, a quarter, or a year. As shown in Figure 9.1, this statement lists sales revenues minus expenses, with expenses segregated into several categories to provide additional information.

Net income is the residual amount after all expenses (purchased materials, labor, utilities, shipping costs, repair costs, depreciation of buildings

---

*Both quotes from *Forbes*, 4 February 1991, pp. 58–62.

Figure 9.1 Sample Income Statement

XYZ Company
Income Statement
For the Year Ending December 31, 1993

Sales Revenues	$1,000,000
Less: Cost of Goods Sold	−550,000
Gross Profit	$ 450,000
Less: Selling and Administrative Expenses	−150,000
Operating Income	$ 300,000
Less: Interest Expense	−100,000
Income Before Income Taxes	$ 200,000
Less: Income Taxes	−90,000
Net Income	$ 110,000

and equipment, taxes, insurance), and financing costs (interest) are sub-tracted from the total revenues (selling prices times the number of prod-ucts sold) received from customers during the year. In a sense net income is the reward to stockholders for investing in the business. It is either paid to stockholders in the form of dividends or reinvested in the business to finance new assets (for example, land, buildings, and equipment) and thus to generate additional net income in the future. The amount reinvested is referred to as retained earnings and has the effect of increasing the stockholders' equity on the balance sheet. This in turn is likely to boost the market price of the stock and therefore provide a gain for the current stockholder when the stock is sold.

Figure 9.2 Sample Balance Sheet

XYZ Company
Balance Sheet
As of December 31, 1993

Assets		Liabilities & Equity	
Current Assets		**Current Liabilities**	
Cash	$ 20,000	Accounts Payable	$200,000
Marketable Securities	50,000	Taxes Payable	30,000
Accounts Receivable	100,000	Notes Payable	30,000
Inventory	180,000	Other	40,000
Prepaid Expenses	30,000	Total Current Liab.	$300,000
Total Current Assets	$380,000		
		Long-Term Liabilities	
Fixed Assets		Long-Term Debt	$ 80,000
Plant and Equipment	$600,000	Deferred Taxes	100,000
Less: Accum. Deprec.	–240,000	Other	40,000
Other Assets	140,000		
		Owners' Equity	
		Capital Stock @ par	$100,000
		Retained Earnings	260,000
Total Assets	$880,000	Total Liab. & Equity	$880,000

Balance Sheets

The balance sheet is a snapshot at a point in time that reflects the assets used in the business as well as a description of the methods of financing those assets. Figure 9.2 depicts a typical balance sheet.

The balance sheet is so named because the two sides of the sheet are equal: The value of the company's total assets balances with the liabilities and ownership equity. The right side of the statement lists the current assets, which will be used in less than a year, and the fixed assets, which are long-lived. The left side of the statement lists the current liabilities, the obligations that must be satisfied within a twelve-month period, and

Figure 9.3 Sample Statement of Cash Flows

XYZ Company
Statement of Cash Flows
For the Year Ending December 31, 1993

Cash Flows from Operating Activities:

Net Income		$110,000
Adjustments to Determine Cash Flow from Operating Activities:		
Add Back Depreciation	$ 50,000	
Changes in Working Capital	(10,000)	
Total Adjustments		40,000
Net Cash Flows from Operating Activities		$150,000

Cash Flows from Investing Activities:

Increase in Plant and Equipment	($100,000)	
Net Cash Flows from Investing Activities		($100,000)

Cash Flows from Financing Activities:

Increase in Bonds Payable	$ 50,000	
Common Stock Dividends Paid	(60,000)	
Net Cash Flows from Financing Activities		($ 10,000)
Net Increase (Decrease) in Cash Flows		$ 40,000

the long-term debt, which refers to debts payable over a period longer than one year. The owners' equity, also on the left side, is a permanent investment in the company and changes only by an increase or decrease in retained earnings.

Statements of Cash Flows

The statement of cash flows reports the sources and uses of cash in the business. This statement is divided into three sections: cash flows from operating, investing, and financing activities, respectively. Figure 9.3 depicts a typical statement of cash flows.

The statement of cash flows is prepared using the data from the other two statements. This statement highlights the importance of cash flow to the operations of the firm: Funds must be available to meet the obligations of the firm as they become due. If cash payments are not made on a timely basis, bankruptcy could result.

Annual Reports

Companies whose stock is publicly traded normally prepare an annual report to shareholders to keep them informed about the status of their investment and to convince them that they have made a good investment. The annual report includes a letter from the chief executive officer (CEO), who highlights the significant events of the past year, often describes the overall strategy of the firm, points out any significant changes that are anticipated, and discusses the future outlook. Next comes a description of the business(es) of the company, including the primary products and customers. The financial data of the company then appears with a summary of key data and ratios, the three basic financial statements, and a number of footnotes describing the accounting policies of the company and elaborating on important numbers contained in the three basic financial statements. Management then acknowledges its responsibility for the financial data and also includes the report of an independent certified public accountant stating that the financial records have been audited and the reported results accurately reflect the results of operations of the company. Finally, the annual report lists the officers of the company as well as the members of the board of directors (most directors are usually not officers of the firm, but several directors may also be officers).

Financial information is often expressed as a ratio or a percentage in addition to being presented as whole numbers, as in the following:

Net Income/Sales = Return on Sales

Net Income/Stockholders Equity = Return on Equity

Because returns are expressed as ratios, it is possible to compare the performance of one company with another or to compare the current performance of a company with its earlier performance. Comparisons of whole numbers have less meaning. In addition to "return on sales" and "return on equity," a number of other ratios commonly are used as standards for measuring the financial status of businesses.

Financing a Business

The funds to purchase the assets used in a business come from investors, who buy stock in the company; from creditors, who lend money to the company; or from retained earnings.

Stock issued by a public company (one that is traded on regularly at a stock exchange) increases the stockholders' equity in the firm and provides cash to purchase new assets. Stock that has been issued by a company (and thus registered with a stock exchange) and that is outstanding (owned by a stockholder) may be traded. Company stocks are owned by any individual or organization that has money to invest and is willing to assume the risk of owning a portion of a company. Stockholders include individuals, insurance companies, pension funds, colleges, trusts, charities, banks, foundations, and religious organizations. Every stockholder is interested in the same thing—earning a good return on the investment.

The *Wall Street Journal* and many other newspapers report daily on the trade of stock, the total number of shares traded each day, and the price at which each share is traded. The activities of the stock exchanges are regulated by the Securities and Exchange Commission (SEC), a government agency. The SEC requires all companies whose stock is publicly traded to publish specified financial information so the stockholders or potential stockholders are informed about the financial affairs of the companies.

Creditors are willing to lend money to companies in order to earn a good return (interest) on their loan. Loans are made in various ways. Companies sometimes issue long-term bonds that guarantee to pay a fixed rate of interest to the bond holder. Like stock, long-term bonds are usually traded publicly. Companies also obtain loans from banks much as individuals do. In addition, suppliers often ship products to a company on credit, stipulating that payment be made at some future time.

Bankruptcy

If a business cannot generate enough profit and therefore enough cash to pay its outstanding obligations on a timely basis, it can declare bankruptcy. There is a prescribed order in which the funds generated by the liquidation of the business are disbursed to creditors: first, to the government for taxes due; next, to secured creditors and then unsecured creditors; next, to preferred stockholders; and finally, to common stockholders.

In case of a bankruptcy, it is unlikely that the common stockholders will receive anything since nothing will be left after the higher-ranking claims are satisfied. Therefore the risk taken by common stockholders is greater than the risk associated with other types of investment and the reward, or return, to common stockholders must be greater to entice them to invest.

Conclusion

There are many facets to the successful operation of any business. For a business to succeed, all stakeholders in the business must be rewarded. The typical stakeholders in any business are customers, shareholders (owners), employees (including management), suppliers, and the community. Customers expect to receive a good-quality product, on a timely basis, with an appropriate amount of service, and at a competitive price. Shareholders expect to receive a return on their investment consistent with the amount of risk being taken. Employees expect an interesting, secure job in a safe environment at a competitive rate of compensation. Suppliers expect to be fairly compensated on a timely basis for the goods and services supplied to the firm. The community expects the firm to be a "good citizen" by complying with all of the applicable laws and regulations and by supporting the welfare of the community. And the business, to be successful, must satisfy the needs of all of these stakeholders.

10 Preparing for Graduate and Professional Schools

George M. Reeves, D.U.

Dean of the Graduate School and Special Assistant to the President, University of South Carolina

Richard B. Lawhon, Ph.D.

Director of the Instructional Developmental Project, University of South Carolina

Senior Voices

Kym

I have decided to go to graduate school for reasons complex and simple. Primarily, I love my field of study and wish to know more about it. Education is more than a preparation for entry into the business world as a productive worker. Because I did not go to college for job training, I have not gained any. What I hungered for was liberal arts training, for answers to the many questions I have about the human condition. After four years of diligent study, I now realize that the questions are much more fascinating than their answers, and I have so many more. Graduate school seems like the perfect opportunity to explore the human condition on a deeper level.

Another reason for choosing graduate school is my fear of the world outside the protective boundaries of ivy walls. Unlike the real world the university community represents a haven where I can explore new ideas and solve problems unfettered by the traditional bounds of conception. I also find that I feel most comfortable in the classroom. My mind feeds on information and ideas. The process of intellectual discovery is the most stimulating aspect of life. There is so much to know, and I cannot stop now. ■

It's been almost four years. Time that once seemed to drag now flies. Classes, papers, and projects you thought would never end are nearly completed. Before long, spring will arrive, and you will graduate— your college career will be over. Or will it?

Maybe you already plan to attend law school or medical school, or to obtain a master's degree in business or a Ph.D. in English. Perhaps you will be taking graduate courses that will prepare you to teach or getting advanced training in an allied health field. If so, congratulations; you are about to experience one of the most exciting periods of your life.

More than likely, though, you haven't quite reached a decision about graduate school. You may be tired of schoolwork, or you may be curious about your chances in the job market right now. Most of us feel that way when we are about to finish college. Graduate school represents a major commitment in terms of time, money, and energy, so it makes sense to consider your options carefully. In this chapter we'll do just that. By obtaining an overview of the world of advanced degrees, you'll be better equipped to make your own decision about graduate school.

The Decision to Attend Graduate School

Both the students quoted in the "Senior Voices" boxes in this chapter have made up their minds to enroll in graduate school, but for quite different reasons. One wants to stay in what she regards as the cloistered world of academia, while the other (see page 145) is convinced that further study will prepare him for extraordinary success in the business world. Both may be able to realize their ambitions, although academia and the business world are no longer quite as separate as they once were. In any event, both students believe that graduate study will enhance their futures.

If you have not yet made up your mind about graduate school, don't worry; you're in good company. Not every senior is able to contemplate graduate school with the self-assurance of these two honors students. Some seniors with excellent records still are not sure which direction they want their careers to take, and others are drawn by the lure of immediate employment. Graduate school is certainly not for everyone. In fact, only about one of every five graduates in the arts and sciences will go on to graduate school within a year of graduation. In the technical and professional fields—business, education, engineering, health, public affairs, social services—the number is only one in thirteen, although a great many graduates in these areas will enroll in postbaccalaureate study at some later time in their lives.

Seniors who are considering graduate or professional school may have to answer several questions to make a decision:

1. Is graduate study really worth the time and expense?
2. If I go to graduate school immediately, how will I pay for it?
3. Will I have to borrow a lot of money?
4. Is it better to work for a few years after graduation?

Answers to such questions depend on both the individual and the field of study. In general, the more advanced the degree, the higher the income and career satisfaction, although this relationship is far from absolute. For example, in the field of business and finance, an M.B.A. (master of business administration) is becoming a standard credential for middle and higher management. Even so, some of the most successful and creative business leaders hold no more than a bachelor's degree. Similarly, a Ph.D. (doctor of philosophy) is not a necessary credential for management, but it can be very rewarding for those who go into college teaching or become research specialists in corporations. For the business student who wants to become a world-class specialist in some aspect of his or her field of interest, the Ph.D. is essential. As for the M.B.A. and other master's-level degrees in business and finance, many students choose to work for a few years before attempting graduate study. This is often a wise choice, especially for students who have some doubt about their credentials for admission. The applicant with several years of experience and strong career motivation may be able to compensate for an uninspired college record. Graduate admissions officers are quite aware of such students and frequently will give them an opportunity to prove themselves worthy of admission to a master's program. There are scores of nationally accredited M.B.A. programs in the United States, and some are specifically formatted for business employees who want to study only in the evenings and on weekends. Some are offered via a "distance education" mode such as interactive television or live instruction offered away from the originating campus. Thus the capable student in business has many options.

So do engineering students. American engineers are in short supply, which means that a bachelor's degree in almost any field of engineering can lead to rapid employment at a very good starting salary. Consequently, most American engineering graduates opt for immediate employment rather than graduate study. This trend is so pronounced that many engineering schools have been forced to recruit foreign students for their graduate programs in order to keep the programs viable. Yet the graduate who proceeds immediately toward the master's degree can enter the profession at a higher level than he or she could with only a bachelor's degree. In addition, some engineering colleges offer a combined B.S.-M.S. program that enables students to earn both degrees in five years, an option that strong engineering students certainly should consider. For those who are hesitant, there will be abundant opportunities for graduate study later. For example, about two decades ago a group of distinguished engineering schools agreed to make master's-level courses available to practicing engineers in the workplace through the new technology of distance education. One result of this program is the National Technological University, which offers master's degrees nationwide as a cooperative effort of the founding universities.

Researching Graduate Schools

As you can see, answers to many of the questions you and other seniors have about graduate study vary widely, depending on the field in which you study. And choosing the right program for yourself won't be easy. At major research universities the array of graduate degrees offered can sometimes confuse even faculty and administrators. But having a large number of degree options should not intimidate you or any other potential graduate student. If you are a careful shopper, you can find a program of study, a degree, and a university that seem tailored just for you.

But how does one make the decision to go to graduate school and then choose the right place to go? Opinions vary about which criteria are most important, but some of the issues you should consider include the following:

1. How genuinely interested are you in this field?

2. Does your past academic record suggest potential for graduate study?

3. Do graduate degrees in your field have prestige?

4. Will your family and friends support your decision?

5. Can you find an appealing job with just a bachelor's degree?

6. Will your long-term career options will be brighter with a graduate degree?

7. Can you handle the financial strain of graduate study?

As you strive to answer these questions, keep in mind that a good decision is one that balances your excitement about studying in a particular field with real-world possibilities for finding a job in that area. Let's consider a series of steps you can take that will help you make a decision.

1. **Talk to people who hold graduate degrees.** Ask them to recall their graduate school days. What good and bad times did they have? How do they feel about their degrees today? Do they think it was worth the effort?

2. **Ask your favorite professors for advice.** Encourage them to be candid about your academic habits; their opinions about your ability

to handle graduate study will help you make realistic plans—which sometimes means you should aim higher while keeping your goals within reason.

3. **Visit a graduate school and talk to the people who work there.** They can help you form general impressions and understand a bit about what life will be like as a graduate student. Ask them for catalogues and brochures—and don't forget to ask them how to apply for financial aid if you think you will need it.

4. **Schedule yourself for the entrance examination required by the programs that interest you.** The catalogues will tell you which test(s) to take. Plan to take the test as soon as possible (preferably not later than the fall of your senior year in college) so that you will have enough time to retake it if necessary. Remember that graduate programs normally make their decisions about admitting students—and especially about awarding fellowships and assistantships—no later than early spring for the academic year that begins the following autumn.

5. **Call, write, or, if possible, visit the actual academic department in which you would like to study.** Try to arrange a meeting with the department chair or the graduate director. If you have not already applied for admission to the program, take along a copy of your transcript and your test scores. The person you see may be willing to look at them and tell you whether you appear to qualify for admission. Ask about academic matters such as course loads, professors who may become your mentors, time limits for your study, resources available to you (libraries, computer labs, study spaces, studio space, and so on), and potential financial support options (such as fellowships, assistantships, and loans).

6. **Discuss your plans with your spouse, family, and friends.** Their patience, understanding, and encouragement will help you through your busiest times in graduate school—when you feel overwhelmed and isolated.

7. **Apply to at least two, and preferably three, programs.** These will cost from $35 to $50 each, but you need to give yourself options in case your first choice doesn't pan out.

Types of Advanced Degrees

When you begin reading graduate school catalogues, you need to know what to look for. This simple overview of typical graduate degree programs will give you a preview of what you will find when you sit down to examine a university's graduate bulletin. You probably will see distinctions made between *professional* degree programs and *graduate* degree programs—although differences between the two are not as clear as they once were. Both are degrees that you pursue after you receive your bachelor's degree, but each offers you a chance to reach different goals. Basically, you might think of a professional degree program as one that helps you develop the skills necessary for a career in a specific type of work. Medicine, law, pharmacy, journalism, nursing, social work, and business administration are among the better-known fields in which professional degree programs are offered. A graduate degree also helps you develop expertise in a particular field, and, in the case of the Ph.D., takes you a step further and prepares you to teach at a college or university or to conduct high-level research. English, history, political science, foreign languages, math, engineering, education, and the sciences are some of the more familiar areas in which you find graduate degree programs.

The alphabet soup of graduate degrees offered at large universities can be misleading—to say the least. During the past couple of decades, degrees have become so specialized that they often have to be explained. Such traditional degrees as the Ph.D., Ed.D. (doctor of education), M.S. and M.A. (masters of science and arts, respectively) have been joined by dozens of new ones, especially professional degrees. The M.B.A. has long been familiar to business majors and to employers in industry, but master's degrees in international business, personnel and employee relations, taxation, and other specialized programs are becoming more popular as well.

Master's degrees in education also have proliferated. If you want to teach or work in a school system, you can study for a masters in at least fifteen areas, ranging from early childhood education to rehabilitation counseling. A similar situation exists in allied health fields—so named to indicate that these fields differ from the traditional ones in medicine (the M.D.) and nursing (the M.S. or M.N.).

One way to sort through the graduate degree maze is to separate (in your mind, at least) traditional degrees that prepare you for teaching as well as for other employment in a field from newer degrees that primarily train you for employment in a field. This distinction is more than a little arbitrary, but it will be useful to you as you consider a graduate program that suits your needs and interests. In somewhat the same manner that we separated graduate degrees from professional degrees, you can fit the graduate degree programs available to you today into two broad groups.

In one are the M.A., M.S., and Ph.D. degrees. These degrees are awarded in virtually all academic disciplines; they imply broad knowledge as well as a high level of special training in that discipline. To hold one of these degrees, you must specialize in a particular field, but you must also demonstrate that you have reasonable knowledge of the entire discipline. For example, a Ph.D. in English requires that you learn a good bit about literature, linguistics, rhetoric, and composition, and that you develop extensive knowledge of a field within one of those areas; that is, a graduate student in English may specialize in nineteenth-century American literature. The differences between traditional masters and doctorates essentially involve the amount of study you do and the depth of your research in the field. Generally, a Ph.D. candidate will study at least twice as long as an M.A. or an M.S. degree seeker.

The other general category features degrees with titles that do not include words like "arts," "sciences," and "philosophy." These degrees are still called masters and doctorates, but they designate specific skills or knowledge in an academic area without simultaneously implying that you have enough general knowledge in an academic discipline to qualify you to teach in it. For example, a master of public administration (M.P.A.), public health (M.P.H.), business administration (M.B.A.), media arts (M.M.A.), or social work (M.S.W.) would prepare you quite well for a professional career in industry or government, but such degrees normally would not qualify you to teach at a college or university.

The Graduate School Experience

As you read a graduate catalogue, you also will notice that course requirements are unlike those you had to meet to get your undergraduate degree. You will take fewer courses, and it may not take you as long to earn your graduate degree as it did your bachelor's. Moreover, you will probably not sign up for as many class hours during a specific term as you did in undergraduate school.

Fewer courses and fewer hours don't mean that graduate study is easier, however. You study in much more depth the subjects that interest you, and you must develop more patience in graduate school. Not only must you study longer, but your concentration and accuracy must improve.

During a typical week in graduate school, you will spend from three to nine hours in class; if you study in a field that requires laboratory work, you may spend at least that many hours conducting experiments in a lab. Visiting the library becomes almost a daily occurrence—so much so that many graduate students are given reserved study areas (called carrels) in which notes and reference materials may be stored. If your graduate school career includes a stint as a teaching assistant or a research assistant, you will spend from ten to twenty hours per week working at those jobs.

As you can see, there is little time for recreation or leisure time pursuits. But graduate school doesn't last forever, and most students enjoy the friendships formed with other students who share similar interests and the frequent association with faculty mentors. Since many graduate students are preparing themselves to teach in college someday, their graduate instructors often give them special attention and guidance. Modeling themselves—at least in part—after a favorite graduate school professor is almost unavoidable for graduate students, and most do not mind the long hours they spend listening to and learning from such mentors.

Careful examination and reexamination of ideas and phenomena in your field are also characteristic of the disciplined, time-consuming research that will be required of you in graduate school. You will write more in graduate school. If you study one of the basic sciences, your formal course work may not take more than a year or two. After that you will spend seemingly endless hours in the laboratory, where experiments will run continuously. Lab work at night and on weekends is not unusual. In the humanities and social sciences your formal courses are likely to be more numerous, and you will read, read, read, and write, write, write. The library will be your laboratory. Initially, you will write lengthy essays in which you comment about research done by other scholars. In time you will be expected to undertake some original analysis or creative work in the field you are studying.

Whatever field you enter—the basic arts and sciences, the fine arts, health sciences, the various professional areas—you will have the opportunity to become an expert and to experience the excitement of creative endeavor and intellectual discovery. And in most academic programs, and in some of the professional programs, you will be required to write a thesis or a dissertation and thus to display your achievement to others.

Getting the Most Out of Graduate School

As you become better trained, you also focus more exclusively on smaller and smaller areas within your field. You will need even more patience—and perseverance. Sooner or later, you may decide that your graduate work matters only to you. And, to a considerable degree, you'll be right. But that feeling, while scary in some ways, also helps explain the unique appeal of graduate school—and allows you to find the patience and the motivation to do your work. In other words, if you remember that you are in graduate school because you wanted to be there—not because someone talked you into it—you'll do fine. Your graduate study has to sustain you, not anyone else. For example, as a Ph.D. candidate in history, you will be expected to make original contributions to our understanding of some significant event from the past. To do that, you will need freedom—freedom to pursue your interests, to test your ideas, to develop your theories, and to conduct experiments that interest you. Graduate school gives you that freedom.

There will still be rules and regulations, but, generally speaking, you will take courses you choose and work under the supervision of faculty mentors who are interested in you and in your ideas. When you realize that you are going to spend two or three years of your life studying, thinking, and writing to get a master's degree—and even longer to earn a doctorate—you want to be sure that you will spend that time doing something that interests you. There are no guarantees, of course, but a carefully chosen graduate program offers one of the best chances you have for finding something to do that truly interests you—and prepares you to make a better living and to have a more meaningful life at the same time.

The emotional and intellectual satisfaction offered by graduate study should be primary factors in your decision to continue your education after you receive your undergraduate degree, but don't forget those other considerations that were mentioned earlier. For example, don't waste time trying to separate your thoughts into such categories as "practical reasons" or "emotional reasons" for attending graduate school. Just list as many reasons to go as you can; the more you think of, the easier your decision will be. Then consider the time involved in attending graduate school. Your graduate school years will be time well spent—if you don't delay too long after undergraduate school before you enroll. There is no compelling reason for you not to postpone graduate school for a year or two if you want to travel, work, serve in the military, or volunteer for a program like the Peace Corps. Sometimes a brief delay will allow you to plan your graduate study better. But it's usually better not to delay too long. As you develop social and recreational interests after college, and especially if you assume such responsibilities as marriage and children, you will find it more difficult to do your best work in graduate school.

Paying for Graduate School

The cost of graduate school is high, and it will continue to rise. The least expensive master's programs cost nearly $20,000 to complete, and Ph.D. programs in many fields can easily exceed $100,000 in total costs. Consequently, few graduate students pay all the costs of their education; as many as 75 percent of full-time graduate students at major institutions receive significant financial support.

Unlike most of the need-based programs in undergraduate school, financial aid for graduate students is more often based on merit. Fellowships are the most sought-after form of aid; they resemble scholarships and usually are awarded only to the top 10 percent of graduate students. Some universities offer special fellowships restricted to minority students and women, and such support may also be available from the government and from large foundations. Fellowships vary widely in value, ranging from as little as $500 a year to as much as $15,000 or more. Although they are usually awarded on an annual basis, fellowships sometimes are renewed for three years (for Ph.D. students) if satisfactory progress toward the degree is maintained.

Relatively few graduate students receive fellowships, so most who need financial aid try to obtain graduate assistantships to pay for their studies. An assistantship not only pays a graduate student a stipend (much like a salary), it allows the student to pay a significantly reduced tuition. The stipend and reduced fees are given in exchange for services performed for the university—usually in the academic department where the graduate student is enrolled. Graduate assistants may teach, supervise labs, grade papers, assist with research, assist with administrative duties, or even help a coach. Generally, they will work no more than fifteen to twenty hours a week, and they will have to take a slightly reduced course load to ensure that they will maintain excellence in their academic work. It is not unusual to find that two-thirds of the full-time graduate students at a university hold appointments as graduate assistants.

Senior Voices

John

I plan to attend graduate school in accounting for three main reasons. First, graduate school at this point in my life seems to be worth the cost. Not only can I afford it, but I am not encumbered by family obligations. Moreover, I am already in the habit of studying and so would not have to adjust my lifestyle. In short, I want to obtain a master's degree sometime in my life, and now seems to be the best time to do so.

Second, graduate school will make me more marketable, will help my future chances of advancement, and will boost my earning power. Accountants who hold a master's degree are certainly more seriously considered by major accounting firms.

Finally, graduate school will give me more time to mature and better establish my long-term career goals, which I have not yet decided on. I am banking on this degree leading to employment for a major accounting firm, which in turn should broaden my career options. I specifically chose the tax program because it will provide me with a specialty should I decide to stay in accounting. Generally, specialization gives a person a better chance of succeeding. In addition, knowledge of the tax consequences of business decisions will benefit me even if I leave accounting. I will save money by knowing how to plan for taxes and how to make investment decisions. In sum, I can't go wrong with this degree. ■

Exercise 10.1 *Discussing the Graduate School Option*

Class discussions can be especially helpful as you consider graduate school because your classmates have many of the same questions you have—and a few you haven't thought of yet. As a class focus your discussion on the following topics:

1. Measuring the cost of graduate school realistically: Is it an investment? If so, how and when will it pay dividends?

2. Finding the money to pay for graduate school: Is all the money on campus, or can you find support from banks or businesses in your community?

3. Finding the ideal location for your graduate school: What are the advantages of an urban or a rural setting? What part of the country do you want to live in for the next few years? Have you considered graduate study in another country?

4. Choosing the best campus atmosphere: Do you want the quiet and relative isolation of a small campus or the excitement (and potentially larger number of resources) of a larger campus?

5. Weighing prestige against convenience: How important is reputation? How will the status of the institution where you receive your degree affect your job prospects? Should you pay the extra cost of a private institution?

6. Understanding the differences between graduate and undergraduate life on campus: Can you have a social life while pursuing a graduate degree? Are there organizations on campuses that are specifically set up to help graduate students?

Conclusion

We've looked at graduate school from a number of different angles in the past few pages. We considered types of degrees, types of programs, differences between undergraduate and graduate study habits and schedules, the motivation necessary for graduate school, and your options for paying the high costs of graduate study—all of which should help as you consider this major career decision.

But those of us who hold graduate degrees consider one other point more important than all these: Believe in yourself. If you are accepted into a graduate program, don't ever doubt that you can obtain the degree. If your academic record is good enough to get you in, you have all the intellectual ability you need. You may not like every professor or every course you take, but no one professor can prevent you from getting your degree. Graduate schools depend on faculty committees to make decisions about students. Essentially, these committees interpret regulations published in the school's catalogue—so read yours carefully, and you will know what is expected from you. If you do the work you are supposed to do, these committees will treat you with respect and make you proud of yourself.

You may hear discouraging stories from people who had unpleasant experiences in graduate school. Listen to them politely—if you care to—but don't immediately assume that you can learn from their experience. Instead, compare yourself to the person who told you the story of failure. Are you and that person essentially alike in character? Probably not. And you will be even less like each other in a few years—if you decide to enroll in graduate school and successfully complete the program. Pursuing a graduate degree is an intensely personal quest. Therefore you should draw fewer inferences from someone else's unpleasant experience than you might have when you considered your undergraduate school or major.

So think hard. And if you decide that graduate study is for you, commit yourself to it as completely as you can. Then, a few years from now when you are asked for advice from students who are considering graduate school, you can confidently encourage them by saying, "Yes. I earned my graduate degree and I'm proud of it; you should go for yours." Those of us who wrote this chapter feel that way. We hope to see you in graduate school.

Personal Life

11 Relationships and Lifestyle Choices

Betty L. Siegel
President of Kennesaw State College

David J. Siegel
Assistant Director of Services for Institutional Advancement, Emory University

Betty L. Siegel
President of Kennesaw State College

David J. Siegel
Assistant Director of Services for Institutional Advancement, Emory University

Senior Voices

Katia

I think my generation is very goal-oriented and very career-oriented, and it's really hard for some people to respect that sometimes relationships are more important than careers. From my perspective, human experience is more important than computer experience.

I have a fear that after college I won't have that community atmosphere—that I'll be on my own. A lot of seniors are already making sure that we all keep in contact with each other, knowing that this is the finale. If we don't schedule appointments or keep up with each other, we're afraid that we're going to lose each other.

I also fear losing contact with those good connections that I've made here in the last three years. I want to make sure that if I go off and do something for two or three years I can still come back to them and use them as references and guidance people—that they'll still be here for me. I seem to be the kind of person who goes out and seeks a mentor, but it's hard to find a mentor that you're compatible with. Luckily, I've just fallen into the offices of some great people, and they have been able to share with me their experiences. Their advice on life and relationships has been incredibly helpful. My school is a unique place.

This year is going to be really important in terms of trying to make some key decisions, but I don't want to put too much pressure on myself that these next few months are going to decide the rest of my life. Making time for relationships is important, so I've got to try not to get too bogged down with homework, resumes, and networking. I just want to try to experience my senior year as much as I can. ∎

As you prepare to depart from college and embark on your life's journey, you may be wondering about the impact and influence that relationships are likely to exert on your pending career and lifestyle decisions. How long, for instance, will you postpone marriage? Would you take a job that requires you to move far away from your family and friends, and if so, how might geographic distance affect your relationships with loved ones? Is it advisable to cultivate friendships with work associates? How will you manage to nurture and maintain close relationships in light of the excessive demands of a busy work schedule? Each of these questions is legitimate, crucial, and worthy of your attention as you prepare to enter into exciting and unfamiliar terrain. In this chapter we will attempt to address some of the lifestyle and relationship issues, choices, and decisions you may face in the near future.

Looking Back and Looking Ahead

What is it about your collegiate experience that you will most fondly recall? Will you revel in the memory of crisp autumn afternoons when the excitement and pageantry of college football games momentarily freed you from your toils in the library? Will you think wistfully about late nights spent sharing pizzas with friends while solving the world's problems and exchanging philosophies of life? Will you remember the way a particular professor inspired your discovery of a new truth or idea, or the caring manner in which a student affairs professional took a personal interest in your development? More likely than not, no matter what memories you take with you from your days as a collegian, you will recognize that "the people make the place."

It may interest you to take inventory of your college or university when you return for some homecoming celebration. As you amble across campus with the seasoned and critical perspective of an alumnus, it may occur to you that the buildings look the same, the students continue to channel their excess energies into weekend rituals of fun and frivolity, and the institution still retains something of the magic you first experienced as a bewildered freshman. What has changed, you will notice, is the faces of students, faculty, and administrators. Not withstanding your loyalty and unswerving allegiance to your alma mater, the campus you once called home may suddenly feel different without your favorite English professor or your cadre of sorority sisters or fraternity brothers.

Just as your college experience has been largely defined by your relationships with fellow students, professors, and school administrators, so too will your "connectedness" to other people continue to determine much about your future as a professional. John Donne's timeless words are a poetic reminder of our interdependence with our fellow humans in the collective and shared adventure of life: "No man is an island entire of itself; every man is a piece of the continent, a part of the main." Indeed, we scarcely make a move that does not, in some form or fashion, affect our companions—girlfriend or boyfriend, husband or wife, friends, parents, or co-workers—in the human experience. We are inextricably joined together. Our decisions and actions have great consequence for ourselves and for those with whom we associate.

Many of you may have chosen one undergraduate institution over another precisely because of a network of people that appealed to you, connected with you, and spiritually pulled you into its folds. You may have decided to spend your time in college in the company of like-minded students, learning something about yourself through your relationships and possibly even defining yourself through your association with partners in the academic enterprise. Even as relationships have been important to you in the past, they are likely to continue to shape many of your decisions about the future.

Deferring Employment

Upon your graduation from college, you will be faced with important decisions. Perhaps nothing is more pressing than deciding what to do professionally. It is the primary topic of conversation between any graduating senior and his or her parents, friends, or other interested parties. Identifying your career interests, writing letters to corporations or graduate schools, and interviewing are likely to occupy a tremendous amount of your time, energy, and effort during your last year in college. The array and diversity of options available to you is truly staggering. Making a career decision is probably not the only choice with which you will grapple. You may entertain notions of going on to graduate school or taking some time off after you finish college.

The vast majority of college graduates seek employment when they finish school. For some it is a natural and logical step, the crowning reward for years of academic labor. Others face financial obligations that make it necessary to get a job. Still others may feel a profound sense of urgency and an eagerness to pursue their professional goals. Indeed, there are many motivating factors for seeking gainful employment.

By the same token, those who do not wish to enter the work force upon graduation have their own rationales. However, because we, as a society, have come to view employment as the appropriate use of one's education, we sometimes fail to recognize or appreciate the host of other options available to the graduating senior. Perhaps you are thinking of deferring employment for graduate school. You may even be amenable to the idea of taking some time off. In either case, it is helpful to make careful and educated decisions before you commit yourself to any plan of action following college.

The Graduate School Option

Many graduating seniors find that graduate school is the most hospitable environment for their immediate or long-range interests and ambitions. In our estimation one can never learn too much. Indeed, some careers require an advanced education; medicine, law, and education are but a few examples. Your particular career objectives may or may not require certification via graduate course work. You may simply wish to continue your education in a field of study that deeply interests you. Some graduating seniors confuse their fondness for their undergraduate days with a desire to commit themselves to further scholarship, and they may elect to work for a couple of years in order to better monitor and assess their allegiance to the notion of graduate school. If you are among the ranks of people who have determined that employment may help them to make a sounder decision regarding continued education, rest assured that such an avenue is entirely acceptable.

Whether you intend to pursue graduate education immediately upon receiving your bachelor's degree or after a period of some years, you must realize that you will likely be making a substantial commitment of time, energy, and resources. The decision to attend graduate school often means postponing earning income or, if you leave the work force after a few years, forfeiting a quality of life with which you may have become comfortable. These words of caution are not meant to dampen or lessen your enthusiasm for graduate education. On the contrary, we firmly believe that short-term sacrifices yield long-term benefits, particularly when it comes to cultivating your talents and interests. It is important, however, for you to be equipped with requisite knowledge of the realities of attending graduate school.

| Exercise 11.1 | *Investigating the Graduate School Option* |

In considering graduate school, it is worthwhile to talk with current graduate students, those who have already received an advanced education, and professionals who may be able to tell you about the benefits of a master's degree or doctorate in their career field. Select a couple of people from each of these groups and arrange to informally interview them about both the specifics and generalities of graduate education. For example, what do they perceive to be some of the pluses of attending graduate school? What do they see as some of the pitfalls? What is the lifestyle of a typical graduate student like outside the classroom or lab? Do (did) they enjoy being a graduate student? Do they have advice, recommendations, or suggestions for you? Is the master's degree or doctorate marketable in the private sector as well as in academe?

The "Time-Off" Option

In certain circumstances you might find the idea of taking a hiatus after graduation appealing. Friends, family, and your own personal barometer may all encourage you to pause before entering the work force, attending graduate school, or committing yourself to some other endeavor. If it is economically feasible, you may wish to travel or devote some time to certain interests. Perhaps the prospect of temporarily supporting yourself through an assortment of odd jobs excites you more than that of immediately assuming career responsibilities. Whatever reasoning you employ to justify an interruption in your education or career objectives, you must make a decision that is compatible with your own best interests. It is perfectly legitimate to want to take time to "sort things out." If you feel that you would benefit from a break in the action, and if circumstances permit you to do so, it may behoove you to indulge.

By the same token, you need to be aware of the consequences of whatever actions you take after graduation. If you plan to delay interviewing for job opportunities, be aware that potential employers are likely to ask you how you have filled your time since graduation. Don't think that you will automatically be knocked out of contention for a job simply because you chose to explore the Rocky Mountains rather than seek employment directly after graduation. A recruiter's satisfaction with your answers, though, will probably be strongly influenced by your ability to chronicle your experiences in ways that sound palatable and reasonable.

Exercise 11.2

Investigating the "Time-Off" Option

Arrange to meet with a college graduate who took time off before pursuing a career. What were his or her motives? What was the decision-making process that led this person to travel or pursue other interests? In hindsight, was the decision to take time off worth it? Did this person have any difficulty explaining his or her decision to prospective employers? What suggestions does this person have for you?

Living Arrangements

Once you have completed college, you will also have to find a place to live. Will you relocate to another community to pursue a career or attend graduate school? Will you share housing with one or more roommates? Or will you perhaps move back home to live with your parents?

Relocating to a New Community

In terms of lifestyle choices, one of the critical decisions you are likely to make in the very near future is where to live. How do you go about finding a community in which to live? Will you live in a large, cosmopolitan city or a smaller, rural town? Geographically speaking, what area of the country appeals to you most? Do you prefer to have schools, museums, professional sports venues, public transportation, and cultural offerings readily available? Or is it more important for you to live in a place that's far removed from the action and energy of the city?

Of course, where you choose to live will be governed in large part by where you choose to work. Before accepting or declining a job offer, then, you'll want to investigate the community in which you will be residing. Most college graduates do not make employment decisions in a vacuum, paying attention only to job descriptions, wages, and benefits. Rather, they also consider the quality of life likely to accompany their job choice, and this almost invariably involves questions about where they will be living. Indeed, an informal survey of your peers may reveal that some of them are more interested in finding the right community than in getting the best job.

In choosing a community in which to live, you need to be aware of your own values, preferences, and interests. For example, if you are interested in plays, symphonies, art galleries, and poetry readings, perhaps you would do well to locate a city that supports the arts. If you like to be exposed to various and diverse cultures and customs, cities with an international flavor may be attractive to you. If you enjoy weekend jaunts to the beach or the mountains, you might want to settle in a town that offers easy access to such amenities. And still other factors may pull you to a particular town; the proximity of friends and family, an agreeable climate, the economy, and a plenitude of young professionals are but a few.

The bottom line is that communities typically develop distinct local flavors, personalities, and characteristics, just as people do. We would be hard-pressed, indeed, to rank-order the best cities in which to launch your career. Such an exercise would assume that all of us think the same way, have the same interests, and place importance on the same issues. Choosing a community in which to live should be inspired by your own individual considerations.

Exercise 11.3   *Finding the Right Community*

Jot down some of the characteristics that you desire in a city or town. Does geographic location make a difference to you? How about size? What are some cities or towns that you would like to call "home" some day? What is it about these communities that appeals to you?

Moving Back Home

One of the issues with which you may have to grapple is whether to move back home after graduating from college. Particularly in times of economic hardship or uncertainty, many graduating seniors opt to live at home with their parents. This arrangement may be temporary, lasting only until the graduate can find suitable employment, or it may be semi-permanent, allowing the new professional to save the money that would otherwise be appropriated for rent, utilities, and food. Whatever circumstances necessitate your potential return home to live with your parents, you would do well to prepare yourself for a lifestyle different from that experienced in college.

Your collegiate career may have been your first introduction to independence. For the most part you have set your own schedule as a collegian, deciding when to study, when to socialize, and when to "call it a night." You have made the important decisions about which organizations to join and which courses to take. You have had some experience in prioritizing your time, energy, and financial resources. In short, you have had an invaluable opportunity to act as a mature and independent individual. Because of your new-found sense of independence, moving back in with your parents may actually feel like "two steps backwards" in your growth and development. You may feel that you are having to sacrifice or forfeit some of your independence by returning to live with those persons from whom you have supposedly become independent.

What you are very likely to find, however, is that your parents have changed, just as you have changed during your collegiate career. By association, your relationship with your parents has probably also taken on some new characteristics. Rather than "taking two steps backwards," you may actually find yourself on the cusp of a new learning adventure in which you and your parents accord one another heightened respect and a mutual appreciation for one another's individuality. You may find that your relationship with your parents has moved to a new level, perhaps one that more closely approximates friendship or companionship and that fosters camaraderie.

Although you will still be your parents' child, you will have taken on a new identity as a mature adult, and your parents are certain to recognize that you are no longer the same person who left their nest years ago.

You may still have to adhere to certain "house rules" and expectations, but keep in mind that these are designed in the spirit of peaceful coexistence, not as some form of punishment or arbitrary restriction. The important thing to remember is that moving back home with your parents can be an enjoyable, educational, and profitable experience, and that it does not necessarily require the forfeiture of your independence.

Living with a Roommate

If moving in with your parents is not a viable option, you still have several other potential courses of action. One is sharing housing with one or more roommates. If you do choose this option, you need to ask yourself several questions. For example, will the person be the same or the opposite sex? Are you likely to get along better with someone you already know, or is it better to live with someone you do not know well?

Remember when you went away to college and were forced to confront living arrangements that differed from those with which you had become comfortable? Perhaps your roommate had a lot to do with your happiness and enjoyment of that first year. Perhaps you learned something about yourself by living with an individual who had different habits, characteristics, and perspectives. Your success in living with a roommate during college may serve as a guide as you determine whether to find a roommate after graduation. As you prepare to make immediate living arrangements, you need to take inventory of yourself in order to discover your own preferences.

Some recent college graduates take on a roommate purely for economic reasons; others may be seeking friendship or companionship; still others may be looking for a combination of camaraderie and financial assistance. Whatever the case, living with a roommate can be both exciting and frustrating. The excitement stems from always having a partner close at hand. Likewise, the frustration stems from always being in close proximity to an individual who may be not at all like you.

If you do choose to live with a roommate, you will have to accept the personal differences you are likely to discover. By the same token, you should expect your roommate to be tolerant and understanding of you as well. The bottom line is that harmonious living involves concessions, compromises, and flexibility. This, of course, holds true whether your roommate is of the same or opposite sex, a cherished friend or a new acquaintance. If you feel that living with someone would only encumber and distract you, and sap energies that you would rather apply to other endeavors, perhaps you should consider living alone, providing you have the financial means to do so. Remember that there is no "best" formula. Your personal preferences should dictate whether you live with a roommate and whether your roommate is of the same or opposite sex and is someone you know or have just met.

Getting Along with a Roommate

Think of the characteristics, traits, and qualities that you liked in a former college roommate. How were these different from your own? How did your perspectives, opinions, and values differ? What did you do to accommodate these differences? What compromises did each of you make for the benefit of a harmonious relationship? What lessons from this experience could prove helpful in future roommate situations?

Relationship Issues

It will be eminently worthwhile for you to begin to think about the role that relationships will play in your life's drama. Just as your college career has placed competing demands on your time, effort, and energy, so too will your professional career require certain things of you. And just as your response to demands in the past has been governed by your personal value system and a carefully considered list of priorities, so too will it be necessary for you to determine the relative importance of work versus the maintenance of your relationships with family and friends. Before you begin to consider how you will manage relationship and work responsibilities, recognize that you are not making an absolute contract with yourself. You will continually find yourself assessing, revising, amending, and changing your values and priorities. By the same token, you must realize that we are not prescribing or recommending a "best method" for addressing this dilemma. It is not our place to stand in judgment of your personal value scheme. Our task is simply to attempt to engage you in thoughtful "self-talk" and prepare you for some of the major relationship issues—at home and in the workplace—you will soon be addressing.

Marriage

One of the more monumental relationship issues that is likely to determine your lifestyle is the decision to get married. It is well beyond the scope and intent of this chapter to tell you everything you need to know about love and marriage. Because intimate relationships are deeply personal and often complicated, advice from an outsider is not always pertinent, even when offered with the best of intentions. Nevertheless, the significance of marriage makes some degree of preparation advisable.

If marriage is in your plans, you need to address several attendant issues. First, how do you go about selecting a mate with whom to spend the rest of your life? Once you have decided to marry, how long will you wait? Should you live together before marriage? How long will you defer parenthood, and what is an appropriate age and stage of life for becoming a parent? What measures will you take to develop a positive and supportive relationship with your in-laws? How will you juggle the demands of a professional career and a family? While several of these questions may not seem that pressing at this juncture of your life, remember that anticipation of future lifestyle choices better equips you to make important decisions. Perhaps the most critical of these decisions will involve the identification and selection of a partner with whom to share your life.

Senior Voices

Christopher

As a senior entering my last year of college, I hope that I have the skills and resources necessary to survive on my own, without having to move back home to my parents. Though I love them dearly, I want to move into my own apartment and enjoy the freedom of living on my own. This is a difficult venture, however, since I must be certain I have a stable income and a reliable means of transportation, among many other things. If I should have to move back home, what will my freedoms be? I wonder if it will be too difficult to live with the parents I have not lived with in over four years. I do believe that I will be able to survive on my own, without the help of my willing parents, and will very much enjoy living away from home.

One of the biggest concerns I have as a graduating senior is how I will handle saying good-bye to my close friends. Though I went through a similar experience in high school, these are people I have actually lived with for four years. I have watched them grow into adults as they have watched me grow. My friends here are like brothers and sisters and sometimes much more. Though everyone always says they will keep in touch, few ever do. I do not want to lose these people forever. For my own part, I know that I will do all I can to remain in touch with the people who have meant so much to me.

Entering the last year of college is like a large door opening. Sometimes I feel like jumping right through the opening without thinking or worrying about what lies ahead. Other times I am much more skeptical and am concerned about what I may find. I question my own abilities to survive on my own and to continue growing as I have done here at school. I want to be able to enjoy myself beyond my college years. I really want to live on my own or, at the most, with one significant other. I worry about leaving behind the friendships that have brought me not only joy but also adulthood. Regarding these questions, one thing is certain: "only time will tell." ∎

Finding a Mate. The college and university environment is remarkably well suited to the development of close, even intimate, relationships with fellow students of the same or opposite sex. The close proximity bred by classes, common living and dining areas, and the proliferation of clubs and organizations makes it reasonably easy to meet and interact with a variety of students. The free exchange of values and ideas endemic to the college campus gives students a truly unique opportunity to learn something about their companions in the academic enterprise. It is no small wonder, then, that many graduating students fear that they may never again be in an environment so amenable to the growth of intimate relationships, specifically with members of the opposite sex. Such a notion, however, is not entirely legitimate.

Just as college has exposed you to an exciting and different world replete with interesting people, so too will life after college introduce you to myriad opportunities to make new acquaintances. You are likely to find an abundance of people, of both the same and the opposite sex, who share your interests and values, whether they be the arts, sports, fine dining, religion, or a vibrant social life. The key to selecting a mate, then, is to know yourself. What are your interests, values, perspectives, and ideals? If you think about marriage as a lifetime of companionship, it may occur to you that you would like to marry someone who shares many of your worldviews. Once you have identified such a person, the task then becomes one of deciding when to marry, whether to live together before marriage, and how long to defer parenthood.

Deciding When to Get Married. There is no magic formula for deciding on the optimum time to marry. The timing of your marriage will likely depend on a complex set of emotional, practical, and financial considerations. If you are new to the job market, you may determine that you would like to work for a few years and establish yourself professionally before you commit yourself to marriage. If you are concerned that you will not be able to adequately balance the demands of a fledgling career and a new marriage, you may elect to postpone marriage until you become more comfortable and confident in your work habits. On the other hand, you may decide that marriage is something that just can't wait. You may be ready, willing, and able to manage the responsibilities of work and marriage, and it simply may not make sense for you to postpone your betrothal. Only you and your "intended" can decide on the most favorable time for marriage.

Living Together Before Marriage. For convenience or for emotional reasons, you and your spouse-to-be may choose to live together before marriage. If both of you believe that living together will better prepare you for the realities of marriage, and if you have convinced both of your families that such an arrangement is appropriate, sharing living quarters may be a uniquely valuable opportunity. It may be that you will even entertain the idea of living together instead of marrying. Some couples choose this alternative for a variety of reasons, ranging from a fear of life-long commitment to skepticism of the institution of marriage itself. The important thing to remember is that there is no "best" way to express your intimate feelings for your significant other. Because marriage, and even living together instead of marriage, implies a partnership, decisions must be made in concert. You and your partner are in the most logical position to best determine issues of mutual import.

Parenthood

Quite possibly the most important issue you and your partner will address is parenthood. Parenthood is an enormous responsibility, and all decisions regarding parenthood have extraordinary consequences, for both you and your children. If you plan to have children, you must invariably determine an appropriate age and stage of life for becoming a parent. While it may not serve your purposes to pinpoint a specific age, you should discuss a general timetable with your spouse.

If settling into your career is important to you before you commit yourself to marriage, then you will probably want to apply the same ground rules with regard to parenting. Additionally, you may choose not to rush into parenting immediately after marriage so that you can effectively "warm up" to one rite of passage at a time. Financial realities will certainly figure into your timetable, since it costs a lot of money to have and raise children. Whatever decisions you and your spouse make concerning parenthood, remember that choosing to have children is not something that should be taken lightly. Educate yourself, be prepared for tremendous responsibilities, and be willing to accept the emotional as well as financial commitment that will be required of you as parents.

Work Versus Relationships

When beginning a new job and adapting to a new lifestyle, you will probably work extra hard to prove your dedication and commitment. Unfortunately, this increased exertion in the workplace will usually cause you to ignore other important responsibilities. One of the most difficult tasks that you will face throughout your career—but especially as you begin a new position—is balancing your personal health and happiness with your professional goals. Often your personal relationships with family and friends suffer from some degree of neglect as you labor furiously to accommodate the demands of a hectic work schedule. Letters to old college buddies may be left unwritten, weekly telephone calls to your parents may be forgotten, and weekend getaways with your friends may be postponed again and again. You may become discouraged as you find yourself declining invitations to attend a party or to have dinner with your old roommates, and you may lament the fact that you don't seem to have the time to invest in a serious romantic relationship. All the while, you may worry about the message you appear to be sending to your friends and family—that you don't care about them anymore now that you have a job.

It should comfort you to know that those closest to you likely will understand the sometimes unyielding requirements of your career. In fact, your peers will probably be experiencing similar dilemmas themselves. Nevertheless, relationships demand nurturing, maintenance, and effort if they are to prosper. Just as you make provisions for other important areas of your life—exercise, worship, and personal interests—so must you allow yourself to restore and rejuvenate your relationships. It may help you to adopt a plan of action whereby you can commit yourself to the task of "keeping up" your close personal friendships.

For example, you may want to reward your hard work at the office with a regularly scheduled dinner with friends at a favorite restaurant. If you are living far from your family, perhaps you can arrange to phone home every week at a mutually agreed-on time. You may even decide to write letters every so often, say, on the first of every month. If "making" time for your friendships seems contrived, perhaps you would be better served by limiting the time and energy that you appropriate to other tasks and activities so as to make more time for your friends. The key is not to lock yourself into a rigid schedule and subject yourself to yet other time constraints. The benefit of scheduling is simply in reserving private time for yourself in which you can devote full attention to personal friendships.

The critical issue here is that you will soon find yourself making decisions about your personal and professional goals. You may decide and demand that you can "have it all," that you will work feverishly to advance your career while concomitantly reserving time and energy for your friends and family. You may come to realize that "having it all" means living life at a frenetic pace, and instead of trying to "burn the candle at both ends," you may elect to devote more of yourself to either work or personal relationships. You may even resolve to compromise between the two extremes, immersing yourself in your career for a couple of years until you reach a comfort level that allows you to attend to your personal relationships. Again, there is no "best" way to treat the issue. It all comes down to making decisions that mesh with your personal values, preferences, and interests.

Mentors

Just as the steady and nurturing hand of an interested professor guided and encouraged your best efforts as a collegian, so too will you find professional mentors who tend to inspire personal excellence. You probably have a favorite professor who stands out as having had the most significant influence on you during your college years. You may have admired this person because he or she established a positive relationship with you that affirmed your abilities and gave you the confidence needed to succeed. For much the same reason that you admire a particular instructor, you may also come to admire someone with whom you work, someone who can once more affirm your abilities and boost your self-confidence.

If you have made yourself worthy of such an individual's support, this person could become your mentor. A good mentor can help you to clarify and achieve your goals by offering practical advice, by introducing you to others who might be helpful, or simply by listening to and sustaining your dreams and hopes when they are threatened by adversity or doubt. Your mentor can also become your chief source of reliable feedback, helping you to develop your leadership qualities, your philosophical attitudes, and ultimately the recognizable style you use to get things done your way (Collins and Scott, 1978).

You might be surprised to learn that many current chief executives, in explaining how they have ascended to their positions of leadership and influence, attribute much of their success to a significant mentoring relationship established early in their careers. Indeed, mentors can and do serve the alternating roles of friend, educator, and advocate. The key is to align yourself with professional role models whom you particularly respect for their integrity, wit, wisdom, tenacity, aggressiveness, vision, adroitness, attention to detail, or ability to make employees feel valued. The workplace abounds with sensitive managers and supervisors who have a genuine interest in the welfare of their employees. Most of these managers would embrace the opportunity to help groom, cultivate, or otherwise channel the unbridled potential that they observe in their young recruits. Your manager would probably be honored to serve as your unofficial mentor, because it would mean that you have identified him or her as someone after whom you would like to model yourself.

Of course, certain circumstances might impair or inhibit your ability to "get close" to your manager or another such professional whom you would like to have serve as your mentor. Some managers may be reluctant to form close relationships with employees for fear that special attention accorded one worker may be perceived as favoritism by the other workers. If mentoring is conducted properly, however, these perceptions can be effectively managed.

Exercise 11.5   *Finding a Mentor*

Write down the names of employers or professors who have influenced you in the past. Next to the names, list the qualities that you admired in each of these people. What did you learn from them? How did they influence you? What did you do specifically to cultivate positive relationships with these individuals? What might you do as a professional to forge such a relationship with potential mentors?

Co-Workers

As an ambitious college student you have worked very hard to complete the requirements of your major field of study. You have demonstrated a desire and a will to succeed through the choices you have made. However, when you leave the familiar surroundings of the college campus and begin your new career, you will eventually find yourself performing in a team situation. Consequently, you must now focus on group as well as individual success.

Joining the Work Team. As an aspiring team member you must pass a series of individual tests. First, you must try out for the team by submitting a resume and by interviewing for a position. You must qualify for the team by meeting certain performance standards and expectations; you should consider your eventual selection a great honor because not everyone who tries out makes the team. Next, you must make the transition from a rookie or trainee to a respected member of the team. This transition not only requires knowledge about your individual strengths but also forces you to relate to your associates in a way that benefits the entire team.

Though you and your teammates obviously have specialized roles to perform, the success of the team transcends the individual performances. You will succeed together or fail together. Your "personal best" comes to mean performing in a way that best assists, enhances, and complements your teammates as you all strive to fulfill a shared goal. In short, as a new member of one of the specialized teams that make up your employer's work force, you will be expected to assume responsibility for the success of others, something you may never have done before.

Thus it is crucial for you to foster positive relationships with your new associates. Because virtually all work experiences are cooperative, collaborative activities, they require a strong bond of trust. Not only must you prove yourself worthy of your co-workers' trust, you must also respect their unique qualities and strive to establish a relationship based on equality, equity, and shared power. You must also actively cultivate relationships with your co-workers, both personal and professional. Being an active listener, taking the time to communicate effectively, promoting civility, being optimistic, breaking bread together—these are just a few of the limitless ways in which you can make positive overtures to your co-workers.

Being a good team player, or even an effective manager, means understanding, accepting, and respecting the differences you perceive in your co-workers. There is usually much more diversity in the workplace than in the typical college classroom. It is fruitless to expect your co-workers to behave, think, feel, and communicate exactly as you do. As David Keirsey and Marilyn Bates point out,

> People are different in fundamental ways. They want different things, they have different motives, purposes, aims, values, needs,

drives, impulses, urges. Nothing is more fundamental than that. They believe differently: they think, cognize, conceptualize, perceive, understand, comprehend, and cogitate differently. And of course, manners of acting and emoting governed as they are by wants and beliefs, follow suit and differ radically among people. (1978, p. 2)

Though competition in the workplace is inevitable and necessary, a skilled team player understands the rules of competition. Any competitive setting, including the workplace, is governed by a set of written and unwritten standards. As a new employee you will be expected to learn how your organization handles competition. Though competition can enhance your job performance by encouraging initiative, innovation, and excellence, a team member whose ambitions are aligned with those of the team always plays by the rules and plays fair. Of course, this is a cardinal rule in any relationship. One way to promote positive relationships among your co-workers is to discourage internal competitiveness and strife. Blind ambition, at the expense of others, has no place in a work environment.

Moving Up in the Organization.   One of the first professional transitions you will make is from being a rookie or trainee to being a respected team performer. The next logical step is for you to become a team leader. Then, as you continue to develop leadership skills, you might become a manager. No matter what your individual ambitions are, your transition from college to the work world will require you to become an effective team player, and an essential part of this task is the development of positive relationships with your managers and co-workers.

The development of positive relationships with your work associates may take a new twist when you are tapped for a management position. Indeed, you may find yourself in a supervisory role much sooner than you ever anticipated. How will you deal with your new subordinates, the same people who were your equals a short time ago? Different managers have different styles. Some choose to have little or no social contact with their workers for fear that their authority will be compromised when they try to hold subordinates accountable for specific job responsibilities. Others experience no conflict in socializing with their workers. It all comes down to a matter of personal style. Indeed, you may find that you need to experiment to identify your particular management style. You may have experienced some of these relationship dilemmas as you assumed a leadership role in your fraternity or sorority, or in a campus organization. Because most of us wish to be well liked by our peers, moving into a position of leadership—where unpopular, even unpleasant, decisions may affect our relationships with team players—can sometimes make us feel uncomfortable.

You must also consider the very real possibility that you may be managing individuals substantially older, and perhaps even more experienced, than you. Such a scenario will be especially likely if you are in a fast-track management training program. The resentment and jealousy of your subordinates may serve as divisive forces that compound the difficulty of your day-to-day duties as a manager, severely limiting your effectiveness to work with people and accomplish important tasks. There's no question about it—mutiny can quickly undermine your best efforts. To gain the support and confidence of your workers, you may find it helpful to intentionally develop productive relationships with these individuals. For instance, respecting the expertise, talents, and abilities of your workers is eminently more valuable than trying to pass yourself off as the "know-it-all college grad." Experts like to be consulted and utilized for their talent, even if they don't occupy a position of official leadership in an organization.

In sum, you must remember that people, or human resources, are the machinery that drives organizations. Therefore the web of interpersonal relationships is critical. People join organizations because they want to feel valued and needed as human beings (Bolman and Deal, 1991). How well you help create a positive climate as a manager, one that is satisfying and fulfilling for your employees, is vital and thus worthy of your best efforts.

Exercise 11.6 | *Getting Along with Co-Workers*

Before you can learn to understand and accept the differences you find in your co-workers and develop productive relationships with them, you must have an accurate understanding of yourself. One way to secure this understanding is to take the Myers-Briggs Type Indicator test. Your college's career counseling center or psychology department should have someone on staff authorized to administer this test. After you have taken the test and identified your particular "type," read the portrait or description of the other types, particularly your opposite.

This information will prove invaluable as you strive to develop relationships with your co-workers. For example, if you are a "sensation type," you will approach a problem by gathering facts and considering practical and sensible solutions. On the other hand, if you are an "intuitive type," you will depend more on speculation, hunches, and inspiration to solve a particular problem. These differences can obviously lead to misunderstandings and team disharmony unless each worker fully understands and accepts his or her co-worker's differences, realizing that one type is not superior to the other.

Conclusion

It is hard to predict what your life will be like in the future. Who knows what job you will hold, what responsibilities you will have, where you will live, what your spouse or children will be like? Ideas or causes that you embraced yesterday may yield to various and sundry other interests tomorrow. For example, who could have foretold that the "flower children" of the 1960s would one day be doctors and lawyers and businesspeople. Indeed, many of us may scarcely recognize ourselves years hence. But as mysterious and uncertain as the future is, you have probably already begun to formulate some notion of what you hope your life will be like.

As you prepare to leave college and tackle the exciting challenges that lie ahead, you will inevitably find yourself facing tough decisions about your future lifestyle and relationships. In this chapter we have presented some of the options and dilemmas to come. What we are advocating is that you take all reasonable steps to acquaint yourself with issues that will soon have great relevance for you, that you anticipate and prepare for some of the realities of lifestyle and relationship choices, and that you realize the importance of "self-talk" and listening to the dictates of your own personal value scheme when making decisions.

Finally, we want to emphasize the sensitive nature of relationship issues in comparison to other, somewhat less personal issues. Someone once said that life is metaphorically akin to juggling two kinds of balls— rubber and glass. The rubber balls represent the concerns and cares of one's job—dealing with the boss, striving to meet quotas, managing daily responsibilities, and the like. If the juggler happens to drop the rubber balls, they will bounce back relatively unblemished. Glass balls, by contrast, are analogous to relationship issues. And if the juggler drops them, they may shatter. Great care, then, must be taken to protect relationships from permanent damage. In all relationship matters, whether they involve co-workers, friends, or family, you must remember that your actions and your choices are of great consequence.

References and Resources

Bennis, Warren. (1989). *On Becoming a Leader.* Reading, MA: Addison-Wesley.

Bolman, Lee G., and Terrence E. Deal. (1991). *Reframing Organizations: Artistry, Choice, and Leadership.* San Francisco: Jossey-Bass.

Boyer, Ernest. (1987). *College: The Undergraduate Experience in America.* New York: Harper & Row.

Braiker, Harriet. (December 1989). "The Power of Self-Talk." *Psychology Today* 23, no. 12: 23–27.

Campbell, Joseph. (1949). *The Hero with a Thousand Faces*. Princeton, NJ: Princeton University Press.

Collins, Eliza, and Patricia Scott. (July/August 1978). "Everyone Who Makes It Has a Mentor." *Harvard Business Review* 56, no. 4: 89–101.

Covey, Stephen. (1989). *The Seven Habits of Highly Effective People*. New York: Simon & Schuster.

Epstein, Joseph. (1980). *Ambition: The Secret Passion*. New York: Dutton.

Keirsey, David, and Marilyn Bates. (1978). *Please Understand Me: Character and Temperament Types*. Del Mar, CA: Prometheus Nemesis.

12   A Diverse America: Implications for Minority Seniors

Laura I. Rendón
Associate Professor of Educational Leadership and Policy Studies, Arizona State University

Tracy Robinson
Assistant Professor of Counselor Education, North Carolina State University

Senior Voices

Gloria

As I embark on my senior year of college, many thoughts fill my mind. Although I will not graduate until next December, the anticipation, excitement, uncertainty, and eagerness is as much alive in me as in everyone entering the last semesters of their college career.

Education is an integral part of my life and one that has been fostered by my family and friends. Neither of my parents finished high school, so they have always considered education the way to a better life. Their support and encouragement have engineered my years in school and made me strive for excellence. Most of my friends are in college, and we push each other to do well. Education also plays an important role in my sorority, Delta Gamma, which is a big part of my life and helps me to stay focused on studies and keep things prioritized.

Receiving my degree will be a success not just for me, but also for my family and for many young Hispanics out there. I am very involved on campus in activities and within the administration. To me it's no big deal; however, I am constantly reminded that by being seen in such important positions, I serve as a role model to Hispanic youths. I am considered a success because I attend college, work part-time, am active on campus, and balance good grades with family and a social life.

University life has allowed me to build character, confidence, an identity, and self-esteem. Recently I wondered about attending graduate school and what I would do during the semester between graduation and school. It was not until just a few days ago that I found my answer. My director at Orientation Services informed me of an internship offered through the National Orientation Directors Association, which would fill the time between graduation and graduate school. He also gave me information about top-ranked graduate programs in the field of college student personnel. Now while finishing courses, I can be found fine-tuning my resume, sending it out, filling out applications, and visiting campuses to begin the next step of the ongoing process of education.

Currently I am employed as Student Director of Orientation Services and as a Peer Mentor at the Peer Support Center. I never considered myself a leader, role model, or anything special. In the past year I have found myself in leadership positions and enjoying them. Being creative, planning projects, supervising staff members, and being in charge has given me newfound energy to go out and make something of myself. My work with students on campus helped me decide that student personnel was my calling. I feel comfortable in meetings and most importantly, I enjoy the work I do with students. I truly believe that things happen for a reason, so I don't worry too much about the future because I know God has a plan for me and He will not let me down.

Believe it or not, I don't feel nervous at all about graduating. I know that I possess the qualities and skills needed to succeed in the real world, and with the love and support of my family and friends behind me, I can accompish all my goals. I remember reading somewhere that the two things needed to succeed were roots and wings: Roots to know where you come from and wings to fly. My family instilled in me the history and heritage of my people and family; my degree is for me and for all those before me who did not have the ways or means that I have. With wings, everyone has the potential to soar and succeed. My family and friends have been the driving force behind many of my accomplishments. If it were not for them, I might have given up. But I didn't and I won't. Now all I can say is Look out world, here I come! ■

Are you African American, Mexican American, Puerto Rican, Asian American, Native American, or Alaska Native? If so, congratulations, because as a college senior, you are well on your way toward earning one of your first tickets to economic and career success:

the baccalaureate degree. You have reached a life milestone very few of your peers have attained. Out of the more than one million bachelor's degrees awarded in 1989, for example, only a small percentage were earned by members of minorities: 5.7 percent by African Americans, 2.9 percent by Hispanics, 0.4 percent by Native Americans, and 3.8 percent by Asian Americans. By comparison, white students earned nearly 85 percent of all bachelor's degrees!

This chapter is dedicated to these minority seniors, many of whom are the first in their family to earn a college degree. This chapter is also dedicated to those seniors who understand that they are living in a diverse society, that the world is changing, and that their future will differ from that of their predecessors. The aim of this chapter is to help all of you—white and nonwhite—understand the dynamics of a changing population, to help you come to grips with key transitional issues you will confront. As you embark on your life journeys, you will witness many more milestones, challenges, and opportunities for personal growth and career success. While the focus here is on students of color, we hope all of you will read this chapter with an eye toward understanding that the future belongs to those who emerge from college well equipped to lead as well as to work in concert with people from diverse cultures, backgrounds, and experiences.

A range of attitudes exist concerning cultural differences. For example, people with an ethnocentric attitude regard their own culture as superior to others and may even exhibit hostility or aggressive behavior toward people in other cultures. Other people adopt an attitude of "live and let live"—they accept and respect cultural differences. Multiculturalism, in which differences are nurtured and people feel comfortable with others from a variety of cultures, is considered an ideal state.

In this chapter we outline demographic shifts that are changing our lives. We also discuss key transitional issues that students of color will face, and we engage you in some exercises designed to make you think about yourself and your readiness to confront the diverse world in which you live.

Demography and Diversity

African Americans comprise 12 percent of the nation's population, Latinos 9 percent, Asians nearly 3 percent, and Native Americans approximately 1 percent. By the year 2000, it is projected, one in three Americans will be a person of color (Hodgkinson, 1985). Demographers also predict that the entire U.S. population will increase by approximately 12 percent. Depending on the particular ethnic/racial group, however, the rate varies. For instance, between 1980 and 1990, the white population increased by only 6 percent, while the African-

Table 12.1 New Entrants to the Labor Force

Group	Current Percentage of Labor Force	Percentage of Labor Force, 1985–2000
White males	47	15
White females	36	42
Nonwhite males	5	7
Nonwhite females	5	13
Immigrant males	4	13
Immigrant females	3	9

SOURCE: Johnston and Packer, 1987.

American population increased by 13.2 percent, the Native American by 37.9 percent, the Hispanic by 53 percent, and the Asian and Pacific Islander by an astonishing 107.8 percent. In the future nearly 60 percent of the estimated projected increase will occur among people of color (Stone and Castaneda, 1991).

What accounts for the more rapid growth rate among people of color? For one thing, on average, these groups are younger than whites. Moreover, African Americans, Puerto Ricans, and Mexican Americans have higher fertility rates (children per female) than whites. Population growth rates among Asians are attributed primarily to Asian immigrants since Asian-American women of child-bearing age have lower fertility rates than white, African-American, and Latino women. Also, the white baby boomers of the 1950s have aged, so they have lower fertility rates. And although the adolescent population has decreased due to declines in fertility rates, the population rate has not declined because more people are living longer due to advances in medical technology and to improved nutrition.

Shifting demographic trends have implications for the future work force. According to *Workforce 2000* (Johnston and Packer, 1987) the majority of the new entrants to the labor force will not be white males. Table 12.1 shows that 42 percent of the new entrants to the work force will be people of color and immigrants, which means that the work force will be more diverse, racially and culturally. Table 12.1 also shows that white women will play a bigger role in the work world.

Exercise 12.1

Tracing Your Family History

Do a "genogram." That is, trace your family history back as far as you can. Focus not only on who your ancestors were but on where they came from, what languages they spoke, what customs they observed, what political conditions they faced, and so on.

Coping with a Diverse World

1. Given demographers' predictions about the racial/ethnic make-up of America in the year 2000, discuss what you need to do to prepare to coexist in a world populated by diverse cultures. Focus your discussion on the following questions:

   a. What are the hopes and fears of the white population in a multicultural society?

   b. What are some of the myths that surround race and ethnicity in this society?

   c. In what ways can whites and nonwhites influence the political and social development of America?

   d. What does multiculturalism mean, and what are the forces that created it?

2. Have a group of students from diverse backgrounds play Bafá Bafá, a cross-culture simulation game developed by R. Garry Shirts, Simile II, 218 Twelfth St., P. O. Box 910, Del Mar, CA 92014. After playing this game, discuss what you learned about yourself and about your values and beliefs about other cultures.

Characteristics of People of Color

Although racial/ethnic groups—Latinos, Asian Americans, African Americans, Native Americans, and so on—share certain characteristics, they are not monolithic and should not be regarded as such. The resilience of these groups over time is evident as measured by strong kinship and familial ties, coping/survival skills in confronting institutional racism, and significant educational and occupational advancement. Unfortunately, alcoholism, unemployment, poverty, dysfunctional families, and crime are problems associated with these groups. And focusing on such problems while ignoring the groups' many strengths contributes to myths about people of color that cultivate ignorance and impede racial unity.

Latinos

The term *Latino* is widely used to refer to persons with Spanish ancestry—Puerto Ricans, Cubans, Central and South Americans, Latin and Mexican Americans. Important cultural and regional differences exist among Latinos. Often, however, data are presented in the aggregate, so that distinctions among the Hispanic subgroups become difficult to discern.

Of the more than 19 million Latinos in the United States, 62 percent have roots in Mexico, 13 percent in Puerto Rico, 11.5 percent in Central and South America, 5 percent in Cuba, and 8 percent in other countries. Over the previous decade the Hispanic population increased by more than 53 percent. Currently, Latinos comprise 9 percent of the total U.S. population, up from 6.5 percent in 1980.

Nearly 50 percent of Hispanics are below age 20, with children ages 5–13 representing the largest age group by percentage, comprising nearly 20 percent of the entire Hispanic population. Among whites the comparable figure is 10 percent, and among African Americans it's 12 percent. Moreover, there were no population decreases noted in any of the age categories for Latinos. In terms of educational attainment, 60 percent of the Hispanic population had completed high school in 1986. Common to most Latinos is the use of the Spanish language as well as strong ties to family and cultural pride. The month of September is now recognized as National Hispanic History Month.

Mexican Americans. Among Latinos, Mexican Americans are the fastest-growing group, with the population growing from 8.7 million in 1980 to the current 12.1 million. The roots of the Mexican-American community spread from colonies established by Spain and Mexico over ten generations ago in much of what is now known as the American Southwest. The higher rate of immigration among Mexican Americans gave rise to their rapid population growth. Although Mexican Americans are concentrated in eight states, 75 percent of them live in California, Texas, New York, or Florida. Many Mexican Americans have strong ties to their mother country and take great pride in celebrating fiestas such as Cinco de Mayo (May 5th), a Mexican holiday commemorating the defeat of French imperialists in Puebla in 1867. Another national holiday is September 16, when Mexico celebrates gaining its independence from Spain in 1821.

Puerto Ricans. As of 1988 there were 2.5 million Puerto Ricans in the United States and 3.3 million Puerto Ricans in the Commonwealth of Puerto Rico. Nearly 80 percent of all Puerto Ricans in the United States reside in New York, New Jersey, Illinois, Florida, or California (*Hispanic Policy Development Project*, 1984). Puerto Ricans also have strong ties to the island, as evidenced by frequent migration to and from Puerto Rico and by strong cultural pride.

Asian Americans

Currently, Asian Americans number 6.5 million, or just under 3 percent of the population. Over 60 percent of Asian Americans are foreign born, primarily in China, the Philippines, Japan, East India, Korea, and Vietnam. The Asian-American population has been growing steadily over the past two decades. In the 1980s, for example, the population growth rate was 141 percent, amounting to 1.6 million people, primarily due to immigration. And some demographers predict that by the year 2000, the Asian-American population will double.

As for Mexican Americans, California is home to many Asian Americans. This is largely attributed to the Chinese who were recruited in the 1800s to work as laborers and on the transcontinental railroads. Hawaii, New York, New Jersey, Illinois, Texas, and Washington are also home to many Asian Americans.

Like other racially diverse groups, Asians often are seen as monolithic. However, Asian newcomers speak hundreds of languages and dialects, and they have a variety of specific national or regional ties. In spite of the myth that Asian Americans are model minorities with few problems (a myth supported largely by the fact that 35 percent of Asian Americans age 25 and older have graduated from college), many Asian Americans, particularly Hmong and Cambodian, are beset with financial and personal difficulties, such as poverty and trouble with the English language.

Despite their heterogeneity, Asian Americans share some common values, such as stoicism, family and group interdependence, and interpersonal harmony. These values may conflict with dominant American values of competitiveness and individualism.

African Americans

African Americans have rich cultural traditions, including valuing family and attaching importance to education and spirituality. They are drawn from diverse cultures and countries in Africa, the Caribbean, and Central and South America. Comprising 12 percent of the population, they are the largest group of color in the United States. During the 1980s, the African-American population grew 13.2 percent, from 26.5 million to 29.9 million, mostly due to natural causes (more births than deaths) rather than to immigration. And although the adolescent population of African Americans increased, high homicide rates among adolescent males offset the high rate of growth.

Approximately 85 percent of African Americans live in cities and in metropolitan areas. During the early 1900s some 60 percent of all African Americans resided in rural areas. However, in the great migration of 1910–1940, the majority of African Americans left the farms of the South and moved to northern cities in search of employment and better living conditions. Today, most African Americans reside in the South (U.S. Department of Commerce, 1986). States containing the largest number of African Americans are New York, California, Texas, Illinois, Florida, and Georgia.

As of 1985, African Americans and whites age 25–29 had attained educational parity in terms of median years of school completed.

Native Americans

In 1980 Native Americans numbered 1.4 million, less than 1 percent of the total population. Although far fewer in number than African Americans, Asian Americans, or Latinos, Native Americans have experienced considerable growth since 1950, from approximately 360,000 to 1.4 million as of 1980 (Fries, 1987). Although a smaller group than African Americans and Hispanics, Native Americans have experienced considerable growth within the last decade. As of the 1990 census, there were 1.9 million Native Americans for a 37.9 percent change over a ten-year period (Vobejda, 1992).

Important differences set many Native Americans apart culturally from the American mainstream. For example, Native Americans emphasize coexisting with nature, intuitiveness, family and community cooperation, and simplicity. Such differences may promote conflict for Native Americans in a society oriented toward assimilation, progress, and competition.

Unlike African Americans and Latinos, nearly half (48 percent) of Native Americans live in rural areas. Many live on reservations or trust lands, in Alaskan Native villages, or in rural settlements or small towns. Like other groups of color, Native Americans reside throughout the United States; however, the majority live in the West (49 percent) or the South (27 percent). California, Oklahoma, Arizona, and New Mexico are home to 45 percent of the total Native American population, while North Carolina, Washington, and South Dakota also have high Native American populations.

There are about 250 Native American languages, many of them spoken by only a few people. Today, there are approximately 517 tribes recognized by the federal government (Peregoy, 1993). The tribes vary in languages, customs, and traditions (Sue and Sue, 1990). Over half of the Native Americans living on reservations speak their native language at home.

Native Americans have increased their high school graduation rates dramatically in the last two decades, from 51 percent in 1970 to 60 percent in 1988.

Alaska Natives

Alaska is home to three distinct indigenous groups—Eskimos, Aleuts, and Native Americans—that comprise 14 percent of the state's population. Of the 64,103 Alaska Natives, 34,144 are Eskimos (Inupiaq and Yu'pik), 21,869 are Native Americans from North American tribes, and 8,090 are Aleuts. Alaska Natives are a young people as well, with 46 percent below the age of 20 in 1980.

Altogether twenty Alaska Native languages exist, none of which were written before the arrival of Russian settlers in the late eighteenth century. The first written Alaskan language was Aleut, which uses a Slavonic alphabet. Alaska Natives have a rich history, and culture and language are quite valued.

Key Transitional Issues for Students of Color

People of color are frequently misunderstood because they are so diverse. As a nation we tend to want to erase differences among people and make everyone conform to a set standard. But people of color have resisted conformity and assimilation, believing that differences should be valued and accepted and that, despite differences, people can live together harmoniously. In the words of Johnetta Cole, president of Spelman College, a historically African-American women's college in Georgia: "We are for difference. For respecting difference. For valuing difference. Till difference doesn't make any more difference." As a person of color, you will be confronted with many conflicts in a society that is still working on valuing difference.

If there is anything that characterizes the senior year, it is transition. You are moving from one world to another, from an established set of friends and relationships to new ones, from an academic environment to a career environment, from a familiar geographic location to a new, unknown setting. While transitions can be exciting, they can also be scary: They test our judgment, our ability to adjust, and our maturity. Key transitional issues you will likely have to confront include (1) identity formation, (2) relationship development, (3) conflict, (4) racism and sexism, (5) civic responsibilities, (6) finances, and (7) career/graduate school options.

Identity

As you anticipate graduation and wonder about your future, you are probably searching for answers to questions such as the following:

1. Who am I?
2. What do I want to do with my degree?
3. What am I capable of doing with my life?
4. How am I going to accomplish the goals I have set?

Such inquiry is part of the never-ending process of identity formation.

Clearly, asking such questions can be unsettling since you are dealing with high levels of uncertainty. However, the process is important. It is crucial that you spend time getting to know yourself and learning to

Maria

Decisions, decisions! What to do? Where to go? Do I want to go straight for my masters in social work after graduation? It's only two more years of school. Or should I go for the advanced standing and finish my masters in a year and a half? Do I get married after graduation to my boyfriend of three years, or can he wait two more years until my schooling is done? Do I want to stay in Indianapolis after graduation, or do I seek jobs in other states? Too many things to think about.

I feel like a high school senior all over again; except this time these decisions are more crucial. I will soon be out seeking a real job in my prospective field and possibly getting married and maybe even moving out of state. After high school marriage was the furthest thing from my mind, and I didn't know what I wanted to do with the rest of my life.

I'm ready to graduate and start my new life in the field of social work, but along with graduating comes anxiety about having to make some drastic decisions involving school, my personal life, my career, and family—all of which I'm not sure I'm ready to make. If I really think about it, I know I will be able to make these decisions—I guess it's just the fear of the unknown. I got through the unknowns and anxieties of college with the comfort and support of my friends, my boyfriend, and my family.

College years weren't so bad in regard to seeing my friends because we could come and visit each other at our respective campuses, but now it's different. Some of us are settling down with a significant other, we're going off to other states for jobs in our chosen fields, or we're continuing our education; therefore, we don't get to see one another very often.

As for my boyfriend, we've been together for three years and have talked about marriage but decided to wait 'til after I graduate. He has been out of school for five years and now it's my turn to finish. This poses many problems for me. He has a house here in Indianapolis; do I look for jobs here? Do we get married after I graduate and be a newlywed while getting my masters? Do we wait a few more years until all my schooling is done?

I am very close to my family, and so I don't really want to live too far away from them. While I went to Indiana University, Bloomington, I talked to my mother at least once or twice a week for a whole semester. Imagine if I lived in another state; my phone bill would be outrageous!

I am beginning to feel major senioritis, especially since I was chosen to represent the seniors of my college and give my perspective of "a day in the life of a student" to all the incoming freshmen. I got to wear a cap and gown and walk in a processional with the chancellor and many deans of schools. My whole family was there taking pictures. Walking along in my cap and gown, I was wondering, "Where is my diploma, and where do I go once I get it?" ■

cultivate your solitude. Remember, you are an individual with your own interests, your own likes and dislikes; you must resist trying to be who other people would have you be. If you need help resolving identity issues, talk to a college counselor or to your mentor, if you have one.

Relationships

Relationships with others provide us with a feeling of connection and a sense of belonging. The absence of such relationships gives rise to stress, unhappiness, and feelings of isolation. Not all relationships, however, are positive. Unhealthy relationships, characterized by dominance and disrespect, can impede personal growth and sabotage professional development. Moreover, the more you know about yourself, the more successful you will be in establishing relationships that are mutually gratifying. Forming relationships is a lifelong endeavor.

Bear in mind that during your twenties you will experience momentous identity shifts. With this in mind, ask how these shifts may affect your relationships. More and more people, male and female, are staying single longer, a state that need not be synonymous with loneliness. In fact, remaining single can be an asset as you take the time to develop your career and attend to important intrapersonal changes.

If you are married or involved in a serious relationship, however, you need to ask yourself the following questions:

1. Is my partner supportive of my professional goals?
2. Does he or she encourage me to be the best that I can be?
3. Do I sacrifice my ambition to please him or her?

How you respond is important because you are at a critical juncture where relationships will have a major impact on your entire life. If you are contemplating marriage, for instance, you must consider whether you and your potential spouse will be able to handle all the changes to come. Regardless of your age, relationships impact your life, so you need to establish positive, healthy ones.

Conflict Management

Conflict is inevitable, whether you are in graduate school or on the job. In fact, it is important to personal growth and development. Unless you learn how to manage conflict, however, it can work against you.

Fortunately, you can learn to manage and resolve conflict better. First, you must accept that conflict not only is inevitable but is not always bad. This knowledge should make you less likely to avoid conflict when it occurs. Second, you must communicate to resolve conflict. Sometimes we suffer needlessly because of an inability or unwillingness to let our feelings be known. Other times, even when we do express our feelings, such communication does not always change the other person's thinking or actions. Nonetheless, the very act of communicating to resolve conflict is an act of personal empowerment. Finally, you must recognize that the resolution to a conflict often is not consistent with your wishes. Part of being an adult is accepting that not all situations go the way you want them to.

Racism and Sexism

Racism and sexism exist. These discriminatory practices primarily affect women and people of color, but men and whites can be victimized as well. In any event, whenever people are valued or devalued primarily because of immutable characteristics—such as gender or race—the concept of meritocracy is convoluted.

Sometimes racist or sexist acts are covert and thus more difficult to detect. An example might be hiring and promotion policies. Although denying hiring and promotion opportunities solely on the basis of a person's gender and/or race/ethnicity is illegal, such discriminatory acts do occur. In these cases, other reasons, such as inferior work quality or insufficient professional experience, may be given to justify the decision not to hire or promote someone. Examples of overt racist or sexist acts might be derogatory name calling or sexual harassment in which an employee is asked to engage in sexual activities in order to be retained or promoted.

Although dealing with discrimination is never easy, it is possible. If you feel you are being discriminated against, you need to document your case in writing. An Affirmative Action officer can be a valuable resource. In addition, some organizations have employee assistance counselors who mediate conflicts between an employee and an employer. The most important thing is to know your rights, but you must also be sure that discrimination on the basis of race or gender is the root cause of your problem.

Racism/Sexism

1. As honestly as possible, answer to yourself the following questions:

   a. Who are your closest friends?

   b. Are they racially/culturally similar to you? Why or why not?

   c. What were you taught about people who were different?

   d. How do you feel about people who are racially and culturally different from you?

   e. How do you feel about the new entrants to the work force?

   f. How do you feel about the rapid population growth rates among people of color?

   g. What is your definition of racism?

   Based on your answers, might you be guilty, even subconsciously, of racist or sexist thinking?

2. With a group of friends, watch and discuss the 1988 Frontline-produced presentations "Racism 101" and "Eyes on the Prize." How did you react to them? Did viewing the shows change your attitudes? How?

Civic Responsibility

For the most part, students of color have very close ties to their communities. If you attended college close to home, you might be thinking about whether you should stay close to home or move farther away. The resolution of the dilemma is not easy. If you remain where you are, you have the opportunity to assume a leadership role in helping to build and strengthen your community. On the other hand, more lucrative opportunities might exist far from your home environment. Yet if you leave, you will be contributing to a "brain drain" of educated persons who can work effectively to build their communities.

Be aware that whatever choice you make, you can find ways to give something back to your community and your culture. No matter where you are, you can be working on issues that affect minority groups. These issues are of central concern to just about every local, state, and federal organization, and you can take part in shaping the issues as well as resolving them.

Indeed, seniors of color are very committed to their communities. One senior said, "I cringe every time I hear a student who says that he wants to major in business because he wants to make a lot of money. Not me. I am interested in social change." One of the ways you can give something back to your community is by being a role model. For example, you might visit elementary, junior high, high school, or college classrooms and talk to students about the importance of staying in school. Other ways to contribute include volunteering in community-based organizations that work with underprivileged youths, doing volunteer work at women's centers, conducting research on issues affecting people of color, or donating to scholarship funds for college students of color.

You also have a responsibility to your college or university. Graduating from college makes you an alumnus of your college. In this role you should plan on staying in touch with your college, offering to help recruit students of color, sponsoring a special activities with the Alumni Center, and working to see that financial aid exists for students of color. Find out if there is an African-American, Hispanic, Native American, or Asian-American alumni organization. If there is, join it and support it.

Exercise 12.4

Deciding Where to Locate After College

One of the most important decisions you will have to make upon college graduation is whether to pursue a career in the community you were raised in or elsewhere. Discuss the advantages and disadvantages of either choice.

Exercise 12.5

Addressing Pressing Social Problems

What do you believe are the five most critical issues facing this country in the next twenty years? How do you believe you can become involved in addressing these issues?

Leadership

More and more of our country's leaders are coming from racially diverse backgrounds. In fact, this may be the last generation in which middle-aged white males dominate the leadership of our society. Yet, there is still a dearth of leaders from a variety of cultural backgrounds. Because of your college background, you have the unique opportunity to become a leader at the local, regional, or national level.

Leaders usually excel in two things: (1) They have a strong command of the issues they advocate and (2) they have good interpersonal skills. Therefore they are able to inspire others to accomplish the tasks before them. Some leaders are born, but most of them are made. You can become a leader, but first you must understand your strengths and your weaknesses.

It would also help if you learned more about leaders from various backgrounds. Read biographies of and autobiographies by figures such as Martin Luther King, Cesar Chavez, Jesse Jackson, Barbara Jordan, Felisa Rincon de Gautier, Thurgood Marshall, and Jaime Escalante. What can you learn from the experiences of these prominent leaders? What made them good leaders? What was their philosophy of leadership? What obstacles did they face, and how did they overcome them? Then look around you. Are there any people of color serving as leaders on your campus? In your community? Get to know them, and learn from their example. Ultimately, you can draw on the experiences of others as you develop your own leadership style.

Exercise 12.6

Developing Leadership Skills

1. Make a list of leaders from minority backgrounds in your college or community. Interview them, and ask them the following:

   a. What are the characteristics of a good leader?

   b. Who are your role models? What are the qualities you admire in them?

   c. What advice would you give to students about becoming leaders?

2. Make a list of talents or qualities you have that you feel will enable you to be a good leader, as well as the qualities that you need to develop in order to enhance your leadership capacity.

Finances

At this point some of you are thinking of going to graduate school while others are ready to enter the job market. Some of you are "flip-flopping." As one senior said, "Sometimes I wonder if I should pick a school first and then a job, or find a job and then a school." Whatever your intentions, you need to do some financial planning.

If you are going to graduate school, you should inquire as early as possible about financial aid packages for graduate students of color. Many colleges and universities offer such packages, but you need to apply early. For example, more financial aid is now available for students of color and women entering math- and science-based fields of study, disciplines traditionally dominated by white males.

If you are getting a job, you need to construct a budget and figure out what your basic living expenses will be. Be sure to include the amount of money that you will have to use to repay your college loans, if you made use of them. Also, try to save some money. It is always wise to set aside funds that you may need later, especially if you plan to go to graduate school and/or start a family at some later time. You might discover that you have to postpone buying that long-awaited brand-new car. But keep in mind that used cars depreciate less and may be a better value in the long run. The key here is to discipline yourself to stick to what you can afford while trying to save money for emergencies and other life goals. Also keep in mind that home ownership is still the best investment you can make, albeit at a future time.

Exercise 12.7	*Planning Your Finances*

1. If you are planning on going to graduate school, write to the financial aid office of the university you plan to attend. Inquire about financial aid opportunities for minority students, including fellowships, graduate student assistantships, and so on. How much aid will the school be able to provide? Will it be enough?

2. If you will be paying back money on loans you obtained to help you go to college, draw up a budget that includes all your expenses. How much will you have to earn to live comfortably and be able to make monthly payments on the loan(s) you owe?

Careers

One of the most critical issues you will confront is how to choose the right job. You might want to consider going to the counseling center and taking some tests that help identify the kinds of careers that are compatible with your abilities, background, and personality. It is also helpful to talk with a career counselor. And, you might want to interview some people who are employed in fields or jobs you are considering.

Those of you going on to graduate school will want to make sure you link your program of study to your career interests. Graduate students are usually assigned advisors to help with this process, so be sure to schedule an appointment (as early as possible) with your advisor to go over your academic and career goals. You might be interested in knowing that people of color are least represented in professions such as mathematics, science, medicine, college-level teaching, and computer science.

Exercise 12.8	*Rating Jobs/Occupations*

Make a list of the jobs and occupations that are perceived as prestigious in society, as defined by status and importance. Do the same with jobs perceived as not prestigious, as defined by low status and less importance. What are the immutable characteristics (gender, race, ethnicity) of jobs on each list?

Graduate School

While the good news is that you will soon earn a bachelor's degree, the bad news is that a bachelor's degree has less value than it once did. Not only are more people earning undergraduate degrees, but more are earning graduate degrees as well. For example, in business more employers are looking for MBA's, and in engineering employers are seeking employees with advanced degrees. While a bachelor's degree remains vital and necessary to obtain a white-collar job, it simply doesn't guarantee what it once did.

If few minorities are earning bachelor's degrees, even fewer are earning master's and doctorates. If you are thinking of going on to get a master's degree, a doctorate, or a professional degree in law, dentistry, architecture, or medicine, be aware that many opportunities for students of color are available. First, think of the program of study in which you are interested. Remember that going to a college because it is close to a boyfriend or girlfriend can be problematic if it is inconsistent with your own career needs and desires. Second, find out which graduate schools have the best programs in your chosen area and write to them. Ask for information about the program, the application process, and potential financial aid. Determine whether the program requires that you take the Graduate Records Exam (GRE), Miller Analogies Test (MAT), or other admissions tests (some graduate schools require none). If a test is required, you should enroll in a test preparation workshop and/or buy test preparation books (available in most bookstores and libraries), especially if your test-taking skills are not strong.

You will also need to have strong references from, for example, a former professor or current employer. Graduate schools do want students of color, but these students, like their white counterparts, must have a strong academic background, excellent references, experiences that relate to the chosen program of study, and a well-written narrative on their goals and the way the program is related to achieving them.

Don't take this application process lightly. It is not a bad idea to apply to more than one graduate school; some waive application fees for graduate students with restricted financial resources. You might also want to find out if the graduate school has any minority faculty members who can serve as mentors, and you should find out whether there are minority organizations, offices, or other groups on campus that address minority issues. If such resources exist, establish contact with them. University life can be very alienating, so you need to cultivate a support network of fellow students.

There are also national projects designed to recruit minority students to graduate school. For example, Hispanic students can contact Project 1000 (1-800-327-4893), which helps Hispanics through the graduate school admissions and applications processes at universities throughout the country. Also, the National Hispanic Scholarship Fund offers scholarships for Latino students. Similarly, the American Association of University Women Educational Foundation (1-202-720-7603) offers graduate fellowships for women. Be sure to conduct library research for more information on the following fellowships: The National Science Foundation Graduate Fellowship, the Ford Foundation Predoctoral and Dissertation Fellowships for Minorities, and the McKnight Black Doctoral Fellowship. Your school library most likely has resources on grants and fellowships for students.

Conclusion

The senior year is indeed a critical transitional period. Yet, it is a time of celebration as well: You are finally attaining a bachelor's degree! It is also a time to look to the future—to make decisions about whether to go to graduate school, get a job, get married, and so forth. Finally, it is a time to prepare to live in a changing world marked by cultural diversity. You will make transitions in your own unique way. We hope your senior experience will help you with future life transitions. One minority senior eloquently expressed the impact of her senior year: "My senior year has given me an edge on life as well as a positive outlook on what awaits me in the future. I will gain a diploma that will probably land me a job, but I have also gained more than I could possibly ever hang on my wall."

References and Resources

Alaska Department of Labor, Research and Analysis Section. (September 1985). *Alaska Population Overview, 1985 Estimates*. Juneau: Alaska Department of Labor.

Carter, D. J., and R. Wilson. (1990). *Minorities in Higher Education*. Washington, DC: ACE Macmillan.

"The Demographics of Diversity: Asian Americans and Higher Education." (1989). *Change* (November/December).

Fries, J. E. (1987). *The American Indian in Higher Education: 1975–1976 to 1984–1985*. Washington, DC: Center for Education Statistics, U.S. Government Printing Office.

Hispanic Policy Development Project. (1984). *The Hispanic Almanac*. Washington, DC: Hispanic Policy Development Project.

Hodgkinson, H. (1985). *All One System: Demographics of Education, Kindergarten Through Graduate School*. Washington, DC: Institute for Educational Leadership.

Johnston, W., and A. Packer. (1987). *Workforce 2000: Work and Workers for the 21st Century*. Indianapolis, IN: Hudson Institute.

Peregoy, J. J. (1993). "Transcultural Counseling with American Indians and Alaskan Natives: Contemporary Issues for Consideration." In J. McFadden (Ed.), *Transcultural Counseling: Bilateral and International Perspectives* (pp. 163–192). Alexandria, VA: American Counseling Association.

Quality Education for Minorities. (1990). *Education That Works.* Cambridge, MA: M.I.T. Quality Education for Minorities Project.

Stone, A., and C. J. Castaneda. (1991). "Vietnamese Set the Pace for Ethnic Growth." *USA Today,* June 10, p. A3.

Sue, D. W., and D. Sue. (1990). *Counseling the Culturally Different: Theory and Practice.* New York: John Wiley.

U.S. Department of Commerce, Bureau of the Census. (1987). *Projections of the Hispanic Population of the United States: 1983–2079.* Washington, DC: Government Printing Office.

———. (March 1986). *We, the Black Americans.* Washington, DC: Government Printing Office.

———. (April 1985). *Nosotros.* Washington, DC: Government Printing Office.

———. (1983). *Condition of Hispanics in America Today.* Washington, DC: Government Printing Office.

Vobejda, B. (1992). "Asians, Hispanics Giving Nation More Diversity." In J. A. Kromkowski (Ed.), *Annual Editions: Race and Ethnic Relations 92/93.* Guilford, CT: The Dushkin Publishing Group.

Williams, G., Research and Analysis Section. (July 1993). *Alaska Population Overview: 1991 Estimates.* Juneau: Alaska Department of Labor.

13 | Interpersonal Communication

Mabry M. O'Donnell

Professor of Speech Communication, Marietta College

Senior Voices

Dave

As a former president of two clubs, I had the opportunity to use "group techniques," or should I say, attempt the use of group techniques, such as parliamentary procedure and committee work. Unfortunately, I came off as being rigid, formal, and oppressive. The group did not talk at the meetings, so I never knew that their goals and ideas had changed from mine. Had I "listened to" the silence, I could have modified, but I didn't and was eventually forced to resign. To be an effective communicator one has to listen. So listen. ■

Every college senior looks forward to graduation with a sense of anticipation. Some of you will enter the work force, others will pursue graduate study, and still others may accept a position with a volunteer agency. Many of you also may marry or move in with a significant other at some time after graduation. All of you, however, no matter what you do beyond college, will live in a world where you must communicate with other people every day of your life. In most cases the key to achieving happiness and success is communication, the kind of communication most often described as interpersonal communication.

In this chapter we will broadly define interpersonal communication and examine some of the ways it affects you. We will also focus on the often overlooked area of nonverbal communication and on that important but often underdeveloped skill of listening.

What Is Interpersonal Communication?

By definition interpersonal communication is concerned with those activities that involve interactions between ourselves and others. Because we live in organized societies, it is virtually impossible for us to avoid interpersonal communication. As social beings we all learn, relate, persuade, play, and help—and we depend on interpersonal communication to do so. The *quality* of the interaction between individuals distinguishes skillful communication at the interpersonal level; there, the basic building block of interpersonal communication is the dyad of two persons.

Interpersonal relationships are (1) unique, (2) irreplaceable, (3) interdependent, (4) disclosing, (5) intrinsically rewarding, and (6) scarce. Above all, interpersonal relationships are necessary for survival. As Jean Paul Sartre observed: "In order to get at any truth about myself, I must have contact with another person. The other is indispensable to my own existence, as well as to my knowledge about myself."

Consider the relationship you have with the person to whom you are the closest. Would you describe it as unique, unlike any other in the world? It's probably also irreplaceable; again, there will never be another like it. As you reflect on your particular interpersonal relationship, you will become aware of your interdependence. Because of your closeness, there is mutual disclosing, a characteristic that sets this relationship apart from superficial ones. Finally, in rare moments of reflection, you may become aware that this relationship is both rewarding in and of itself (that is, intrinsically so) and scarce.

Interpersonal communication activity involves six elements—sender, message, channel, receiver, feedback, and noise—that interact simultane-

Figure 13.1 The Elements of Interpersonal Communication (Simplified)

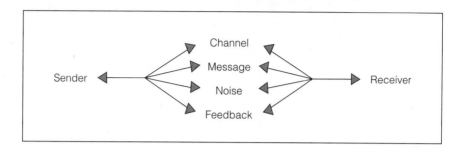

ously and not necessarily in sequential steps (see Figure 13.1). The sender is the person who sends the verbal or nonverbal message. The verbal message may take either oral or written form. Interpersonal messages travel by channels (such as person to person, FAX, telephone, smoke signals) to a receiver, who gives feedback, either intentionally or unintentionally. The overall communication process is affected by "noise"—physical, psychological, or both. Thus effective interpersonal communication takes place only when noise is kept to a minimum.

Exercise 13.1

Interpersonal Relationships

List six characteristics applicable to a *quality* interpersonal relationship. For each characteristic note specific ways in which it applies to your relationship with the person you are closest to.

How Effective Are You at Interpersonal Communication?

Even at this point in your college career, it's not too late to assess your effectiveness at interpersonal communication—and to improve your skills. For example, what do you regard as your strengths and weaknesses? Have you learned anything about communication during your four years of college? How well do you communicate with your roommate or suitemates? Boy- or girlfriend? Friends? Professors? Parents? For instance, have you conversed recently with your roommate, or do you ignore each other? If you have suitemates, do you ever engage them in a meaningful conversation? Perhaps you leave one another phone messages; do you even recognize their handwriting? Do you genuinely communicate with your boyfriend or girlfriend, or do you take that person for granted, seldom explaining what is on your mind? (Remember, silence is itself a profound act of communication.) Likewise, how do you interact with your friends? And what is your interpersonal communication relationship with your professors? Do you feel comfortable going to their offices or stopping after class to ask a question? What about your communication with your parents? How much has that improved since you left home for college? Do you avoid having conversations with them?

Asking yourself how well you communicate at present is not an exercise in futility. Each of the individuals or groups mentioned here has a counterpart in the world beyond college. Your future success, happiness, and satisfaction depend in large measure on perfecting your skills at interpersonal communication. In Abraham Maslow's well-known hierarchy of needs, the highest category is termed *self-actualization*—that is, becoming the best person you can be. And without interpersonal communication skills you may never achieve self-actualization.

Persons in Community

While we may regard ourselves as independent, self-reliant individuals, we are at the same time persons in community. It does not matter whether the community is comprised of you and one other as friends or a couple, you and several others in a family, you and a number of others in an organization, or you and thousands of others in an identifiable political community. The quality of your communication with and in these several communities directly impacts the quality of your life as well as the lives of all the others with whom you communicate. John Donne's often-quoted aphorism that no one is "an island, entire of itself" remains as true today as it was almost four hundred years ago.

In the computer age we commonly blame errors on the "garbage in, garbage out" syndrome. Similarly, "garbage out, garbage in" aptly characterizes failed attempts at communication in an interpersonal relationship—an individual sent out garbage that was received and then returned in kind. We all send and receive messages, and we can avoid the frustration of "garbage out, garbage in" by consciously striving to improve our interpersonal communication skills.

Nonverbal Communication

As you consider the range of your communication skills, remember the world of nonverbal communication, in which messages are conveyed through channels other than the spoken (or written) word. No matter how stone-faced and impassive we think we may be, we constantly send nonverbal messages via (1) body language, (2) artifacts, (3) proximity and territoriality, (4) touch, (5) silence, and (6) paralanguage. Nonverbal communication has several key attributes:

- It is culture bound.
- It is primarily attitudinal.
- It serves many functions.
- It is ambiguous.

Body Language

How we stand, sit, walk, and gesture conveys a message or perhaps a whole series of messages. The nature of these messages is shaped in part by the culture in which we live. In some cultures broad gestures are a natural and vital component of the communication process, while in others the use of gestures is inappropriate. The same is true of facial expression and eye movements. For example, Americans accustomed to greeting passers-by with a friendly smile will be viewed with suspicion in Europe. Similarly, in the United States, in most cases of direct communication, eye contact is looked upon favorably as a mark of truthfulness and credibility. Among South Americans and southern Europeans, however, prolonged eye contact is considered a sign of hostility. And Asians lower their eyes as a sign of respect. By contrast, blinking and winking is not regarded with approval. During the 1991 Persian Gulf War a neuropsychologist analyzed the nervous blinking of Iraq's Saddam Hussein during a news interview. According to the researcher a person speaking before a camera "normally" blinks between 30 and 50 times per minute; more than 50 is considered high. Hussein reportedly blinked 113 times per minute, a frantic rate indicative of extremely high stress.

Artifacts

We also communicate nonverbally through and with the artifacts we employ. "Artifact" in this context refers to clothing, hair style, jewelry, perfume or cologne, furniture, art objects, automobiles, and even the places we live in. If you are meeting someone for the first time, consider what would be communicated by the following:

- A man sporting long hair
- A woman wearing long dangle earrings
- Someone chewing gum
- Someone chewing tobacco
- Someone giving off an overpowering fragrance
- A man wearing an earring
- Someone driving a $100,000 car
- Someone riding a bicycle

Exercise 13.2   *Interpreting Artifacts*

Imagine that you have posted a note advertising for a roommate. When someone calls about this, by mutual arrangement you agree to meet at a certain place and time. What would your reaction be if the person arrived thirty minutes late, left his or her bicycle leaning against the front window, and came in wearing a soiled T-shirt, cut-offs, and sandals? What might these artifacts communicate?

Proximity and Territoriality

An increasingly important aspect in the understanding of nonverbal communication is the study of spatial considerations, known as proxemics and territoriality. Proxemics refers to how our treatment of our personal space sends messages. For example, how far do you stand from someone with whom you are unacquainted? If someone edges closer to you in a line, do you hold your ground or try to edge a bit farther away? How is the furniture in your dorm room arranged? Is everything pushed back to the walls, leaving open space in the middle, or have you and your roommate expressed your territoriality by marking off separate zones through the location of furniture?

Touch

One area of nonverbal communication about which we must be especially sensitive is tactile communication, or haptics. Haptics involves those messages that are communicated by touching and being touched. In this type of nonverbal communication, care must be exercised lest someone take your effort at communication in the wrong way. While most of us accept a certain amount of touching communication from relatives and loved ones, we are not as open to such communication from strangers. If you are one of those persons inclined to touching as a means of communication, you might consider withholding such gestures until you are absolutely certain you will not offend someone. Restraint is recommended especially in the case of tactile communication with the opposite sex; a male in a position of authority may be perceived as sexist for patting the shoulder of a female subordinate, while touching on the part of the female subordinate or new acquaintance might be regarded as an effort to win favor.

Exercise 13.3   *Interpreting Tactile Communication*

List five people you have touched today. What was their interpersonal relationship to you? List five people who touched you today. Did any of them offend you by doing so? Can you think of an occasion when your touching might have offended someone?

Silence

Much like touching, silence communicates meaning. Silence, strictly speaking, is the absence of speech, but it does not reflect the absence of communication; silence communicates as surely as the spoken word. For example, if you are attempting to communicate with someone who says nothing in return, you may conclude that the response is negative or, at the least, that the person is not interested in what you have to say.

Paralanguage

Like silence, paralanguage can communicate meaning, intentionally or unintentionally. Paralanguage is the study of the vocal but nonverbal dimensions of speech. We send paralingual messages when, for example, we speak much more rapidly or at a higher pitch than we do normally, perhaps due to nervousness, stress, or anxiety. One common manifestation of paralanguage occurs with persons who have to say essentially the same thing over and over again. How often have you visited a museum or tourist attraction and been struck by the guide's memorized spiel? Through the prerehearsed, monotonous delivery the guide was communicating his or her boredom with the job and desire to hurry through it in order to be finished. Paralingual messages also may be conveyed in the volume, resonance, pauses, and quality of one's speech. For instance, have you answered the phone hurriedly, unthinkingly answering in an extremely unpleasant voice? Finally, when we respond to the paralanguage of a message, our paralingual feedback should be appropriate to the situation. For example, if your roommate came in with the news that his or her mother had just died, chirping "Don't worry about it" would be inappropriate.

Exercise 13.4 | *Using Paralanguage*

1. Think about a situation in which you used paralanguage. Was it intentional or unintentional? What types of paralanguage did you use? What did they communicate?

2. Say "I love you" six different ways. How does paralanguage change the meaning of the three words? What meanings did the different versions convey?

Exercise 13.5 | *Analyzing Nonverbal Communication*

Bring five large pictures from magazines to class. Analyze the nonverbal communication in each picture. What nonverbal messages are being conveyed? How?

Listening as an Acquired Skill

One of the places where our nonverbal responses is most obvious is in the communication activity of listening. Perhaps surprisingly, of all the types of communication in which we are engaged on a daily basis, we spend more time listening. For example, one study of college students found that 53 percent of their communication time was spent in listening, with only 17 percent given to reading, 16 percent

Figure 13.2 Trends in Listening Activity Among College Students

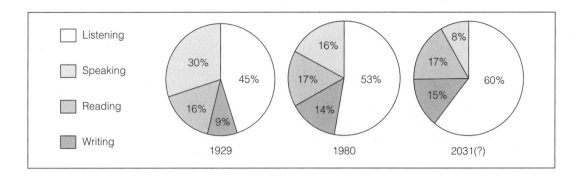

SOURCE: DeVito, 1990, p. 105.

devoted to speaking, and 14 percent dedicated to writing. Figure 13.2 compares current levels of communication time with past levels and projects possible future levels.

Bad Listening Habits

Unfortunately, most of us are such poor or inefficient listeners that we sabotage the communication process. Readily identifiable bad listening habits include the following:

- Pseudolistening—pretending to listen
- Stage-hogging—talking more than listening
- Selective listening—listening for what interests us
- Insulated listening—avoiding the unpleasant
- Defensive listening—taking offense at what's said
- Ambushing—exposing the speaker's weaknesses
- Insensitive listening—giving inappropriate responses

Undoubtedly, we have all been guilty of one or more of these bad listening habits. Perhaps the classic circumstance for observing many of these traits in action is the social occasion. In such a setting some people are inevitably exposed as pseudolisteners, revealed as such by their eyes drifting away from you and looking for someone or something more

Karen

Life between my freshman and senior years was anything but dull. It took only one semester at a large state university for total disillusionment with higher education to set in and for me to begin a circuitous journey that ended with my graduating from Marietta College and going on to law school.

You might be thinking, "That's very interesting, but what does it have to do with interpersonal communication?" The answer is, everything! It is one thing to get an A in Speech 101, but it is another to successfully translate academic success into effective interpersonal communication skills. Unfortunately, success in the former does not guarantee success in the latter.

As a perfectionist my biggest fear has always been that I might one day actually mess up. After two years of law school, I now realize that it's not what you know; it's what other people *think* you know. Effective communicators can and will be able to talk their way through any calamity. Remember the deodorant commercial with the slogan "Never let them see you sweat"? My philosophy is, if you are listening to what your parents, siblings, spouses, bosses, and professors are saying, you won't have to worry about sweating, because 99 percent of effective interpersonal communication is listening to what is being said. If you are spending more time talking than listening, chances are you're missing the message.

From this point on, as you hone your interpersonal communication skills, remember three things: (1) Even if you have no clue what you are doing, act like you do. (2) If number 1 fails, resort to listening; you'd be surprised how much more effective your interpersonal communication skills will become. (3) If numbers 1 and 2 fail, then never ever let them see you sweat! ■

interesting. Or, at the same gathering, we often wind up trying to engage in conversation with a stagehogger, who is far more interested in a captive audience than in listening. There also may be a selective listener, who nods perfunctorily at your comments until some topic strikes a responsive chord—for example, "Well, let me tell you!" Meanwhile the insulated listener avoids dreaded topics while demonstrating interest in the most irrelevant matters. The defensive listener hears all comments as attacks, prompting him or her to repel your attempts at communication. Perhaps no one is less desirable at a social event than an ambushing listener, who attacks your every word with comments like "You're wrong about that!"

"Where did you hear that?" or "Let me set you straight about that!" In some ways, however, the most exasperating conversationalist is the insensitive listener, whose response is always the same, no matter what you say—for example, "That's nice" or "That's wonderful"—regardless of whether your message actually was nice or wonderful. As W. H. Auden put it in his poem "At the Party": "A howl for recognition, shrill with fear, / Shakes the jam-packed apartment, but each ear is listening to its hearing, so none hear."

The more fundamental issue, however, is whether and how often you have engaged in any or all of these poor listening practices. If you have been guilty of these offenses, why have you done so, and what might you do to change?

Exercise 13.6

Rating Your Listening Skills

1. Consider the last party you attended. How many of your listening responses were inappropriate? How many of the people at the party behaved similarly?

2. Interview a classmate. At the conclusion of the interview, summarize the ideas presented. Based on the interviewee's response to your summary, how would you rate your own listening skills? What should you work on?

Reasons for Poor Listening

Before we plunge too deeply into self-accusation about our listening failures, we should take comfort by examining some of the reasons. If the study cited previously is true, we may spend over half of our time listening, a condition that may result in message overload. There are also times when we're too preoccupied to devote full attention to the speaker's comments or when our own capacity for rapid thought causes our concentration to waver. Sometimes we simply don't exert the necessary effort, for careful listening requires physical exertion. External noise over which we have no control also may interfere with our roles as effective listeners. Occasionally, a listener may have a physiological hearing problem that prevents effective listening, no matter how hard he or she is trying. At times we as listeners make faulty assumptions about what's being said, too often concluding that "we've heard it all before." In a world too often dominated by the tyranny of appearances, it is tempting to conclude a lack of apparent advantages from time spent listening. Certainly, many of our shortcomings as listening communicators may come from lack of training.

Improving Your Listening Skills

Whatever your shortcomings as a listener, your skills will be improved if you do the following:

1. **Talk less.** Talking less does not mean keeping absolutely silent but simply listening more carefully.

2. **Get rid of distractions.** Closing the door or turning off the stereo is often the simplest way of getting rid of distractions; another way of eliminating distractions is by paying closer attention.

3. **Don't judge prematurely.** Not judging prematurely suggests that you are giving the speaker the benefit of the doubt, not prejudging what's being said as something that's been said many times over.

4. **Look for key ideas.** Searching for key ideas means active listening in which, instead of letting your mind wander, you seek to analyze as you listen.

5. **Ask questions.** If the communication setting permits it, ask questions in order to be certain you understand.

6. **Paraphrase.** Paraphrasing is a way to compare what you think you heard with what the speaker thinks was said.

Improving Your Responding Skills

If, on the basis of improved listening, you are expected to respond, what will be the most appropriate responses? Depending on the situation you might offer any one of the following responses: advising, judging, analyzing, questioning, or supporting.

You might also ask yourself if both your listening and your responding might not benefit from the "you" attitude. If you are going to improve your listening skills in particular and your interpersonal communication skills in general, you need to think about the other person involved. Martin Buber, the well-known philosopher, wrote of changing one's thinking from "I-it" to "I-thou." In terms of interpersonal communication, the "you" attitude means treating the person who is speaking or to whom you are listening as a person about whom you care, not merely a thing or an object—an "it" in Buber's construct.

In any relationship, whether two or twenty people are involved, communication will improve if we stop thinking about the "I" (ourselves) and start thinking about the "you" (Buber's "thou"), the other person or persons with whom we are attempting to communicate or improve communications. If every one of us thinks only of what "I" want, communication will be limited because this is an entirely selfish motivation. On the other hand, asking what "you" need or want is much more likely to reduce barriers and improve communication flow.

Conclusion

Within this brief chapter we have considered the characteristics of effective interpersonal communication, a practice both necessary for survival in the world beyond college and fundamental to your happiness and self-actualization. You now recognize how instrumental a heightened awareness of nonverbal and listening skills are to effective communication. As you move into life beyond college, practice these communication skills carefully, always adopting the "you" attitude. Your expectations will be fulfilled.

References and Resources

Adler, Ronald B., and George Rodman. (1991). *Understanding Human Communication,* 4th ed. Orlando, FL: Holt, Rinehart & Winston. Every aspect of human communication—intrapersonal, interpersonal, and public—is covered in this easy-to-read volume.

Adler, Ronald B., and Neil Towne. (1990). *Looking Out; Looking In,* 6th ed. Orlando, FL: Holt, Rinehart & Winston. Color photographs, diagrams, cartoons, and exercises make this a practical guide to interpersonal communication for ages 18 to 80. An excellent, up-to-date annotated bibliography is included at the end of each chapter.

Boyd, Malcolm. (1990). "Listen Between the Lines." *Modern Maturity* (June/July): 13. Boyd forces us to realize that we often don't say what we mean and therefore that others don't hear what we mean. We need to be honest, listen carefully to the verbal and nonverbal messages, and avoid making assumptions.

DeVito, Joseph A. (1990). *Messages: Building Interpersonal Communication Skills.* New York: Harper & Row. This book takes a personal approach to nonverbal communication. The readers can test themselves in such areas as perceptions of love, conflict styles, interviewing techniques, and language usage. Suggestions for improvement are included in each chapter.

DeVito, Joseph A., and Michael L. Hecht. (1990). *The Nonverbal Communication Reader.* Prospect Heights, IL: Waveland Press. Many studies in nonverbal communication are explained and discussed. Checklists help the reader understand how to replicate the studies.

Disby, Victor. (1990). "Stop Talking and Listen: The Elmer's Glue Principle." *Cosmopolitan* (August), pp. 136–37. Disby suggests a method by which we can learn to think before talking.

Guarendi, Ray. (1990). "How to Talk So Your Kids Will Listen." *Redbook* (September), pp. 150f. This article analyzes barriers to communication in family relationships and makes suggestions for ways to establish and maintain real communication.

Katz, Albert M., and Virginia T. Katz. (1983). *Foundations of Nonverbal Communication: Readings, Exercises, and Commentary.* Carbondale: Southern Illinois University Press. The approach in this volume is more academic in the sense that the articles included are written by some of the foremost experts in the field of nonverbal communication, such as Edward T. Hall, Albert E. Scheflen, and Ray L. Birdwhistell.

Leathers, Dale G. (1976). *Nonverbal Communication Systems.* Boston: Allyn & Bacon. Anyone interested in nonverbal communication will find it interesting to compare this older study of nonverbal communication to more recent ones. Much historical background missing from newer sources can be found here.

Malandro, Loretta; Larry Barker; and Deborah Barker. (1989). *Nonverbal Communication.* New York: Random House. This book discusses all the relevant aspects of nonverbal communication from body size to personal distance. Good definitions, examples, and ideas for future research are included in each chapter.

Tanouye, Elyse T. (1990). "What Is Your Staff Afraid to Tell You?" *Working Woman* (April), pp. 35–37. Hearing bad news or criticism is unpleasant at first, but managers who purposely draw it out of employees gradually develop a thick skin. Furthermore, they develop better management skills because they understand what is going on—they know about the good, the bad, and the potentially disastrous in time to handle each.

14 Personal Finances

Lee Allen Scott, Sr.

Senior Vice President for Investments, Prudential Securities

Keisha

I've never felt anxious about managing my money. I've had a check-ing account since I was 16, I balance my account monthly, and I have never bounced a check. In addition, while I use my credit cards frequently, I always manage to pay off my debt.

But now that I've graduated, the term *money* is transforming into *finances*. My school loans will need to be paid, as will insurance pre-miums and income taxes. And it's all my responsibility. Graduating involves more than finding a job and a place to hang your diploma. It means preparing for the future and ensuring your security. I've concentrated so hard on my educational and career goals that I've neglected to form any financial goals. Needless to say, I'm feeling a lot of anxiety about these new responsibilities. ∎

Managing one's personal finances becomes more complicated every day. New and different saving and spending options, combined with more complicated tax laws, make planning for your financial future both difficult and time-consuming. Nevertheless, you must do some planning if you wish to attain even your most basic financial goals.

The key step in this process is creating a budget and using that budget to guide you in your major decisions: purchasing a car and/or house, getting married, continuing your education, and so on. Thus in this chapter we will discuss how to create a personal financial inventory and how to budget your resources. In addition, in today's world of rapid social, family, and economic change, you need more than ever to be aware of and knowledgeable about the many different aspects of your financial life that will have a direct bearing on your future happiness and success. Given this shifting landscape, we will also examine opportunities for investment, types of insurance, taxes, and the need for estate planning.

The Personal Financial Inventory

Although as an undergraduate you might scoff at the need for completing a comprehensive financial plan before graduation, your senior year is the optimal time in your life to begin such a project. The financial plan is a blueprint of your financial design. As your circumstances change, you can always modify the plan, just as you can add to the basic structure of a building you've designed. The object is to create a basic design that provides direction and focus.

Figure 14.1 shows a brief financial data sheet that can serve as the basis for a comprehensive financial plan. As this personal data sheet suggests, you should identify anything that might have a bearing on your personal finances and record this information. The data sheet documents all your current assets and liabilities (debts), and serves as a starting point for planning financial growth. Specifically, the personal financial inventory serves the following functions:

- Provides a permanent document for personal data
- Enables the establishment of particular goals and objectives
- Gives consistent format for comparing goals to actual results
- Highlights financial issues that must be resolved, such as educational loans, taxes, medical and life insurance, investments, children's education, and retirement

The importance of having a financial plan cannot be overemphasized. It has been shown time and time again that those who have a written,

Figure 14.1   Blueprint for a Personal Financial Data Sheet

PERSONAL DATA SHEET

I.   Personal Information

NAME: _____   Sex: Male ____   Female ____

(first)   (m.i.)   (last)

Residence: _____   Phone: _____

Date of Birth: ___/___/___   Social Security Number: _____

Occupation: _____

Name of Employer: _____   Title: _____

Business Address: _____   Business Phone: _____

SPOUSE

NAME: _____

(first)   (m.i.)   (last)

Date of Birth: ___/___/___   Social Security Number: _____

Occupation: _____

Name of Employer: _____   Title: _____

Business Address: _____   Business Phone: _____

CHILDREN   **EDUCATION ***

Name	Birth Date	Dependent Yes-No	Age Child Will Begin	Child's Assets	Annual Cost (Today's $)	Years of Schooling
____	____	____	____	____	____	____
____	____	____	____	____	____	____

* If you would like to provide any of your children with a private, college or graduate school education, please record the information requested.

II.   General Remarks

Are there any matters which are of particular concern to you? Describe.

_____

_____

III.   Assets

	Current Value	Owner* C,S,J	Taxable or Non-Taxable Return	Return			Current Value	Owner* C,S,J	Taxable or Non-Taxable Return	Return
Checking Accounts:	___	___	___%	___%	Municipal Bond Funds:		___	___	$___	$___
	___	___	___%	___%					$___	$___
Savings Accounts:	___	___	___%	___%	Stocks/Mutual** Stock Funds:		___	___	$___	$___
	___	___	___%	___%			___	___	$___	$___
CD's: Maturity					Personal Property					
___	___	___	___%	___%	(furnishing,		___	___		
___	___	___	___%	___%	jewelery,		___	___		
					art, etc.)		___	___		
Money Mrkt Funds:	___	___	___%	___%						
					Business Interests:		___	___		
Government Securities:	___	___	___	$___	$___		___	___		
	___	___	___	$___	$___	Other Assets:		___	___	$___	$___
Corporate Bond/Funds:	___	___	___	$___	$___			___	___	$___	$___
	___	___	___	$___	$___						

*As used here and throughout questionnaire C=client, S=spouse, J=joint.

**Include only traded securities. Closely held corporate stock should be recorded under Business Interests.

SINGLE PREMIUM ANNUITIES

Company	Current Value	Owner C. S. J	Interest Rate	Purchase Date	Beneficiary* CL,SP,CH,OT	Annuitant* CL,SP,CH,OT
____	____	____	____	____	____	____

*CL = Client; SP = Spouse; CH = Child; OT = Othe

NOTES AND MORTGAGES RECEIVABLE

Description	Current Value	Owner C. S. J	Taxable Income +/-	Non-Taxable Income	Interest Rate	Cap.Gain Maturity	Ratio*
____	____	____	____	____	____	____	____

* For receipts resulting from the sale of an asset, please indicate the percentage of each principal payment withich is capital gains.

(continued)

Figure 14.1 (continued)

REAL ESTATE

	Current Value	Owner C. S. J	Taxable Income +/	Net* Cash Flow +/-	Mortgage Balance	Mortgage Rate	Mortgage Maturity
Residence							
Vacation Home							
Other (Describe)							

* Total Income minus expense for maintaining property. This amount may exceed taxable income.

IV. Liabilities

List debts *not previously recorded.*

Nature	Balance Due	Debtor C. S. J	Monthly Payments	Due Date	Interest Rate

V. Retirement Plans

Type *	Employee C. S	Current Value	% Vested	Annual Contribution Employee Employer	Annual Rate of Return	Retirement Benefit Lump Sum or Monthly	Age Available	Death Benefit

* = IRA, K = Keogh, Q = Qualified Plan, N = Non-Qualified Plan

VI. Insurance

LIFE

Company	Insured CL. SP	Owner CL. SP	Face Amount	Beneficiary CL.SP.CH.OT	Cash Value	Policy Loans	Annual Premium	Type*

* W = Whole Life, G = Group, T = Term

DISABILITY

Company	Insured CL. SP	Monthly Benefit	Waiting Period	Age Paid to	Annual Premium	Type*

* I = Individual, G = Group

VII. Income, Expenses, Tax Data

Please list your estimated income this year from the following sources.

	Amount by Recipient	
Source	Client	Spouse
Salaries		
Self-Employment		
Bonuses		
Social Security		
Pensions/Annuities		
Trusts		
State Tax Refund		
Short Term Capital Gains/(Losses)*		
Long Term Capital Gains/(Losses)*		
Other Taxable Income**		
Other Non-Taxable Income*		

* Only include gains or losses that have occurred this year.
**Do not include income from previously listed investments.

Please record the following items in annual amounts.

Total Family Living Expenses *or* Expected Annual Savings (exluding retirement plan contributions)	
Filing Status*	
Number of Exemptions	
Alimony Payments	
Unreimbursed Business Expenses	
Total Itemized Deductions	
Total Tax Credits	

*J = Joint, S = Single, H = Head Of Household.

VIII. Objectives

PERSONAL NEEDS

For each of the following areas indicate the *monthly* pretax income required by your and/or your family. State your objective in current dollars. Also rank each in order of importance (1 = most important).

	Amount	Rank
Disability Income Need:	_____	_____
Retirement Income Need:	_____	_____
Retirement Age:		
Client _____		
Spouse _____		
Survivor Income Need:		_____
Today	_____	
After children are independent	_____	

Investment Concerns

Please categorize your tolerance for investment risk.

Risk Tolerance
High (H), Medium (M), Low (L)   _____
Rank the following investment characteristics in order of importance (1 = most important)

	Rank
Income	_____
Growth	_____
Tax Avoidance	_____
Liquidity	_____
Diversity	_____

IX. General Information

Are you covered by Social Security? (Y, N) _____
Is your spouse covered by Social Security? (Y, N) _____
Are you self-employed? (Y, N) _____
Is your spouse self-employed? (Y, N) _____
What would you consider a reasonable pretax average annual total return (growth plus yield) on your investments? _____ %
What would you consider a reasonable pretax average annual yield on investments chosen for their income potential? _____ %

What would you consider a reasonable average annual inflation rate to anticipate? _____ %
Do you have a will? _____
Date of will _____/_____/_____
Total debts to be paid off at death _____
Amount of emergency fund to be set aside in the event of death _____

X. Portfolio Details (As of   /   /   )

In order for us to serve you more effectively, it is important that we have detailed information concerning your specific investment holdings. Please provide the following information. It is assumed that this material has been previously recorded in summary form.

Stocks

No. of Shares	Name of Security	Owner C. S. J	Date Acquired	Basis - Cost/Share	Current Price/Share	Taxable Income	Non-Taxable Income
			/ /			$	$
			/ /			$	$

Bonds

Description	Face Amount	Owner C. S. J	Date Acquired	Basis- Cost	Current Price	Coupon Rate	Maturity Date	Taxable Income Y//N
			/ /					
			/ /					

Mutual Funds

No. of Shares	Name of Fund	Owner C. S. J	Date Acquired	Basis- Cost/Share	Current Price/Share	Taxable Income	Non-Taxable Income
			/ /			$	$
			/ /			$	$

comprehensive plan are much more likely to achieve their financial goals than are those who plan but fail to commit it to writing. Although at this point in your life you may find this data sheet far too extensive, you should begin to fill in the details about your assets and liabilities. As your financial situation changes, you should record the changes on a regular basis. In fact, you should develop the habit now of reviewing, correcting, and updating at least semi-annually and preferably quarterly.

Cash Flow Analysis/Budget

Once you complete the personal data sheet, you can establish the priorities according to which you will allocate your total resources. Only with a *written* plan, however, can you use your assets most effectively. Spending without a plan often leads to excessive debt, lack of proper protection against risks, and failure to achieve the financial independence that so many of you have as your basic financial goal. Keep in mind that once you are out of college, you will be called on by salespeople, each claiming that his or her product meets your most important and immediate need, whether it be car insurance, mutual funds, life insurance, or so forth. Listening to salespeople without regard to your plan can lead to a serious cash shortage.

Faced with the temptation to purchase unplanned-for goods and services, many people resort to institutional credit, often through credit cards. Thus they run a double risk: purchasing without regard to their financial plan and making heavy investment payments that are no longer tax deductible. This spending pattern has produced an explosion of debt throughout the United States in recent years. And because changes in the tax laws have caused interest payments to become extraordinarily expensive, such payments generally should be avoided. A few notable exceptions include home purchases, business investments, and/or investments for continuing education in order to satisfy financial and/or personal goals and objectives.

The key point is the need to prepare a cash flow analysis/budget (Figure 14.2) to guide you in living within your means. The following two suggestions will help you budget more efficiently:

1. Write a check to a money market account at the start of each month and then live on what is left. A rule of thumb is to set aside 10–20 percent to meet unexpected contingencies and to provide a stream of savings.

2. Check the balance in your checkbook at the same time each month (after rent, car payments, and so on) and make sure it is growing according to your financial plan.

Figure 14.2 Cash Flow/Budget

CASH FLOW/BUDGET

MONTHLY INCOME	Jan	Feb	Mar	Apr	May	Jun	Jul	Aug	Sep	Oct	Nov	Dec
Wages and Salary												
Dividends from Stocks												
Interest on Savings, CD's, Bonds												
Capital Gains												
Other (Pensions, Soc Sec, etc.)												
TOTAL MONTHLY INCOME $												
MONTHLY EXPENSES												
Mortgage Payment or Rent												
Automobile Loans												
Personal Loans												
Charge Accounts												
Income Taxes												
Social Security												
Real Estate Taxes												
Transportation												
Life Insurance												
Homeowners Insurance												
Savings & Investments												
Contributions												
Household Maintenance												
Furniture												
Gas												
Electricity												
Telephone												
Water												
Other Local Government Services												
Food												
Clothing												
Medical												
Entertainment												
Club Dues												
Vacation Home Mortgage												
Education Expenses												
Other Expenses												
TOTAL MONTHLY EXPENSES $												

TOTAL MONTHLY INCOME: $_____

TOTAL MONTHLY EXPENSES: $_____

DISCRETIONARY MONTHLY INCOME: $_____

(Subtract your expenses from your income)

Remember, your personal financial inventory and cash flow analysis/budget must be completed in detail in order for you to be in a position to consider other major aspects of financial planning.

Risk Management/Insurance

R isk is defined as the probability of something happening other than what you expect. An integral part of your personal financial plan should be insurance to protect you against unforeseen expenses for which you cannot adequately budget. As you think about insurance, the key question to ask yourself is whether you are protecting yourself and your family in the event of death, disability, lawsuit, liability, or loss of property. Those of you who will be working for major companies will have many needs met in the most cost-efficient way through company employee benefit and welfare programs. These programs generally are comprehensive in nature and include not only a core of required benefits (for example, life, medical, dental, disability, and retirement) but also additional options for tailoring coverage to meet your specific needs.

In determining your future insurance needs, you should carefully weigh the following: (1) life insurance, (2) health insurance, (3) disability insurance, (4) homeowners insurance, (5) automobile insurance, (6) liability insurance, and (7) apartment dweller/condominium insurance. In short, you must consider how your insurance needs will change upon graduation from college, taking into account your new lifestyle and health needs, and the special requirements of those of you who have dependents, a spouse, and/or children.

Life Insurance

Life insurance provides a death benefit to the beneficiary you name and takes one of two basic forms—term or whole life. At the risk of oversimplification, term insurance is a policy whereby you pay a premium for a specific amount of protection. The younger you are when you buy a term policy, the lower the premiums. Thus it is advantageous to buy term insurance at the earliest possible age. Remember, however, that term insurance accumulates no cash value through the life of the policy. You are paying for protection only, not for savings. By contrast, the premium for whole life or permanent insurance is higher than the premiums for an equivalent amount of term insurance, but the policy not only provides a death benefit but also accumulates a cash value. Again, the younger you are when you buy the policy, the lower your premiums will be. Although some people believe that permanent insurance is always better than term insurance, there are times when permanent insurance is simply too expensive for your income level and financial plans. In those instances term insurance may be the answer.

Before purchasing life insurance, you should sit down with a knowledgeable, qualified insurance professional and decide how much insurance is appropriate given your financial resources. You can then purchase a proper blend of term and permanent life to satisfy your needs. Should you decide on term, be sure to choose a policy that permits later conversion—without medical examination—to permanent life. Finally, in the event that you become disabled, you will want a policy with a waiver of premium provision, which allows the insurance to be continued without any additional premium payment.

Medical Insurance

Everyone should be aware of the need for adequate medical insurance, which provides protection against accidents and sickness. The premiums for this insurance are very expensive. Most employers provide access to group insurance, which is normally the most affordable and most comprehensive medical coverage available. Some employers require the employee to pay a portion of the premium.

A major problem for many college graduates is that their medical coverage under their parents' and/or school's group insurance program terminates after graduation. A number of alternatives, however, are available. Those fortunate enough to secure jobs with employers who provide employee benefits will be covered almost immediately. In the event that you have not secured employment where insurance is offered or are attending graduate or professional school, current law allows for coverage to continue if you participated in a group insurance plan prior to graduation. Once begun, insurance may be continued under certain circumstances for periods up to thirty-six months. However, it's your responsibility to pursue this option.

In the absence of that option, you still need to maintain medical coverage. In order to keep the premiums as low as possible, you should buy medical insurance with a high deductible and co-insurance. To illustrate, consider a policy with $500 deductible and a co-insurance of 80 percent/20 percent. Under this plan, if you were to incur $1,000 worth of medical expenses, the insurance company would cover you according to this schedule: $1,000 − $500 = $500 x 80% = $400. Thus you would have to pay $600 in medical fees. Your financial plan and budget will help you determine whether you can meet the deductible amounts.

The danger you face is that if you don't have medical insurance and a major illness or accident occurs, you might be devastated financially. Moreover, if your parents help you out in such circumstances, they might also face disastrous consequences. Medical insurance can provide protection.

Disability Insurance

The risk of disability (the inability to work) is far greater than the risk of death for individuals under age 65, and the expenses stemming from a disability are a tremendous burden on the family as well as the disabled individual. For some people Social Security may provide adequate coverage. Others who participate in employee benefit programs are probably eligible for or automatically included under company disability programs. If you need to purchase your own disability policy, you can keep the premiums relatively low by choosing a policy that features a waiting period (six months or longer) before benefits kick in. A recommended level of coverage would be a policy that pays 50 to 60 percent of earnings.

Homeowners Insurance

Those who own their homes need fire, comprehensive liability, and theft insurance in amounts that, insofar as possible, provide for replacement costs of the structure and its contents. In addition, a good homeowners policy protects the individual owner and his or her assets in the event that someone else is injured while on the property.

Automobile Insurance

Most states now mandate minimal levels of personal liability coverage. You should carefully review your auto insurance policy, not to meet the minimum levels of liability, but rather to ensure that it provides enough coverage to protect against a personal injury lawsuit.

Liability Insurance

A comprehensive umbrella personal liability policy of $1 million or more provides relatively inexpensive protection from a lawsuit. The importance of this coverage cannot be overemphasized because courts continue to award plaintiffs increasingly escalating monetary settlements in civil proceedings.

Apartment Dweller/Condominium Insurance

This type of policy is very similar to homeowners insurance except that it applies solely to risks associated with contents (furnishings, clothing, and so on).

Income Taxes

Tax planning is a natural extension of the basic planning and budgeting processes that have been discussed previously. The purpose of tax planning is to understand current tax laws so that you can take every advantage to maximize investment performance, increase your net disposable insurance, and reduce tax burdens. Basic concepts in tax planning that will affect your personal finances include (1) debt management, (2) asset conversion, and (3) tax deferral.

Debt Management

Perhaps the most insidious erosion of purchasing power results from debt incursion. During the 1980s we saw an explosion of consumer debt brought on largely by favorable tax laws. In 1986, however, those laws changed abruptly to the detriment of the consumer. Consequently, you should exercise great caution in using credit cards. Consider this rule of thumb: Use credit cards only in the event of an emergency or when purchasing within a preestablished budget. Too often people fall into the trap of using credit cards and absorbing exorbitantly high nondeductible interest costs while at the same time paying taxes on interest earned in taxable savings accounts, certificates of deposit (CDs), and/or money market funds. Thus, in the absence of a cash reserve, you should avoid incurring credit card debt. Save your credit card for an emergency.

Asset Conversion

Simply put, asset conversion means taking assets that are taxed as ordinary income and converting them into tax-free or tax-favored income. To illustrate, consider a couple in the 28 percent tax bracket (which is not unusual for recent college graduates) where both spouses work and can get a 6 percent interest rate on tax-free municipal bonds. To achieve the same after-tax yield, they would have to find CDs, Treasury bills, or money market accounts yielding 8.33 percent. This spread becomes even more significant if state tax rates are involved. Therefore conversion of taxable investment income to tax-free income through the purchase of municipal bonds can be desirable in many cases. Table 14.1 shows the relationship between tax-free and taxable investments. For example, if you are in the 28 percent tax bracket, your CD or money market account would have to pay 5.56 percent interest in order to equal the yield on a 4 percent tax-free municipal bond.

Table 14.1 The Relationship Between Tax-Free and Taxable Investments

	Tax-Free Yield (%)						
	4.00	5.00	6.00	7.00	8.00	9.00	Tax Bracket (%)
Taxable Yield (%)	4.71	5.88	7.06	8.24	9.41	10.59	15
	5.56	6.94	8.33	9.72	11.11	12.50	28
	6.00	7.50	9.00	10.50	12.00	13.50	33

Tax Deferral

Another tax strategy is deferral, which means postponing current tax liability to some future time. The strategy involves investing a portion of your income in a tax-deferred retirement account. After retirement you will pay taxes on the investment and all interest it has earned. In all likelihood, however, because your retirement income will be relatively low, you will pay less tax than you would have at the time you earned the money. Four common methods of deferring taxes are individual retirement accounts (IRAs), Keogh plans for the self-employed, 401(k) plans through your employer, and annuities. Deferral of taxes using all or any of these methods enables your investment to grow at a much faster rate.

To illustrate the benefits of tax-deferred compounding, assume that two investors, each in a 28 percent bracket, invest $100,000 and each earns the same 8 percent rate of return. One pays taxes on earnings before reinvesting, while the other's investment earns tax-deferred interest. The tax-deferred investment will grow to more than $465,000 in twenty years, while the taxed investment will grow to less than $306,000.

Investments

After you have completed your personal financial data sheet, prepared a budget, insured yourself against risk, and planned for taxes, you should consider a long-term investment program. Economic uncertainty, new financial instruments, and changing laws and regulations are just three reasons that people need a financial strategy to meet their individual needs.

One of the objectives of financial planning is to create a diversified portfolio based on your assets, income, tax bracket, goals and objectives, and, most importantly, risk tolerance. It's critical that you begin to save and invest as early in life as possible. If you want the money for a car or graduate school next year, however, be sure to invest in liquid investments—that is, those that can be readily converted to cash. Some investments, such as trusts and IRAs, cannot be relied on for buying homes, cars, and the like since conversion to cash results in severe penalties. In the case of trusts, funds may simply not be available in time. Stocks and mutual funds can be cashed in, but often at a high cost. Thus you need to choose investments that will best serve your needs.

In order to understand your own risk tolerance, you need to understand the concept of risk in relation to investments. Risk may be defined as the uncertainty of your return on an investment. For example, a high-risk investment could easily lead to partial or total loss of your capital. Risk and return are correlatives of each other. In general, the greater the perceived risk, the greater the anticipated return; similarly, the lower the risk, the lower the expected return. You can minimize risk through a diversified and balanced portfolio.

In general, diversification and asset allocation (in stocks, bonds, mutual funds, cash, and real estate) yield higher returns than single-asset investing. In order to achieve diversification, you need to understand the options available to you. The investment pyramid in Figure 14.3 categorizes investment options according to risk and can help you structure a balanced portfolio. Note that the pyramid is divided into three sections: (1) low-risk "safe foundation" investments, (2) moderate-risk growth investments, and (3) high-risk aggressive-growth investments.

The base of the pyramid consists of conservative investments. Every sound investment plan rests on this kind of solid base, which represents your long-term security. Investments in this category could include your home, money market funds, bank accounts, CDs, pension plans, Treasury bills, deferred annuities, permanent life insurance, government securities, high-grade bonds, and bond funds (including zero-coupon, government, and investment-grade municipal bonds).

The middle section contains moderate-risk investments. These can include stocks, mutual funds, convertible and corporate bonds, real estate, equipment leasing, oil and gas income funds, precious metals, and stock options. As we ascend the pyramid, we move from more conservative growth instruments such as blue-chip stocks or convertible bonds to the more aggressive growth instruments, such as some mutual funds and real estate.

Finally, the top section contains high-risk ventures in which you might invest the dollars you can afford to speculate with. For example, you might purchase new-issue stocks, commodity futures or options, low-quality bonds (those rated BB or lower), precious gems, collectibles, and oil- and gas-drilling partnerships.

The key point to remember when analyzing your portfolio in terms of the investment pyramid is that each person's situation is unique and that no one pyramid is right for everyone. For example, you might focus

Figure 14.3 Investment Pyramid

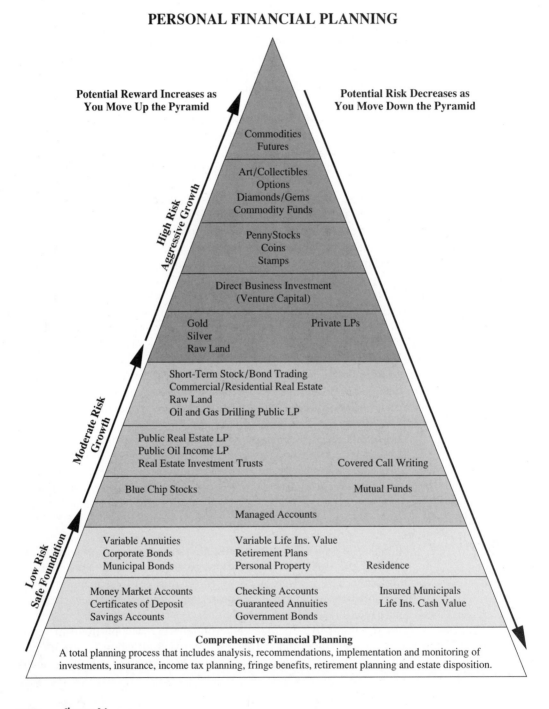

PERSONAL FINANCIAL PLANNING

Potential Reward Increases as
You Move Up the Pyramid

Potential Risk Decreases as
You Move Down the Pyramid

High Risk
Aggressive Growth

Commodities
Futures

Art/Collectibles
Options
Diamonds/Gems
Commodity Funds

PennyStocks
Coins
Stamps

Direct Business Investment
(Venture Capital)

Gold
Silver
Raw Land

Private LPs

Moderate Risk
Growth

Short-Term Stock/Bond Trading
Commercial/Residential Real Estate
Raw Land
Oil and Gas Drilling Public LP

Public Real Estate LP
Public Oil Income LP
Real Estate Investment Trusts

Covered Call Writing

Blue Chip Stocks

Mutual Funds

Managed Accounts

Low Risk
Safe Foundation

Variable Annuities
Corporate Bonds
Municipal Bonds

Variable Life Ins. Value
Retirement Plans
Personal Property

Residence

Money Market Accounts
Certificates of Deposit
Savings Accounts

Checking Accounts
Guaranteed Annuities
Government Bonds

Insured Municipals
Life Ins. Cash Value

Comprehensive Financial Planning
A total planning process that includes analysis, recommendations, implementation and monitoring of
investments, insurance, income tax planning, fringe benefits, retirement planning and estate disposition.

your investments in the top or risky portion of the pyramid at a very young age knowing that time has a means of working out negative situations. As you get older, however, shifting toward the base of the pyramid is normally advised because of the lack of available time to rebound from negative market fluctuations.

Keep in mind also that investing in stocks over a long period of time has proven to yield a higher return than investing in bonds, money market funds, cash, Treasury bills, and CDs. How you divide your investments between stocks and bonds, however, depends on your age—the younger you are, the greater the proportion of the investment portfolio that should be oriented to equity investments.

In sum, investment is critical to building long-term wealth because of the potential need for supplements to social security and normal retirement plans. Because investments compound over a long period of time, the earlier you begin building your portfolio, the more gain you will accrue.

Estate Planning

Although a discussion of estate planning directed to college seniors in transition may seem inappropriate, estate planning remains an important, and often misunderstood, part of everyone's life. In simple terms, estate planning is lifetime planning for the transfer of assets after your death, in accord with your wishes, and at the least possible tax cost. A properly structured estate plan allows you to choose your beneficiaries, provide for the management of assets, and eliminate or reduce taxes. If improperly structured, an estate could pass to unintended beneficiaries or be reduced in value by unnecessary taxes or unsound investments. Your will, drafted by a competent attorney, should address these issues.

Unfortunately, even though experience has proven the wisdom of executing a properly planned will, many Americans continue to die without a will. If you fail to draft a will, your probate property will be distributed according to the laws of the state in which you were residing at the time of your death. This may result in unnecessary federal and state death taxes.

To be valid, a will must be created and executed in accordance with specific state laws. If you have thought of drafting and executing a will without an attorney, *don't!*

Conclusion

In this chapter we have examined the complex subject of personal financial planning by identifying some basic concepts that should provide you with the knowledge needed to develop an effective financial plan. As you plan for your financial future, remember the importance of writing the plan down, budgeting, setting priorities, managing risk, developing investments, and planning for taxes. Equally important, remember not to use credit cards, try to do it yourself, risk more than you can afford to lose, buy anything if you do not understand the risk, or leave yourself exposed to risk. If you follow the simple steps outlined here, your financial future should be a bright one.

References and Resources

Hallman, G. Victor, and Jerry S. Rosenbloom. (1981). *Personal Financial Planning—How to Plan for Your Financial Freedom*, 2nd ed. New York: McGraw-Hill.

Leimberg, Stephan R., and John J. McFadden. (1990). *The Tools and Techniques of Employee Benefit and Retirement Planning*, 2nd ed. Cincinnati: National Underwriter Company.

Leimberg, Stephan R., et al. (1990). *The Tools and Techniques of Estate Planning*, 8th ed. Cincinnati: National Underwriter Company.

———. (1988). *The Tools and Techniques of Financial Planning*, 3rd ed. Cincinnati: National Underwriter Company.

Wollack, Richard G. (1985). *The Financial Desk Book—Your Complete Guide to Financial Planning, Investments, Taxation, and Estate Planning*. Emeryville, CA: Richard G. Wollack, Consolidated Capital Communications Group.

15 Healthy Lifestyles

Lisa Ann Mohn

Director of Health and Welfare Programs,
University of South Carolina

Lisa Ann Mohn

Director of Health and Welfare Programs,
University of South Carolina

Senior Voices

Jenny

Like many of you, I have been on a "wellness rollercoaster" since I began my freshman year. When the dreaded "freshman fifteen" pounds became a reality, I decided that something had to give. The first step was identifying exactly what wellness meant. This is not an easy task, but through experimentation and, most importantly, education I achieved a better understanding of what health and wellness encompass. Unfortunately, many people measure health and wellness solely in terms of physical fitness and body image. A sound diet and regular exercise are certainly an integral part of a healthy lifestyle, but the most valuable lesson I have learned concerns the more abstract aspects of health.

For me wellness means accepting yourself while always pushing ahead. It means realizing your limitations but maintaining your expectations. It means staying in touch with your emotions and constantly reevaluating yourself. In short, wellness is a state of body *and* mind. Looking back over this four-year journey, I realize that the acquisition of knowledge and motivation are the keys to a healthy lifestyle. If you have the tools to make a change and the desire to do so, a positive outcome is inevitable. ∎

As with other aspects of life, college graduates have varying experiences with their health behaviors after they leave the college environment. In fact, we could group graduates into three general categories: (1) those who don't change many of their habits, (2) those whose health and lifestyle behaviors actually worsen, (3) and those who make a conscious effort to improve their health and wellness. The course you take will depend on the value you place on your health, the competing priorities in your life at any given time, and the risks you believe you'll face if you change or don't change.

In this chapter we'll outline some of the options you'll be facing, along with the negative and positive consequences of the choices you'll make. To some of you this will be new information; to others it will merely be review. What is important is that you realize the extent to which you have control over your health. Genetics and luck play a part in how each of our lives will unfold, but what we *do*, consciously or unconsciously, will most likely be a greater determinant of our future health.

Your Future Health Options

To help you begin considering your options, let's discuss the three categories mentioned previously. On the one hand, you can choose to maintain many of your old habits after leaving college. Whether this is good or bad will naturally depend on your prior commitment to a healthy lifestyle. Like many college students you may not have practiced the healthiest behaviors, and whatever you did may have been because of convenience or happenstance. For instance, if yours was a typical college diet, you may benefit simply by being in a different environment (for example, having a kitchen of your own for the first time). Likewise, college students often do not get enough sleep, but this may change because of fewer demands on your time and more privacy.

On the other hand, your health may suffer. Perhaps it was easier to get regular exercise when you played on intramural teams or could stroll from the dorm or classroom to the gym. Maybe it was easier to access regular medical care when it was already paid for and was offered right on campus. The important thing to realize is that if you don't make a conscious decision to stay healthy and practice positive lifestyle behaviors, your health probably will suffer.

The graduates whose health and lifestyle suffer noticeably after college often feel they have no choice in the matter. Many times this change is due to increasing demands on their time. It may be hard to imagine now that you could have *more* demands on your time, but for some the world outside of college holds responsibilities that college didn't. Even with all the demands, in college you may have had more control than you'll ever have over your schedule. To an aspiring professional a new job can mean putting in many hours of overtime. A simple task like eating can become more complex when it involves going to the grocery store and preparing meals, as opposed to walking to the dining hall, presenting a mealcard, and filling a tray. While this happens to many graduates, it doesn't have to. Once again it is a matter of making your health a top priority.

If this all sounds rather discouraging, take heart. Some people find it easier and more rewarding than ever to begin and maintain a healthy lifestyle after college. Often these people found the demands and stress of college overwhelming but experience a greater sense of control over their time now that they are in a different environment. The transition from college can involve so many dramatic lifestyle changes that many seniors find the motivation to embark on untried paths and begin anew.

| **Exercise 15.1** | *Assessing Your Current Health* |

As you begin to determine your future health status, it may be helpful to assess where you are now. Draw a line down the middle of a sheet of paper. Head one column "Strengths" and the other "Weaknesses." Now consider how healthy your behaviors are in the following categories: Nutrition, Fitness, Stress Management, Weight Control, Tobacco Use, Alcohol/Other Drug Use, Sexuality, Emotional Support Network, Medical Self-Care, and anything else that comes to mind. Place these items in the appropriate column. This chart should give you an idea of where you'll need to start working to improve your health and wellness.

What Is Wellness, and Why Is It Important?

Most people are familiar with the concept of health, but the term *wellness*, and all it embraces, may be new to you. We include a discussion of wellness here to remind you that taking care of the precious commodity you call your body means more than simply living a long time or avoiding illness. Achieving wellness also means feeling good. Many people in society, including college students, accept a low level of wellness as normal. Perhaps you or some of your friends spent your college years feeling mediocre much of the time—tired, hung over, out of shape. Unless you are ill with a temporary infection or a chronic disease, however, feeling "blah" is not the way it's supposed to be! According to the wellness perspective you don't avoid fast food just because the fat can raise your cholesterol level, but also because you feel sleepy and sluggish after eating it. You don't exercise just because it's good for your cardiovascular system and weight control, but also because you feel alive and energized and proud of yourself after a workout.

Embodied in the idea of wellness are two important concepts: self-responsibility and moderation. Self-responsibility is crucial; healthy behaviors don't just happen. There has to be some conscious effort and action on your part. Most people tend to take the easy way out, thinking they can buy their health: They wait around until they get sick, and then pay doctors to heal them. This approach is probably not ideal. While we can't control everything that happens to us, we certainly can maximize our own potential for health and well-being.

Moderation is another key component to wellness, because our excessive behaviors tend to be most detrimental. Being well—emotionally, physically, and spiritually—means balancing all the areas of your life. Therefore being obsessed with anything, even if it's a healthy behavior like exercise, can be unhealthy. You don't have to become a vegetarian, give up sex or alcohol, run fifty miles a week, or do anything else that dramatic in order to practice a wellness lifestyle. Keep in mind that the goal is to maintain health and prolong life but that *quality* of life is essential to the meaning of wellness.

Starting on the Road to Healthy Behaviors

How, then, do you achieve wellness? Let's focus on the following specific areas: (1) nutrition, (2) exercise, (3) weight control, (4) stress management, (5) sex, and (6) alcohol and other drugs.

Nutrition

Perhaps you're a skeptic. If you keep up with the news, you have probably come across conflicting media reports about how beneficial this or that nutritional practice is. It may have seemed that one month oat bran helped to lower your cholesterol and another month it didn't. If you look carefully, however, you will find that the major reputable sources on health issues—the American Cancer Society, the American Heart Association, the surgeon general—agree on what's best for us to eat. Moreover, they base their recommendations on a large body of research data, not on the findings of one or two random studies.

The bottom line is that complex carbohydrates and high fiber, including lots of fresh vegetables, fruits, and whole grains, are in, and fat and cholesterol are out. For example, the build-up of plaque on the walls of the arteries as a result of high cholesterol can lead to cardiovascular disease and atherosclerosis. Because this build-up takes place over many years, you may not reap immediate benefits from lowered cholesterol. Nevertheless, you're not too young to be concerned about this. Likewise, a diet rich in animal fats and low in fiber has been linked to cancer of the colon, and high-fat diets are also thought to play a part in the development of breast cancer. Certainly, people who follow the recommended diet may experience more "regularity" in their digestive systems. And a high-carbohydrate, low-fat diet is definitely the diet of choice for weight control because fat is more than twice as calorie-dense as protein and carbohydrates. In addition, you will find that you can eat a larger quantity of food when your diet is low in fat. Finally, a growing body of research indicates that in a diet featuring an excess of calories, those coming from fat are most likely to be stored as body fat; the body burns excess calories from carbohydrates much more efficiently.

How are these recommendations translated into actual eating practices? In broad terms you should meet your daily caloric requirements using the following breakdown of nutrients: 10–15 percent protein, 20–30 percent fat, 55–70 percent carbohydrates. In other words you should consume 2 servings of dairy products (preferably skim or low-fat sources), 2 servings from the meat/fish/poultry/bean/nuts/legumes group (emphasizing low-fat choices by limiting intake of red meat and pork, and including nonanimal protein sources), and fruits and vegetables (5–7 servings per day) and grains (4–8 servings per day, emphasizing complex carbohydrates like whole wheat bread, brown rice, and so on).

Exercise 15.2

Assessing Your Nutritional Habits

Before you can begin to change your eating habits, you need to know what they are. This quiz helps you evaluate your nutritional choices. The more points you get, the better your nutritional health is.

For each question answered "yes," give yourself 1 point. Then add up your points and compare them to the total possible.

Circle point score if applicable to your diet:

PART I

1. I usually do not eat more than a total of 6 oz. of meat, fish, or poultry each day.   1 point

2. I do not eat red meats (beef or pork) more than 2 times a week.   1 point

3. I remove fat or ask that fat be trimmed from meat before cooking.   1 point

SOURCE: Prepared by Dr. Roger G. Sargent, Professor, Department of Health Education, University of South Carolina. Used with permission.

4. I have no more than 3 fresh eggs per week, either in other foods or separately. 1 point

5. I sometimes have meatless days. 1 point

6. I usually broil, boil, bake, or roast meat, fish, or poultry. 1 point

TOTAL POINTS EARNED _____

PART II

7. I have 2 servings of milk or milk products each day. 1 point

8. I drink low fat or skim milk (1% or less butterfat) rather than whole milk. 1 point

9. I eat no more than 2 moderate servings of ice cream or ice milk per week. 1 point

10. I use butter, margarine, and oils sparingly. 1 point

TOTAL POINTS EARNED _____

PART III

11. I have at least 5 servings of fruits and vegetables each day. 1 point

12. I eat at least 1 vitamin A or beta carotene rich selection (broccoli, carrots, sweet potato, greens, tomatoes, winter squash, cantaloupe) each day. 1 point

13. I eat at least 1 vitamin C rich selection (citrus fruits, honeydew, watermelon, tomatoes, broccoli, greens, asparagus, potatoes) each day. 1 point

14. I eat vegetables from the cabbage family (broccoli, cabbage, cauliflower, Brussels sprouts) several times a week. 1 point

15. I cook vegetables without fat. 1 point

TOTAL POINTS EARNED _____

PART IV

16. I generally eat whole grain breads and cereals. 1 point

17. Cereals that I eat are usually high in fiber. 1 point

18. Cereals that I buy are low in added sugar. 1 point

19. I eat brown rice instead of common white enriched rice. 1 point

20. I would generally have at least 6 servings of bread or cereal grains each day. 1 point

TOTAL POINTS EARNED _____

PART V

21. I am usually within a healthy weight range. 1 point

22. I have no more than 1 (for women) to 2 (for men) drinks per day, no more than a few times per week.   1 point

23. I do not add salt to food after preparation and prefer foods salted lightly or not salted at all.   1 point

24. I try to avoid food high in refined sugar and add it sparingly to coffee, tea, and recipes.   1 point

25. I always eat a breakfast of at least bread or cereal and fruit or fruit juices.   1 point

TOTAL POINTS EARNED _____

Circle the number of points earned for each part of the quiz. Place totals in lines designated at end of columns.

YOUR NUTRITIONAL RATING

	Excellent	Good	Fair	Poor	Your Score
PART I	5–6	4	3	2	_____
PART II	4	3	2	1	_____
PART III	5	4	3	2	_____
PART IV	5	4	3	2	_____
PART V	5	4	3	2	_____

TOTAL POINTS EARNED _____

Excellent 24–25
Good   19–23
Fair   14–18
Poor   9–13
How do you rate your score? _____

If you are planning to do more cooking after college, you will be in a good position to modify your eating habits. When you prepare a meal, you have total control over the ingredients and the method of preparation. You may have to experiment a bit to find out which healthy foods you enjoy, such as the wide array of low-fat, low-calorie salad dressings, spreads, and the like.*

For those of you who will still be eating out often, be aware that eating healthfully means examining the menu with a critical eye. Method of cooking is one way to determine a dish's healthfulness. For example, baked, broiled, or steamed foods are better for you than fried foods. And

---

*The References and Resource section at the end of the chapter lists several cookbooks you might consider if healthful cooking is a new concept for you or you'd like to expand your repertoire of healthful meals.

fresh fruit and vegetables are more likely to have retained their fiber, vitamins, and minerals than those heavily cooked. You should also be conscious of portion sizes. It's easy to gain weight when eating out frequently because portions are often too large for moderate eaters. Thus consider splitting a main course with a friend while each of you has a side salad or else taking half your meal home for lunch the next day—a great way to cut down on costs when you're just starting out.

When shopping for food, it's important to be skeptical of advertising hype, particularly relating to fat and cholesterol. Do not take what manufacturers tell you at face value. Manufacturers often label something as "cholesterol free" since everyone wants to jump on this popular bandwagon. Note, however, that, unless it contains animal products, the item never had dietary cholesterol in it to begin with. You should also be aware that an item can contain no cholesterol and still be high in saturated fat (called serum or blood cholesterol), which can raise the cholesterol levels in your body.

Another common misperception in the world of food products relates to labeling foods "low-fat" when in fact a large majority of calories in the product comes from fat. One example is processed lunch meat. Ninety-two percent fat-free may sound like a healthy, low-fat product. But if you read the label, you will see that a relatively low-calorie serving contains two or three grams of fat, giving you perhaps 40–50 percent of the calories from fat. Remember the recommendation of no more than 20–30 percent fat in your diet per day; thus the lunch meat is a high-fat product. Another example relates to milk. Two-percent milk surely sounds like it contains little fat. However, whole milk only contains 4 percent! The measurement you're being given is by weight, but if you calculated the calories coming from fat in the product, you would find that 50 percent of the calories come from fat in the whole milk, and 35 percent from fat in the 2-percent milk. This is why 1-percent or skim milk is the better choice.

It's easy to calculate the percentage of fat in a product by following a few simple steps:

1. Consult the product's label for nutrition information per serving. A sample label might show the following data:

    SERVING SIZE: 4 ounces

    SERVINGS PER PACKAGE: 2

    CALORIES: 280

    PROTEIN: 6 grams

    CARBOHYDRATES: 26 grams

    FAT: 17 grams

    SODIUM: 180 mg

2. Convert grams into calories according to the following conversion data:

1 gram of protein = 4 calories

1 gram of carbohydrate = 4 calories

1 gram of fat = 9 calories

3. Multiply the number of fat grams in the product (17) by the number of calories per gram (9) to determine the total fat calories in the product (153).

4. Divide the total fat calories (153) by the total calories in a serving (280).

5. Multiply the number you get (.55) by 100 to determine the percentage of fat in the product: 55 percent.

Finally, remember to read labels cautiously. You may not have noticed that in our example there are two servings in the package. While this doesn't change the percentage of fat in the product, it does mean you would be getting twice the fat and calories you thought you were getting if you consumed the whole package. Sometimes, the manufacturer's idea of a serving would only match the appetite of a child!

Fitness

You're no doubt aware that a fitness craze is sweeping the nation. In many ways this has been a positive trend. People who want to exercise have more options than ever before: more classes, more fitness facilities open at convenient times, and more home exercise videos. People who don't already exercise, however, can be intimidated by the world of fitness. And some people believe that unless they participate in the real "in" sports of the superfit or follow a high-powered exercise regimen, they may just as well not bother.

Whichever characterization applies to you, remember that movement of any kind is better than the life of a couch potato. Even activities like regularly walking a few blocks to the bus or taking the stairs instead of the elevator will have some impact on your fitness level. While ideally you should exercise at the "prescribed" level indicated later in this section, you can still benefit from movement of any kind. In other words, people who maintain even a small amount of fitness, which can be gained from recreational pursuits like gardening, generally live more healthful lives than people who get virtually no exercise at all. Most young, healthy people coming out of college are naturally going to fall in a fitness category above the lowest level; however, it's easy to get increasingly sedentary as you age.

Types of Exercise Programs. If you are ready to embark on an actual program of exercise or are trying to maintain your present exercise level, a number of factors will influence what type of exercise you should undertake. For example, if you enjoy competitive sports, your community may offer leagues organized by the city or town, local churches, businesses, or community centers, and may include sports such as softball, volleyball, tennis, bowling, and others. In addition to recreational benefits, competitive sports are a particularly good way to make friends if you have relocated to a new town. Beyond the social and recreational benefits, this type of interaction does not usually require a commitment of more than one or two sessions per week. The major drawbacks to these programs are that people sustain relatively high rates of injury (the weekend athlete syndrome), particularly if they don't do any other type of exercise, and that they usually don't provide a sufficiently arduous or frequent workout to ensure really good conditioning. To combat both these drawbacks, supplementing participation in competitive sports with some other exercise during the week can be an ideal solution.

Another popular exercise program is weight training, either with machines or free weights. While this has traditionally been a male pursuit, in the past ten or so years many women have taken up weight training for fitness or competition. Weight training activities are excellent for building muscle mass, reducing body fat, and providing tone and shape to your body. The main drawback is that weight training is not an aerobic activity, which is the type of exercise most beneficial to your health. Nonetheless, experts are recommending that people use weight training to supplement an aerobic exercise program, particularly for weight control. Not only does weight training conserve muscle mass, the major component of our bodies that burns calories, but it helps to maintain bone mass (particularly important for women, who lose bone mass rapidly after menopause, making them susceptible to osteoporosis).

The best exercise program, however, features aerobic activities—swimming, jogging, brisk walking, cycling, vigorous one-on-one racquet sports, to name a few. For one thing, aerobic exercise strengthens the cardiovascular system, which improves the overall health and has many feel-good benefits: more energy, less stress, better sleep, weight loss, and improved self-image. For another, aerobic exercise tends to increase endurance and to lower blood pressure and cholesterol levels.

To get the most out of your aerobic exercise program, you need to follow some minimum criteria:

- **Mode:** Pick an exercise that you enjoy and will continue. You can cross-train using different exercises, as long as they cumulatively meet the other criteria listed here.

- **Frequency:** Exercise at least three times per week. You will see greater improvements, however, if you gradually build to four to six times per week and maintain this frequency. Take at least one day a week off to allow your body to recover.

- **Duration:** Exercise for at least twenty to thirty minutes at a time. Even when you begin, it's important to maintain exercise for twenty minutes, although this may mean you need to slow down periodically.

- **Intensity:** Monitor the intensity of your workout. In order to get aerobic benefits, your heart must be beating at a target heart rate.

Exercise 15.3

How Hard Should You Exercise?

Determine your target (exercise) heart rate by completing the blanks in the following formula

220 - ___ = ___ X .60 = ___ **(lower end of target)**
    (your age)   (beats/minute)

220 - ___ = ___ X .75 = ___ **(upper end of target)**
    (your age)   (beats/minute)

For example, if Jan is twenty years old, her maximum heart rate is about 200 beats per minute. (She never wants to exercise at that intensity.) Her target heart rate would be 60–75 percent of 200, or 120–150 beats per minute. If she measures her heart rate a few minutes into her workout and finds it lower than 120, she knows that she has to work a little harder. If she finds that it's much more than 150, then she knows she needs to slow down.

Suggestions for Success in Exercise Programs. To get the most out of your exercise program, try doing the following:

1. **Find an exercise partner.** If you are trying to begin a program or are having trouble continuing one, a friend's support and motivation can be invaluable.

2. **Begin slowly.** There's nothing more discouraging at first than having aching muscles for a week. Keep in mind that your body is a fine-tuned "machine" that needs time to become fit.

3. **Think of exercise as a lifelong commitment, and choose exercises you can continue for a long time.** Fitness is not stored; you need to exercise regularly. Keeping it up is a lot easier than starting over, too.

4. **Have more than one exercise option.** Jogging is great, but are you willing to run in sweltering heat or in the rain? The health club near work may be a great alternative for you, but what do you do if you want to exercise on weekends, on a business trip, or on vacation? Cross-training also offers a way to avoid the boredom of doing the same old thing every day.

5. **Consult your physician.** If you are 40 or younger, and healthy, you probably do not need a physical exam before beginning an exercise

program. However, if you have any doubts, if you have a preexisting medical condition, or if a past injury may pose some limits or risks, consulting with your doctor is recommended.

6. **Don't use the excuse "I don't have time."** Schedule exercise into your day as you would business appointments and social engagements, and don't let anything interfere with it. Finding time is often a matter of setting your priorities to include exercise.

Weight Control

We are a weight-conscious society. While the health hazards of obesity have been known for a long time, it is important to have a realistic approach to weight control. If you have gained weight in college and now feel you are ready to lose it, follow the principles of good nutrition and exercise outlined here. If you feel the structure of an organized weight control program would benefit you, use a critical eye in examining your options. The multibillion-dollar weight loss industry has not gotten so rich because people have been successful in their weight loss efforts. In fact, if they had been successful, these diet programs would have rendered themselves obsolete. Your best bet is a sensible approach. Most communities have worthwhile programs available through local hospitals or the Weight Watchers organization. The following guidelines should help you evaluate any weight management program:

1. **Be alert for gimmicks.** If something seems too good to be true, it probably is. There are absolutely no magic formulas, combinations of foods, or anything else that will burn fat at a faster rate than your body knows how to. The equation is simple—if you burn more calories than you take in, you'll lose weight.

2. **Be wary of plans that exclude or severely limit intake of a major nutrient group.** There are foods in each of the major food groups that represent better and worse choices, but there's no food you should have to avoid totally in order to lose weight.

3. **Be skeptical of extravagant claims.** For example, avoid any program that promises a weight loss of more than one to two pounds per week. Your body simply cannot burn fat at a faster rate than that. If the scale shows a weight loss of more than two pounds or so, you can bet that the excess (and even part of the two pounds) is due to water weight, which is only temporary.

Some college students have weight problems that do not involve being overweight. Eating disorders such as bulimia and anorexia nervosa are an all-too-common phenomenon, especially among female students. If you have experienced an eating disorder but have not yet sought help for it, it is not too late. For some, getting out of the stressful college environment can help with recovery. For others, a reputable program or mental health professional in the community can guide treatment. Even if you do not have an eating disorder, you may be one of the millions of young people who has somehow gotten the message that they don't look good enough, that they aren't thin enough. It is no wonder that, in a society which seems to value excessive thinness above health and positive self-esteem, even preadolescent girls have reported feeling fat and going on diets. Perhaps this would be a good time to seek out classes or begin reading about self-esteem and body image, and to discover ways to enhance these to become a happier, healthier person.

Stress Management

Most college students experience stress at various times throughout the school year, and for some this is more the norm than the exception. In fact, your stress level may be something you are most looking forward to changing when you finish college. Depending on your personality and your future circumstances, this may be a very real possibility. However, it's probably unrealistic to think that your existence after college is going to be free of stress—particularly at first. With graduation from college comes change, and with change comes stress. Even pleasant occurrences like a new job, a new apartment, a new car, different sleeping habits, and a change in financial or marital status can be stressful just because they are new. And several changes simultaneously can be especially overwhelming. Finally, to be perfectly realistic, life doesn't always go according to plan. If, for example, you haven't gotten a job yet, are concerned about money, and don't have an ideal housing/roommate situation (or have to move back in with your parents), things may be stressful for a while.

The most important thing to remember in managing stress is that you always have some measure of control over your life and certainly over your attitude toward things that happen to you. Events aren't inherently stressful. It's the meaning we give to the events that largely determines whether they are going to affect us emotionally and physically. Therefore try to follow this rule of thumb: Determine whether you can change something that is causing you stress. If you can, do it to whatever degree possible. If you can't, don't become obsessed with it—let it go and try to maintain a positive outlook. In this way you are taking constructive measures to change a negative situation (thereby reducing stress) or modifying your attitude about a situation (which also reduces stress). It's a win/win strategy.

Sex and Alcohol

Although college students are at a particularly high risk of developing problems related to sexual activity and/or alcohol, these risks don't vanish immediately just by virtue of graduating from college. We know that college is a time of experimentation and that students often act in extreme and immoderate ways. Many students who partied heavily in college naturally cut down on the amount they drink once they've graduated. People who become sexually active in college or before may still continue this behavior but feel less of a need to "score" with many partners as they increase in age and maturity.

Certainly, you have the ability to make good decisions in these areas. Hopefully, you learned early on that sexually transmitted diseases are an epidemic on college campuses. Many of the most common diseases, such as herpes and human papillomavirus (which causes venereal warts), do not have a cure and may recur frequently. This means that a person who became infected with one of these viruses in college may remain contagious for years. Between these diseases and the steadily increasing numbers of people contracting HIV, which causes AIDS, you need to be cautious about your sexual decisions. Abstinence, monogamy, and condoms are still the best prevention strategies available.

While the temptation to drink often and to excess may be somewhat diminished out of the college environment, there are still risks. Driving under the influence isn't any safer because you're older. Also, while most college students who drink heavily do not become alcoholics, some of them do. You may need to honestly assess your situation if you drank heavily in college and continue to do this even out of the college environment. The risk of developing problems with alcohol later in life increases with the years of heavy drinking one undertakes. The bottom line is, you may have gotten through college unscathed, even if you partied a lot, but there are no guarantees that you'll remain problem-free forever. If you feel you might have lost control of your drinking, seek help—soon. A local chapter of Alcoholics Anonymous or a county drug treatment program are good places to start.

Being a Good Health Care Consumer

One of the new challenges you may face when leaving the college environment is making provisions for your own medical care. When you were living at home, your parents probably made the arrangements for you to get regular check-ups and to seek professional help when you were ill. At college you probably had access to a campus medical facility or at least to a school nurse to guide you to appropriate community resources. Recent graduates often find themselves in a new locale with no ties to the medical community, leaving them feeling lost and confused as to how to begin establishing these ties. A factor that compounds this issue is that people often don't think about health care until they are sick, which is not the best time to be making important decisions.

Seeking Medical Care

Fortunately, you can take specific steps to reestablish a medical support system. While no tried-and-true methodologies exist, the following will give you some idea of the options:

1. **Obtain a referral from a friend.** It certainly doesn't hurt to have a personal recommendation from someone who has been pleased with the care he or she received. Keep in mind, however, that the person making the referral may look for different qualities in a medical provider than you do. It may be helpful to ask not only whether the doctor provides good care but what it is about this person that your friend likes. For instance, personality and "bedside manner" are qualities that are more important to some than to others.

2. **Contact the local medical society for information about doctors in your area.** It can provide you with a list of licensed physicians and their medical credentials, and let you know if they are taking new patients at this time. One thing you may be interested in is finding out which doctors are "board certified" in a particular specialty. Once medical students complete school and are licensed by the state, they may call themselves doctors. However, to be more than a general practitioner, one must complete a residency in a specialized field (family practice, pediatrics, orthopedics, and so on) to be board eligible and must pass a proficiency exam in that specialty to be board certified. While being board certified does not guarantee a physician's competence, it assures a minimum standard of training and proficiency.

3. **Consult the Yellow Pages to find a convenient location.** Depending on the type of doctor you're looking for, you may prefer one closer to work than to home. Finding a physician in this manner is certainly not ideal, however. At the very least you may want to call the office with some questions, such as how long the doctor has been practicing, how many days you can expect to wait for an appointment for urgent as well as routine concerns, what the rates are, and if the office will file the insurance for you directly.

Do not underestimate the importance of finding a physician you like and trust—and doing so before getting sick. This recommendation includes dentists, eye doctors, and any other type of provider you might expect to have to see at some point. If you wait until you are sick, it is more difficult to call as a new patient and expect an immediate appointment. Also, people who lack a personal physician are likely to resort to more expensive alternatives like emergency medical clinics (referred to by some as "the doc in the box") or hospital emergency rooms. In the case of an emergency room visit, you can expect to pay at least $100–$200, and the waiting time, particularly for nonemergencies, can be several hours. These services play an important role in our medical care system, but they are not the most appropriate options in nonemergency situations. If you have a personal physician in the community, you can usually consult with him or her, or with someone taking calls for them, at all hours of the day, thereby likely helping you to avoid a long and costly visit elsewhere.

Exercise 15.4

What Do You Want in a Physician?

Take a few minutes to mentally review past experiences you've had with the medical profession. List the qualities you feel are most important in a medical provider. Compare this list with that of your classmates or friends. Discuss the merits of the criteria on your list, and compare your view with others. This may expose you to some new perspectives and ensure that you can justify your own reasoning.

Knowing Your Rights and Responsibilities as a Patient

In our society doctors are held in very high regard in their role as healers. However, many people end up feeling intimidated in their interactions with the medical community, and feelings of intimidation do not make for a very good doctor/patient relationship. To get the most from your medical care, you must know your rights as a patient.

Ethically speaking, it may help you in your interactions to remind yourself that in the doctor/patient relationship you are a consumer. Fancy credentials and years of training aside, when you seek care from a medical provider, you are a consumer purchasing a service and are entitled to expect professional and courteous treatment. This includes a respect for your time. While many doctors' offices are busy, you should not be forced to wait an hour or more without an explanation or an apology. You also have the right to expect that all your questions will be answered patiently and courteously by everyone in a doctor's office, from the receptionist on up. It is particularly important that you ask as many and as detailed questions as necessary to understand the diagnosis, recommendations for testing and treatment, and potential effects of medications. Remember, while *the doctors* are the experts, it is *your* body, and you are entitled to understand everything that is being done to it. If you are not treated in a professional manner, make your complaints known immediately. If you still do not get the desired results, find another doctor.

Your medical care is a partnership. Just as you should be able to expect certain things from your doctor, you are responsible for taking an active role in your care. Communicating with your medical practitioner is perhaps the most important of these responsibilities. Your provider needs accurate information about your health history, behavioral risks, and current symptoms. He or she is also entitled to know what you are willing to undergo in terms of medical treatment. For instance, if you are prescribed a medication that makes you ill, you're better off letting your doctor know than suffering in silence or discontinuing it to the detriment of your health.

Concerning issues such as confidentiality and access to your medical records, variations occur on a state-by-state basis and according to which type of medical entity is involved (that is, a private physician's office or a hospital). Some issues are governed not by the law but by the accepted ethics of the medical profession. Should you have questions, problems, or concerns, contact your local medical society, state board of medical examiners, or the state attorney general's office for further information or clarification.

Conclusion

This chapter has outlined several areas of health and lifestyle that you can examine, and perhaps modify, to get the most out of life. It's important to set realistic goals for yourself, as behavioral change does not come easily or quickly for most people. Be patient with yourself and strive to move in a positive direction, rather than achieve your ultimate goals all at once. Some people find it helpful to develop a structured plan for behavior change, as they are less likely to lose sight of their goals and more likely to be practical about carrying them out. The last exercise will give you a format to do just that. Good luck!

Exercise 15.5 — Contracting for Change

Now that you've learned about aspects of wellness, you may feel the desire to make changes to improve your own health. This behavior change contract should help by giving you some structure and providing a reward at the end! To draw up this contract, do the following:

1. List specific behaviors you want to change, and specify what the ideal behaviors are.
2. Describe how you will go about making the changes. List substitute behaviors and changes in the environment to make it supportive of the changes.
3. Identify some negative thoughts you have that keep you from changing the behavior.
4. Think of what you can say to yourself that might be helpful.

5. (Optional) Choose a support person(s). Specify what that person's responsibilities will be.

6. Establish a system of rewards for yourself when you meet your goals. Also specify any potential rewards for meeting subgoals.

7. Date and sign the contract. If you designated a support person, have him or her do so as well.

References and Resources

General Resources

Boston Women's Health Collective. (1984). *The New Our Bodies, Our Selves*. New York: Simon & Schuster.

Cooper, Kenneth H. (1982). *The Aerobic Program for Total Well-Being*. New York: M. Evans.

Davis, Martha; E. R. Eshelman; and M. McKay. (1988). *The Relaxation and Stress Reduction Workbook*. Oakland, CA: New Harbinger.

Hirshmann, Jane R., and C. Munter. (1988). *Overcoming Overeating*. New York: Fawcett Columbine.

Hutchinson, Marcia G. (1985). *Transforming Body Image: Learning to Love the Body You Have*. Freedom, CA: Crossing Press.

Travis, John W., and Regina Sara Ryan. (1988). *Wellness Workbook*. Berkeley, CA: Ten Speed Press.

Cookbooks

American Heart Association. (1991). *The American Heart Association Cookbook*. New York: Times Books/Random House.

Brody, Jane. (1990). *Good Food Gourmet*. New York: Bantam Books.

———. (1985). *Good Food Book: Living the High Carbohydrate Way*. New York: Norton.

Hinman, Bobbie, and Millie Snyder. (1988). *More Lean and Luscious*. Rocklin, CA: Prima.

Robertson, Laurel; Carol Flinders; and Brian Ruppenthal. (1986) *The New Laurel's Kitchen*. Berkeley, CA: Ten Speed Press.

Wesler, Cathy R., ed. (1992). *Cooking Light Cookbook*. Birmingham, AL: Oxmoor House.

IV Responsibilities to Community

16 Leadership

Steven D. Blume

Chair of the English Department, Marietta College

Stephen W. Schwartz

Dean of the McDonough Center for Leadership and Business, Marietta College

---

Senior Voices

Leah

Mr. Mac Award, September 2, 2000

"President McDonough, Dean Godow, Dean Schwartz, Dr. Blume, and distinguished faculty and friends: It is with deep honor and pleasure that I accept this year's Mr. Mac Award from the McDonough Center for Leadership and Business. Thank you for deeming me worthy enough to be in Ted Turner's company! This is special to me for two reasons. The first is this: Unlike for some of our past Mr. Mac recipients, Marietta College (and the McDonough Leadership Program) is my alma mater. Being recognized by my alma mater tells me that while I was a student I made a contribution that you remember; that since shaking my hand at graduation seven years ago, you have watched me progress; and that you believe I am making contributions to my profession and my community. The second reason is that this is the year 2000, which marks an incredible period for all of us. I remember as a child calculating how old I'd be in 2000 and dreaming that people would be driving rocket ships. Well, I am definitely 29, but my car is not rocket charged—not yet anyway. Perhaps it will be in another seven years, and what will get us there is leadership, the kind of leadership produced here at Marietta and at other schools and in other environments across the country."

This is the introduction to my dream speech, which I wrote for my final leadership course at Marietta College. When I came here in 1989, MC was on the cutting edge of leadership study. My peers and I were to become just the third class of the program, and we were excited about this. I can still clearly remember what attracted me: a letter from Dean Schwartz describing the program and the invitation to explore my leadership potential regardless of whether I read Keats or the label off a ketchup bottle. This ketchup bottle image was what struck me.

My study of leadership has taught me that I can be and do anything I want as long as I have respect for everyone and everything affected by me. This is a scary time to be a college graduate, and it may take me a while to get from a job to a career. I may never be considered for the Mr. Mac award—but I can be anything if I dream it and believe it. ∎

Each of you reading this chapter has experienced leadership—in some cases as leader, in others as follower. Those of you who have held leadership positions signified by a title—such as president of the Students for Environmental Action—are easily identified as leaders, past or present. But leadership need not be tied to title or office, and many of you have played leadership roles simply by sharing your expertise and/or by influencing others. For example, you may have responded to a question in class in a way that caused your peers to think about the issue under consideration in a new way or that steered the discussion in a new and enriching direction. In a bull session over coffee or in the dorm, you may have raised an argument that led someone to change his or her view of a specific issue. In other words, you functioned as an opinion leader. In an organization you may have assumed the role of keeping the discussion on target or ensuring that everyone present had the opportunity to contribute. In short, you have acted as a leader in any situation in which your advice or behavior led others to act or think in a new way or caused others to be involved. Each of you has also played the role of follower many times, and if you've ever thought about the relationship between leaders and followers, you've probably realized that the roles are interchangeable.

In this chapter we will identify various leadership roles and explore the dynamics of leadership as you will meet them after graduation. We will also explain why, as you approach graduation, you need to begin thinking deliberately about the nature of leadership and about your readiness to assume the leadership roles that will be expected of you—in the workplace and the community.

Exercise 16.1	*Types of Leadership*

Think about some situations in which you have acted as a leader. Did your influence stem primarily from the position you held? Have you practiced leadership behavior in instances in which you did not hold such a position?

Constraints on Leadership

"Why the rush?" you might be asking. Isn't the fuss about an international leadership gap just one more attempt to sell newspapers and air time? Yes and no. Yes, it's true that almost every generation throughout history has complained about leadership gaps and leadership failures. That's not to say, however, that we don't need better leadership. We do.

Consider the words of John W. Gardner on that subject. In *On Leadership* Gardner writes: "People need to know the worst about the evils to be remedied, the injustices to be dealt with, the ambushes lying in wait for the unwary, the catastrophes to be averted by measures born of foresight." This is a world, after all, "only fitfully committed to justice, often unloving and unlovely." As you prepare yourselves for your roles as adult citizens functioning outside of the confines of academe, you must be aware of the needs waiting to be served, and you must think about whether you are obliged, as citizen-leaders, to serve those needs. If your education has helped you to develop a sense of hope, a belief in social responsibility, and a sense of personal efficacy, then you are ready to act: to take your place in the world and help make it a little better. However, you must also be aware of obstacles to leadership.

Exercise 16.2	*Leadership and Change*

Leadership almost always involves change. Think specifically about what you wish to change and why you wish to change it (1) in an organization or institution of which you are a part and (2) in an organization or institution with which you have in some way come into conflict. How might you effect such a change?

Radical Individualism

As you think about the choices you might have to make as a citizen, you need to think also about the conflict between the traditional obligations of citizenship and the recent trend toward "radical individualism." Certainly, since the late eighteenth century, individualism has been an essential component of American life. It is a strand in the American tapestry, one that we generally regard as being strongly tied to our overall commitment to individual freedom. Nonetheless, we must also recognize the other side of the coin: that individualism, carried to extremes, can undermine the ability of a democracy to achieve a national vision and consensus.

To put this conflict into concrete, contemporary terms, think a bit about the debate over gun control. Even while individuals lobby vigorously—and successfully—to maintain the right to bear arms, we live in fear of growing violence in a society that appears to undervalue human life. How do we balance the rights of the individual and the rights of the community to keep itself safe from those who would abuse the ownership of firearms? Is there a point at which a sense of the common good should take precedence over our sense of individual rights?

Some observers characterize the Reagan-Bush years as a period of unrestrained greed and individual acquisitiveness. President Clinton's proposal for a national service program is based on his belief that each of us has an obligation to serve society and that such service is not an act of altruism but an act that balances self-interest and the national interest. To explain the balance, Benjamin Barber, a professor of political science at Rutgers University, uses the analogy of people living in a rooming house. If a fire breaks out on the top floor, you, as a boarder living on the first floor, can choose to ignore the fire—after all, it's not your room—or you can sound the alarm and help extinguish the fire—after all, you do live there! Helping to put out the fire is not an act of sacrifice on your part. Neither is it a wholly selfish act of self-preservation. Rather, it is an act for the common good of all who live in the house—the community of which you are a member.

Whether a current political platform emphasizes self-interest or the common good, you, as future leaders, need to think carefully about your choices. Consider the words of Dino DiDonato, former director of leadership programs at Marietta College: "What is needed . . . are ways to work cooperatively for the good of all while preserving initiative and individual creativity; ways to meet the needs of communities and organizations while at the same time protecting individual liberty." Your reflections on your future as a citizen-leader can help resolve the tension between radical individualism and the responsibilities of citizens in a republic. Future leaders need to learn to act effectively not just for self-gain but also for positive change.

Complex Bureaucracies

Still another reason to consider your role as a leader resides in the nature of our contemporary bureaucratic organizations. Such organizations are necessary to our social and economic viability. However, as Howard Prince, dean of the University of Richmond's Jepson School of Leadership Studies, states:

> Bureaucratic organizations tend to become less flexible and more impersonal, thereby working against the expression and development of leadership. Increased complexity leads to increased specialization and the need for ever increasing coordination and control mechanisms, all created by well meaning, bright people. In the extreme, the power of centralized control leads to conformity and stagnation, thereby altering in a very adverse way the conditions that might otherwise make it possible for leaders to emerge and develop.

Obviously, organizations will not disappear. What is needed, therefore, is leadership to find new ways to redesign organizations to address the problems of the next century.

Exercise 16.3   *Thinking About Leadership*

Think about your own views of leadership. What characteristics do you associate with leadership? What specific behaviors indicate leadership? Does leadership behavior depend on holding a leadership position? What is the relationship between leadership and power? Is leadership positive or negative, and on what assumptions do you base your judgment?

Preparing for Leadership

Some of the assumptions that have guided your education may not have prepared you for leadership roles as effectively as they might have. The concept of specialization, for example, which has dominated American higher education since the turn of the century, may be the greatest enemy of leadership. Specialization tends to focus our attention on the minute and the fragmented. For instance, in the classroom you learn a great deal about the behavioral assumptions of psychology or about deconstructive approaches to understanding literature. But you may not gain the broad vision that allows you to see the whole picture, and the ability to see the whole picture is essential to effective problem solving.

In addition, the traditional lecture course perpetuates the notion of instructor as authority and student as passive learner. Moreover, classes have provided clearly defined parameters constraining your behavior: descriptions of what you were responsible for learning, how you were to learn it, and how you were to demonstrate what you learned. In short, your education placed you in a clearly defined role in which your behavior was reactive rather than proactive. Furthermore, it often encouraged you to remain within the limits of assignments rather than to move beyond. It certainly did not encourage risk taking.

Certain innovations in education, however, may have given you an understanding of the roles you will almost certainly be called on to play. One such innovation is collaborative learning, in which small groups of students work together to complete tasks. In contrast to more traditional assignments, the collaborative assignment often requires students themselves to define and develop the details of the project. Other forms of active learning may have involved you in critical thinking, problem solving, and synthesis of conflicting ideas, all of which are crucial to leadership.

In another sense, however, your education has suited you for leadership. At a national conference on leadership, Larraine Matusak of the W. K. Kellogg Foundation said that higher education—whether intentionally or as a by-product—has created in you the inclination to be leaders by freeing you "from superficiality, from prejudice, from the need to control, from fragmentation, from narrowness—from the risk of merely settling for single-focus opinions." Those of you who have had the privilege of education have become "intellectually competent, able to think, to ask questions, to examine assumptions, to see errors in reasoning . . . in a phrase *to lead more effectively.*"

Exercise 16.4 *Leadership and the Classroom*

Contrast your performance in a course in which you merely sat and listened to a lecture and a course in which you were an active participant. In which class were you most comfortable? What were the sources of your comfort? In which class did you experience the most discomfort? What were the sources of your discomfort? From your overall experience as a student, what have you learned about your willingness to assume the risks and responsibilities of leadership?

Leadership Models

The Traditional Leader

The traditional view of leadership is based on the notion of the leader as sole authority. The leader is the "boss," and everyone else assumes the subordinate position of follower. Leaders in the traditional mold usually make decisions unilaterally with minimal input from followers, whose primary role is to ensure that the leader's goals and objectives are met. Such a view implies the maintenance of the status quo, perpetuated by a series of managers who initiate procedures. Organizations headed by such leaders tend to create a bureaucratic structure, which reinforces the importance of the traditional leader. In these organizations, creativity, innovation, and shared responsibility are seldom encouraged; the followers of such authoritarian leaders are reactive rather than proactive.

The Charismatic Leader

While the traditional leader derives his or her position from the organization, another kind of leader—the charismatic leader—derives leadership from followers who attribute to the leader special personal qualities, like courage, wisdom, or fatherly concern. Because these qualities inspire confidence, people enthusiastically embrace programs and procedures instituted by such leaders. However, popular support notwithstanding, the charismatic leader does not necessarily set his or her agenda with the wishes of the followers in mind. In fact, a charismatic leader may be as authoritarian as any other traditional leaders.

The term *charismatic* is not a value judgment but a neutral description. History is full of leaders who were loved by the populace but who fulfilled their personal agenda rather than the agenda of the people; Benito Mussolini, Adolf Hitler, and Fidel Castro are but a few. While the people may have been willing to follow them "into the bowels of hell," these dictators set their agendas with personal goals in mind. In contrast, other charismatic leaders, such as Mahatma Gandhi and F. W. de Klerk, developed their goals from a sense of the common good.

The Contemporary Leader

As we approach the end of the twentieth century, we find traditional views of leadership giving way to other forms in which leaders and followers exist in a more mutually interdependent relationship. This relationship is characterized by the view of the organization as a community, and when we look at an organization as a community, we find that the roles of leaders and followers are ambiguous and dynamic.

Consensus Leadership. One example of this interdependent relationship is consensus leadership, a phenomenon in which group process is more important than personality in defining the nature and role of the leader. In this relationship the group is the primary agent in creating an agenda; the leader acts more as facilitator, aiding the group in discovering an agenda. Therefore the consensus leader expresses group rather than individual authority, and the continuance of his or her authority is dependent on the group. Even the personality of the consensus leader is determined by group needs.

Transactional Leadership. According to James McGregor Burns, in his book *Leadership*, "the relations of most leaders and followers are *transactional*—leaders approach followers with an eye to exchanging one thing for another: jobs for votes, or subsidies for campaign contributions." The transactional leader attends to meeting the needs and expectations of the followers and to the marginal improvement of the followers. Leader and follower exist in a balance in which the contribution of each is recognized and rewarded. Self-interest, usually of a short-term nature, is at the heart of the bargain. As Thomas Cronin observes in his essay "Thinking and Learning About Leadership," transactional leadership is a practical necessity for getting a job done and, for politicians, for staying in office. Pork barrel legislation is a traditional example of transactional leadership.

Transformational Leadership. Whereas transactional leadership most often involves an exchange of commodities, transformational leadership is characterized by a moral dimension. In Burns' words "the transforming leader looks for potential motives in followers, seeks to satisfy higher needs, and engages the full person of the follower. The result of transforming leadership is a relationship of mutual stimulation and elevation that converts followers into leaders and may convert leaders into moral agents." Of key importance in Burns' definition is the phrase "relationship of mutual stimulation," for it describes the engagement between leader and follower that enables the follower to reach the heightened awareness required of transforming moral action. The transformational leader is able to inspire and clarify in followers a vision of the good life, a desire to move toward that life, and a sense of how to achieve it. Moreover, the relationship of mutual stimulation is based not just on power but also on shared values and aspirations (even where these are not articulated). In fact, followers choose these leaders because of their shared interests. Again in Burns' words, "moral leadership emerges from, and always returns to, the fundamental wants and needs, aspirations, and values of the followers [and] can produce social change that will satisfy followers' authentic needs." Burns cites Franklin D. Roosevelt as a modern example of a transformational leader.

Transformational leadership signals an evolution in the relationship between leaders and followers. It involves a mutuality in which people's roles and responsibilities shift in response to situations and individual talents. The result is what Max DePree calls "roving leadership." In such a model, leadership occurs not in a hierarchy, but in a community. Leadership becomes everyone's responsibility, and each member's expertise provides leadership opportunity.

Servant Leadership. Leadership that is particularly concerned with the community is called servant leadership. Articulated most fully by Robert K. Greenleaf in his book *Servant Leadership*, this model views the leader specifically as servant. Greenleaf takes the notion from a story by Herman Hesse, *Journey to the East*, in which the actual leader of a group of travelers turns out to be the camel master—both leader and servant.

Influence Relationship Leadership. A recent model synthesizes many contemporary views of leadership. As Joseph C. Rost, in *Leadership for the Twenty-First Century*, states:

> Leadership is an influence relationship among leaders and followers who intend real changes that reflect their mutual purposes. From this definition, there are four essential elements that must be present if leadership exists or is occurring:

1. The relationship is based on influence.
    a. The influence relationship is multidirectional.
    b. The influence behaviors are noncoercive.
2. Leaders and followers are the people in this relationship.
    a. The followers are active.
    b. There must be more than one follower, and there is typically more than one leader in the relationship.
    c. The relationship is inherently unequal because the influence patterns are unequal.
3. Leaders and followers intend real changes.
    a. *Intend* means that the leaders and followers purposefully desire certain changes.
    b. *Real* means that the changes the leaders and followers intend must be substantive and transforming.
    c. Leaders and followers do not have to produce changes in order for leadership to occur. They intend changes in the present; the changes take place in the future if they take place at all.

4. Leaders and followers develop mutual purposes.

    a. The mutuality of these purposes is forged in the noncoercive influence relationship.
    b. Leaders and followers develop purposes, not goals.
    c. The intended changes reflect, not realize, their purposes.
    d. The mutual purposes become common purposes.

Exercise 16.5   *Influence Relationships and Leadership*

Analyze your leadership behavior during your college years in terms of Rost's definition. In particular, what were the influence relationships you were involved in as both leader and follower? Within these relationships, what was the nature of the influence? Describe the movement of influence from leader to follower, follower to leader, and follower to follower. What real changes were intended? By what process did leaders and followers arrive at agreed-on mutual purposes, and did these mutual purposes become common purposes?

Leadership and the Workplace. As we move toward the twenty-first century, we become more aware of significant changes occurring in the workplace. Shifts in population mean that by the year 2015 the workplace will indeed be multicultural, and former minorities may well enjoy majority status. Thus new attitudes toward race and gender will be needed. The shift from an industrial base to a technological, information economy will further necessitate new conceptions of leadership, which emphasize new paradigms and tasks. We must all be aware of such changes and their effect on our attitudes and behaviors in the world of work and in the community.

Clearly, recent conceptions of leadership grow out of notions of community that extend not only to public areas of social life but to the workplace as well. As Rost and others argue, community in the workplace involves mutuality and interdependence, a sharing of power whose purpose is the empowerment of the "other." Where such mutuality exists and is a goal, two factors are essential:

• People must feel as if they are important and share in the power of decision making.

• People must not be made to think that their contributions are unimportant and so choose not to contribute at all.

When individuals are made to feel that their participation is irrelevant or insignificant, or that they have no place in the group, they are essentially being marginalized. Performance is often tied intimately to how valued people feel in their group or organization. In any leadership relationship people can choose the degree to which they will participate. Making people feel as if they matter encourages fuller participation.

Exercise 16.6

Leadership and Group Dynamics

Choose a partner and do the following:

1. Individually consider an experience involving others in which you felt you mattered. How did the behavior of other members of the group demonstrate your importance to them? How did your own behaviors demonstrate that you felt important? How did your behaviors affect the group as a whole?

2. Consider an experience involving others in which you felt marginalized—that you did not matter. How did the behavior of other members of the group communicate your lack of importance to them? How did your own behaviors demonstrate that you felt unimportant? How did your behaviors affect the group as a whole?

3. Share those experiences with your partner.

4. Discuss what behaviors you found to be empowering. To be marginalizing.

Leadership and Gender. Theorists who have studied the influence of gender roles in leadership positions argue that women are often most effective in making others feel as if they matter. In fact, in the *Harvard Business Review* article "Why Women Lead," Judy B. Rosener asserts that women describe their leadership specifically in terms of transformation. In contrast to male leaders, who describe their leadership activities in terms of organizational status and the transactions that result from their relationship to their subordinates, women describe their activities in terms of their ability to encourage subordinates to transform their self-interest to the interests of the larger group. Women achieve their goals by encouraging widespread participation, sharing power and information, and enhancing the self-worth of others. In Carol Gilligan's words, women in leadership positions operate through "a morality of responsibility." Their view of leadership consistently recognizes the "other" and is shaped by the importance they attribute to the preservation of relationships. The tendency of males, however, is to employ "a morality of rights," which often ignores the human factor. Men base decision making not on relationships but on issues of hierarchy, competition, and rules.

Applied Leadership

Four people are sitting around a table that has a small pie in the center. Their task is to divide the pie fairly (though not necessarily equally). What questions might they ask in order to ensure the fairness of the division? How might a person's view of leadership influence the mode of division? How might gender influence the mode of division? What leadership lessons might you draw from the different methods?

Leadership and You

Contemporary views of leadership, though they differ in detail, are similar in one important respect: They reject the traditional, hierarchical notion of leadership, the primary function of which is to keep power and control in the hands of a few, thereby maintaining the status quo. The newer conception is far more dynamic. It embraces the notion not only that power is shared among leaders and followers but also that in the sharing of power can be found the most effective and energizing solutions to problems. In short, sharing power among the many produces distinct benefits. First, it brings the richness of diversity to the task of problem solving, thereby generating solutions that might otherwise remain obscure; second, it creates a new cadre of people actively involved in the relationship known as leadership.

Such approaches have begun to permeate the thinking of contemporary organizations, including many corporations. For example, in *Leadership Is an Art*, Max DePree, CEO of the Herman Miller Furniture Company, speaks of the practice of "roving" leadership. In roving leadership power is not distributed according to rank or position, but rather according to whoever has the ideas and skills germane to the problem at hand.

You may already have observed the kinds of changes in conceptions of leadership that we have been describing. Consider the very structure of the college or university you are attending. Are decisions made by the trustees alone? By the administration alone? By the faculty alone? Rather, isn't it true that decision making is shared with the students as well, that decision-making groups such as curriculum committees are composed of faculty, administrators, and students? If you are involved in the life of your community, haven't you observed in the groups of citizens who contribute so many hours to performing community service a mixture of people from all walks of life and a variety of socioeconomic classes? As you listen to both national and local news, how often do you hear about community problem-solving models in which ordinary citizens take the initiative to define the problems that face them and choose which of these problems they should solve as well as the method for solving them?

In other words, your experiences have probably already prepared you for this fact: that you are about to enter a world that is, with respect to leadership issues, radically different from the traditions you may have grown up with. When you leave college and enter the workplace and the community in which you finally choose to live, you must be open to those differences and prepared to utilize these new approaches.

Exercise 16.8

Traditional Versus Alternative Leadership

Recall a situation in which you, as part of a group, were involved with a traditional, hierarchical leader. Were you satisfied with the outcome in terms of both process and product? If not, how might one of the alternative modes of leadership discussed here have made a difference? What specific steps might have been taken to arrive at a more fulfilling solution for all members of the group? How could power have been shared with others to create a win-win decision?

Conclusion

Is your readiness for leadership really important? Absolutely! Change is everywhere, and we must be ready both to adapt to it and to shape it. Society, by its nature, will always have needs. In the seventeenth century the poet John Donne observed: "Soldiers finde warres, and Lawyers find out still / Litigious men, which quarrels move . . . '' Today, ethnic groups continue to war with one another; countries as well as socioeconomic groups clash over scarce resources; the world abounds in poverty, ignorance, and greed. This world needs the leadership that your generation can provide, and you need to find ways to accommodate both your individual wants and your responsibilities as citizen-leaders. Will this be easy? Probably not. Should you make the attempt anyway? We've already answered that one. How do you maintain the courage and optimism to do impossible things? Try and keep on trying. In Lewis Carroll's *Through the Looking Glass*, Alice gives voice to despair—"There's no use trying, one can't believe in *impossible things*"—only to be corrected by the White Queen: "I dare say that's only because you haven't had much practice. When I was your age, I always believed impossible things for half an hour a day. Why, sometimes, I've believed as many as six impossible things before breakfast!" This chapter is an invitation for you to believe impossible things and then act to make them possible.

References and Resources

Barber, Benjamin. (1993). Keynote address, Ohio Campus Compact, Athens, Ohio, April 2. The thesis of this keynote is that colleges and universities have an obligation to pass on to students the need, in a democracy, to be good citizens. Barber asserts that national service is one of the most effective means for teaching the lessons of citizenship.

Burns, James McGregor. (1978). *Leadership*. New York: Harper & Row. *Leadership* is a landmark text surveying leadership primarily in the political arena. In it, Burns distinguishes between power wielding and leadership and then between transactional and transformational leadership—a distinction that has revolutionized thinking about leadership.

Cronin, Thomas. (1984). "Thinking and Learning About Leadership." In *Contemporary Issues in Leadership*, 2nd ed. Boulder, CO: Westview Press. Cronin asserts that, although the ability to be a leader cannot be taught, leadership study is nevertheless essential to helping students understand leadership and its issues and recognize effective (and ineffective) leadership when they experience it.

DePree, Max. (1989). *Leadership Is an Art*. New York: Dell. Written by the CEO of the Herman Miller Furniture Company, this text focuses on the obligations of a leader to the community he or she leads and on the covenant between leader and followers. By first meeting the needs of individual people, leaders also meet the needs of their organizations.

DiDonato, Dino. (no date). "What We Teach and Why." Unpublished document, Marietta College.

Gardner, John W. (1990). *On Leadership*. New York: Free Press. John Gardner surveys the current state of leadership in America and asks probing questions about our capacity as a nation to act for the common good. Ending his thought on a hopeful note, he indicates the tasks that leaders must undertake as well as the qualities of leadership that will enable them to complete their tasks.

Gilligan, Carol. (1982). *In a Different Voice*. Cambridge, MA: Harvard University Press. Gilligan examines the socialization processes that differentiate the moral development and interpersonal styles of men and women.

Greenleaf, Robert K. (1977). *Servant Leadership*. New York: Paulist Press. Greenleaf diverges from the conventional view of leaders to describe leaders as servants to those they lead. He applies this view of leadership to trusteeship, business, education, and churches.

Matusak, Larraine. (1993). Keynote address, Conference on Leadership and the Liberal Arts. Marietta College, Marietta, Ohio, April 16, 1993.

Prince, Howard. (1993). Plenary address, Conference on Leadership and the Liberal Arts. Marietta College, Marietta, Ohio, April 17, 1993.

Rosener, Judy B. (1990). "Why Women Lead." *Harvard Business Review* (November/December).

Rost, Joseph C. (1991). *Leadership for the Twenty-First Century*. New York: Praeger. Rost provides a history of leadership study as well as an analysis of Burns' definition of leadership. He concludes that the twenty-first century will require a definition of leadership suitable to a postindustrial society.

17 Making Your Way Toward Citizenship

Suzanne W. Morse

Director of Programs, Charles F. Kettering Foundation, Dayton, Ohio

Suzanne W. Morse

Director of Programs, Charles F. Kettering Foundation, Dayton, Ohio

Senior Voices

Elizabeth

When I think about my growth as a member of my community, I owe much to my experience in college. I believe that the spirit of a liberal arts education opens us to a world of ideas, encourages us to think, whether it be by considering themes in literature, studying lifestyles and cultures, examining historical patterns—almost any focus. If we are awakened by the winds of possibility and encouraged to relate what we learn about worldviews to our own lives, then inevitably we will come to question our roles in the progress of our times, of our society. My experience has led me into an active role, making my own choices rather than passively accepting the changes all around me. I participate in political rallies, speaking out publicly for causes I believe in. My education has encouraged me to think, act, and speak, but also to listen. Part of active citizenship means productively and constructively sharing all of our gifts—intellect, energy, skill—to shape our communities. As I prepare for graduation, I do feel charged with a responsibility to apply my education toward public good. I think that universities should strive to instill this goal in all of their students because, after all, the future belongs to us. ■

W hen we use the phrase "making our way," we imply in both tone and substance that we are not quite there. Thus, with regard to our lifetime commitment to citizenship—its rewards and trials—most of us are making our way. The process is active rather than passive and involves us in learning about the nature of citizenship and the obligations of citizen; training ourselves to talk, think, and judge publicly; and committing ourselves to act on our public judgments. As we prepare for the next century, we need to recognize that citizenship extends from the microcosm of the community to the macrocosm of the nation. In this chapter we will discuss what it means to be a citizen and why citizenship is such a crucial role.

Defining Citizenship

T he term *citizenship* often implies something finite. That is, if you or your parents are born in a country, you have earned the title of citizen. The popular belief is that citizenship involves the basic knowledge acquired in high school government or civics classes: the functions of the three branches of government, the electoral process, and the importance of voting. Add in such things as obeying laws, understanding the Bill of Rights, and knowing how a law is passed, and most people think they have "made their way" to citizenship. Such, however, is not the case.

Thomas Jefferson, one of the "Founding Fathers" of the American nation, contended that in order to be called "citizen," every member of the community had to be involved in the business of society. To Jefferson citizenship meant membership in the larger community—namely, being a member of the "public." In Jefferson's day community was a tangible, definable concept: People lived in geographic communities and participated with their neighbors in their collective affairs. Their deliberations and conclusions reflected—and directed—issues of the public interest.

The Constitution and the Bill of Rights do not define citizenship. Nevertheless, citizenship is a legal construct that implies membership, rights, responsibilities, and protections—a mutual relationship between citizen and state. Citizenship is neither a grand scheme for securing public office nor a role fulfilled simply by voting or by obeying all the laws. Nor is it an abstract concept; the statement "I am a citizen" indicates that its status is real and recognizable. The "office" of citizen receives the most attention when a perceived right or privilege is threatened. Indeed, while the popular definition refers to the "rights" of citizenship, the concept is much broader than that. According to Barber (1984), the most important fact about citizens is that they are members of a *political* community. The civic identity applies only when citizens interact with one another. Therefore, citizenship entails not just the rights of the individual; it also involves the interactions and responsibilities of all citizens in a democratic society.

Exercise 17.1   *The Office of Citizen*

Have you ever considered citizenship to be an office? What responsibilities does this office entail?

Learning About Citizenship and Politics

Chances are you came to college knowing more about citizenship than you thought you did. In fact, your civic life started before you can remember; you were schooled in citizenship long before you took government or civics classes. As noted previously, citizenship involves far more than voting or holding elective office. It is related to that part of your lives that is common and public. And what does this have to do with the senior year experience? Everything.

Your initial experiences in citizenship probably derived from your interactions at home and in school. For instance, if as a child you learned to be seen and not heard, that mode of behavior likely carried forward. If, on the other hand, early on you were encouraged to express opinions and views, to make decisions on important issues as a family unit, and to see your own needs in relation to those of the larger group, then you learned some very different things about life in the larger public world. In a wonderfully revealing book, *The Altruistic Personality*, Samuel and Pearl Oliner (1988) illustrate the influence of childhood experiences. The authors studied the behavior and early life of non-Jews who lived during the era of Nazi domination in Europe. What they found, almost to the person, is that those who were willing to help the Jews in their time of need had been well treated and respected as children. By contrast, those who were unwilling to help had usually come from authoritarian backgrounds, characterized by some form of abuse or a general attitude of disrespect. Thus we live what we learn, read, and experience. Keep in mind, however, that while our early observations and experiences influence us, they do not cast our values and attitudes in stone.

You are also exposed to citizenship through what you read and hear. Some of the classics in literature—for example, George Eliot's *Middlemarch* or Aristotle's *Nicomachean Ethics* or Pericles' "Funeral Oration"—are one influence. Popular media in the form of newspapers and magazines, television shows and films, and even comic strips are another. While we may not agree with everything we read and see and hear, these sources all contribute in some way to civic learning.

Yet another way you learn about your role as citizen is by exposure to and opinions about politics. The words *citizenship* and *politics* are combined in the heading to this section for a simple reason—*politics is what citizens do*. Yet people often recoil when politics is mentioned. Most of us feel excluded by or want no part of the singular, partisan-interest version that we hear about on the evening news. It is generally conceded that politics is best left to the devices of the elected politicians, that it has little or nothing to do with our role in society. That, of course, is the problem.

Politics in a democracy is not about winning and losing elections; it is the process by which citizens and elected officials decide how they will live together. The representative system of government was not intended to exclude citizens' input, although there are those who think that citizens are incapable of making good public choices. According to this view, if citizens had a real voice in the decision-making process, the nation would fall prey to special interests and private pursuits, and would never discover any common purposes. Ironically, that is precisely what has tended to happen, primarily because citizens were *not* involved rather than because they were.

The idea of democracy originated with the ancient Greeks, who believed that each person had public responsibilities in addition to private ones. The Greek version of democracy had many flaws, not the least of which were racism, sexism, and classism. A prime virtue, however, was a conception of the citizens' role: one that involves action, participation, and choices, and that is central to the function of the democratic system.

What, then, does all this have to do with you? To answer this, let's look at where you think you were when you came to college, what has happened to you in the past three or so years, and finally, how you perceive your civic role after college or university life.

Exercise 17.2 *Civics Check*

	Yes	No
Before College		
1. In school or at home, did you participate in group decisions?	_____	_____
2. Was interaction encouraged at school?	_____	_____
3. Did members of your family participate in the community?	_____	_____
At College		
1. Have you participated in college community life?	_____	_____
2. Did college help you have a better idea of what is expected of you as a citizen?	_____	_____

	Yes	No
3. Have you been a part of a group decision either in or outside of class?	_____	_____
4. Was the decision better as a result of group participation?	_____	_____

Exercise 17.3 *Politics Check*

	Yes	No
1. Do you feel a part of the political system?	_____	_____
2. Have you ever voted?	_____	_____
3. Have you ever attended a group meeting (for example, dorm, neighborhood, or community) to decide something?	_____	_____
4. Do you feel that elected politicians can solve our national problems?	_____	_____
5. Do you feel that you and others like you can influence the solutions to problems?	_____	_____

Exercise 17.4 *Practicing Citizenship*

Based on your responses in these two exercises, how have you practiced being a citizen? Take some time to think about an incident that you remember that exemplifies your notion of citizenship. In thinking about this experience, ask yourself three questions:

1. Did it involve other people? How?
2. Did it involve government?
3. Did it involve a collective action?

Potential responses could range from helping a needy family, to voting, to building a community shelter for the homeless. What is important to realize is that while your example may have involved only one person (you) or a singular action (voting), it could have also involved the broader notion of citizenship and politics discussed previously—discussion, participation, action. And herein lies the purpose of these exercises: To fulfill your own desires and expectations about the larger world we all share, you and I and everybody else must have an idea not only of what is expected of us but also (more importantly) of what we need to do.

Wanted: Citizen

If someone asked you to list your qualifications for the job of citizen, what would you say? Law-abiding? Voter? American? Despite the virtues of all of these, you really have not said anything about what skills you might bring to the job. For example, do you know how to talk and listen to other people about matters of common concern? Are you capable of thinking about issues in terms other than black or white—or "my way or no way"? Can you imagine a different way of solving problems or envision the many people who will be needed to solve the problem? If you had the know-how and the resources, could you put a solution into place? Do you have the will to take the necessary actions?

Exercise 17.5	*Qualifying for the Office of Citizen*

Qualifying for the Office of Citizen

To help you think through your qualifications for the office of citizen, begin by listing the five most pressing problems in our country. Then list several potential solutions to each of these problems. Are these solutions viable economically? Do they depend on government action? How might individual citizens help solve these problems?

Of these, which do you think government alone can solve? Before you answer, bear in mind that the government has limited resources. For example, the federal budget deficit is a daunting reality, state and local governments are cutting services, and nobody wants to pay more taxes. Your list might include the environment, poverty, homelessness, education, world peace, and so forth. Even with unlimited resources and abilities, governments alone cannot solve these problems. There are conflicting demands and interests; there are underlying causes that money alone cannot correct; and finally, even the partial solution requires personal and public will.

Of course, it's easier to think of problems as belonging to others. Most of us prefer to let others solve problems for us—in this case, our elected representatives, be they presidents, mayors, or members of Congress. Unfortunately, such abdication of responsibility has no place in a democratic society, because the problems we face as a nation and as a world cannot be solved solely by governments, no matter how efficient.

As you think about your list of problems, consider for a moment that some of the public problems we face have been around for decades. For example, despite our high standard of living, one out of eight American children goes to bed hungry. Many of our fellow citizens are homeless. Education at the primary and secondary levels is widely accepted to be "in crisis." Finally, many neighborhoods are drug-infested and crime-ridden.

And yet, despite our affluence and our advanced technology, we have not been able to cure these ills. Clearly, something else is needed.

What, then, does citizenship require in a democratic society? Active citizenship is about choices. In fact, politics is the process by which a group of people decide how they will live together and govern themselves. These choices are public choices, and making them requires civic skills. Acts of citizenship are shared acts, not individual ones. In contrast to personal decision making, they require the ability to make informed, rational decisions in concert with a community of fellow citizens.

Skills Needed for Civic Life

As you might suspect, this business of being a citizen is not easy work. It takes time and effort to discuss, reason through, and solve difficult problems. Specifically, the skills needed for effective participation in civic life include public talk, public thinking, public judgment, public imagination, and courage to act.

Public Talk

You know how to talk. You spend a good portion of your day doing it. But public talk is not just speech. It includes a whole range of communication skills: listening, cognition, agenda setting, and mutual inquiry. As Barber (1984) points out, "Political talk is not talk *about* the world; it is talk that makes and remakes the world." In short, political talk builds a community. Good civic conversations, according to Minnich (1988), are public: "At its best, the public is where we find—through conversation with others—a deeper level of understanding of our opinions and a level of understanding of ourselves and others."

To learn this basic skill of democracy, citizens must talk. Pericles had this conception of talk in mind when he said that the Athenians "taught themselves first through talk" before taking action. So must we.

Public Thinking

You know how to think. But "public" thinking is not an individual activity. Rather, it is a collective skill requiring mental interaction with others, a habit of thoughtfully considering problems and issues with others in mind. Essentially, public thinking requires that citizens examine issues in more inclusive ways while also connecting them to the larger world. Philosopher Hannah Arendt called this skill the "enlarged mentality": We must think in the place of everybody else.

Public Judgment

Public talk and public thinking are building blocks for another skill required in a functioning democracy—public judgment. Political or public judgment is not personal judgment. Whereas personal judgment is concerned with what "I" will do, public judgment refers to what "we" will do. First and foremost, public judgment deals with uncertainty; it is required when no rule can be applied directly, which is why we have judges and juries. Arendt (1963) gives a practical example of what this concept means in her work on the war crimes trial of Nazi S.S. officer Adolf Eichmann. She states that Eichmann lacked reflective (that is, public) judgment. Even in his trial Eichmann maintained that he had done nothing wrong in overseeing the massacre of hundreds of thousands of Jews. He felt no obligation other than to follow orders.

Public judgment is required because of the uncertainties that surround public issues. Because public judgment implies that what we can know together as citizens we cannot know alone, it is imperative that we be exposed to diversity, pluralism, and notions of what brings us together, not what divides us.

Public Imagination

We all like to think we have an imagination—it makes us more interesting. But, beyond that, imagination is required for our civic role. Imagination, says Michael Denneny, is that strange ability to make present what is absent and to make ourselves absent from our immediate perspective and present to some absent perspective. This means that imagination gives us the ability to put ourselves in the other person's position and understand that viewpoint. Imagination makes judgment possible. As Wallace Stevens said, "Imagination is the power of the mind over the possibility of things"; we need it as citizens.

Courage to Act

Beyond all these skills for a participatory democracy—talk, thinking, judgment, imagination—is the courage to act. The courage to act comes from the interaction of the other skills. A good example of this type of courage is the Civil Rights Movement, which was predicated on the civic capacity of a group of people to think, judge, imagine, and then act on a societal problem. Specific events and stimuli caused certain actions, but the movement itself arose out of long years spent practicing civic skills out of the public eye. The Southern Christian Leadership Conference's program of citizenship education courses at the Highlander Center in Tennessee, the Mississippi freedom schools, and the work of local groups and churches were instrumental in helping to develop those skills and then move them from the private to the public arena.

Another vivid example of the courage of a people to act occurred in Denmark. The Danes have had a remarkable history of marching to a different drummer. For instance, they were the first of the European nations to outlaw slave trading and were early providers of public education for citizens. However, it was their conduct in 1943 that will forever honor them. In the early days of the Nazi occupation of Denmark, no attempt was made to round up Jews as had been done elsewhere. But in September 1943, the Danes received word that deportation and imprisonment would occur during the Jewish holy days in October. Within forty-eight hours after the secret warning, 7,220 Jews had been contacted, hidden, and moved to safety by their non-Jewish fellow citizens. Only 464 Danish Jews were taken to the Theresienstadt concentration camp. Why did the Danes get involved? They, as a nation and a people, had the capacity to judge a situation and to act courageously.

Perhaps the participants in the Civil Rights Movement and the Danes were no different from you and me, but they had a conception of their place in the larger world that is the essential element of citizenship. As both examples show vividly, citizenship requires people to act in concert: to think and talk together, and to judge the best course of action. Also, it shows clearly that citizenship does not begin and end with voting. The majority of African-Americans could not vote before 1965, but many of them were busy developing a broader set of civic skills that enabled the movement to proceed.

Thus, as you prepare to embark on the next phase of your life's journey—whether it be employment, professional school, or even some time off for travel—you need to be mindful of what you have done in college that has given you the civic skills necessary to contribute to a functioning democracy. Unfortunately, many of us leave college with little or no notion of what we are supposed to do or how our college experience has prepared us to be citizens. Thus you need to think with your fellow students and faculty about the connections between your college life and your civic self. As a nation we must make our way toward a brand of citizenship that is broader than and different from what we know. Our future prosperity—or deterioration—depends on it.

Exercise 17.6   *Conducting a Town Meeting*

As a supplemental exercise, you might consider sponsoring a town meeting–style gathering in which you and your fellow students discuss issues facing the nation. The National Issues Forums, a nationwide, nonpartisan network of citizens groups, can provide a host of materials to assist you in this process. Issues books on such topics as racial inequality, AIDS, and the environment present material in a multiple-choice format that forces participants to consider all sides of the issue and its potential solutions. For more information, call Ms. Pat Ginan at 1-800-221-3657.

| **Exercise 17.7** | *Bridging College and Citizenship* |

Based on your answers to the "Civics Check" and "Politics Check" exercises, how has college influenced your preparation for citizenship? Specifically, what experiences in college have taught you the civic skills discussed here, and how? The following questions should help you formulate some answers.

1. Were you a member of a group (fraternity, sorority, club, professional society)? How did the group function?

2. How did the campus political system (student government association, administration/faculty/student interaction, campus/community relationship) operate? Was it "politics as usual," focused on winning and losing?

3. What course work exposed you to the public dimensions of our lives? What did it teach you?

4. What teaching methods (participatory, authoritarian, noninteractive) were you exposed to? Did they reinforce some notion of your role as a citizen of the classroom or the community?

5. How did you relate to students who differed from you in attitudes, values, background, race, or gender? Did you gain a better understanding of where others are coming from?

6. What community service experiences did you have, either on or off campus? Did you want to "help" someone, or did you see it as mutually beneficial to both parties? What did you learn?

Reflect back now. What did each of these experiences do to affect your view of how the world works? What did each of these interactions do to prepare you for citizenship? Take a look at your institution's catalog and see if you can find words in the mission statement like *to prepare for responsible citizenship, to develop qualities of leadership, to shape good citizens,* or *service to society.* Think about these purposes as you reflect on your experiences. Your college years were intended to do many things, one of which was to prepare you for a larger role in society and not just a profession or a career. How did it do that? How have your attitudes toward those larger responsibilities and the skills needed to fulfill them been fostered?

Citizenship Communitywide and Nationwide

We have focused on what your experience has been thus far. In the remainder of this chapter, we need to examine the larger context: the community and the nation.

There is a movement afoot nationwide to recruit people—especially young people—for service to the country. This movement has its roots in our history of compulsory military service. In the absence of a military draft, however, many feel that younger Americans should serve their country through other activities. In fact, applications to the Peace Corps are up. Moreover, programs exist throughout the country, as do bills in Congress, designed to encourage young people to serve in the community, the nation, or even the world.

Former President Bush's initiative, "A Thousand Points of Light," was a symbol of the renewed commitment to something beyond one's own narrow interests. Under the Clinton administration, this commitment is being defined as an obligation of citizenship. The belief in service beyond that to oneself is consistent with a long history of programs and opportunities for participation. For example, ongoing programs like VISTA and the Peace Corps offer the opportunity to serve at the national and global levels, respectively. Your campus career placement office probably has information on these and other service opportunities. In addition, many programs recruit volunteers to serve both on and off campus in a variety of capacities. For instance, the Campus Outreach Opportunity League (COOL) has been instrumental in establishing student-initiated volunteer programs on campuses throughout the country. Campus Compact is an organization of over two hundred college and university presidents committed to community service opportunities for their students. In addition, individual campuses (no doubt including your own) maintain a file of service opportunities for the local community and beyond. Indeed, many colleges give credit for such service.

A national service initiative is another crucial piece in this public service mosaic. Congress has passed legislation designed to generate over a billion hours of community service. The legislation will funnel some federal work/study funds to community service work, as well as set aside money for service programs and allow for partial cancellation of student loans. Thus, students will be able to work in the community without jeopardizing themselves academically or financially.

Service opportunities vary broadly, but a common underlying principle is that citizen participation is critical to the solution of major problems. As we consider the community service issue, two questions become especially important: (1) How is the agency or community benefiting from the service of the individual? and (2) How do volunteers relate the experience to a larger conception of what it means to be a citizen? For our purposes the key to the service experience rests in what it teaches that can be applied later in life and what it implies about our responsibility for our common lives. At its very heart, a good service experience exposes the participant to a novel environment, problem, or group of people. For example, a student might choose to do a community service project at the local food bank. Here, the student would confront the overwhelming need for and the limited supply of food, the problem of distribution (that is, the mechanics of getting the food to the neediest people), the bureaucracy of distribution and the many agencies that can be involved, the fact that hunger is just one symptom of larger issues, and, finally, the realization that what could be done is not being done. This is a real civic experience. In addition to the simple act of helping people by dispensing food, it involves a whole range of learning opportunities that will make that student a better citizen. Combining all of the above with the opportunity for the student to reflect with his or her fellow workers or classmates about the experiences yields a full spectrum of theory, practice, and reflection.

Seeing the Civic Tapestry

The emphasis on community and public service today should not be considered a one-to-one match with civic responsibilities. Just as citizenship goes beyond voting, so it reaches farther than service. In fact, you might think of voting, participating in the cultural and civic life of the community, and performing community service as the building blocks of citizenship. Indeed, they are important parts, but the responsibilities of citizenship are greater than the sum of these parts. In order to have a properly functioning democracy, we must have people who see the larger tapestry, not just the loom, the threads, and the pattern.

How often have you heard it said that "you've got to see the big picture" in reference to corporate takeovers, airport expansions, scientific innovations, and the like? Put another way, some people may argue, "Don't sweat the small stuff," but the civic tapestry is about both the small and the big things. In order for our democracy to flourish, we have to see the big picture but also remember the small steps and the people needed to take them. Former Czechoslovakia President Vaclav Havel summed up the argument: "Let us make no mistake. Even the best government, the best parliament, and the best president cannot do much by themselves. Freedom and democracy, after all, mean joint participation and shared responsibility."

Havel reminds us that the civic tapestry is made up of a whole range of steps and people. There are roles for all to play—and all must do their part. The problem is finding the time for public life. You have been caught in this web in balancing your college workload with other responsibilities. Indeed, what the Greeks taught us is that in that workload we must include our private as well as our public responsibilities. In fact, their word for those who did not participate in deciding the affairs of the community was *idiotes*. Citizenship is our right, but it is also our responsibility.

Exercise 17.8	*Becoming a Citizen*

What were your responsibilities as a citizen on your campus? What experiences in and outside of class have prepared you for your role of citizen after college? How do you plan to make use of what you have experienced in college to be a citizen after college? In terms of the aforementioned civic tapestry, how would you like to and/or how do you plan to try to make a difference with some of the small stuff in the next few years?

Conclusion

A multitude of challenges face the nation as we approach the twenty-first century—the environment, education, the inner cities, at-risk children, and so forth. As you think about what has been said in this chapter on citizenship and community service, you may be wondering how your generation will deal with the problems at hand. What choices need to be made to build a better world? To answer such questions, take time with your fellow students and faculty to think about what you want for the world of the twenty-first century. Consider the steps, large and small, that it will take to get there. As you begin this process of thought, discussion, and judgment, keep in mind this assurance from anthropologist Margaret Mead: "Never doubt that a small group of committed citizens can change the world; indeed, it is the only thing that ever has."

References and Resources

Arendt, Hannah. (1963). *Eichmann in Jerusalem: A Report of the Banality of Evil.* New York: Viking Press. Arendt reports on the war crimes trial held for Adolf Eichmann in 1960 in Israel. While Eichmann's crimes against Jews epitomized evil for most, Arendt saw his actions in political as well as personal terms. She called him thoughtless in a public sense: He had no capacity to think or judge a situation beyond his own needs or circumstances. His allegiance was to a narrow set of rules, regulations, and prejudices.

Bellah, Robert N.; Richard Madsen; William M. Sullivan; Ann Swidler; and Steven M. Tipton. (1991). *The Good Society.* New York: Alfred A. Knopf. Bellah and his colleagues point out that we live in, work in, and function through institutions like home, school, church, and so on. Therefore we must understand how to better manage and change them. The authors explain how to think, discuss, and act differently on the social and economic issues that face all citizens working through institutions.

Barber, Benjamin R. (1984). *Strong Democracy: Participatory Politics for a New Age.* Berkeley: University of California Press. Barber argues that a democracy must have the full, active participation of its citizens to function effectively. Furthermore, he contends that the system of representation often destroys our capacity and incentive for self-government. This is an excellent blueprint for reconnecting citizens with their government.

Berkowitz, Bill. (1987). *Local Heroes.* Lexington, MA: Lexington Books. Berkowitz shows through powerful biographic vignettes how individuals working in concert with others can change things in their communities. The anecdotes demonstrate how to build a different kind of community life that involves citizens and solves real problems.

Dionne, E. J., Jr. (1991). *Why Americans Hate Politics.* New York: Simon & Schuster. Dionne examines how the American political process, as it was originally envisioned, has failed. The nation has become divided in its responses to issues because politics (and politicians) have defined the issues in such partisan ways that consensus is nearly impossible.

Evans, Sara M., and Harry C. Boyte. (1987). *Free Spaces: The Sources of Democratic Change in America.* Chicago: University of Chicago Press. Evans and Boyte remind us of the need for citizens to have places to practice politics. They give a particularly important treatment of the historical exclusion of groups from public life and their struggle to find free spaces. The authors contend that free political spaces move people from their private to their public selves.

Gardner, John. (1990). *On Leadership.* New York: Free Press. Common Cause founder and former secretary of health, education, and welfare, Gardner draws on his years of study and work to provide valuable lessons about leadership. He identifies ways in which large numbers of people can wrest leadership from "the few."

Minnich, Elizabeth K. (1988). "Some Reflections on Civic Education and the Curriculum." *The Kettering Review* (Summer), Dayton, OH: The Kettering Foundation.

Oliner, Samuel P., and Pearl Oliner. (1988). *The Altruistic Personality.* New York: Free Press. The Oliners prove, among other things, that the way we function as adults both politically and socially is due in large part to the way we were treated as children. A study of Gentiles who helped Jews during World War II versus those who did not showed that adults from authoritarian, rigid families were less inclined to get involved or to help a fellow citizen. They were adverse to risk. The converse was true for the "rescuers," who had better self-concepts and were able to think beyond their own needs. This is an excellent treatment of how individuals are conditioned to respond.

Schlesinger, Arthur M., Jr. (1991). *The Disuniting of America: Reflections on a Multicultural Society.* New York: Norton. Schlesinger discusses what it means to be an American. He addresses boldly both the positive and negative aspects of ethnic awareness and recognition.

18 Contemporary Social Problems

Rick Eckstein

Assistant Professor of Sociology,
Villanova University

Senior Voices

Dean

When I was growing up, I had many things to look forward to: a good job, a beautiful home, a family well provided for—even a world free from war and hate (which were topics I only read about in history books). As a child, I was friends with everyone, and thought everyone was friends with me. I trusted everyone.

As I grew older, became "grown up," this future I had looked forward to as a child came to seem unreal. Currently, with unemployment rising, crime increasing, and the likelihood of my owning a home decreasing, my future is bleak. With the recent Gulf War, war became a part of my life, and not just history. And the recent L.A. riots proved that not everyone loves everyone. I still trust, but not everyone.

I became even more aware of how much my childhood vision was just a fantasy when my mother recently became unemployed. When I accompanied her to the unemployment office, I looked around. I looked at the long lines, at the many people, at the sad faces. And what struck me was that everyone—men, women, black, white, old, young—everyone was represented there. I closed my eyes, I looked around and saw myself.

We are all in this together. ■

The world has changed dramatically in the last ten years. Social problems such as unemployment, homelessness, discrimination, and poverty have become more than just abstract moral issues, and no longer limit their targets to "others." Today's graduating college seniors are more likely than ever to actually experience many of these harsh circumstances. For example, you will work harder than your parents worked, earn less money than your parents earned (accounting for inflation), and own fewer homes than your parents owned. You are more likely to spend time without health insurance, more likely to lose your white-collar job, and more likely to be assaulted. By many accounts, the post–baby-boom generation's (those born after 1964) living standards will be lower than their parents'. Yours will be the first American generation to experience downward mobility.

This chapter is not designed to depress you. Nor is it intended to expose the United States as a corrupt and immoral nation in need of a good revolutionary cleansing. Instead, it seeks to help you "know your enemy." In this case the enemy is a host of social problems that will almost certainly affect you, your friends, and your families. We tend to view our own problems as individually based rather than as socially based. For instance, if we don't get a good job after college we blame ourselves for not working hard enough or for majoring in the wrong field. Similarly, the 1992 Los Angeles riots are often blamed on lazy, amoral individuals with no respect for "law and order" or an honest day's work. However, such an analysis ignores the complex social circumstances surrounding these seemingly individualistic actions.

In this chapter we will examine how the decline in our standard of living, or what might be called the demise of the American Dream, is rooted more in *social* issues than in *personal* troubles. Thus, in order to maximize your chances (and your friends' and family's chances) of living the American Dream, you must think about addressing and solving these larger social problems. Your individual biography is partially shaped by forces beyond your personal control. Much of this book offers optimistic advice on maximizing personal growth and satisfaction after leaving college. A lot of this advice assumes you will be getting a good-paying job with leadership responsibilities. Hopefully, this will be the case. However, this book would be negligent if it failed to warn you about the serious problems you and your classmates may face, not to mention the significant hardships of total strangers. The best leaders are those who never underestimate potential obstacles. These social problems are potential obstacles.

The Demise of the American Dream

Each of you probably envisions a slightly different version of the "American Dream." Still, most of us have been exposed to the stereotypical image of an adult couple (one of whom works outside the home), 1.7 kids, a dog, TVs in every room, a minivan (formerly a wood-paneled station wagon), and a white picket fence. When forced beyond such stereotypes, most of us equate the American Dream with a decent job, home ownership, good health, some children, a quality education, and a crime-free life. In addition to the substance of the American Dream, there is also a correct procedure to obtain it. We must work hard, stay in school, make the best of our talents, and avoid distractions such as sex, drugs, and rock and roll. Selling crack to unsuspecting schoolchildren and selling junk bonds to unsuspecting senior citizens are not proper ways to achieve the American Dream (although the punishment for these deeds is very different).

For some people associated with certain social groups, achieving the American Dream has always proved difficult. For instance, women are frequently paid less than men who hold the identical job, and on the whole, women with college degrees will earn about the same as men with only a high school diploma. African Americans also have found barriers on their aspirations to achieve the American Dream. For example, a recent government study found that light-skinned people were three times more likely to receive job offers than dark-skinned people applying for the same position at the same time with the same credentials.

However, the current demise of the American Dream affects individuals even from traditionally advantaged groups. While extra obstacles still suppress the upward mobility of women and certain minority groups, declining living standards are now evident everywhere. As you start your senior year, you are probably worrying more and more about what lies ahead. You hear frequent horror stories about the dismal job prospects. Fewer recruiters visit the campus, and the ones who do come have fewer, and lower-paying, jobs to offer. Your 3.7 GPA may *hurt* your chances of attending graduate school or medical school. Friends with management degrees are flipping burgers at a fast-food joint; others with petroleum engineering degrees are changing oil rather than drilling for it. Many are living with their parents until they "get on their feet." This is the American Dream?

As mentioned earlier, we tend to blame ourselves for this seemingly unfair deal of the cards. Perhaps a little less beer or a little less sorority activity might have given us a better chance. In addition to blaming themselves, members of traditionally advantaged groups also may blame members of traditionally disadvantaged groups for this economic strife—it's those damn quotas and affirmative action programs that keep us from getting jobs. In any case, whether we blame ourselves or other people, we are still not recognizing the *social* origins of these problems, which may have little or nothing to do with an individual's desires or actions. It will be much harder to revive and to realize the American Dream if we keep defining it in personal rather than social terms.

Wages and Jobs

What are your job prospects after college? Career counselors across the country have noticed a steady decline in total job openings over the past several years. For instance, there were 10 percent fewer jobs offered to college seniors in 1991 than in 1990. This trend cuts across all fields and majors except for nursing, which currently has more jobs than applicants. Business majors will face as many problems as liberal arts majors. In fact, one recent study suggests that liberal arts majors actually have an advantage over business majors when applying for certain jobs (Useem, 1992). Even accounting majors, once seemingly immune from employment downturns, are receiving fewer job offers.

Decreasing Wages and the Wage Gap

Those jobs that are available tend to pay less now than ever before. For example, the average industrial wage in the United States is about $15 per hour. This is 25 percent higher than the average 1973 wage of about $12 per hour, but when you adjust for the rising cost of living since the early 1970s, this $15 per hour wage is only worth about $10. In other words, people making the "average" wage in most jobs can do less with their paychecks now than they could twenty years ago. Moreover, American workers earn less than their counterparts in other industrialized countries. For instance, the average wage for industrial workers in Germany is over $20 per hour, in Japan almost $20 per hour, and in Italy about $19 per hour. By contrast, twenty years ago, American workers' wages in the United States were more than 1.5 times higher than German workers' wages.

This downward mobility has been much more noticeable among workers without college degrees. In fact, until 1987 college-educated men and women were actually enjoying modest increases in their purchasing power. Unfortunately, this trend has slowed since 1987 and even reversed itself in the early 1990s (Newman, 1988). A college degree no longer necessarily insulates workers from becoming what some people call "dump-

Monica

I took my first sociology class my junior year at a public high school in South Carolina. It was much like my other classes at the time: generally boring and repetitive, with an occasional interesting moment. The majority of the grade for the class was based on group projects exploring some facet of a current social problem. My group worked well together, and we presented what I thought was a pretty good project. After the class was over, the teacher called me over to her desk. She sat silently frowning for a moment, and then said, "I want you to be perfectly honest with me. You know you can trust me, right?"

I responded, "Yeah, sure," although I believed nothing of the sort.

"You did this entire project yourself, didn't you?"

Well, I certainly hadn't expected to hear that. I could only stammer, "No, of course not . . . what . . . I . . ."

"Okay, fine," she snapped, not believing me for a second. As I was walking to my next class, I tried to make sense of her question. At last it came to me—I was the only member of my group who was white. It was inconceivable to my teacher that African-American students could contribute to a well-done project that a white student had also been involved with. The fact of the matter was that I had done much less work on the project than two of the others in the group. However, I was given more credit for the work simply because of my skin color.

This is but one relatively subtle incidence of racism; the sad truth is that this kind of unfair treatment goes on all the time, and often passes by unnoticed. I discovered at a relatively early age that the ideology that all people are treated equally in the United States and need only work hard to achieve success is nothing more than a malicious illusion. It didn't matter that two of the other students worked harder on the project than I did; I received the credit for it because I was white. ■

ies"—downwardly mobile professionals. Starting salaries are declining in all so-called white-collar sectors such as finance, operations, marketing, sales, and engineering (*Business Week*, 1992). Midlevel managers in the United States generally make less than their counterparts in France, Japan, and West Germany. Corporate chief executive officers (CEOs) are the one group of American "workers" whose salaries have fared well in recent years.

Indeed, the pay gap between CEOs and other workers is greater in the United States than in any other country. In Japan, for instance, the typical CEO (average salary = $375,000) makes about ten times more than the typical unionized worker. In the United States CEOs (average salary = $1.2 million) make almost twenty times more than unionized manufacturing workers. Similarly, the gap between the richest and poorest Americans—sometimes called the polarization of wealth—is greater in the United States than in any other industrialized country. This gap has been increasing steadily for over a decade. In the United States the very rich *are* getting richer while everyone else is getting relatively poorer.

Unemployment

Unemployment is another growing social problem. Depending on which set of "official" government indicators you consult, the unemployment rate during 1992 was either 7 percent (Bureau of Labor Statistics) or 10.5 percent (Census Bureau). However, even the higher figures from the Census Bureau may underestimate the severity of the problem because they tend to define very narrowly the population of unemployed persons. For example, official unemployment figures do not count "discouraged" workers—those who have previously searched for work but have given up. Also, many homeless people who have never "registered" with the government fail to be counted in unemployment statistics. In addition, workers searching for full-time jobs but settling in the meantime for part-time positions are counted as fully employed by the government. Finally, those working full-time for wages significantly less than in their previous jobs are considered fully employed. Thus official government figures tend to ignore people without jobs (the discouraged or otherwise invisible) while counting underemployed people as though they were in positions commensurate with their training and expectations. When discouraged and underemployed workers are considered, the unemployment rate in the U.S. approaches 15 percent (Mishel and Frankel, 1991).

As with other social problems, we tend to blame individuals for employment—if people weren't lazy and really wanted to work, they could get a job. Now, as more and more of our friends and relatives find themselves unemployed or underemployed, such individualistic explanations are not as convincing. After all, we know these people; they aren't just anonymous faces on the nightly news who we assume never worked a day in their lives. Those of you about to graduate are probably willing to work hard and show up on time. But will this attitude alone get you a job where you can fulfill your vision of the American Dream? If not, what are you going to do about it?

Home Ownership

How many of you really want to live with your parents after college? Unfortunately, young people are finding it harder and harder to purchase their own homes. Even rents are falling beyond the means of many recent college graduates. For some, moving back in with the family is the only option short of taking a bed at the YMCA or sharing a place with several roommates. In 1979 almost one in four people under age 25 owned a home. By the early 1990s, fewer than one in five people under age 25 owned a home. In fact, if you are younger than 45 years old, you are significantly less likely to own a home now than you would have been prior to 1980 (Mishel and Frankel, 1991). Those persons ages 25 to 35 have been hardest hit by this trend.

Clearly, the declining wages discussed in the previous section have a great impact on your ability to avoid homelessness. In addition, surging real estate values in the early 1980s compounded the difficulty facing first-time home buyers. For example, in the 1980s mortgage payments for married homeowners ages 25 to 29 swallowed about 33 percent of their total income. By contrast, in the 1960s, mortgage payments required only 20 percent of total income. The median family income of all homeowners in the early 1990s was about $35,000—slightly higher than the median income for all American families. Controlling for inflation, in 1967 the median family income of homeowners was around $26,000—well below the median income for all American families. Renting is also becoming more expensive, thereby making it more likely that people will be without any sort of shelter. For instance, in the early 1970s renters spent about 23 percent of their income on housing; by the late 1980s the average rent required almost 30 percent of income. Only those in the highest income categories, who use a smaller percentage of their income for shelter, have not experienced declining rates of home ownership.

Health Care

The United States and South Africa are the only two industrialized countries in the world in which citizens do not have universal access to basic health care. In fact, people in many nonindustrialized nations also have unfettered access to primary medical care. Americans, however, must depend on private insurance companies to help them pay for medical services. Individuals, or perhaps the companies they work for, pay insurance companies, which in turn subsidize all or some medical costs. If individuals or companies cannot or choose not to purchase health insurance, it is almost impossible to pay for even basic medical care unless you are very poor and covered by government insurance (Medicaid). Presently, about 37 million Americans lack health insurance.

Infant Mortality and Social Class

The United States is an amazingly unhealthy country despite its image as a technological superpower. One way to measure a society's health is its infant mortality rate—the percentage of infants who die before reaching the age of one. In 1990 one out of every 100,000 American babies died before reaching one year of age. This was a slight decrease from 1985 when the rate was 1.1 out of every 100,000 live births. However, this apparent improvement is tempered when the U.S. rate is compared with the rates of other countries. For example, in 1985 the United States ranked seventeenth in infant mortality and by 1990 ranked twenty-fourth. So, even while the U.S. rate is falling, it is dropping faster in other countries. Indeed, the major industrialized countries all have significantly lower infant mortality rates than the United States (for example, 0.5 in Japan and 0.6 in France). Amazingly, even nonindustrialized countries such as Cuba, Costa Rica, and Jamaica have lower infant mortality rates than the United States.

However, there is a wide disparity of infant mortality rates among different racial, ethnic, and class groups in the United States. A recent study by the Centers for Disease Control reported that infant mortality rates among the poor were three times higher than for the nonpoor (Duke, 1992). In addition, rates were slightly higher for African Americans (regardless of social class), 33 percent higher for Native Americans, and 79 percent higher for Filipino Americans. Thus the color of your skin, your heritage, and your social class play a large part in determining whether you will live to see your first birthday.

Effective prenatal care is the single best way to prevent infant mortality. It is no coincidence that infant mortality rates are highest among those who lack health insurance. Babies die in the United States because their parents are forced to choose between food and health insurance policies that may cost $4,000 per year for an individual and much more for a family. During the 1980s, the number of families whose health insurance was paid for by an employer declined 40 percent (Barlett and Steele, 1991). As this trend continues, more families will face these very hard decisions. Even with insurance, the quality of health care in the United States depends on the social class composition of the neighborhood. For instance, Beverly Hills has one internist for every 566 people; a scant mile and a half away, South Central Los Angeles has one internist for every 19,422 people ("Wasted Health Care Dollars," 1992). Poor people also contract tuberculosis at rates significantly higher than nonpoor people. As with infant mortality, this is due to the absence of preventative care and early diagnosis. The main cause of this lack of preventative care is the absence of health insurance.

Causes of Soaring Health Care Costs

But how can such problems exist when the United States spends more per capita on health care than any other country in the world? Over 12 percent of the U.S. Gross Domestic Product goes toward health care of one kind or another. By contrast, Canada and Germany spend about 8 percent of their total resources on health care while England and Japan spend about 6 percent. Yet in all of these countries, everyone has universal access to basic health care, especially routine preventative care. Many place the blame for excessive health care costs on doctors. Indeed, doctors' salaries are about 60 percent higher in the United States than in Canada, but then, total fees are almost 300 percent greater in the United States than in Canada. So where is all the money going?

The biggest cause of soaring fees is hospitals that use expensive machines and charge ridiculous rates for goods and services knowing that insurance companies have been willing to foot the bill. For example, I recently went to the emergency room with a sprained ankle suffered during a basketball game. Although I was there for about two hours, I was only busy for about fifteen minutes worth of dialogue, X-rays, and treatment. And those fifteen minutes of treatment cost $249! My "emergency room brief," which amounted to giving a nurse my name and address, cost $26. A lukewarm icepack used while in the wheelchair cost another $6. A pair of crutches cost $41. Fortunately, because I have health insurance, I had to pay only $15, with my insurance company picking up the balance.

Clearly, these types of unnecessary charges contribute to skyrocketing insurance premiums and the growing number of people who cannot afford them. In addition, a study by the Rand Corporation in the 1980s found that doctors and hospitals routinely perform unnecessary procedures (including surgery) in order to pad bills and increase profits ("Wasted Health Care Dollars," 1992). Nor are insurance companies without blame. The insurance industry is one of the most profitable sectors of the entire economy, yet healthy companies routinely deny coverage to people they define as "high risk." A favorite technique of insurers is refusing to cover any ailments emanating from "preexisting conditions." Thus, for instance, people needing heart surgery may be denied coverage because their arteries clogged before the policy was obtained.

Pharmaceutical companies also contribute to the exorbitant cost of health care in the United States. The General Accounting Office found that these companies charge 32 percent more for prescription drugs in the United States than they do in Canada ("Prescription Drugs," 1992). For example, McNeil Laboratories charges 484 percent more for Tylenol with codeine in the United States. Because Canada has a centralized health insurance system (which uses bulk purchasing) and regulates drug prices, these companies must sell drugs in Canada at prices closer to actual costs. Given this, it's hardly surprising that the pharmaceutical industry was the most profitable sector of the U.S. economy during the 1980s.

Health Care and You

It's no wonder that 37 million Americans, many of them children, must do without health insurance. It's no wonder that companies are finding it harder and harder to provide health insurance for their employees. This is the reality you face after leaving college and are no longer covered by your parents' or your school's health insurance plan (assuming they have one). You and your family may face dropping your health insurance to pay for food. Or you may find yourself in the same position as a young girl from Washington who got sick two years ago while visiting relatives in British Columbia. Her condition was extremely serious, and she was treated in a public hospital in Vancouver even though her family was not Canadian. After she had strengthened, the Canadian hospital sought an American hospital to continue caring for her. Not a single hospital in the entire United States was willing to take her. They said it was just a business decision since her family could not afford health insurance and the hospitals, as private profit-making organizations, were uninterested in footing the expensive costs. Just a business decision. Your daughter may be the next business decision.

Crime

In terms of homicides, the United States is the most violent society in the entire world, with a homicide rate about three times higher than in all other countries and more than seven times higher than in other industrialized countries. Each year the United States has 22 homicides for every 100,000 people. By contrast, Northern Ireland, racked by civil strife for decades, has a homicide rate of 11 per 100,000 people; supposedly Mafia-torn Italy has about 5 homicides per 100,000 people each year. Guns are the biggest cause of teenage deaths in the United States. The United States also has the highest rate of rape in the industrialized world—twenty-three times higher than Italy, for example. It is getting harder and harder to avoid violence in the United States.

Typically, increases in crime are met with calls for increased law enforcement and stricter sanctions. The way to reduce crime, it is argued, is to put more cops on the beat and to punish criminals more severely. However, compared to other industrialized nations, the United States already has the most police officers (2.7 for every 100,000 people) and the second highest incarceration rate (455 out of every 100,000 people). It is also one of two Western industrialized countries (South Africa is the other) where capital punishment is legal and utilized. Given these facts, more cops, stricter laws, more jail time, and more executions will not reduce violence in our society. If these punitive measures were really effective, the United States would have the lowest homicide rate rather than the highest. Indeed, one recent study shows no relationship during the 1980s between increases in punitive actions and crime rates (Arvanites, 1992).

Calls to increase punishment are rooted in the belief that maladjusted individuals with moral deficiencies commit crimes, and that harsh responses will teach these criminals right from wrong. According to the tenets of the American Dream, just as people succeed or fail based on their own personal fortitude, individuals choose to live either lawfully or lawlessly. As with other social problems, our dominant worldview does not examine the more general social conditions that may foster success, failure, law obedience, or law breaking. But by examining these larger, non-individualistic social factors, we might conclude that increases in violent crime may be a response to deteriorating social conditions and escalating social problems. At local, state, and federal levels, crime rates increase during periods of economic hardship. Executing criminals and building more jails will not solve unemployment, homelessness, and hunger.

Urban Unrest and the "Riots" of 1992

The 1992 violence in Los Angeles and other cities following the not-guilty verdict in the Rodney King beating trial illustrates the different ways we can define and address social problems such as crime and unemployment. Former Vice President Dan Quayle was among many who asserted that the "riots" primarily resulted from a breakdown in family values and from people's total disrespect for law and order. In short, some sort of moral deficiency caused those individuals to engage in criminal behavior. According to this logic, the Rodney King verdict was disappointing, but it didn't mean people had to act so brutishly. And allegedly these were the same morally deficient people who won't work, parent too many babies, and cheat the government's welfare programs. For the former vice president the problem of "urban decay" is caused by urban dwellers themselves rather than more general social factors.

The Terminology of Social Unrest

Rioting Versus Celebrating. The very words *riots* and *looting* clearly place blame for these events on the individuals involved rather than on more general social conditions. Compare the word *riot* to *celebration*. In

1985, after the Villanova University basketball team won a national championship, fans "celebrated" by breaking store windows, overturning cars, lighting fires, and pummeling alleged Georgetown fans. After Ohio State beat Michigan in a 1969 college football game, Buckeye fans tore up the city of Columbus, prompting Governor James Rhodes to say that "boys will be boys" when celebrating. Less than a year later, Rhodes sent the National Guard to Kent State University where anti–Vietnam War student "rioters" were setting fire to the ROTC barracks. Although the damage following the football game was much more extensive than damage from antiwar protests, troops were not sent to Columbus and four people were not shot there. The students at Kent State were not so lucky.

Rioting Versus Revolting.   Also consider replacing the word *riot* with the word *revolution*. *Riot* implies a mob of uncontrollable savages taking to the streets with little concern for life, liberty, or private property. In a riot, violence and destruction become ends in themselves. As one juror in the Rodney King case said, people in South Central Los Angeles were just looking for an excuse to be violent. In her mind the acquittal of the police officers who were videotaped beating King gave these rioters their excuse. *Revolution*, however, implies a more thoughtful and calculated response to actual or perceived oppression and injustices. Revolutionaries are actively trying to change social structures and challenge conventional and traditional forms of social organization. Here, violence is an acceptable means to a legitimate end—a more beneficial society. So, riots are caused by individuals who for some reason can't seem to understand the importance of social order while revolutions are caused by unbearable social circumstances that may lead individuals to rise up and overthrow what they see as the sources of these painful conditions. Whether we use the word *riot* or *revolution* probably depends on where we rank in the social hierarchy and whether we will gain or lose from any major social transformation.

Think about the birth of the United States as a nation. The American colonists saw a "revolution" to shed the oppressive shackles of British rule; the English saw a bunch of crazy "rioters" who had no respect for law, order, and tradition. The definitions of the same actions differed depending on a person's relationship to the status quo. So, the violence in Los Angeles and elsewhere is defined as a riot by those of us who benefit (or think we benefit) from existing social arrangements. For us to call these actions a revolution would mean we acknowledge the serious structural flaws in our society that may lead some people to violence.

Looting.   Another term that was used frequently during the 1992 uprisings was *looting*. But, as with the word *riot*, it forces us to look only at individual behavior rather than at larger social issues. Looting implies an almost systematic disregard for private property and private ownership. Given an excuse, morally deficient individuals will just take as much as they can. However, while television images portrayed most people taking televisions and VCRs, this was not a fair representation of the situation. As insurance investigators noted, the first items taken from stores were milk and diapers—hardly compelling television. Instead of calling these people looters, we could call them great parents willing to risk their lives for their children, who would still ingest and egest even though their neighborhoods were in flames. Rather then saying the absence of "traditional family values" led people to steal, we could say that "traditional family values" were beautifully displayed by these parents.

Analogies can be drawn to other recent events that, while yielding similar results, are not defined as looting. For instance, the savings and loan "crisis" of the past several years will probably cost U.S. taxpayers at least $200 billion, a lot more than the estimated $1 billion in property damage in Los Angeles ("The Riots," 1992). Notice the choice of words. A "crisis" just sort of happens, but "looters" are consciously responsible for their actions. But by examining the savings and loan "crisis" more critically, it actually looks very much like another "looting." These financial institutions went bankrupt generally because their officials made terrible loans (with depositors' money) that were never paid back. Often, these officials knew about these risky loans but did not seem to care since they also received enormous commissions (often several million dollars) for each loan. Thus bank officials and borrowers made huge sums of money while the average depositors will be forced to pay themselves back through government insurance funds primarily supported by depositors' taxes!

It seems fair to say that these bank bosses "looted" property (deposits) that was not theirs. And almost every single banker involved in this scandal was white and rich. Have we ever considered the possibility that the deficient morals and family values of rich, white people caused them to loot the savings and loans? Hardly. Poor people loot; rich people merely exercise bad judgment. Overall, so-called white-collar crimes (such as embezzlement and tax evasion) account for almost two hundred times more stolen property than so-called blue-collar crimes (bank robberies, burglaries, muggings). The difference between the estimated costs of the L.A. "riots" and S&L "crisis" perfectly illustrates this more general fact. Yet, we rarely see a headline proclaiming that "Citizens of Beverly Hills *robbed* the U.S. Treasury today by willfully withholding income taxes." Nor did we see headlines stating that "Poor, unemployed South Central L.A. residents *forgot* to pay for their milk and diapers at the 7-11 today."

The Social Roots of the "Riots"

Challenging Dan Quayle's (and others') explanation for urban unrest means moving beyond purely individualistic explanations and considering the sorts of social problems discussed in this chapter. Rather than insisting that personal moral deficiencies caused these so-called riots, it may be that endemic social problems such as unemployment, expensive health insurance, and high rents encourage more people to act in "riotlike" ways. If these structural social problems generate events like the urban unrest of 1992, then we must solve these problems rather than simply blaming the victims of these problems for bringing pain onto themselves. If we don't address these social problems, there may be many more "riots" and "revolutions" waiting for the next generation of college graduates like yourselves.

About one out of every two adults in South Central Los Angeles is *officially* unemployed, but remember the previous discussion of official and unofficial unemployment figures. Many of those working full-time are still poor. While there may be individuals who simply do not want to work, abundant evidence suggests that there are fewer and fewer jobs available in South Central Los Angeles. In addition, because of current government policies, it is more beneficial for a poor family to receive assistance (including Medicaid) than to work at a minimum-wage job. But does this mean urban residents have improper values? Why blame poor people for making a decision that serves the best interest of their families? Did they set the minimum wage at a level that guarantees poverty? Did they make the rules about government assistance?

Discrimination and Urban Unrest

Although we might not like to admit it, racism exists in this society. People are judged as inferior or superior solely on the basis of irrelevant physical characteristics. Generalizations are made about individuals based on the same irrelevant characteristics. As mentioned previously, a recent government study (in Chicago) showed that white applicants received almost three times more job offers than black applicants applying for the same positions and demonstrating identical credentials. Another recent study by the Federal Reserve Board found that banks were much more likely to grant home mortgages to whites than to blacks regardless of income and collateral. Finally, a police department just outside Philadelphia is being sued because it allegedly targets and pulls over cars driven by people with relatively dark skin. The erroneous, racist generalization at work here is that darker-skinned people are more likely to be carrying drugs than lighter-skinned people. FBI data contradict such an assumption, yet this police department acts as if it were true. Did Rodney King's skin color have anything to do with his treatment or with one officer calling him a gorilla? How many other Rodney Kings are out there who were not videotaped? This sort of discrimination has nothing to do with a city dweller's values or morals, but it certainly may lead to some unrest.

Understanding Racism

As a class discuss how we tend to assign social meaning to physical char-
acteristics.Consider what it would be like if people were organized hier-
archically based on nose volume or toe length or beard thickness. And
note that, once these irrelevant characteristics have been socially defined
as relevant, people treat them as if they are relevant. Is it really clear that
there are "subspecies" of humans based on clearly identifiable differences
in skin color? If there is no real biological basis for the concept of race,
why does it exist? Might it be an ideological construction that helps justify the unequal distribution of wealth, power, and prestige found in many
societies?

Capital Flight and Urban Decay

Over the past fifteen years American companies have been steadily moving factories out of urban areas. Some of these plants were relocated in
sprawling suburban areas where overhead was cheaper and executives
had a shorter ride to work. Between 1978 and 1982 alone, South Central Los Angeles lost 70,000 jobs to capital flight. Many of these jobs paid
above minimum wage and included fringe benefits; most replacement jobs
paid minimum wage and had no benefits. Other companies fled not only
the cities but the country as well. Since 1979, for example, Cleveland has
lost 37 percent of its factory employment to either domestic or international capital flight ("The Riots," 1992). Many of these companies were
prosperous before moving but desired higher profits.

A specific form of capital flight is called "redlining," in which banks
systematically deny loans to the communities in which they operate. The
term refers to banks that drew red lines on a map around certain "high-
risk" communities. They would accept deposits from these residents but
would not loan money to help them buy or renovate homes and/or businesses. When banks practice redlining, they act as conduits for sucking
capital out of poorer neighborhoods and funneling it to wealthier neighborhoods. South Central Los Angeles has over 500,000 people but only
19 bank branches, many of which refuse to grant loans to local residents.
So, when Dan Quayle wonders why these urban residents don't take
some pride in their neighborhoods, he may want to ask the banks the
same question.

Fiscal Policies and Urban Unrest

Decisions by elected and nonelected elites have also contributed to the
growing unrest in American cities. In 1980 federal grants accounted for

14 percent of the average city's budget, but by 1990 only 5 percent of city funds came from Washington, DC. This shift was the direct result of cuts under the Reagan and Bush administrations in programs that primarily served poor, urban residents. Los Angeles experienced a 70 percent reduction in federal money for job training programs, public works projects, and school lunch programs. One member of the Reagan administration justified the cutback in school lunches by reclassifying ketchup as a vegetable, thereby eliminating the cost of purchasing other vegetables. These cutbacks in urban aid helped stoke the urban embers that were already burning. Cities like Los Angeles now have few choices. They can cut services and/or raise taxes, leading middle-class people to flee for the suburbs (they can afford to move) and increasing the distressing living conditions of poorer residents (who can't afford to move or are discriminated against when they try). Pools and schools close, hospitals and fire stations shut down, bank loans dry up—and none of it due to a lack of family values.

It's not that the federal government was saving money by reducing aid to cities. Rather, it merely took this money from the cities and used it elsewhere—namely, military spending. In theory military spending, like any government spending, has the potential to create jobs and economic activity. So, any cutbacks in urban programs that helped fund military projects could have benefited cities as long as any military jobs created were in these urban areas. Unfortunately for Los Angeles and other cities, this theory never turned into reality. Residents in 80 percent of America's largest cities pay more to the military (as a percentage of their total taxes) than they get back in local military contracts and jobs. In 1990, for example, Los Angeles residents paid $4.7 billion in "military taxes" but received only $1.5 billion in military contracts. In other words, the federal government's fiscal policies transferred over $3 billion of wealth out of Los Angeles and into mostly suburban areas. Indeed, one of the biggest beneficiaries of this transfer of wealth was Orange County—just a few freeways removed from South Central Los Angeles. However, South Central residents would have a better chance of getting a job on Mars than in Orange County, where mass transit barely exists.

Government policies also encourage capital flight from the United States to other countries. For example, corporations pay no taxes on earnings from overseas operations, and the recently implemented North American Free Trade Agreement (NAFTA) will probably make this sort of capital flight easier. A similar agreement was reached between the United States and Canada a few years ago. Since then, many Canadian unions have claimed that high-paying industrial jobs have been moving south to the United States, where wages are lower and government regulations are lighter. With NAFTA, Mexico becomes part of the picture, and there is every reason to expect an ongoing flight of capital toward more profitable grounds.

Dealing with Urban Unrest

If the moral deficiencies of city dwellers caused the 1992 uprisings, then we should do whatever is necessary to instill "correct values" in young people. However, if these larger, less individualistic social problems are primarily responsible for these uprisings, then the task for present and future leaders is much more challenging, although no less important. Recent attempts to partially address these underlying social factors, however, may not be effective. For example, the federal government recently passed a $1 billion urban aid bill that would channel money to loans and other capital projects necessary to revitalize economically depressed cities. A billion dollars is a big chunk of change for you and me, but compared to funding for other government programs it is a drop in the bucket. Indeed, the government spent more money on police overtime and National Guard troops during the uprisings! Ironically, failing to fix the root causes of the unrest will merely intensify the need to spend more money on law enforcement.

In the same congressional session in which legislators wrestled with the immensity of this billion-dollar package, they also approved funding for twenty B-2 stealth bombers, which will cost about $2 billion *each*. Not only has this plane not performed up to expectations during testing, but its original purpose, to evade Soviet radar, is no longer even valid. Still, $40 billion plus will be spent on these planes. The 1991 Persian Gulf War cost an estimated $70 billion with the United States responsible for about $15 billion. In order to garner support for the war, President Bush agreed to "forgive" all government-backed loans to Egypt—totaling about $7 billion. This means Egypt doesn't have to pay them back; the U.S. government (hence, the taxpayers) will foot the bill. Similar deals were also made with other countries. By the same standards the U.S. government could "forgive" all federally backed small business loans and mortgages to poor, urban residents right here in the United States. How likely is this?

Both former President Bush and President Clinton support "weed-and-seed" programs and "enterprise zones." The former entails "weeding" out drug dealers from urban areas and "seeding" the communities with day care centers, Head Start programs (for preschoolers), and job training courses, all sponsored with government money. In the most recent federal budget, a mere $500 million has been targeted for these programs; President Clinton has not indicated whether he will try to increase this amount. In addition, weed-and-seed programs ignore some of the deeper reasons why people are dealing drugs in the first place. One person's moral decadence is another person's only opportunity for high-wage employment.

Enterprise zones create tax incentives for business owners if they open up plants, factories, and offices in depressed urban areas. While this sounds great on paper, it ignores a crucial point: Many of these "new" businesses will be leaving other urban areas. One city's enterprise zone is another city's capital flight. For instance, suppose a company with a thousand employment slots moves from Philadelphia (a nonzone area) to Los Angeles (a zone area). The company benefits from lower taxes and higher profits, and Los Angeles residents have a thousand more decent jobs to which they can commute via mass transit. Meanwhile, Philadelphia has a thousand extra unemployed people who may get increasingly testy and even violent. Of course, this capital flight and increasing unrest may qualify Philadelphia for enterprise zone status and all the accompanying business tax breaks. Perhaps a year or two later the company that originally fled for California will return east for lower taxes and higher profits. Philadelphians will be working again! As for the folks in Los Angeles . . .

Exercise 18.2

Defining Poverty

Either as a class or in smaller groups, imagine that you are a "poor" family of four—two adults, a 6-year-old child, and an infant. Work out a monthly budget for this family: food, clothing, housing, day care, health insurance, and so on. The typical budget usually comes out somewhere between $20,000 and $25,000. However, the U.S. government's official definition of a "poor" family of four is one earning about $13,000. So, after setting up this "extravagant" budget, you need to cut out all the luxuries—if any.

Based on this exercise, what do you think about the government's official definition of poverty? Do you still think having a job guarantees that you won't be poor? And two income families are also frequently poor. If you were forced to choose between buying health insurance and food or heat, what would you do? Do you have a better understanding of why poor people living in horrible conditions might act in desperate ways?

Conclusion

A few months ago I returned to Ohio for my tenth reunion. It was thrilling to learn about the diverse paths my friends have taken. Catching up was great fun, but there was also a lot of pain. Divorces, layoffs, lousy health insurance, eternal renting, and even violence had crept into our lives. In the early 1980s the oil industry was booming, and many of my friends secured terrific jobs with oil companies thinking that they were on their way to the American Dream. One is now an entry-level attorney and the other is living with parents. They told me that other former engineers are working at 7-11s or driving trucks. The sad part was that these were smart, hard-working people who were victims of circumstances beyond their control; yet, they somehow felt like failures. My friends conceded that maybe social problems ought to be taken seriously *before* getting out in the so-called real world.

I tell my current students the same thing. Maybe I'm wrong about all these endemic social problems. Maybe unemployment, poverty, and violence won't affect you. But the reality out there, painful though it may be, is hard to ignore although we often spend four or more years of college inventing new ways to ignore it. Prepare yourself for this reality. The author of Chapter 20 will drive home what it means to have been educated in the liberal arts. One thing he will stress is problem solving. In this chapter I have suggested that solving personal troubles may require that you address larger, less personal social issues. There *is* a connection between your declining health benefits and urban unrest. There *is* a connection between your inability to buy a home and the increasing polarization of wealth and income in the United States. There *is* a connection between enjoyable personal relationships and government military spending. Your education, regardless of where you go next, should help you understand these relationships. Without understanding there will be no solving.

References and Resources

Arvanites, Tom. (Forthcoming). "Increasing Imprisonment: A Function of Crime or Socioeconomic Status?" *American Journal of Criminal Justice.*

Bartlett, Donald, and James Steele. (1991). *America: What Went Wrong.* Kansas City, MO: Andrews & McMeel. Based on an award-winning series in *The Philadelphia Inquirer,* this book argues that government policies have increased inequality over the last decade, leading to a demise of the so-called American Dream.

Bowles, Samuel, and Herbert Gintis. (1986). *Democracy and Capitalism.* New York: Basic Books. Bowles and Gintis argue that a truly democratic society is difficult, if not impossible, given the contradictions of a capitalist mode of production.

Dolbeare, Kenneth. (1986). *Democracy at Risk.* Chatham, NJ: Chatham House. This book examines how increasing inequality in our society threatens the core values of liberal democracy.

Duke, Lynn. (1992). "Study: Infant Mortality Underreported for Some." *The Philadelphia Inquirer* (8 January), p. 2.

Eitzen, D. Stanley. (1992). In *Conflict and Order.* Boston: Allyn & Bacon. This is a fine introduction to how sociologists examine issues such as inequality, racism, sexism, and education.

Ferguson, Thomas, and Joel Rogers. (1986). *Right Turn*. New York: Hill & Wang. The authors outline how large corporations gained control of both major political parties to influence fiscal policies during the 1980s.

Goodman, Robert. (1979). *The Last Entrepreneurs*. Boston: South End Press. Goodman shows how local governments compete with one another to attract companies. These businesses often play cities and states off against one another to obtain the best tax breaks. This usually hurts the local community even when there are more jobs available.

Harrison, Bennett, and Barry Bluestone. (1988). *The Great U-Turn*. New York: Basic Books. This book traces the effects of corporate and governmental policies on the American standard of living.

Kozol, Jonathan. (1992). *Savage Inequalities*. New York: Crown. Kozol documents movingly the vast inequalities among U.S. public schools.

Leone, Robert. (1986). *Who Profits: Winners, Losers, and Government Regulation*. New York: Basic Books. Leone presents the unintended negative consequences of allegedly beneficial governmental regulations and other fiscal policies.

Levy, Frank. (1988). *Dollars and Dreams*. New York: Norton. This is a clear documentation of the decline of U.S. living standards during the 1980s.

Mishel, Lawrence, and David Frankel. (1991). *The State of Working America*. Armonk, NY: Sharpe. This is an easy-to-understand empirical documentation of the collapse of living standards in the United States and how this disproportionately hurts poorer people and young people.

Newman, Katherine. (1988). *Falling from Grace*. New York: Free Press. Newman examines how downward social mobility affects members of the so-called middle class.

Nussbaum, Bruce. (1992). "Downward Mobility: Corporate Castoffs Are Struggling Just to Stay in the Middle Class." *Business Week* (23 March), pp. 57–63.

Page, Benjamin. (1983). *Who Gets What from Government*. Berkeley: University of California Press. Page explains how the federal government's social welfare programs actually shift wealth from poorer people to richer people.

"Prescription Drugs 32% Cheaper in Canada Than U.S." (1992). *The Miami Herald* (22 October), p. A10.

"The Riots: Just as Much About Class as Race." (1992) *Business Week* (18 May), p. 47.

Useem, Michael. (1991). *Liberal Education and the Corporation*. Hawthorne, NY: Aldine de Gruyter.

"Wasted Health Care Dollars." (1992). *Consumer Reports* (July), pp. 435–49.

Confronting Moral Challenges

Ralph Lamont Mosher
Professor Emeritus, Boston University

John M. Whiteley
Professor of Social Ecology, University of California at Irvine

Senior Voices

Harold

I believe that everybody does consider himself or herself a moral person. However, morality lies in the eyes of the beholder: What I might consider the morally correct thing to do, another person may disagree with. I think that religion is a good example of this. Consider the zealots in India who murdered travelers in the name of their god Kali: They believed that they had to kill people to be allowed a place with their god. There are many forms of religion, and all have different views of morality. Some assert that it's wrong to be a homosexual or to have an abortion while others say it's ok. Another example of how morality lies in the beholder can be seen in the KKK: Some members of the KKK honestly believe that what they are doing is right. Personally, if I'm about to do something wrong or if I have done something bad, this little voice inside me nags away until I rectify the behavior. I believe that everyone, to some extent, hears these voices, whether it be a voice of justice or a voice of caring, and makes decisions based on their past experiences and upbringing. ■

I n this chapter we highlight some of the moral dilemmas left unsolved or unaddressed by the current generation of citizens and leaders. (For further discussion of this issue, see Chapter 17, "Making Your Way Toward Citizenship.") We also present some of the moral dilemmas that current college graduates may confront and share the methods used by several of their contemporaries to cope with actual dilemmas.

In the pages that follow, we will identify two sets of parameters for thinking about moral challenge. The first set concerns the importance of learning from the societal context. Entitled "Do As I Say," this section will delineate the flawed context provided by contemporary America. The second set of parameters is far more hopeful. With a group of colleagues we have been researching moral reasoning and moral action in late adolescence and young adulthood. In the section entitled "Do As I Do," we present examples of the moral challenges reported recently by young adults and share what they thought about them and how they acted on them at the time. A recurrent theme in this chapter is that college students can learn from the difficult experiences encountered by others who have gone before them.

"Say It Ain't So, Joe"

A s the story goes, Joe Jackson got the nickname of "Shoeless Joe" when, to rest sore feet, he took off his spikes during a minor league game. He has been described as one of the best natural hitters in baseball history. Only Hall of Fame immortals Ty Cobb and Rogers Hornsby have surpassed his lifetime batting average of .356, compiled over thirteen major league seasons. He was a sure-fire Hall of Famer going into the 1919 World Series, which his team, the Chicago White Sox, was favored to win. Gambling was well established at that time, however, and going along with some teammates, Jackson accepted $5000 to help throw the World Series to the Cincinnati Reds.

Eight players, including Jackson, were indicted by a Chicago grand jury. While a jury ultimately acquitted the players, the baseball commissioner, Judge Kenesaw Mountain Landis, banned them from the game for life:

NOTE: The authors wish to acknowledge the significant collaboration of a number of colleagues in the data collection and presentation of results for this chapter. Drs. David Connor and Kathy Kalliel conducted almost all of the moral dilemma interviews in the process of completing their doctoral dissertations at Boston University. The moral dilemmas excerpted in the chapter are based on Dr. Kalliel's dissertation, as are the tables of women's and men's dilemmas and their resolutions. Dr. Mark Porter, Professor James Day, and Ms. Norma Yokota-Norwood are additional colleagues in a broader collaboration examining the relationship of moral reasoning to moral action in young adulthood.

Regardless of the verdict of juries, no player who throws a ball game, no player that undertakes or promises to throw a ball game, no player that sits in conference with a bunch of crooked players and gamblers where the ways and means of throwing a game are discussed and does not promptly tell his club about it, will ever play professional baseball! (quoted in Dickey, 1982, p. 65)

"Say it ain't so, Joe" is the perhaps apocryphal remark of a young fan to his hero when "Shoeless Joe" was banned from baseball for life and the fan wanted reassurance that Joe had been banned unjustly.

Seventy or so years later another baseball hero, Pete Rose, former player and manager of the Cincinnati Reds, was also banned from baseball for life for gambling. For Rose, as for "Shoeless Joe," the ban cost him baseball's highest honor, certain induction into the Hall of Fame. Even though well over half a century passed between the incidents involving Joe Jackson and Pete Rose, the appropriate lessons were not learned, and personal tragedy followed for yet another athlete.

The challenges of moral action and inaction are compelling in the years of early adulthood. While few college graduates will meet their moral challenges in the glare of publicity that confronted Joe Jackson and Pete Rose, the challenges themselves likely will be even more difficult. How those are handled at the time can influence the rest of one's life.

Do As I Say

Daily the media showcase the apparent decline and corruption of traditional American values and morality. Sports, long celebrated as an emblem of American values, has recently become a symbol of the decline of those values. Pete Rose was banned from baseball for gambling and sent to prison for income tax evasion. All-American basketball player Len Bias of the University of Maryland died of a cocaine overdose less than twenty-four hours after being the first pick in the National Basketball Association draft. World record holder Ben Johnson was stripped of his Olympic gold medal and of his world record in the 100-meter dash because he tested positive for banned steroids. And these examples are but the tip of the iceberg.

At a different level, Stanford University, one of the most prestigious universities in America, has been accused of inappropriately charging the federal government hundreds of thousands of dollars for such things as improvements in and flowers for the president's residence and for maintaining the mausoleum of the university's founder and namesake. Junk bonds and corporate takeovers have been the source of incredible fortunes and have resulted in criminal indictments and long jail sentences for individuals associated with Wall Street.

It is estimated that mismanagement and fraud in the savings and loan industry ultimately will cost American taxpayers over $500 billion. For past generations of bank robbers—men and women without much formal education—"plying their trade" meant wielding a gun for comparatively modest stakes. For some of today's leaders in the savings and loan industry—men and women with the finest education America can provide—the proverbial bank robbery was accomplished much more lucratively with the stroke of a pen. Their accomplices in these modern-day bank robberies were not get-away drivers, but highly educated and high-priced lawyers, politicians, appraisers, and accountants.

The level of cynicism and moral inconsistency among some of our nation's leaders also has been distressingly apparent. An attorney general of the United States during the Nixon administration (the *highest* legal officer in the country) said, "Watch what we do, not what we say," and then in testimony under oath could not remember what he did. In the Reagan administration, Oliver North, for whom patriotism was a stated motive and who virtually wrapped himself in the flag, "couldn't remember" critical events or players in the Irangate scandal. The Irangate investigation became a modern morality play in which the seemingly exemplary all-American Marine colonel was both a hero and a sacrificial victim of the moral failures (lying to Congress, lying to the people, lying to the press) of leaders in the highest echelons of government. The dean of the Boston University School of Communication gave a powerful commencement speech on the critical need for morality in the media, only to be charged with plagiarism. Portions of the speech were lifted virtually word for word from the writings of a film critic for the Public Broadcasting Service. Examples of such moral hypocrisy appear daily.

Writing in 1939, Robert S. Lynd drew attention to a list of overlapping and contradictory assumptions in American life that had developed over different eras. These assumptions, in his view, had become a part of the culture that was passed on *uncritically* to subsequent generations. Among those assumptions was the following: "Honesty is the best policy. But: Business is business, and a business man would be a fool if he didn't cover his hand." The "business is business" ethic noted by Lynd can be found repeatedly in American life and reflects inconsistency in basic cultural values.

But all is not inconsistency and hypocrisy, and the business community also presents some of the best in basic cultural values (see Chapter 8, "Applied Ethics"). Consider another example. Warren E. Buffett, an investor from Nebraska, recently became chairman of Salomon Brothers, a Wall Street firm facing huge civil and criminal penalties for violating rules governing the auctions of U.S. Treasury securities. In connection with the scandal, Buffett was invited in 1991 to testify before the House Subcommittee on Telecommunications and Finance. He outlined a very different ethical standard:

The nation has a right to expect its rules and laws to be obeyed. At Salomon certain of these were broken. Almost all of Salomon's 8,000 employees regret this as deeply as I do; and I apologize on their behalf as well as mine. My job is to deal with both the past and the future. The past actions of Salomon are presently causing our 8,000 employees and their families to bear a stain. Virtually all of these employees are hard-working, able, and honest. I want to find out exactly what happened in the past, so that this stain is borne by the guilty few and removed from the innocent. To help do this, I promise to you, Mr. Chairman, and the American people, Salomon's wholehearted cooperation with all authorities. These authorities have the power of subpoena, the ability to immunize witnesses, and the power to prosecute for perjury. Our internal investigation has not had these tools. We welcome their use.

As to the future, the submission of this Subcommittee details actions that I believe will make Salomon the leader within the financial services industry in controls and compliance procedures.

But in the end, the spirit about compliance is as important or more so than words about compliance. I want the right words and I want the full range of internal controls. But I also have asked every Salomon employee to be his or her own compliance officer. After they first obey all rules, I then want employees to ask themselves whether they are willing to have any contemplated act appear the next day on the front page of their local paper to be read by their spouses, children and friends with the reporting done by an informed and critical reporter. If they follow this test, they need not fear my other message to them: Lose money for the firm and I will be understanding. Lose a shred of reputation for the firm, and I will be ruthless. I welcome your questions. (Buffett, 1991)

Buffett is eloquent about the importance of the "spirit of compliance" and the importance of each employee serving as his or her own compliance officer. It is an exacting challenge he places on each employee to contemplate how his or her children would respond to such actions if they read about them on the front page of the newspaper.

Buffett's testimony notwithstanding, the current generation of citizens and leaders are passing on a flawed moral legacy. There are examples of both the best and the worst to learn from. This section, "Do As I Say," took its title from the sworn testimony of Nixon-era Attorney General John Mitchell, who urged listeners to focus not on what government leaders said, but on their actual deeds. Then he claimed not to be able to remember what he did.

A far better record of action in response to moral dilemmas is provided by recent college graduates. In the next section, entitled "Do As I

Do," they report actual moral dilemmas of young adulthood, recount what they did when confronted with the dilemmas, and perhaps most helpful, share their reasoning.

Do As I Do

The set of moral issues facing contemporary America is long and ambiguous enough to cause widespread social debate. This debate may reflect the abandonment or the failure of traditional American values and institutions (for example, the family, the school, the church). Or it may reflect an increasingly divergent culture and society that tolerates relativism, many moralities, or none at all. Certainly the Bill of Rights empowers active citizenship and free expression. Consequently, as the current generation of young Americans begins life after college and subsequently moves into positions of leadership, the moral and legal challenges embedded in their society will be inescapable: affirmative action, sexual harassment, voluntary euthanasia, a woman's right to privacy and a fetus' right to life, to name just a few.

Of concern to young adults are both the *personal* and the *work-related* moral dilemmas that they will face almost immediately after graduation. In one sense they may seem much less earth-shaking than the problems outlined in the previous section. Nonetheless, because they are personal, they are every bit as important to individuals as the larger or broader social/civic dilemmas.

The Sierra Project

As authors we have not been subject to the personal pressures of young adulthood for over three decades. Therefore of far greater immediacy and relevance is a longitudinal study of moral reasoning and moral action that we have been conducting since 1975 with the cooperation of a group of students and former students at the University of California, Irvine. These students had been volunteers in a "character education" study named the "Sierra Project" after the freshman residence hall they all shared as freshmen. These "Sierrans" had collectively governed the residence hall, establishing rules and penalties for violations; taken part in a weekly seminar focused on social and moral issues such as racism, sexism, equal opportunity, and so on; written weekly logs of their experiences that were shared with the project staff; met personally and in groups with the staff (which included a number of undergraduates living in the residence hall as residence assistants as well as faculty members); completed a formal curriculum; and taken part in community service projects in Irvine and surrounding communities (see Loxley and Whiteley, 1986).

The Sierrans' moral reasoning and their personal and social development were measured several times during their undergraduate years and compared to that of a "control group" in another residence hall. The essential finding was that the varied activities and experiences of the Sierra Project had a positive impact on the moral reasoning and principled thinking of the participants.

When we began the "Sierrans Revisited" project, nearly a decade had passed since these students graduated from college. The chance to follow up on a sample of fifty of those former students in order to learn how they now defined moral issues and, in particular, what moral choices they made in the face of personal dilemmas, was both unique and appealing. These students were living primarily in Southern California and in the Pacific Northwest. In our initial interviews we asked former Sierrans to "tell us about their moral lives" at age 30. More specifically, we began with a leading question: "Tell me about a moral dilemma you have faced recently or a moral decision you are currently making."

In spite of some uncertainty, we found that the Sierrans were willing to be interviewed, and the stories of the moral domain in their lives were rich in meaning. Excerpts follow from moral dilemmas recounted by three Sierrans. Part of these narratives and the considerations that moved the subjects to act as they did are included. We shall then summarize the variety of moral dilemmas they described and the actions they took to resolve or temporize the problem(s) they faced.

Case Study: Maria

Maria is a 29-year-old Hispanic woman who works in a medium-sized manufacturing business as an office manager. The firm is small enough that she knows the owner and manager, yet large enough that there is an unskilled and semiskilled work force of several hundred employees.

Maria's Moral Dilemma. The moral dilemma Maria described involved the behavior of the shop foreman, who had responsibility for the hiring and supervision of the unskilled personnel.

> I worked at a large plant where the men and women out there, they're mainly men, but they're all under this foreman. Now, I would say that 70 percent of all workers are illegal,* and so they feel very threatened, of course; and they are afraid of losing their jobs. This gives the foreman more power over them and I believe he's a man who uses that consciously or unconsciously; I think he

---

*This term is used to refer primarily to citizens of Mexico who are in the United States in violation of federal immigration laws. As a group they are particularly vulnerable to exploitation by the unscrupulous.

does. I had been confronted with a phone call about two years ago, when a woman called to tell me that she didn't want to give her name, that she didn't want to get into trouble in any way, that she had asked for a job. She had gone for a job interview. . . . He didn't come right out and tell her, but that if she would sleep with him, he would give her the job, if not, she didn't have a job. She didn't have a job because she wouldn't sleep with him and that she was just thinking about it, that she should call and we should know about it.

He seemed like a really nice man and I confronted him with this problem; I felt it was best to confront him with this problem. . . . He felt because he was Latin, the boss would think the worst and think it was true. I didn't tell the boss for this reason. He and his brother run the whole company, they do all the work and don't get paid more than family and family friends who just read the newspaper and magazines. An ex-employee that was fired and called me up to let me know because . . . every time like on unemployment, a claim is filed against us, I prepare the case. I take care of all the personnel records, I fix the case for it, and I have to go to court for it. . . . I'm only going by what the termination report I get from the foreman out there and all my payroll records. But I'm not in contact really with the men out there. We won our case. . . .

And so this man who isn't receiving unemployment insurance, he called me to say that . . . he was going to appeal it. But beside appealing it, which he could do . . . he just wanted to let me know because he knew we weren't aware of the situation, but that the foreman was very unfair. He believed the foreman was very unfair, that every year the employees would be forced to contribute $20.00 to the boss's Christmas present. The foreman would pocket half the money. The employees made $3.35 to $5.00 an hour for hard work at an assembly table so that $20.00 was a lot of money. The man was threatened for his job on several occasions. Once he wanted to contribute $5.00 but the foreman threatened him with his job. The foreman ordered the lunch truck for the workers and was getting a kick-back. The boss knew that and didn't care. I didn't know it but in this industry everyone did this. What the owner didn't know was on their one-half hour lunch hour, the workers were forced to go to that one lunch truck. If the employees went to another lunch truck, they were threatened with their jobs and got a verbal notice; and if it happened again the workers would be fired. This man had disobeyed two times and the last time, the man had used another lunch truck since it was cheaper and he was hoping not to get caught. Also, the foreman verbally abused the workers, and yelled at them. The foreman didn't want the workers to become friends with each other and forced them to buy their lunch from the truck and not bring their lunch from home. The men had to sit at their dirty, greasy work areas for lunch and not talk to friends or anyone.

I believed this worker and did not want to go talk to the foreman since I was afraid he might convince me not to go to the boss and he would put doubt in my mind. The owner should be aware of that and work it out. I decided to go tell the owner and then ask if they could notify the court they weren't going to contest the appeal, that they could begin to pay unemployment. The boss was really upset about the contribution and conditions about lunch. The owner did not fire him since he was dependent upon him. I went with the gut feeling that the [fired worker] was telling the truth. Even though the foreman was polite and businesslike with us in the office, it was hard but I believed it was true. I remembered the phone call from two years ago. Sometimes when a person comes from a low socioeconomic background, they've been prejudiced against, the minute they get a little power, they use it on someone else. (quoted in Kalliel, 1989, pp. 87–89)

Maria was asked to explain the reason she chose to bring the foreman's behavior to the attention of the boss.

I think that I had like an outrage in me in the sense that, all that was going on out there and for how long. It was the injustice of how they were being treated. Once I believed that it was justified . . . Come on, how much more fortunate I am than they; I can find another job or I could pay the premium. How big a deal is it that the worst thing that could happen happens. I lost my job. Okay. I don't have my insurance any more. I'll deal with that when it comes. I'm so much better off to start with than these men out there. I guess that gave me putting it more into perspective and not thinking that the whole world was mean. Or what is going to happen to me. (quoted in Kalliel, 1989, p. 90)

Commentary. Maria made a reflective decision to inform the owner of her company about the abusive and dishonest behavior of the foreman. She did not blow the whistle rashly; rather, she made up her mind over time and cumulatively. One can observe the progression in her thinking as it was affected by a series of abuses of the workers by the foreman: his "casting couch" job interview with the woman applicant; his pocketing or skimming of part of the workers' Christmas gift to the boss; his forcing workers to sit at their dirty work benches while they ate a solitary lunch; his discriminatory hiring and firing of employees, a majority of whom were illegal immigrants without legal protection, medical and retirement benefits, or job security. The illegal aliens were particularly vulnerable to being threatened by the foreman with the loss of their job and had little recourse when he was yelling at them.

Maria's decision to act appeared to be about equal parts moral judgment, the expression of moral outrage, and an empathic response to the plight of the workers. As she expressed it, "I had an outrage in me in the sense that, all of this was going on out there and for how long. It was the injustice of how they were being treated." This is what Carol Gilligan (1982) refers to as Kohlberg's "voice of justice [and rights]," a voice Gilligan associates with the moral thinking of men. In Gilligan's view women are more likely to base their moral judgments and actions on the principle of care and a nonpossessive love in personal and social interactions. We shall come back to these two theories of morality shortly.

Recognizing how much better off she was than the workers, Maria demonstrated real concern for their welfare throughout her employment. To lose her job would not have been nearly as "catastrophic" as it would have been for the workers. Indeed, she was willing to risk her job to make life "less mean" for the employees. (This makes her an unusual individual in the overall sample of Sierrans, who generally did not care to risk their jobs over a moral claim.) Some months earlier she had confronted the foreman over his offer of a job for sex. She did not report the sexual blackmail to the boss, who might have fired the foreman because he was a Latino. Maria is also Hispanic and was especially understanding of the many handicaps of poor, victimized workers. Her specific concern and caring for the 70 percent of the work force in her company who are illegal immigrants was especially evident. To Maria they work in a twilight zone within American society—lacking medical insurance and job security, laboring in difficult conditions, and subject to the abuse of the foreman. The majority are paid, at most, minimal wages.

Maria's outrage at how unjustly and meanly the workers were treated is understandable. This "righteous anger" appears to be a powerful motor driving her moral action. Maria's moral actions (confronting the foreman on the sexual harassment issue, going to the owner about further violations, expending effort on behalf of the fired employee, seeking to improve working conditions so they will not seem universally "mean") originate in personal moral judgments concerning an unfair system and the unfair treatment of the work force.

Maria's moral judgments, however, appear to grow out of both a voice of justice and a voice of caring. The concern for justice comes through loudly and clearly: "I had an outrage . . . for what was going on and for how long. It was the injustice of how they were being treated." Equally striking is the voice of caring: "Seventy percent of all the workers are illegal and so they feel very threatened, of course, and they are afraid of losing their jobs. This gives the foreman more power over them and I believe he's a man who uses that power . . . against them." To cite Gilligan's paradigm, then, Maria speaks with the two voices of judgment and caring.

What additional moral criteria or principles lie behind the two voices of justice and caring in Maria's case? Clearly, she has a strong sense of fairness and a capacity for righteous anger where injustice is an institutional norm of the workplace. She expresses sympathy and caring for the workers, sharpened perhaps by a recognition of their common ethnic roots and a sense of her own good fortune compared to their tenuous, vulnerable position. The moral affect is powerful in helping her formulate her response to the dilemma. *Not* to act would be to join in the oppressive treatment of the workers by the foreman.

The moral imperative for her is to treat others in the same way she wants to be treated. She does not express this imperative in words, nor does she say she is acting to obtain the best deal possible for a majority of the workers. She does act toward the workers as if they are persons of worth, deserving of dignity and respect in the difficult conditions under which they are required to work. Last, but by no means least, she decides to act on her moral imperative and her core principles. She could have pulled back at several points along the way but did not. Poignantly, she also observes that "when someone comes from a low socioeconomic background, they've been prejudiced against, the minute they get a little power they use it on someone else."

Symbolically, by interposing her moral assessment and action, she tries to balance the arbitrary, capricious use of raw power by the foreman. This seems to be the plot of yet another contemporary American morality play. It underscores an earlier point: Moral challenge is not exclusively or even primarily the stuff of Bush-Gorbachev summits, closely argued debates and decisions of the Supreme Court on abortion, or of the brutality/racism of the Los Angeles Police Department. Rather, all the elements of moral challenge in this society appear in the day-to-day lives of ordinary citizens.

Case Study: Kyoko

Kyoko is a 27-year-old woman of Japanese ancestry who is a social work trainee in a family service agency. Her direct supervisor is an experienced social worker. One important role of professionals in her agency is to render expert testimony in court cases involving child welfare and child custody.

Kyoko's Moral Dilemma.　The moral dilemma Kyoko described revolved around whether to testify in a child custody dispute that involved sexual abuse. She believed that even though she had been working with the child directly and her supervisor had not, his testimony before the court would have been more influential because of her perceived inexperience.

Recently I was in a situation where I was asked to testify in a court custody/sexual abuse case. I was a trainee so my supervisor should have testified but he did not want to. He wanted me to. I had the best information about the family. I had direct contact with the family. The supervisor suggested that when the subpoenas were being served to leave the building so we would not get served. Should I follow what my supervisor said and avoid legal complications or do I testify in behalf of my client since I have information that would help the client in his life situation? He said: "let's have you testify or no one testify," but he did not want to testify. "Let's all leave; let's not get involved, not have our input in the situation." The dilemma was knowing how difficult these types of cases can be, the issue of being a trainee, not being experienced, going into court, having all that inexperience pointed out, being a trainee and feeling like a fool, somehow thinking that if I was going to have this happen the supervisor would go to court. But once it happened I felt pressured by the supervisor to take this on. The feeling that I had important information, and that in the absence of this information the child could be placed in a dangerous situation.

I had about two days to think through the dilemma. First, I thought about what was at risk at the court trial. What types of decisions were going to be made based on the evidence presented during the trial? To me, what was at risk was a child's well-being. It appeared that the child's court-appointed attorney was heavily biased against the mother and towards the father. The father was serving as his own attorney and appeared, in my few contacts with him, as very manipulative. The court was sick of this case coming up over and over and wanted to put an end to it. The way to do it was to focus the blame and pathology solely on the mother and mandate that sole custody be given to the father. In my work with the child, I felt that it would be unhealthy and a dangerous situation for him to be in. First, I weighed the risk here and felt the child would be in danger.

The second step, I thought who was best qualified to present the information to the court and was it okay for us to duck that responsibility and to leave the kid hanging? I came to the conclusion that it was not morally all right for us to duck the responsibility; someone needed to be there to present the information.

The third step was deciding who, me or my supervisor, would make the presentation. I felt angry towards my supervisor for being so warm and supportive on the surface, yet when I looked beyond that I realized that there was a very firm line being drawn that, "if anyone is going to, you are going, I don't plan to go, I don't feel I have the information to provide since I do not work directly with the child," which is ridiculous since many times the trainees see kids in this situation and supervisors will go and testify in court cases. So I had to decide the best person to present the evidence was the supervisor in terms of being credible and an experienced expert in the field but given the unwillingness, the responsibility fell with me. There was either very little evidence, no evidence, or me. I felt I owed it to the child to put in my two cents. I decided to contact a lawyer and have a subpoena served. (quoted in Kalliel, 1989, pp. 90–92)

Kyoko was asked to explain why she chose to testify, what the moral dilemma was for her, and how she resolved the dilemma. She focused on her inexperience as a trainee and on the way her testimony could be devalued by the court. She also stated that the welfare of the child was at risk and that her testimony could contribute to keeping the child from being placed in a "dangerous situation." Her moral judgment was unambiguous: "I came to the conclusion that it was not morally . . . right for us to duck that responsibility; someone needed to be there to present this information—it was either very little evidence, no evidence, or me" (quoted in Kalliel, 1989, pp. 98–99). Kyoko's moral action was to arrange to be subpoenaed so that she could testify.

Commentary. Kyoko made a carefully reasoned decision to testify in court personally in the child custody dispute. Her highly experienced supervisor had not only declined to testify himself but suggested that the members of his team leave their building to avoid being served with a subpoena that would have compelled their testimony. "To me, what was at risk was a child's well-being" (again, one can hear the voice of Carol Gilligan's "caring" as moral concern). The provision of care to people in need is an institutional aim of the social work profession. One explanation of Kyoko's action was that she was actualizing a core value of her chosen profession. In the specific instance the legal issue (in contrast to the moral dilemma) was which parent would have custody of the child. The father, who was acting as his own attorney, seemed "very manipulative" to Kyoko, and the court was reputedly "sick of the case." One way to resolve the issue was "to focus the blame and the pathology solely on the mother and mandate that sole custody be given to the father."

Kyoko's thinking is illustrative of parts of several theories on the origin of moral action. Her interpretation of the dilemma (an integral step in both Kohlberg's [1984] and Rest's [1986] models of moral action) facing her was clear. She articulated the issues succinctly: whether as a social worker trainee she knew enough to testify and whether as a social worker she had the right to "duck" testifying on behalf of a client when she was in sole possession of information she believed to be crucial to the child's well-being. Her conclusion was that she had a moral responsibility to act, even if she could put in only "two cents worth." Her knowledge of the child and his father, and her empathy and caring for a bewildered minor, also contributed to her decision to act on his behalf when all of the other professionals seemingly wanted only to be free of the case.

Case Study: Gilberto

Gilberto is a 27-year-old Hispanic man who is a kindergarten teacher in a public school. His classroom is designated by the school as bilingual. According to the educational policy of his school district, Gilberto is to offer instruction only in English for children of Hispanic background who have poor language skills in Spanish.

Gilberto's Moral Dilemma.   The moral dilemma Gilberto described involved his belief that this policy is wrong for children who are low in proficiency in both their dominant language, Spanish, and their second language, English. The dilemma for him was whether to conform to school district policy, which required teaching in English—in his view, providing inferior instruction—or teaching at least initially in Spanish and offering a higher-quality instruction.

> I teach kindergarten and I teach in a bilingual classroom and that, in itself, is a moral dilemma, teaching bilingual education. But the decision that I'm making now . . . is . . . in regard to the placement of the children. Initially, when the children are put into the bilingual program they are tested for language dominance so they are tested for Spanish dominance and English dominance. So they are giving us scores in A, B or C or whatever. So with new bilingual legislation and our district's idea of bilingual education there seems to be a trend beginning, before it was taught, now it's a trend. It started a new program and they've given it one of those big names and the trend is now that if a child is low in his dominant language which in this case is Spanish and obviously low in English, he would be immersed, in other words taught in English only. Which, to the uneducated . . . sounds like the ideal thing to do but in previous years it has been proven as being not the most efficient way of teaching.
>
> And so, what I'm being faced with now is taking five or six children in my classroom and deciding whether they are going into this program or not. This is a difficult choice because . . . I haven't taught that long but I have developed a certain idea as to what I'm doing and how I am educating these children. And I do have very definite beliefs and one of these beliefs is if you build a child's language ability it will show as success in reading especially, which is the key to the whole elementary education system. So . . . the thing now is if you teach them nothing but English and so they're getting locked in, as far as I'm concerned, they are losing a great deal of time when they could be learning

concepts that would be useful in reading and you would be teaching them in a language they would understand, you know. Now they're missing out just because the district seems to think this is the right thing to do now. So it's a very difficult choice to make. (quoted in Kalliel, 1989, pp. 138–139)

Gilberto decided to act on what he thought was best for the children and was teaching in Spanish when representatives of the school district came to observe his classroom instruction:

They showed up on me and I was doing a lesson (in Spanish) and "Isn't this your PVP group? . . . Why were you conducting the lesson in Spanish?" Well then they would write me up as needing improvement in following district policy or one of the other BS grades which they have which is ultimately their way of getting back at you for not playing the game as they wish you to play it. I suppose obviously the grossness of the error I commit would come into play, they wouldn't fire . . . I have tenure, for one thing. So that's a certain degree of protection. I have clout because I'm a good teacher. I have the respect of fellow workers because I'm a good teacher. There are a lot of things going for me and yet. . . . My ego would be bruised, I don't know. Now, they won't fire me, not for something like this. They would reprimand me and reprimand me and reprimand me again. And say, "That Gilberto he's so unruly." (quoted in Kalliel, 1989, pp. 138–39)

Commentary. Gilberto was willing to act on his conviction of what was best for children in his classroom. He offered instruction in Spanish for the benefit of children who had low proficiency in both Spanish and English. He was willing to act against a school system rule he felt to be wrong because it penalized children with poor language skills.

Gilberto's empathy for the plight of these children is evident. He cares about the difficulties of a small group of the children in his classroom, and maintaining the quality of his relationships with those students is his first priority. He does not seem to be actively proposing broad policy changes or making recommendations on improving bilingual education in the school system; his preoccupation has been with five or six children only. The central moral issue for him was that the school was wrong about these children and the way they should be taught. "Question authority" was a watchword of the student radicals of the 1960s and 1970s. Gilberto is questioning authority in principle (or in the principal of the school) and is breaking school policy. Like many moral problems in teaching, the issue here is both personal and professional, although Gilberto is largely immune from retaliation by the authority structure of the school.

Gilberto offered a rationale for his action, "a certain idea as to what I am doing and how I am educating these children." Further, he was acting on a belief that "if you build a child's language ability it will show as success in reading especially, which is the key to the whole elementary education system."

With this rationale Gilberto relied on his professional judgment on the suitability of English as a second language rather than the school system rule and instructed minority children in their native language. Even though he forecast how the system would harass him ("they would reprimand me and reprimand me and reprimand me again"), his decision did not constitute a great risk. He has tenure, and in his words, "I'm a good teacher with clout."

Moral Development After College

In our study of moral action in young adulthood, we asked respondents two basic questions: (1) What actual dilemmas do you identify as characteristic of your work and personal lives? and (2) What factors determine your moral behavior?

Moral Dilemmas of Young Adulthood

The forty Sierrans interviewed as part of the Sierra Revisited project described more than eighty moral dilemmas in their personal and work lives. A partial taxonomy of those real-life challenges and the actual moral solutions they chose is presented in Tables 19.1 and 19.2.

What remains to be said about our subjects and the moral issues they face? First, their dilemmas are fairly mundane—one is almost tempted to dismiss these stories as the stuff of "As the World Turns." Indeed, it may be that soap operas have the wide appeal they do primarily because they raise profound personal and moral issues. And the moral lives portrayed in soaps are sharply drawn and explicitly detailed. Perhaps the soaps are the richest, most widely generalized force for adult moral education available to us.

We say that only partially in jest; we don't wish to trivialize the pain, the victories and the defeats, and, most importantly, the moral and human profundity of these real dilemmas. Indeed, however familiar and commonplace the dilemmas may seem to the reader, they are nonetheless profound experiences for those who face them. Classic moral "voices" or issues of evil and good, justice and injustice, compassion and noncaring, guilt, courage, fear, and so on reoccur even in our small sample. But they are new and perplexing and painful to individuals experiencing them for the first time.

Determinants of Moral Behavior in Young Adulthood

The former Sierrans identified a relatively diverse array of factors as determining their moral behavior.

Table 19.1 Young Adult Women's Moral Dilemmas

Subject	Content of the Moral Dilemma	Moral Action
1	Whether to return to (live with) a former, unfaithful boyfriend	Did not reestablish relationship
4	Whether to use disposable but nonbiodegradable paper diapers rather than cloth diapers	Decided for disposable paper diapers, "against the environment"
5	Whether to share study notes with law school classmates	Decided not to share study notes
7	Whether to have an affair with another man	Decided to remain faithful to her husband and not have the affair
10	Whether to give her employer several months' advance notice that she will be leaving	Decided to do "the right thing" and notify her employer
11	Whether to notify her employer/owner of her company that a foreman was mistreating and exploiting the workers	Informed the employer about "kick-backs" and sexual harassment
12	Whether to continue to deal with a customer who devalued her because she was a minority female	Decided to continue to deal with the customer, who "is always right"
13	Whether to move in with her boyfriend	Decided to live together
15	Whether to continue having an affair with a married man	Decided to break off the relationship
18	Whether to resume a relationship with an ex-fiancé	Decided not to resume the relationship
19	Whether to testify in a court custody/sexual abuse case despite her trainee status in social work	Decided to testify for the child

SOURCE: Adapted from Kalliel, 1989.

Consideration of One's Own and Others' Well-Being. A woman law student, for example, initially loaned her detailed lecture notes to a friend, only to see the friend score higher on a test on torts. Because of the cutthroat competition for grades and the relationship of grades to election to the *Law Review*, she decided not to help further. "I don't like it but that's how it is." Also, a married woman was considering an affair with a co-worker: "I feel responsible to my husband, I know he loves me and I knew immediately I should say 'no.' That's what I did."

The Family. Mothers were especially influential in the moral decisions and actions of young adult women (much less so for the men). Mothers were persons with whom it was possible to talk, and they served as role models for decision making and as explicit/implicit sources of standards by which to live. Approximately 80 percent of the women subjects talked through the moral issues they were facing with family members: mothers, sisters, less often brothers. Fathers were rarely mentioned, however,

Table 19.2 Young Adult Men's Moral Dilemmas

Subject	Content of the Moral Dilemma	Moral Action
3	Whether to do part-time military-related work that contradicted his beliefs	Decided to do the work: "It's the convenience of the job and money and interest versus what I believe in"
6	Whether to pursue a romantic relationship with a young woman	Decided not to go further with the relationship
8	Whether to tell a female friend that her husband was having two affairs	Decided not to tell
9	Whether to enforce a fraternity rule to remove a pledge who used drugs	Enforced the rule; pledge was ostracized
14	Whether to tell his parents that his sister was living with her boyfriend	Decided to hint that his sister was living with the boyfriend
16	Whether to abandon bilingual instruction of Hispanic students as directed by his principal	Decided to teach kindergarten in the same bilingual format despite the administration directive
17	Whether to change jobs despite a pay reduction that affected his family	Made the change of jobs
20	Whether to usurp his business associate's power in their company	Moved ruthlessly to force the associate out of the company

SOURCE: Adapted from Kalliel, 1989.

with the notable exception of three Sierrans whose actions were particularly exemplary (Day, 1992).

The Quality of Interpersonal Relationships. Figuring prominently in the decisions of young adult women was the possibility of repairing a relationship and continuing to trust or to care when hurt by another person. This was especially true with potential boyfriends and with ex-boyfriends or ex-husbands.

Religion. Across the sample as a whole, religion was reported as relatively unimportant in making moral decisions, but it was very influential for those subjects (10–15 percent) who were actively religious. "Then my boyfriend moved in. I felt I had let myself down. I had a standard to follow: the rules of the church and I set it for myself and said: there it goes!"

Society and Its Norms. The influence of society and what is regarded as conventional behavior were not widely reported. One exception to this was the following: "I decided it was a moral decision when in my Lamaze class, the teacher brought up both issues [cloth versus disposable diapers] and then said: 'You know they're not really disposable' and the whole class said, 'What?' First, it is against the law to throw the disposable diaper out and this is what the industry meant for you to do with the disposable diaper [but] they were really not biodegradable."

Particular Codes.   Religious, business, and professional norms were frequently cited.

- **Marriage vows:** "It's just not right to do that to your spouse and it would hurt my husband terribly. I know he loves me."
- **Professional ethics:** "I believe [even as a beginning social worker] that I need to do everything I can to help and protect others."
- **Business code:** "I decided to continue my account with this client even if he was both racist and sexist toward me as a minority woman. 'The customer is always right.'"

In the workplace morality beyond self-interest and self-protection generally was temporized at the point one's job or livelihood was at risk. For a number of what were termed "everyday heroes," however, perceived injustice, the immorality of war-work, or the abuse of employees in the workplace evoked clear moral actions (Day, 1992).

Personal Moral Norms and Principles.   One or more personal (that is, internalized) moral norms or virtues were mentioned by many of our sample: "I don't think it's right to lie . . . that would have been deceitful." Personal moral principles included consideration of one's own rights as well as those of others (voices of justice and caring) and consideration for the well-being of others and oneself (altruism and caring): "My most basic moral concern is to oppose racial inequality wherever I can."

Feelings.   Both negative and positive feelings were associated with moral action.

- **Negative:** Fear for others involved in the dilemma and outrage at the situation: "I was very distraught. . . . I started feeling guilt, resentment, and anger."
- **Positive:** "I do what feels right. . . . I felt awesome after I decided not to resume a relationship." "I had the feeling: God's happy! And I got peace; it's the right thing to do."

These references to the power of feelings to affect moral action were more prevalent than we had anticipated. The notion of "what feels right" seems to be an important influence on moral action.

The Sierra Project: An Overview

Day (1992) expressed one of our more basic findings as follows:

> There appeared to be a conspicuous lack of points of reference to which our subjects turned when faced with moral dilemmas. For the most part, it appeared to us that when the subjects considered

moral dilemmas in their lives, they did so in terms of narrow definitions of self and of consequences for others. With a few exceptions they spoke rarely of well-formulated or consistently available principles, did not refer to institutional or communal sources of moral support, did not rely on identifiable moral heroes and examples, and rarely spoke of seeking the advice of friends, family, or partners. Few of our interviewees had talked about religion or more broadly confirmed "spiritual" contexts for assessing and considering the consequences of their actions.

For the Sierrans we studied, deciding what to do when confronted with a moral dilemma seemed to be a largely secular process. The impression given was that choosing whether to report an unethical foreman or to follow a moral business practice differed little intellectually from choosing what model of car to buy or apartment to rent. Moral resolution from thinking to action was ironically "amoral," and moral criteria were not strongly present in the decision making of both groups. Affect, by contrast, was strongly experienced in many of the dilemmas and in connection with their resolution.

Conclusion

As the results of the Sierra Project might suggest, the need for ethical education is as apparent now as it was when the project was conceived. Moreover, how to provide this education remains a profound issue. As you prepare to move on to the next phase of your life, you can be certain of one thing: You will face moral dilemmas. As you struggle to resolve these dilemmas, remember the words of Warren Buffett: "[Are you] willing to have any contemplated act appear . . . on the front page of [the] local paper to be read by [your] spouses, children, and friends . . . ?"

References and Resources

Buffett, Warren. (1991). Testimony before the House Subcommittee on Telecommunications and Finance (transcribed from the MacNeil-Lehrer NewsHour, September 4, 1991).

Day, J. (1992). *Narrative, Identity, and Audience in the Moral Lives of Young Adults.* Unpublished manuscript.

Dickey, Glenn. (1980). *The History of American Baseball Since 1902.* New York: Stein & Day.

Gilligan, Carol. (1982). *In a Different Voice: Psychological Theory and Women's Development.* Cambridge, MA: Harvard University Press.

Haan, N. (1978). "Two Moralities in Action Contexts: Relationships to Thought, Ego Regulation and Development." *Journal of Personality and Social Psychology* 36: 286–305.

Haan, N.; E. Aerts; and R. A. B. Cooper. (1985). *On Moral Grounds: The Search for Practical Morality.* New York: New York University Press.

Kalliel, Kathy. (1989). The Moral Decision-Making of Young Adults in Actual Dilemmas. Doctoral dissertation, Boston University.

Kohlberg, L. (1984). "Moral Stages: A Current Formulation and a Response to Critics." In *Essays on Moral Development, Vol. II: The Psychology of Moral Development.* San Francisco: Harper & Row.

Loxley, J. C., and J. M. Whiteley. (1986). *The Character Development in College Students, Vol. II: The Curriculum and Longitudinal Results.* Schenectady, NY: Character Research Press.

Lynd, Robert S. (1939). *Knowledge for What?* Princeton: Princeton University Press, pp. 60–63.

Piaget, Jean. (1932). *The Moral Judgment of the Child.* Glencoe, IL: Free Press.

Rest, J. R. (1986). *Moral Development: Advances in Research and Theory.* New York: Praeger.

V

Leaving College

20 Liberal Arts: What Has It Meant?

William C. Hartel

Codirector of the Senior Year Program,
Marietta College

Senior Voices

William

A "liberal arts education" is not schooling in how to act like a political liberal. The term *liberal* is drawn from the word *liberty.* Thus the liberal arts education is one that frees the academician from the normal learning process and immerses him or her in cross-disciplinary scholarship. The liberal arts education represents an expansion of the mind to envelop skills and acquire knowledge far beyond the realm of the ordinary, more specialized higher educational process.

For example, when I was an undergraduate, I chose to major in both music and history. At many institutions this decision might have meant that I would have been very limited in my course selection. However, because I wished to be challenged, and because the liberal arts education demands cross-disciplinary study, I learned much more than music theory and American history. Not only did I graduate with honors in both departments, I also managed to study the philosophy of Kant, the physical laws of Newton, the theories of Einstein, the plays of Shakespeare, the poetic *tao* of Lao Tzu, and the Japanese language. Thus the liberal arts education expanded my horizons and gave me an understanding of things far beyond the realm of the traditional education.

Why learn these things? To some it may appear that I engaged in the study of "things I will never use in my career," as the saying goes. Only someone who has not had the benefit or has never desired to meet the challenge of a liberal arts education would question its value. The liberal arts education above all fosters a love of learning.

It feeds a hunger that is within all of us to understand our world and all its complexities. Thus, freed from the boundaries of a traditional education, the liberal arts education allows one to draw on a deeper realm of knowledge and understanding when faced with life.

As I find myself with little to do over the summer but relax (for the first time in a long while), I am constantly reading new material and reassessing what I have learned. I am not simply studying material to pass an exam. I now appreciate the value of knowledge. Consequently, I am sad that I have only a normal lifetime in which to learn about this world, and I sometimes want to experience more than will ever be possible. I learned to love learning, and that is the greatest gift of the liberal arts education. ■

One of the more satisfying aspects of a liberal arts education is that it is not an end in itself. Unlike many other things in life that are measured by beginnings and endings, there may be a beginning to a liberal arts education but there is no end. The benefits continue to flow as life itself goes on. When you receive that diploma, only in a very narrow sense is one chapter of your life over. Your liberal arts education has prepared you for the rest of your life! Spelman College president Johnnetta Cole has stated that a liberal arts education "doesn't just educate you for the first job, it educates you for all jobs. Not just for the first few days after graduation, but . . . for living for the rest of your life." You will use the knowledge and skills that you have acquired continually as you pursue your roles as responsible citizen, conscientious worker, and caring participant in more intimate personal relationships. In this chapter we'll show you how.

Lifelong Learning

We are all aware that our society becomes more technologically complicated every day. We are also aware of the multiple consequences arising from this complexity. According to which prophet you honor, these consequences are both bad and good. In any event, we can agree on one thing: Those people who are the most adaptable to change and who know how to use positively their increasingly available leisure time will be the most satisfied and fulfilled.

Adaptability to Change

One of the essential elements of the liberal arts is the examination of process. In other words, it is not so much the history of the world, the development of economic systems, the existence of literature, or the make-up of chemical units that is important to the learner. Rather, it is the methodology of the examination of history, economics, literature, or chemistry. Put in rather simplistic terms, the essence is more in the how and why than in the what. These tools of questioning and examining are crucial for the individual's successful adaptation to change.

The study of the liberal arts is always placed within the context of human development. As you have studied the liberal arts in a more formal manner, you have been examining the human condition in a historical context. Undoubtedly, one of the prevalent themes has been that of change and adaptation. Regardless of the comments of critics on specific events in history, the tone of this theme has been one of hope and optimism. After all, it is out of Western society that the very concept of progress originated. Thus the liberal arts tradition has revealed to you that societies do cope with change and that change has always been, in fact, a triumph of the human condition. The message of the liberal arts is this: You can play an essential role in your own fate!

Perhaps it has become increasingly difficult to accept what once was taken for granted—that "progress" is inherently good. However, it is the liberal arts that has aided our contemporary society in questioning what more and more technology has meant for our physical environment. The outcome has been an increase in the number of people who are asking if we ought to reevaluate our concept of progress. There are those, for example, who are seriously contemplating such issues as whether trees and rocks also have rights. Such issues, which might have appeared ludicrous one hundred years ago within the Western world, will become more and more visible in the years to come. Your liberal arts background will help you not only ask the serious questions but also frame solutions.

There are those "savants" who tell us that our modern society is undergoing a paradigm shift the likes of which has not been experienced since the invention of the printing press and the subsequent emergence of the print culture. These same observers are pointing out that, perhaps for the first time in human history, we are realizing that such a shift is occurring while it is occurring and therefore are trying to develop the language to understand and to adjust to the shift. We must use the tools and the skills suitable for one technology in order to be able to discover the tools and skills necessary for the emerging technology. To avoid what is often termed "paradigm paralysis," those who are able to change must become the activists for the new technology.

The term *liberal* itself indicates a freeing; thus, in its ideal sense, your liberal arts education should free you from a narrowness of purpose, the destructiveness of superstition, and a shallowness of spirit. With what result? We hope that it has strengthened your resolve to act, your ability to analyze more clearly, your capacity to articulate clearly, and your tolerance of ambiguity. Certainly, your education has not made you perfect, but it has given you the tools to adapt successfully to change.

Use of Leisure Time

One of my former students, now a practicing attorney, told me that, when he talks with other lawyers, he can always tell which ones had a good liberal arts education because they are the ones who can talk intelligently about something other than law. What a terrific recommendation for a liberal arts education!

Earlier I noted that such an education frees one from a shallowness of spirit. In doing this, the liberal arts education heightens the imagination, strengthens curiosity, and encourages creativity. Such an education helps us to see life as more than pursuit of material pleasures and gain or a game of simple survival. Giving us the resources to make rewarding use of leisure time, therefore, is another benefit of the liberal arts education—one of those ingredients that add the proverbial spice to life.

As my former student observed, your education has intensified your oral communication skills. Conversation and discourse in general should be concerned not just with the exchange of basic, essential information but should be stimulating, expansive, and interesting! This is not to suggest that all liberal arts graduates must become witty raconteurs, but rather that they should have developed the communications skills necessary to guarantee that they will not be crashing bores.

Likewise, your appreciation of the written word has been honed. Undoubtedly, you are not only a better writer but also a better reader; your expertise goes beyond the reading and writing of memos, basic instructions, and simple explanations.

Those who have developed good written and oral communication skills can enrich their lives through exposure to the works of other skilled "communicators"—writers, actors, artists, and the like. For instance, watching actors bring to life the words of a noted playwright or screen or television writer can give you a respite from the mundane. Reading a novel, essay, biography, autobiography, or some other well-crafted prose or verse will provide a necessary boost to your life. Adding to your experiences the information gained through stimulating, informative, and/or entertaining newspaper and magazine articles brings depth and breadth to your daily routine. And your ability to appreciate a museum, a concert, a play, or a dance performance is enhanced. While your education probably has not made you a connoisseur of dance, for example, it might very well have given you the opportunity to explore the aesthetic benefits that this art form might hold for you.

You have, however, gone beyond the more formal application of the aesthetic sensitivity. Your appreciation of tone, structure, and form will allow you periodically to bring about personal renewal through contact with your physical environment. For some of you this might entail a simple stroll in a verdant park; for others it might involve the observation of a stimulating blend of oddly shaped buildings framed by a threatening summer storm. In sum, life becomes more than just existence and a perceived battle for survival. Rather, existence becomes an incredible journey via the senses!

Responsible Citizenship

In Chapter 17 Suzanne Morse shared with you her thoughts about responsible citizenship and the ways in which college has helped you learn the necessary skills for civic life. Finally, she asks the "nagging question": "What do you think your generation will do with the problems at hand?" A liberal arts education has helped you to hone the skills and attitudes you need to tackle that nagging question.

Previously, we discussed how your education should have prepared you to adapt to change and to use your leisure time. In other words, your education prepared you to start along the path of lifelong learning. A satisfying journey down that path will provide you with constant renewal, a willingness to take reasonable risks, a tolerance for ambiguity, and a recognition that life is more than simply the pursuit of material pleasures and gain.

What your education has provided for you is the tools to become a citizen leader. You are now more capable than when you entered college to engage in what Morse terms public talk, public thinking, public judgment, and public imagination, and you now have the courage to act.

Some of you may become leaders in a broader sense than citizen leaders; Chapter 16 elaborates on this issue of leadership. Your generation will provide corporate, academic, and political leaders, for example. Your world of work will provide those opportunities. But every person, no matter what his or her choice of vocation, will have the opportunity to be a citizen leader, to become an active participant in what Morse terms the "hard work" of being a member of the community.

Exercise 20.1

Leadership and the Liberal Arts

List one skill that you might use as a civic leader that your education in each of the four basic liberal arts disciplines (fine arts, social sciences, humanities, natural sciences) has enhanced.

The World of Work

While some individuals may inherit wealth or for some other reason choose not to participate in the world of work, most of us sooner or later find ourselves in the workplace. Perhaps you remember someone asking you what kind of job you were going to get with a liberal arts education. What was your answer then? Do you have a different answer now? Better still, what is the right answer?

One of the desired outcomes of your education is the recognition that in many situations in life there is no right answer. The right answer for you at this time may be that your exposure to the liberal arts has pointed you toward the goal of teaching high school history. For your friend, that same exposure may have resulted in a desire to hitchhike across America before deciding on a career. A person can arrive in the workplace from one of many different paths, and a liberal arts education hardly guarantees the "rightness" of any particular path.

What we hope that it does guarantee is that you learn a process for survival both on the path toward the workplace and within the workplace itself. As noted previously, in our rapidly developing technological world, one of the essential elements for such survival is the availability to change, to be flexible, and to accept ambiguity—in other words, to "roll with the punches." This ability becomes even more crucial when one considers the predictions of current prognosticators that job-holders in the future will have not only several jobs but also several different careers. And it is this ability to change and adapt that your liberal arts education has enhanced. In other words, those who cannot adapt to the constantly changing norms of the workplace might be not only unemployed and/or underemployed but constantly apprehensive, uneasy, and generally dissatisfied. Again, note that your education does *not* guarantee an absence of these conditions—but at least it reduces the possibility.

If the prophets are wrong and if technology has reached its workable limit, does this mean that your liberal arts background will not serve you in a stable and predictable workplace? Indeed not! You may find one job and one career that will be yours for life. Your creativity, your imagination, and your communication skills will make that job and that career fulfilling and satisfying, not only for you but for those you might serve.

Regardless of whether you find that one definitive career or pursue several different career paths, your education should serve you in yet another important fashion. Granted, from the period of the Renaissance, the world of work has loomed as more and more important. This increasing importance is reflected in the works of such diverse Western thinkers as John Calvin, Adam Smith, and Louis Blanc. But you must also recognize the truth contained in the old cliché that "all work and no play" makes for a dull person as well as a probable candidate for early burnout.

By contrast, if your interests are varied, you can find renewal for your career in the fields of play and leisure. You may indeed fall into the category of "all work and no play," but with your exposure to the liberating arts, the odds that you won't are in your favor!

Exercise 20.2

Tolerating Ambiguity

If a tolerance for ambiguity is an important skill for survival in a world of constantly changing career and work demands, list three ways that your liberal arts education has honed that skill.

Personal Relationships

We all seek and long for meaningful relations with others. The family, be it a traditional, extended, or so-called modern one, remains a significant social institution, and you seek healthy family relationships. Moreover, you probably have developed or will develop an intimate relationship with a partner of your choice. Finally, you have probably formed, and will continue to form, friendships, whether with many people or with only a few. These various categories of personal relationships together provide a framework for your lives. Although a liberal arts education is no guarantee that such a framework will be the most sturdy, the most desirable, or the most satisfying, your education probably has enhanced, and will continue to enhance, your personal relationships.

The twenty-first century promises to be one of rapid change. Joseph Rost and others are using such terms as "postindustrial society" to describe this future. As noted previously, your education will better prepare you to deal with this world of ambiguity and to find your way into that impossible-to-describe career of the future. What this means is that you should be relatively secure economically. Chances are that one who is somewhat free from economic concerns feels more secure, which in turn provides a better milieu for fulfilling personal relationships.

Your education has also enabled you to become a better-balanced individual. We hope that one of the consequences of the balance is that you will not become overly absorbed in work but will know how to combine work and leisure. How can you hope to nurture strong personal relationships if all your energy is focused on your career? Of course, you may develop personal relationships with those with whom you work; however, if the only common denominator in such a relationship is work, then it's likely to be a shallow relationship.

Can a liberal arts education change a cold, calculating, and distant person into a warm, empathetic, and caring one? Probably not. But such personality descriptions are relative terms. In addition, an education that frees one from cant and superstition, that opens vistas of human achievement in arts and letters, and that examines the human condition within a historical context might result in a more understanding, more empowering, and more caring individual. And deep and meaningful personal relationships are far more likely to develop within such a context.

Finally, to put it in very simple terms, your education should make you a much more interesting person. You are knowledgeable, you know how to continue to learn, you have a sense of community responsibility, and you have learned something about yourself. As a noted wit once observed, the greatest sin of an educated person is to be dull! Interesting people are sought by others; dull people are avoided.

| **Exercise 20.3** | *Learning About Yourself* |

An important element of your liberal arts education is the opportunity to know yourself. Can you cite at least one new piece of the puzzle called "understanding yourself" discovered through exposure to the fine arts, the social sciences, the humanities, and the natural sciences?

Conclusion

Your undergraduate years have either just concluded or are about to conclude. We hope that this chapter will help you to begin the process of assessing what those years have meant. Within higher education in the 1990s, one of the most important issues that has developed is that of assessment. That is, the "customers" of higher education are asking for—indeed, demanding—accountability from those institutions in the business of education. Various instruments have been created for measuring "outcomes" of a liberal arts education. These measurements are, and will be, based on both acquired skills and acquired information. But the final and most crucial assessment is yet to come for the graduate of the 1990s, and that assessment will be based on the quality of the total life of the graduate.

My intention was not to demonstrate that a liberal arts education will lead to the perfect life or that a lack of such education will assure an "imperfect" life. Rather, I wished to point out that the real purpose of the liberal arts education is to *enhance* one's life. Ideally, your own education will do just that. The concluding chapter in this book addresses the issue of alumni responsibility. Part of that responsibility is helping your institution improve where improvement is needed. However, as you reflect on your education, remember that even the best educational offering must have a willing recipient.

How many commencement speakers on how many thousand of occasions have expressed the sentiments with which I wish to close? I will spare you the flowery phrases, but I will not spare you the essential message: You are the future. And your liberal arts education should have helped you to *be* the future!

References and Resources

Cole, Johnnetta. (1993). "On Campus with Women." *Association of American Colleges* 22(4): 3.

21

The Final Six Weeks

Cheryl Barnard
Assistant Dean of Students at Quinnipiac College

Brian McCoy
Department Manager of Family Practice at Fallon Clinic, Worcester, MA

Senior Voices

Danelle

There's so much to think about when you graduate from college: getting a job, finding a place to live, maybe buying a new car. But the hardest thing for me was saying goodbye to my friends. There were four of us that had been together since our freshman year. We had lived together, attended classes together, attacked late-night pizzas together, and shared our deepest dreams and fears with each other. About two months before graduation, the finality of it dawned on me: Two of us would be leaving the state, and our friendship would never be the same. My friends must have felt it, too. Whereas earlier in the semester we were all too busy to get together, suddenly everyone had time to spend with each other. Our studies as well as our boyfriends suffered, but we needed that time together to say goodbye. We never did share our fears about our upcoming separation, but we had more fun those last two months than we had all year. I suppose it was the last hurrah for our little group. I know that those memories will always be there, and I'll never forget my college buddies. ■

D o you remember the early days of your freshman year? Chances are, you felt anxious about your immediate future, and graduation probably seemed light-years away. Now that you have almost made it, are you a little surprised at how anxious you're feeling again? Back then, you thought graduation would be the easy part. What happened?

The time has come for you to face another enormous change in your life. You are now leaving an institution that has become familiar to you—in many ways, a second home. What lies ahead is uncertain, new, and scary. The uneasiness you may be feeling is normal; fortunately, there are options available to you that can help make your senior year and graduation all you expected it to be.

What are those options? To get an idea, picture yourself standing on a beach and gazing out at the vast ocean, an ocean that represents your life after graduation. On the beach you are safe, but how many of us are able to stay on the shore when the ocean is only a few feet away? Its vastness seems so enticing. As you wade into the ocean and begin exploring this new world, you encounter strong currents and powerful waves. And, even if you decide to head for shore, how can you avoid being knocked down by those waves or sucked under by the currents? With a little bit of knowledge, the right supports, and some encouragement, you can go right back into that ocean and stand confident in the face of those oncoming waves (Sammon, 1983).

In this chapter we will provide you with the knowledge, support, and encouragement to face graduation. Specifically, we will guide you, week by week, through your final six weeks of college, outlining what you need to do, both practically and emotionally, to prepare for the "real world." Key topics include (1) living on your own, (2) coping with returning home, (3) making new friends, (4) overcoming boredom, (5) facing success and failure, and (6) saying good-bye.

Week One: Living on Your Own

I n planning your final six weeks of college, begin with the basics. For many of you, choosing to live on your own represents your next step in achieving independence. Some of you who may have already been living on your own know the trials and tribulations of finding a place to live and paying the bills. For all of you we offer this advice: *Think practical!*

Planning Your Finances

For business majors, *net worth* is a common term that refers to how much someone is worth in dollar amounts. Your financial planning at college probably consisted of pinching pennies and checking desk drawers for loose change so that you could buy that late-night pizza. Now that you will be earning a steady income, you need to figure out your financial status before you put yourself in debt.

Exercise 21.1

Assessing Your Net Worth

To find out your net financial worth, do the following:

1. Figure out your current or future gross monthly income.
2. Subtract taxes—local, state, federal, social security.
3. Subtract any contribution to company benefits—health insurance, life insurance, retirement, profit sharing.
4. Subtract any revolving debt—credit cards, health club memberships, insurance premiums.
5. Subtract student loan payments. Although repayment might not begin for six months after graduation, these payments can throw your budget off if you don't plan for them from the start!
6. Subtract costs of having a car—loan payments, taxes, gas, insurance, upkeep.
7. Subtract housing costs—rent or mortgage, phone, utilities.

These are the fixed costs for which you will be responsible every month. Whatever money is left can be used for variable costs: clothing, entertainment, car repairs, and other basic needs. Remember, one basic need is to eat. For many recent graduates food seems to be the last item on the list of things to buy. The days of cafeteria dining are over, however, and eating out every night can become extremely costly. Depending on your cooking ability, it may be more cost-effective (and certainly better for your health) to purchase a good cookbook and experiment rather than live at the drive-through window.

You will survive. In fact, you may find yourself with money left over at the end of the month. If this is the case, open a savings account. Even $5 a month establishes a history of savings that will help your credit rating and, in the long run, will begin to add up. Having money in a savings account can be a lifesaver in times of emergency such as an unexpected car repair. Financial experts suggest that you have the equivalent of three months' worth of your salary in the bank just in case you should be laid off or unable to work. It may be tough to reach that three-month total, but the struggle will be worth it if something unexpected happens.

A final note on paying bills: Do not be late with payments. Bad credit will haunt you forever! (Many people have been denied mortgages because credit card payments were not made that first summer out of college.) If you are going to be late with a payment, call your creditor. In most cases the creditor will note your call and avoid giving you a bad credit rating. If you get yourself into a deep financial hole, call all your creditors. Many will be more than willing to set up a payment plan that you can afford until you get back on your feet.

Good luck and remember: "A penny saved is a penny earned."

Finding a Place to Live

Deciding where and possibly with whom you will live can be both an exhilarating and disillusioning experience. The thought of having your own place to decorate and set up the way you want is exciting. But there can also be disillusionment stemming from the cost and the time involved in finding a suitable living environment. The key is to take your time, be practical, and find something that fits your lifestyle and wallet.

Exercise 21.2

Thinking About Your Living Options

Before you begin looking for your new living environment, you need to answer some questions:

1. Do you want to live alone? Can you afford to live alone?

2. Do you want roommates? How many people could you live with?

3. What type of living arrangements would you prefer (house, condo, apartment)?

4. How are you going to find your new living environment (realtor, newspapers, word of mouth)?

5. Do you want to try to buy a house?

6. Do you want the option of owning a pet?

The Roommate Option. The first issue to tackle is deciding if you want to live alone or if you would rather share your living space. Perhaps you and a friend have always dreamed of sharing a place, in which case you are all set. If you want to live alone and can afford it, then you are also all set. Difficulty arises when you not only need to find a place to live but also need to find someone to live with. There are a variety of ways you can find potential roommates. One is a roommate referral service. Such services usually cost $25–$75, and many of them do not guarantee the "quality" of the people in their listings. Many newspapers have a "Roommate Wanted" section. Some major companies have housing referral services for new employees. No matter how you find your roommate, you should not only meet face to face but also discuss in depth the type of living arrangement and relationship you expect. One recent graduate corresponded with his future roommate, Taylor, by mail. You can imagine his surprise when he moved in and found out that Taylor was a female.

Types of Living Spaces. The next issue to tackle is the type of physical space you would like. If you want to rent, then you have a variety of options available to you. One of the most common is the privately owned apartment. An example of this is the first or second floor of a two-family house where the owners live in one flat and rent out the other; another example is a condominium that the owner is renting out. Both these types of apartments have advantages and disadvantages. Living in a privately owned apartment usually means that you are going to have greater restrictions on the types of things that go on in your apartment, given the owner's personal investment in the property. (One recent grad, for instance, was not allowed to hang pictures because the owner did not want holes in the walls.) On the plus side, this investment means the owner is more likely to respond to maintenance requests.

Another type of apartment is corporate owned. These apartments usually are situated in a complex owned by investors who hire a person(s) to manage the buildings and/or site. This type of living arrangement also has its advantages and disadvantages. On the plus side, you will be living in an environment where there are a lot of people and sometimes extra amenities (for example, tennis courts, swimming pools, laundry facilities). On the minus side, there are so many units that repairs may take longer.

No matter what type of apartment you choose to live in, make sure you inquire about any additional costs above and beyond your rent (for example, garbage removal fees, parking fees, water fees, pet deposits). Many times these extra costs can add up and turn your dream apartment into a financial nightmare.

Finding an Apartment. After you decide on the type of apartment you want, you need to decide how you are going to go about finding such an apartment. One option is the professional realtor, who will do the leg work for you and show you only those apartments that fit your specifications. *Beware:* A realtor can be your friend or foe. If you consult a realtor, you need to find out the costs involved in finding the apartment. For example, is there a finder's fee? A commission? Will you be paying these additional costs?

When you do find the place of your dreams, you must always read the lease carefully and completely. You will be expected to pay a certain amount to secure your apartment—usually first and last months' rent and sometimes an additional security deposit. You have a right to negotiate these and other items on the lease. For example, one recent graduate talked her future landlord into waiving the security deposit because she was able to provide excellent references from past living arrangements. So take your time and discuss everything before you sign anything.

Another source of information on available living spaces is the classified section of local or regional newspapers. Many times, if the apartments are not listed with a realtor, you will avoid a realtor's fee. You can speak directly with your potential landlord and negotiate a satisfactory lease. Again, however, be sure to ask about any additional fees. Your rent may be $800 per month, but with a first-and-last-month rent agreement, you will have to hand over $1600 before you can take occupancy. Remember, too, that this fee is negotiable and that all arrangements should be put in writing. In sum, striking out on your own without the help of a realtor may be scary, but it might afford you the opportunity to save some of your hard-earned money.

Planning Your Move.   Once you have found your new living space, you will also need to plan your move. You should make a list of those things you need to accomplish prior to occupancy, such as activating utilities, connecting phone service, and hiring a moving company. Another recommendation is to conduct a full inspection of your new residence with your landlord prior to your moving any of your belongings into the new residence. During this inspection you should document all existing damage. This document should be signed by all parties and stapled to your lease. This will save you from being billed for previous damage to the unit. Does this sound like a college room inventory? Exactly! If you can get a copy of this form from your alma mater, then do so. It will be a useful guide.

Buying Your Own Home.   We have talked a great deal about renting; however, some graduates may be able to afford a condominium or house. If you are considering buying rather than renting, we suggest that you go to a bank or mortgage company first. The bank or mortgage company will look at your current income and existing debt and, based on a ratio (income over outstanding debt), will determine what you can afford. If you can get preapproval for a specific mortgage amount, this will help when you begin your search.

With or without preapproval, you can either use a realtor or look through the newspaper real estate section. Keep in mind that realtors who work for the seller are obligated by law to tell the seller how much you can afford. Thus it is important to tell the realtor approximately how much you wish to pay for your new home. And because so many laws protect both you and the seller, certain procedures must be followed in purchasing property. The procedure may vary from sale to sale or state to state, so we recommend that you consult an expert in the field.

Andrea

During my final semester at college, I feel I was in denial. I knew I was graduating, but I did not want to face it. I had been so secure in my environment of four years, I never thought it would end. I was nervous about graduating, because I did not want to lose the secure lifestyle I had developed with my friends and roommate.

It wasn't until after graduation that I started to realize how quickly my four years had passed. I now miss every aspect of college. I wasn't prepared for the drastic changes involved in entering the real world. And I hadn't allowed myself to bring that wonderful college experience to a satisfactory close. ■

Buying a Car

Most recent graduates dream of buying a new car as a reward for having worked hard for four years. Like looking for an apartment, looking for a car offers a mixed bag of thrills and letdowns. The expression "Caveat emptor!" (Let the buyer beware) certainly applies to car purchases. Car dealers have a reputation for wheeling and dealing, and the more you pay for a car, the more the dealer earns. Thus you need to learn about the intricacies of buying a car.

There is a logical and systematic way to purchase a car. First, you must decide what you can afford. Second, you must investigate a car's dependability as well as its attractiveness. Third, you must recognize that this will by no means be your first and only car. The following are some suggestions as to what to think about when looking for a new car:

- **Dependability and repair costs.** Consult the *Consumer Reports Annual New Car Edition*, which will provide you with all pertinent information for making an informed buying decision.

- **Insurance costs.** In most states auto insurance is required by law. Depending on where you live, what kind of car you purchase, and what your driving record is, insurance may cost as little as $400 or as much as $2000 per year.

- **Road costs.** Based on the car you choose, you will need to set money aside for registration, inspection, and taxes.

- **Dealer costs.** When you begin negotiating with the car dealer, remember that the sticker price is a suggested price, not the price you have to pay. To negotiate a better price, ask for the actual dealer invoice, which shows how much the dealer paid for the car, and then discuss with the dealer how much more you are willing to pay. A dealer's unwillingness to negotiate is a good indication of the type of service you may receive in the future. As a recent graduate and, in many cases, a first-time buyer, you also become eligible for rebates direct from the manufacturers. Be sure to ask the dealer; some dealers are reluctant to present all the rebate options because rebates cut into their commission. And if you feel you are being taken advantage of, you can contact the Better Business Bureau or go to another dealer.

Exercise 21.3

Living on Your Own

1. Prepare a monthly budget based on your estimated first-year income. Remember to figure in taxes, rent, utilities, food, gas, student loans, credit cards, maintenance on a vehicle, insurance, entertainment, and clothing.

2. Consult the apartment listings in your local paper. Define the terms used in ten of the advertisements (for example, w/d = washer and dryer). Visit at least one available apartment.

3. Visit a car dealership and talk with the salesperson.

4. Interview a recent alumnus who chose to live independently. Ask what surprises he or she encountered.

Week Two: Returning to the Nest

Many seniors return home to live with their families right after graduation—some because they want to live at home, others for basic economic reasons or convenience. The choice to move home is not a cop-out or an embarrassment and should not be viewed as such. Many seniors feel they have to strike out on their own. If they are unable to obtain an apartment right after graduation, they feel they have failed. *This is a myth*. In reality, moving home represents a viable option for graduates, giving them time to practice budgeting and to save money.

Planning the Move Back Home

If you are considering moving back home, you must be aware that you have grown and changed, and that your family has adjusted to life without you. Furthermore, you may find that your family has not changed. In either event, both you and the family may have developed patterns of behavior and lifestyles that no longer mesh, so that moving back could lead to friction and hurt feelings. Thus you should talk with your family before your return. By discussing one another's concerns prior to your arrival, you may eliminate unnecessary anger and frustration. And whenever problems do crop up, it's important to communicate openly about them.

You may be thinking that you lived with your family for eighteen or so years, so what problems could there be? It's amazing how much you and your family may have changed in the last few years. Reflect on your current lifestyle. Is it consistent with the lifestyle you had when you lived at home? For example, one recent graduate who had become a vegetarian could not believe her mother would not stop serving roast beef at Sunday dinner. Another recent graduate was surprised to learn that her parents had a regular standing "dinner date" for Wednesday nights and that she was not invited.

The key is to negotiate with your parents and siblings. Remember, it's their home. In some ways you will be disrupting the routine established while you were in college. Thus you need to be honest, open, and willing to compromise. Your relationship with your parents is changing from adult-child to adult-adult, and as a young adult you must hold up your end of the bargain. Remember, mutual respect stems from sincere commitment and concern for one another's feelings. Keep this in mind and many of their requests will seem more reasonable.

Exercise 21.4

Thinking About Moving Back Home

If you are considering moving back home, you need to answer some questions:

1. Will your parents expect that you abide by a curfew?
2. What will be your responsibilities regarding household chores?
3. Will you be expected to attend all those family events you missed while you were in school?
4. Will your parents worry if you stay out all night?
5. Will your friends be allowed to stay over?
6. Will your parents approve of your staying overnight at your significant other's apartment?
7. Will you be expected to contribute monetarily (i.e., rent, food, phone bill)?
8. Will you have to share a room/bathroom with your kid brother/sister?

Negotiating a "Living-at-Home" Contract

Some seniors choose to contract with their parents concerning the amount of time they will live at home. By setting up a reasonable time frame, you give your parents an opportunity to assist you for the short term, force yourself to set a goal to shoot for, and enable both parties to treat the arrangement as finite. For instance, it is easier to mow the lawn if you know that in three months you will be off on your own. Likewise, your parents might be more tolerant of your loud music if they know that you and your stereo will be leaving at the end of the summer. In any case, do not stop looking for opportunities for living on your own. Home can become very comfortable, and recent graduates often have a hard time leaving the nest, especially if their savings account keeps growing. Do not forget about your plans to move out and try living on your own.

Exercise 21.5

Things to Do Before Moving Back Home

1. Develop a housing contract with your parents that spells out everyone's rights, privileges, and expenses.

2. Create a list of your expectations about moving home. Have your parents create a similar list. Share your lists with one another.

3. Develop a list of changes you will have to make in your current lifestyle in order to successfully move home.

4. Complete the following statements with your parents:

   a. The thing I am most excited about, when I think about moving home, is . . .

   b. The thing I most dread about moving home is . . .

   c. My parents are great about . . .

   d. My parents cannot deal with . . .

   e. Moving home makes me feel like . . .

   f. Since leaving for college I have changed my feelings about . . .

   g. I hope moving home will be . . .

Week Three: Socializing

Try to recall your first day at college. Were you thinking about how you were going to occupy your time outside of class? Did you wonder if you would find things to do, make new friends, and fit in with the other students? Some of you no doubt became involved quite quickly, while others took a little longer to find your niche. But all of you discovered that the college environment provides an enormous array of opportunities for socializing and keeping busy.

Maintaining Old Ties

Once you leave school, you will face similar adjustments. You might be wondering if you'll be able to maintain your college friendships and how you'll go about forming new ones. Will there be as many opportunities for socializing? Where will you go? What will you do? Whom will you meet?

You're probably thinking, "Why all this talk about keeping old friends and making new ones? The friends I've made at school will be my friends for life, and we'll continue to get together just like we did at school!" The fact is, being part of a college community made it easy to form friendships, and soon you will be leaving that community. Even with the best of intentions to not let your relationships change, circumstances will begin to interfere. For example, some of your friends may move to a different state. Even when a friend moves only twenty miles away, it soon begins to seem as if that person now dwells on a different continent. In addition, the promises of weekly calls and monthly visits become harder to uphold in the face of the demands of your new life, friendships, and interests. Finally, the constant pressures of work may begin to take precedence over socializing.

Forming New Ties

Just as maintaining old ties can be tough, establishing new ties may be equally difficult. In college you were part of a community where all members shared some similar experience not only in the classroom but also elsewhere on campus. You shared a common jargon (names of buildings, classes, popular hangouts). You shared a common physical environment (the library, the gym, the cafeteria, a residence hall). You shared a common vision to foster your intellectual, social, and personal growth. This common experience made it easy to develop a network of friends and acquaintances with whom to socialize.

By contrast, you may find that the work environment has a very different and more limited mission. Most organizations concentrate on improving productivity and give little thought to the personal growth of their employees. In addition, the members of this community will be varied: They will have different organizational roles, priorities, and lives outside of work. This varied environment may not provide you with a network of friends and acquaintances with whom to socialize.

This may be scary, overwhelming, and frustrating at first. But be encouraged by the fact that you will soon find your niche and begin to develop a network of colleagues and, later, maybe some new friends.

The first step you need to take is to assess the culture in your environment. Are you lucky enough to be working in an environment where personal growth and socializing are integral components of the organizational mission? If this is the case, then there will be company softball teams, regular get-togethers outside of the office, and so on. If these types of activities do not exist, then you should not assume that the people at work will automatically replace your college social group. Many organizations frown on co-workers socializing, so remember, before you start planning an end-of-the-week social hour, assess the specific organizational climate and take your lead from other employees. And even if socializing is appropriate in your workplace, it may not be appealing and may actually be disappointing. Unlike in college, where at minimum a few people likely shared your interests, in your work environment there may be no one who has common interests and lifestyles. Don't blame yourself for not making new friends immediately.

The second step is to investigate other ways to find new friends. Your past experiences at college can help you in this endeavor. How did you meet your closest friends in college? If all your friends lived in the same resident hall, then pay particular attention to the type of living accommodations you choose after graduation. Your best bet might be an apartment complex, but be sure to find out what the average age of the occupants is, whether there are community recreation facilities, and if a social committee exists. If you met your college friends on the playing fields, then join a town athletic league or a local health club. Remember, though, that some people use their workout time as private time. Also, keep in mind that it is hard to initiate a conversation during an aerobics class or basketball game, so spend some extra time prior to and after your workout or game hanging out.

Another way to meet people with similar interests is to attend events sponsored by your institution's alumni office. Many colleges have chapters of their alumni groups across the United States, and these groups often sponsor get-togethers. If your college does not have a chapter in your town or city, call the alumni office and see if they can give you the names of any alumni who live in your area. Lastly, join one of the numerous professional/civic organizations (Rotary Club, Saleswomen of America, and the like) or a church or synagogue. Meeting new people will be easier if you become involved outside of work.

Exercise 21.6

Planning for the Postcollege Social World

1. Develop a personal statement regarding the expectations you have about socializing and friendships at work.

2. Have your friends develop a list of those qualities they like about you. Keep this available for positive reinforcement during your first days in the "real world."

Week Four: Becoming Part of a New Community

If leaving the college environment is going to change how and with whom you socialize, you might wonder how you will find opportunities to stay busy. Our best advice is to get involved in activities that interest you, otherwise known as "avocations" (the definition of *avocation* is "distraction from business; diversion").

You may say, "I won't have a problem finding things to do. I always kept myself busy at college." Remember, however, that most colleges have a large variety of resources (student government, student organizations, athletic departments, and so on) providing you with limitless opportunities to become involved. You also had your studies. Believe it or not, you will miss going to classes and doing homework; not having them will create a void in your life. How often did you fill that free hour with extra reading or reviewing? What will you do with a free hour? At first, you might enjoy having nothing hanging over your head and just "hanging out" with nothing to do. But most recent graduates will tell you that after a few months of this inactivity you will long for something—anything—to do.

Where do you find things to fill your free time now that you are in the "real world"? There are still many opportunities available to you; it just takes a little more effort and energy to find them. For instance, towns and cities provide various services to their residents. Park and recreation departments offer a plethora of athletic activities such as softball leagues, ice skating lessons, and so on. In addition, public school systems and/or public libraries usually offer adult education classes. If you always wanted to take a photography course, then sign up now. If you have a particular interest, call your town/city hall and ask for specific information.

Another way you can become involved is by volunteering during your free time. Many nonprofit social service agencies depend on volunteers. Call a local soup kitchen or community center and offer to volunteer several hours a week. This will enable you not only to give something back to your community but also to become part of the new community.

Still another way to keep busy is to become involved with your local church or religious organization. Such organizations may be looking for youth group leaders or teachers for their religious education classes. In addition, many churches sponsor social activities geared specifically for young adults.

Finally, if you can't find something that interests you, consult the Yellow Pages or your local paper's calendar of events. The Yellow Pages provides a myriad of information on just about everything. Likewise, most local newspapers publish weekly lists of upcoming events ranging from meetings of civic organizations to try-outs for local theater and choral groups.

Before you graduate, make a promise to yourself to become involved in one new activity outside of your work environment. This will allow you to avoid a pitfall common to many recent graduates, that of devoting an exorbitant amount of time to their careers. While admirable and often necessary to fulfill expectations, such narrow concentration on a job can be unhealthy and counterproductive. An avocation in your life reduces stress and makes you more productive at work. It may take time to strike a balance between your personal and professional life, but once you do you'll reap rich rewards.

| **Exercise 21.7** | *Joining a New Community* |

1. Read your local newspaper's calendar of events for two weeks. Create a list of events you would be interested in attending.

2. Call a variety of local agencies (such as the town hall, YMCA, or school department) and develop a list of services and organizations that are available to the public.

3. Write a personal statement on what your priority will be—job or avocation.

4. List methods you currently use to alleviate stress.

5. Create a list of those activities you are currently involved in at your institution. Rank-order those activities you would like to continue.

6. Create a wish list of all those things you have always wanted to do.

Week Five: Being Successful

You've landed the job you wanted, you have a place to live, and your friends will all be living nearby. So why do you still have that uneasy feeling in the pit of your stomach? Indeed, as the first day of work rapidly approaches, the feeling grows stronger until, the night before your first day on the new job, you wonder if it's appendicitis. You begin to think back to the day before you started college and realize that this anxiety is similar to what you felt then.

This realization should calm you down sufficiently so that you can think about ways to make this transition a smooth one. Unlike college your new job is probably not going to have an extensive orientation program specifically geared to easing you through this transition. How, then, do you survive?

The first step is to remember that at one time all your co-workers have been the "new kid on the block." No one expects you to know everything about the job. But people do expect you to pay attention, learn your responsibilities, and complete tasks in a timely manner.

The second step is to recognize that every organization has its own "climate" that dictates the way people operate in the organization. Because the corporate handbook does not describe the organizational climate, a portion of your time as a new employee must be spent observing co-workers both at and away from their desks or work stations. Pay close attention to unwritten rules regarding telephone usage for personal calls or length of time for lunch. Note how organizational communication functions and where the "informal" power in your work group exists. Be aware of the dynamics of office politics. Because this information is not instantly available, you must take your time and *observe*. For instance, one recent graduate committed professional suicide by planning a surprise birthday party for her boss. Little did she realize that there was an unspoken rule forbidding celebrations during working hours.

The third step is to understand that it will take time to make a successful transition to your new job. When you first entered college, it took time to discover the ins and outs of the institution. You learned by listening to fellow students and other members of the college community. You may have relied on an older student to provide you with the necessary information, or you may have struck out on your own and learned from trial and error. Similarly, in the workplace there will be many people who can provide you with the necessary information. To make the transition easier, however, you need to strike a balance. If you choose to work without assistance from current employees, you might find yourself ostracized by your co-workers. If you constantly rely on your colleagues to help you, they may feel you are not pulling your own weight.

Finally, be realistic: You don't have to figure this all out on your first day of work. Take the time to orient yourself and assess the climate in which your co-workers operate.

Exercise 21.8

Succeeding on the Job

1. Describe the "organizational climate" of a club or organization you are currently involved with.

2. Create an action plan on how you will deal with office gossip.

3. Interview a recent alumnus on his or her transition to the work force.

4. Develop a "work" philosophy statement and share it with appropriate colleagues. Reflect on the statement as needed.

5. Compose a list of your biggest fears regarding your new career and share this with friends and professors.

Week Six: Saying Good-Bye

Again, think back to your first day as a college student, back to the day you moved into your residence hall room or attended your first class. Graduation must have seemed a distant, hard-to-comprehend event. Now graduation swiftly approaches. Some of you may be apprehensive at the thought of leaving, while others may be impatient to get graduation over with because you can't wait to leave. No matter what your feelings, saying a proper good-bye to college is important.

The Importance of Achieving Closure

Why is it so important to say good-bye and achieve closure on the college experience? The main reason is to allow you to move on. In everyone's life there are certain events, called "marker events," or transitions like graduation that "have notable impact upon a person's life" (Levinson, 1978). How a person deals with the change determines the level of importance of the "marker event." For instance, if college was not important to you, your separation will be easy. If you feel that your college experience has great meaning, however, your separation will be more difficult.

A common reaction to having to say good-bye is denial: "I don't need to put closure on this experience. I am still going to keep in touch with my friends and visit the campus." That may be true, but it is also important to recognize that if you do stay connected, your relationships will be different. You will no longer be an undergraduate, attending classes or living with people you once saw daily. Therefore you will be treated differently by the community and your friends. You will soon be part of a new community—a graduate, an alumnus, and a member of the "real world." You must understand this "new" relationship and achieve closure on the old one.

How do you achieve this closure? There are as many different ways as there are different people experiencing this event. The key is to find the method that works best for you. Think back to how you have said good-bye in the past. Throughout your life you have bid farewell to people and things that have become important to you (camp friends, your first bicycle, high school, childhood friends). In each case you have practiced saying good-bye. Sometimes the method you used was positive, and other times it was not. Take time and think about these experiences. This will allow you to change the things that have not worked in the past.

Perhaps you are thinking, "The college community has not been my central focus, and I really do not feel the need to achieve closure on my experience. I can't wait to get on with my life." If so, your need for closure is not strong. Still, you ought to say good-bye to those things that

did affect you. This may be as simple as attending the graduation ceremony or saying thanks to a professor or administrator who went out of
his or her way for you. It might mean going to the gym to play one last
pick-up basketball game or simply walking the campus. In short, it's
important that you think about how you want to say good-bye and then
do it!

The Hardest Part of Saying Good-Bye

If you ask graduating seniors the toughest part about finishing college,
they will tell you it is leaving their friends. During your college years
many of you have developed friendships that you feel are the strongest
bonds of your life. Think back to your freshman year when you had to
say good-bye to your high school friends. Did you feel the same way, or
is it harder this time?

What makes these good-byes so difficult? In most instances you lived
with your college friends. You probably ate and drank together, and
shared the same tiny quarters, forcing you to relax your guard and be
yourself. These people are part of your college family. They may have
replaced a brother or sister you never had or have been true confidantes.
They were your sounding board for ideas, a source of emotional support
in crises, and a catalyst in your moral and values development. Together
you shared so many things: the anxiety of being a freshman, exams, the
sophomore slump, parties, and so forth. Your college friends seem to
know the real you. How many of you spent long hours talking about your
life, your major, your relationships, your future, the good times and the
bad? Now those times are almost over.

In saying good-bye to friends, start early. As painful as it may feel, it
is easier to start talking about it now rather than waiting until the graduation ceremony is over and it's suddenly time to go. You cannot put the
past few years of your life behind you and just say, "So long!" Although
you might deny the fact that you may never see your friends again, such
a possibility is quite real. There are ways to maintain your college friendships, but you cannot recapture your college experience. You are in a new
place now.

Ways of Maintaining Contact

If you want to maintain contact with your friends, consider the following:

1. **Call each other.** Set reasonable expectations for yourself and your
   friends. While a phone conversation differs from seeing a friend, it is
   "the next best thing to being there." Remember, however, that long-
   distance calling does cost money. With your new budget it is important to think about money and how much phone time you can afford.

2. **Plan social gatherings in advance.** You will find that your new schedule will be demanding. Family events, work, and new friends will take time out of your schedule. Be flexible with one another, and understand that your schedules will not always mesh.

3. **Write.** It costs less than calling, and we all prefer getting letters to bills.

4. **Plan for holidays and weddings.** You may find that these are built-in social occasions where you can spend time together. Try to arrive a day early or spend an extra day. The added time will give you a chance to catch up.

5. **Attend reunions.** Depending on your alma mater, some schools have homecomings and reunion weekends. Don't wait for your anniversary year. Plan to attend as many as you can.

Whatever method you choose, it will take some effort. But this investment will surely pay off in the long run. In saying good-bye, reflect on these lines by Richard Bach (1977): "Don't be dismayed at goodbyes. / A farewell is necessary before we can meet again. / And meeting again, after moments or lifetimes, is certain for those who are friends."

Exercise 21.9

Reflecting on Your College Years

1. View the movie *St. Elmo's Fire* with friends and discuss the characters' problems with "letting go" of their college experience.

2. Generate a list of the people whom you want to say good-bye to and how you will accomplish this.

3. Write a statement on what you think will change after graduation. Share this with friends.

4. List the ways in which you will maintain contact with those people who have grown important to you over the past years.

5. Complete the following statements and share them with your friends.

   a. What I will most miss about college is . . .

   b. What I'm least looking forward to after college is . . .

   c. The person(s) I will find it most difficult to say good-bye to at college is (are) . . .

   d. What I won't miss at all about college is . . .

   e. What I am most looking forward to after college is . . .

   f. If I could give one piece of advice to an incoming freshman about the college experience, it would be . . .

Conclusion

Your final six weeks in college no doubt will be bittersweet. On the one hand, you'll be saying good-bye to many friends and leaving a place you've come to call home. On the other hand, you're about to embark on a new and exciting adventure—one you've spent four or more years preparing for. We hope the information provided in this chapter will aid you on that journey. Good luck, and happy travels!

References and Resources

Anderson, Nancy. (1984). *Work with Passion—How to Do What You Love for a Living.* New York: Carroll & Graf.

Ashton, Betsy. (1988). *Guide to Living on Your Own.* Boston: Little, Brown. Ashton offers a complete guide for recent graduates, including information on budgeting, buying a car, and meeting new people.

Bach, Richard. (1977). *Illusions.* New York: Dell.

Bennis, Warren. (1989). *On Becoming a Leader.* Reading, MA: Addison-Wesley. This practical and stimulating book leads the reader through the exciting process of becoming a leader.

Grothe, Mardy, and Peter Wylie. (1977). *Problem Bosses: Who They Are and How to Deal with Them.* New York: Warner-Tamberlan. This book is a survival guide for anyone who has a difficult working relationship with a boss. It presents twelve survival strategies as well as descriptions of every type of problem boss.

Kouzes, James, and Barry Posner. (1987). *The Leadership Challenge.* San Francisco: Jossey-Bass. The authors examine a variety of leadership topics such as identifying characteristics of leadership, developing leadership qualities, and turning commitment into action.

Levinson, Daniel. (1978). *The Seasons of a Man's Life.* New York: Random House.

Molloy, John. (1981). *Molloy's Live for Success.* New York: William Morrow. Molloy explores the characteristics of successful people and offers specific guidelines for incorporating these characteristics into your life.

Sammon, Sean. (1983). *Growing Pains in Ministry.* Whitinsville, MA: Affirmation Books.

Sheehy, Gail. (1976). *Passages.* New York: Dutton. This is an in-depth examination of the various developmental stages in adult life.

Sinetar, Marsha. (1987). *Do What You Love, the Money Will Follow: Discovering Your Right Livelihood.* New York: Dell. This step-by-step guide tells you how to find a career that utilizes your needs, talents, and passions.

Becoming an Alum

Laura Baudo

Freelance Writer on Education and Illiteracy, New York City

Senior Voices

Olivier

Before I graduated from college, I never gave a thought to the importance of being an alum. I figured all alumni do is give money to the university, and I had given this place too much already over the past four years. As soon as I received my diploma, I really didn't care if I remained involved with the university.

But soon after I graduated, the alumni office sent me a list of people who had graduated over the past twenty years with the same degree as mine and who live in the same geographical area I do. Suddenly I had a valuable tool—a ready-made network for discovering the possible career doors my degree could open. All this simply because I have something in common with the people on that list: I'm an alum.

Now I realize being an alum is a responsibility as well as an honor. I want my degree to retain its value, and I want future graduates to receive the same superior level of education I received. I can help ensure this by becoming an active alum, both financially and socially. ■

Like many things in life, becoming an alum is something that happens to you, not something you choose. When you leave school, you become an alum automatically. Becoming a *responsible* alum is something else altogether—something that takes thought and preparation. In this chapter we will discuss why active alumhood is important and how you can be an active alum.

Why Is Active Alumhood Worth It?

It's the same old story: You get out of something what you put into it. If you put effort into being involved in your alma mater after you leave, you'll reap a number of potential benefits.

An Ongoing Sense of the Worth of Your College Years

It's your choice, really: College can be relegated to your "mental scrapbook" or continue as an ongoing, influential force in your thinking. It can function as a vocational school preparing you for your career or as a lifelong source of philosophical, ethical, and leadership guidance. If you stay in touch with your school, you stay in touch with what happened to you while you were there. You rethink the roles professors played in your life if you hear of their ongoing activities at your school. You continue to learn from the activities you took part in if you hear of other students taking part in the same activities. In short, you get more out of the body of knowledge you gained in school if you stay close to the source of that knowledge.

A Say in the Value of Your Diploma

The life-after-college reality is that people will ask you where you went to school. They will have a sense of the worth of your education based on their impression of the school you attended. Thus it's in your best interests that the outside world have a good impression of your alma mater. You know that a school's reputation is based on recognition, which comes in answer to many questions: Is your alma mater in the news as a research institution? Do its professors have reputations through publishing or speaking? Are the sports teams nationally known? Do graduates achieve prominence? Is the school visible in other positive ways?

Alumni can help the school answer yes to these questions and consequently can help influence the public's perception of their education.

NOTE: The author wishes to acknowledge the contributions of Carol Gilbert, Aaron Handleman, Karen Huebner, Creel McCormack, and Patricia Willis in the writing of this chapter.

A Natural Network

Do you want to explore the possibilities of getting a job in Hollywood? Are you wondering what it's like to be an astronaut? Are you considering a career in the diplomatic corps? One of the easiest ways to connect with people who have done similar things or who can point you in the right direction is by being a part of a group of individuals who have done interesting things. As an involved alum you will automatically be just that. Every year since its inception, your college has graduated hundreds of people who have gone on to do myriad things. As corny as it sounds, you are a part of this extended "family" if you acknowledge the bond of your alma mater. Active alums are people who do acknowledge that bond and who help members of their alumni family.

In addition, this network offers more than just career guidance and aid. The alumni network is a source of information about interests beyond the workplace. You can exchange information about hobbies, travel, recreation, and problem solving. It seems like a long way away, but the day might even come when your children benefit from something they can learn or ask from someone who attended your school.

The Knowledge That You're Doing the Right Thing

In one way or another, you paid for at least part of your education, and you may think you've discharged any obligation you have to repay your college for what you've gained while you were there. The truth is, you haven't. In essence, you've paid for the seeds but not the fruit. College has given you the means to grow into whoever you set out to be. We hope that in four years you've gained sufficient maturity, knowledge, and skills to put yourself on the path to realizing your dreams. Still, you have no idea of how fine a person you can become, how well rounded, how experienced, how charged by the energy of leading a useful life. When you realize you have become that person, you have to acknowledge your debt to the institution that helped nurture your growth. You owe your alma mater not just money (we'll get to the inevitable money part later), but loyalty and commitment. A college is a living entity; its lifeblood is people—not just the people it employs but the people who willingly help it out of affection. An active alum is a donor of that lifeblood.

| Exercise 22.1 | *Becoming an Alum* |

1. Try to picture yourself as an active alum. Can you see yourself getting any of the benefits just described?

2. Write two paragraphs about returning to your alma mater twenty-five years from now. In the first paragraph imagine you've had no contact with the school since graduation. In the second imagine you've been an active alum.

3. Think about graduates you know who are active alums. Can you see what they get out of their participation in their alma maters? If not, get in touch with one and discuss this.

4. In the next three days identify a member of the faculty who you think is an active alum of her or his school. Ask about her or his experiences.

What Type of Alum Will You Be?

Look around you. Can you see which of your fellow students will instantly become active alums and which never will? Can you predict which ones will avoid any contact with the school for a number of years and then resurface? Which do you feel will be you?

In truth there is no "normal" way to become a responsible alum. Your college hopes you will maintain contact from the moment you graduate and become a more active participant in the college's affairs as you move through adulthood. But it doesn't always happen that way. Many students feel the need to sever all connections when they leave college. Some do so because they feel it's the only way to "cut the apron strings" of a bond that was almost too strong, too emotional. Some choose to drop out of sight as a way of underlining their indifference to their younger days. Other reasons may come into play as well.

Some students, however, are active alums from the moment they throw their caps into the air. They instantly join alumni associations and clubs, they keep in touch with professors, and they communicate with the alumni publications from their first month away from campus. Most of these alums stay in touch, but some gradually drift away. Far more students go on to become consumed by their concerns with establishing themselves after school or with taking time off. They keep in cursory touch with the school and respond to one or two of the many mailings they receive each year.

Regardless of what happens right after graduation, a common phenomenon seems to recur when tenth reunion time rolls around: People begin to feel more connected to their alma mater. They often return for that reunion as their first visit since graduation. They begin sending news of promotions, marriages, and children to the alumni magazine. They start contributing to the school in meaningful ways.

Like all rules, even rules of thumb, this one has exceptions. The point is, while it's best for your college if you stay in touch and offer what you can, no doors are permanently closed if you don't open them the minute you graduate. Even if you are quite certain you won't want to become active a year from now, don't discount the possibility of contributing to your school down the road. Not only will you change, but times will, the institution will, and the students will.

Exercise 22.2

Reviewing Alumni Publications

1. Get copies of alumni publications from the alumni office. Take a look at the participation by students whom you've known in past years. Are there any surprises?

2. Look at the topics being addressed to alums. Can you understand why they'd be interested? Can you imagine being interested?

3. Look at what alums write in. Look at when they graduated. Write an imaginary entry for yourself five years from graduation. Ten. Twenty.

What Do Active Alums Do?

The antiquated picture of an involved alum is someone in a raccoon coat, carrying a college banner, attending football games and reunions, and reminiscing while writing checks for fund-raising drives. Chances are, you can't see yourself doing any of the above. Fortunately, to be a valuable asset to your school as an alum, you don't have to. What can you do?

Stay in Touch

After you graduate, you become part of the largest part of your school's constituency. It's simple mathematics. The current population of the school is equal to current enrollment. The current population of the alums is equal to the sum of all surviving members of every class that was ever enrolled in the past. A number of groups of people care about what the school stands for: the administration and faculty, the trustees, the current students and their parents, and alumni. And alumni are both the most numerous and the most powerful. If you keep in touch with what is going on at the school, you can form and voice opinions about policies and spending. You can have an influence over what the school stands for.

In order to participate at all, you must make sure the school knows where you are and what you are doing. You can be an active alum only if the lines of communication are open. You can hear from the school only if they know where to reach you. If you hear from an alumni organization, keep in touch with it also. Many alumni associations act as autonomous power bases outside of the administration's influence. This may be a way for you to stay active in your school's affairs if you aren't interested in school-sanctioned or traditional alumni activities.

Spread the Word

In order to continue to exist, a school must attract students. Even the most selective schools in the nation must recruit students. And some schools find themselves in the unhappy circumstance of having to sweat out every entering class, hoping they have enrolled enough qualified students. From the moment you entered college, whether you realized it or not, you became a recruiter for your school. High school students who observed your attitudes toward your school were observing your school at the same time. If you happened to talk positively about your school, you may have influenced someone's decision to apply and/or attend.

Now that you are graduating, you have a much fuller picture of what your school has to offer. You can speak confidently and knowledgeably about its strengths and assets. You can identify students who would profit from spending time at your school. You can even develop a "sales pitch" that might influence someone who doesn't know about the college or is skeptical. Here's the real shocker: Even if you wouldn't attend the same school if you had it to do all over again, most of the graduates would. That means many prospective students could benefit from spending four years there.

How do you find prospective students for your school? Even if you're not inclined to "mining" for prospects, relax—they will come to you. You go from being a lowly student to being a role model as soon as you graduate. If you have younger siblings, they or their friends would appreciate and respect your advice about prospective colleges. If you've maintained a connection to your high school, you can make your willingness to talk with students known. If you go on to graduate school, work, or the military, you will come in contact with people who have children who are seeking advice about which schools to consider. And finally, your college admissions staff would love to have you as a resource in the geographic area where you settle. If you are willing, they will be happy to have you talk with students who write to the school for information.

By the way, this is a two-way street. Your alma mater will pay attention to your recommendation of a student. If you are particularly impressed by someone, your calling him or her to the attention of your school's admission staff can be a big help.

Exercise 22.3   *Recruiting for Your School*

1. Give yourself five minutes to draw a picture of your college. It can be a single image or a collage of images, and it needn't be realistic or artistic. When the time is up, look at what you've drawn. Does it lead to a word picture you can use to describe the school?

2. Take a minute to identify your college's strengths. Use the following list as a guideline, but feel free to add anything we might have missed.

    a. Overall academic reputation

    b. Quality of the faculty

    c. Access to faculty

    d. Strong departments and programs

    e. Innovative curriculum

    f. Average class size

    g. Tuition cost/financial aid

    h. Work/study options

    i. Location

    j. Library

    k. Computing facilities

    l. Recreational facilities

    m. Size and setting of campus

    n. Variety of social life options

    o. Strong extracurricular programs

    p. Career counseling

    q. Housing

    r. Other support services

3. Ask yourself which students at your school seem happiest (we hope that you are one of them). What is the source of their contentment? Keep this in mind when you talk with prospective students.

4. Give yourself ten minutes to do the following: Imagine yourself as a high school guidance counselor. Someone just like you were as a high school senior asks for a description of your college. Write the conversation you have with her or him.

5. Stop by the admissions office before graduation and talk with an admissions counselor about what you can do to help reach the right students with the message about your school.

6. Go back to your high school and let the guidance counselors know they can count on you as a resource for advising students about your alma mater.

7. If you move from your hometown after graduation, let the local high schools know of your willingness to tell students about your school.

Stay Involved

How many times did you hear the phrase *ivory tower* while you were in school? There's a reason why people talk about colleges this way. They are isolated from the outside world in many ways, and even though the harsh realities of finances and perhaps bleak employment prospects impinge on college life, many of the realities of life beyond academe do not.

To your college, you are a resource from the outside world. You can provide insights and brings a perspective that extend beyond academe. As you progress in other industries, you can show your college how these industries think and act in ways that might be helpful. Colleges can always use the thinking of bankers, marketers, entrepreneurs, retailers, politicians, public relations experts, fund-raisers, social workers, artists, athletes, attorneys, doctors, religious leaders—indeed, members of any profession you can name.

Additionally, you will become a resource from the moment you leave college because you will be able to speak to people who are still in school about that big step you took. As you progress in your career or your search for one, you can offer to speak or write to students about the steps you've taken, the decisions you've made, and the lessons you've learned. In time, you will probably be able to offer significant career counseling for students enrolled in your school—either casually by mail or telephone or in a more formalized way by speaking with students in assemblies, classes, and seminars or one on one. You might even be a graduation speaker someday, giving people sitting right where you once sat advice about what it's like to grow beyond the walls of the school.

If you don't see yourself as a speaker or guide for young people, you can serve the school in other ways. You can help individual departments learn about employment opportunities or grants. You can advise the administration about fiscal realities you deal with that might help them solve the problems with which they regularly wrestle. If you become an architect, craftsperson, investment advisor, or one of dozens of other occupations, your school will be able to use your professional services to help defray operational costs. Individual professors will also welcome your connections for consulting opportunities, for help with field trips, and for aid in their research and case studies.

Eventually, you may be tapped to become a trustee of your school. Beyond being a great honor, this is a great responsibility. Trustees oversee the school's dispatch of its charter. They essentially hire the school's president. They determine the direction of the institution's future and interpret and dictate its philosophy. Trusteeship is the ultimate manifestation of active, responsible alumni citizenship.

Once again, the key is keeping in touch. The school will find ways to use you and your talents.

Be a Leader

If there is a campus problem that concerns you after you graduate, you must remember that it's up to you to organize the solution. Work through the alumni association. Start a concerned alumni committee and communicate with the appropriate people at school. Call and write to your fellow graduates. Get in touch with regional alumni organizations. Be a one-person band if you must, but don't think it's up to someone else to act before you get involved. Similarly, if there is a social issue you'd like to see your school or your fellow alumni involved in, take it upon yourself to be the leader who informs people of the issue and potential responses. Your college is an affinity group. As alumni you are, in one way or another, birds of a feather, and by flocking together you can do beautiful and meaningful things for the world.

Exercise 22.4   *Assuming Leadership*

Identify an issue that is hot on campus now. Can you organize your fellow students into a concerned alumni group that will stay active after you graduate? Set up a steering committee to determine what needs to be done and find people who are willing to help after graduation.

Consider the Serious Side of the Social Side

If you settle in an urban area after school, you are likely to find a regional alumni club there. Some clubs are more social than others. Some function as formalized recruitment arms of the school as well as regular symposia for reports from admissions personnel, development officers, other administrators, and professors. Some barely acknowledge the common bond of a shared alma mater, preferring to act as a travel or recreational affinity group. Most, however, are about both the business of being an informed, active alum and the pleasure of having fellow alums.

If you choose to join such a club, your chances of realizing all of the benefits of being an active alum mentioned in this chapter are greater than if you don't. If you join, you will also find it easier to carry out the responsibilities of being a responsible alum.

Some people are joiners and some are not. You must judge for yourself whether joining a regional alumni organization is right for you. Keep in mind, however, that you will probably be better able to decide if you attend a meeting. And, even if you don't join, you may choose to keep up with the agendas of your regional organization's meetings, in case a topic to be covered interests you.

If there is not a club in your area, you may wish to start one. The development office of your school will be happy to give you guidance and to put you in touch with officers of other clubs.

We should add a word about homecoming. Remember that alum in the raccoon coat with the pennant we mentioned earlier? Get him or her out of your mind when you are considering making a trip back to your school for homecoming. For some, returning to campus is the most natural thing in the world and the first autumn after graduation finds them caught up in the rites of returning. For others, it's that tenth-reunion milestone that prompts them to return. Some don't come back for twenty or thirty years. And some never do. You will know what's right for you, but once again, keeping in touch is the key. If you hear about the school's plans for homecoming, you might find a reason to return that you never would have imagined. If you keep in touch with your professors and fellow graduates, their plans might influence yours. Or you might influence theirs. We talk more about that at the end of this chapter.

Don't Rule Out the Simple Contributions

A while back, the chorus of a private midwestern college visited Atlanta. The organization's travel budget was tight, but the opportunity to perform in a big city was too good to pass up. How did they manage? A convoy of alums picked them up at the airport. They loaned out cars for the duration of their stay. They functioned as tour guides. They put them up in spare bedrooms. One night, an alum threw a dinner party for the group while another baked pies for dessert. Trivial activities? To the contrary. These are truly the little things that mean a lot, that enable a school to offer a broad range of experiences to its students. What's more, the alums got as much out of it as the students did, feeling once again that their alma mater was a place where contributions from the heart counted as much as those from the head or pocketbook.

You will always have something to offer your alma mater if you aren't shy about offering what you have.

The Financial Factor

There's no getting away from it: Alumni donations are critical to a college or university's success. Some of the sums donated by people who were students just like you may be difficult for you to consider ever amassing, let alone donating. Indeed, it may seem like a fairy tale to imagine ever writing a check in any amount to your alma mater. The topic of social responsibility and philanthropy has been touched on in other places in this book, and you have undoubtedly made financial donations of one kind or another at many points in your life.

Most people derive great satisfaction from knowing that the fruits of their labors go to benefit more than just themselves. Giving to your college or university is a good way to benefit many people without having the value of your contribution greatly diluted by unwieldy national advertising campaigns and administrative expenses. What's more, any contribution you make can be earmarked to go specifically where you would like it to go. If you have a particular area of interest, be it departmental, extracurricular, political, or otherwise, you can see to it that the dollars you donate benefit that area directly. And be sure to find out if your employer has a matching contribution program. Your donation dollars can double under such arrangements.

Whether you become a financial contributor as soon as you leave school or later in life, you should read the mailings from your alma mater. They will keep you informed not only of the school's needs but also of some unusual ways for you to give something back. They will also offer you opportunities to see the value of any money you give and to plan for giving in the future.

Once again, all you are called on to do as a senior is to think about the concept of being a financial contributor to your school and to recognize that your feelings may change. Keep in mind, too, that your college values every donation, no matter how small, because they use the percentage of donating alumni as a way of demonstrating the health of the institution to foundations and other organizations that can offer it financial support.

| Exercise 22.5 | *Investigating Alumni Fund Drives* |

If you are interested in how alumni contributions are handled by your alma mater, you might want to visit your college's development office and talk with someone about the various alumni fund drives currently under way. You can also read some of the literature that discusses alumni giving and special fund-raising drives.

Conclusion

No matter what the benefits of being an active and responsible alum, and no matter what the responsibilities inherent in active alumhood, you must take a step inside yourself before you can be a successful alum on the outside.

Wanting to be an active responsible alum comes from acknowledging a bond with your school. It takes some reflection to see the fibers of that bond. That reflection can offer you one of the most powerful mental pictures you'll ever see while in school.

The traditional, traditionally aged student goes from childhood to adulthood while in college. As a senior you have faced many moral crossroads and made many decisions about your values while in school. The direction you went in when you reached those turning points was influenced by the people around you, most notably your friends and your professors.

If you've seen any of the "college buddy" films like *St. Elmo's Fire, Carnal Knowledge, Four Friends, The Return of the Secaucus Seven,* or *The Big Chill,* you've observed that adults believe in the bonds of college friendships. You probably feel those bonds without intellectualizing them, but now, in your senior year, you may want to reflect on the depth of your affection for your college friends and on what you've been through together. You may want to talk with your friends about your plans for staying in touch. You may even want to consider how you as a group are going to become active, influential alumni.

Likewise, you have probably had some professors who had a profound impact on your thinking and on your career decisions. They have been the people you have trusted to tell you the truth about the world. They have willingly labored to help you achieve wisdom. You are about the enter into a new relationship with those professors as a fellow responsible adult. You might want to take a look at your mentors and friends in that light.

These are the people who will star in your memory's movie of college. They will also take with them the picture of you as a student. These "films" will always have an audience. They will endure as masterpieces because they were absolutely true to life. In college you have had your first experience at being taken completely seriously, and one hopes you have had fun doing it. Now is the time to think about that. By getting in touch with what is important to you while you are still in school, you will be getting in touch with why your school can still be important to you after you leave. Through that knowledge you will find the path to becoming an alum who finds enduring benefits and offers a lasting contribution to her or his alma mater.

Index